Non-ferrous metals

Non-ferrous metals

Their role in industrial development

Lotte Müller-Ohlsen

Woodhead-Faulkner
in association with
Metallgesellschaft AG

First published 1981 by J. C. B. Mohr (Paul Siebeck) Tübingen
as *Die Weltmetallwirtschaft im industriellen Entwicklungsprozeß* (Kieler Studien 165) for the Kiel
Institute of World Economics, University of Kiel

This edition published 1981
by Woodhead-Faulkner Ltd, 8 Market Passage, Cambridge CB2 3PF
in association with Metallgesellschaft AG, Frankfurt am Main

Translation: M. Tillack

© Text: Institut für Weltwirtschaft an der Universität Kiel 1981
© Translation: Metallgesellschaft AG 1981
ISBN 0 85941 190 7

Conditions of sale:
All rights reserved. No part of this publication may be reproduced, stored in a retrieval system or transmitted, in any form or by any means, electronic, mechanical, photocopying, recording or otherwise, without the prior permission of the copyright owners.

Design: Geoff Green
Typesetting: Rowland Phototypesetting Ltd, Bury St Edmunds, Suffolk
Printed in Great Britain by
St Edmundsbury Press, Bury St Edmunds, Suffolk

Foreword to the German edition

The Kiel Study presented here by the Institut für Weltwirtschaft (University of Kiel Institute of World Economics) is a study of the world metals economy during the course of industrial development.

This work was inspired by Karl Gustaf Ratjen, Chairman of Metallgesellschaft AG, who has had close ties with the Institute for many years and has always shown great interest in following and encouraging our work. We should like to express our thanks to those who co-operated with us from Metallgesellschaft AG: Dr Thomas Baack, Willy Bauer, Professor Dr Ernst Henglein, Hans Schreiber, Dr Walter Sies, Jakob Wiessler, Professor Dr Peter Wincierz and Frau Ingrid Brosius. They made relevant information available to the author and also gave her every assistance on many problems, particularly of a technical nature.

The section on technical progress in the metal industry (3.3) was contributed by Professor Dr Kurt Meyer. We should particularly like to thank him for this section; the book would have been very incomplete without it.

The author is especially indebted to all those who helped her in this work, particularly Dr Martin Hoffmeyer, Dr Hubertus Müller-Groeling, Bernhard Klein and Ursula Wollesen, who edited the manuscript and suggested a number of improvements.

The Institut für Weltwirtschaft would like to express their thanks to Metallgesellschaft AG, who, in connection with their centenary celebrations, provided the financial assistance which made this book possible.

Kiel, April 1981   HERBERT GIERSCH

Contents

	page
Foreword to the German edition	v
List of tables	ix
List of figures	xiii
Introduction	1

1	The basic principles of the non-ferrous metal industry	5
1.1	The mineralogical raw materials and their metals	5
1.2	Occurrence and deposits of metallic raw materials	9
1.2.1	Heavy metals	10
1.2.2	Light metals	12
1.2.3	Steel improvers	14
1.2.4	Other alloying and special metals	16

2	The production structure of the non-ferrous metal industry	18
2.1	Metal mining and ore dressing	19
2.2	Smelting and refining	21
2.3	Metal processing	23

3	The origins of the non-ferrous metal industry	25
3.1	The discovery of non-ferrous metals as industrial materials	25
3.2	The Industrial Revolution – the generative force for the non-ferrous metal industry	28
3.3	Technical progress	34
3.3.1	Preparation of the crude ores	34
3.3.2	Extraction of metals	41

4	Factors determining the demand for non-ferrous metals	63
4.1	Properties and fields of application	63
4.1.1	Heavy metals	64

Contents

		page
4.1.2	Light metals	71
4.1.3	Steel improvers	74
4.1.4	Other alloying and special metals	79
4.2	Substitution processes	80
4.3	Levels of development and industrialization	82

5 The pattern of consumption of non-ferrous metals — 92
- 5.1 The product structure of world consumption — 92
- 5.2 Regional and national trends in consumption — 99

6 Growth and change in the pattern of non-ferrous metal production — 106
- 6.1 World mining — 106
- 6.1.1 Development and product structure — 106
- 6.1.2 The international structure of mining output — 111
- 6.2 Smelting and refinery production — 125
- 6.2.1 Development and product structure — 125
- 6.2.2 The international structure of smelter and refinery production — 132
- 6.3 The commercial structure of the mining and smelting industries in the Western world — 147

7 The supply situation of the principal consumer countries — 159
- 7.1 The supply of mining products and primary metals — 159
- 7.2 The importance of secondary recovery — 165
- 7.3 The role of stockpile holding — 176
- 7.3.1 Commercial stocks — 177
- 7.3.2 Strategic reserves and other measures to safeguard supplies — 180

8 Trends in world trade in non-ferrous metals — 187
- 8.1 Origin and determining factors — 187
- 8.2 Essential features and changes in the structure of trade — 188
- 8.3 The regional pattern of trade — 193

9 Pricing in the non-ferrous metal markets — 198
- 9.1 Pricing at the metal exchanges — 198
- 9.1.1 The London Metal Exchange — 198
- 9.1.2 The New York Commodity Exchange (COMEX) — 202
- 9.1.3 The Metal Exchange in Penang — 204
- 9.2 Pricing outside the metal exchanges — 204
- 9.3 The current price structure — 205

10 The price trend in the non-ferrous metal markets — 211
- 10.1 The functioning of the markets — 211
- 10.2 The price trend — 214

11 Attempts at regulation in the non-ferrous metal markets — 220
- 11.1 Attempts at control of the copper market — 220

Non-ferrous metals

		page
11.1.1	The Sécrétan Syndicate (1887–89)	221
11.1.2	The Amalgamated Copper Company (1899–1901)	221
11.1.3	The Copper Export Association (1919–23)	222
11.1.4	Copper Exporters Incorporated (1926–32)	223
11.1.5	The International Copper Cartel (1935–39)	224
11.1.6	The Intergovernmental Council of Copper Exporting Countries (CIPEC)	224
11.2	Attempts at control of the zinc and lead markets	226
11.2.1	The European Spelter Convention (1908–1914)	226
11.2.2	The International Zinc Cartel (1931–34)	226
11.2.3	The Lead Smelters' Association (1909–14)	227
11.2.4	Other lead cartels before the Second World War	227
11.2.5	Post-war attempts at regulation of the zinc and lead markets	228
11.3	The International Tin Agreements	229
11.3.1	Early attempts at regulation of the tin market	229
11.3.2	The International Tin Agreements 1931–47	230
11.3.3	The International Tin Agreements since 1954	232
11.4	Cartel policy in the aluminium market	236
11.4.1	Aluminium cartels before the Second World War	236
11.4.2	Market regulation after the Second World War	239
11.5	Cartel formation and control of the nickel market	240
11.6	Attempts to regulate metallic raw materials within the framework of the Integrated Programme for Commodities	240
12	**Development prospects and problems of the world metal economy**	246
12.1	Medium- and long-term prospects for supplies of raw materials	246
12.2	Supply policy responsibilities	257
Appendix		265
	Explanatory notes on the tables	265
	Tables	267
Bibliography		291

Tables

		page
Table 1.	Technical data on the principal industrial non-ferrous metals	8
Table 2.	By-products of copper and copper production from non-cuprous ores in the United States, 1975	11
Table 3.	The discovery of the principal non-ferrous metals	25
Table 4.	The introduction of major stages in copper extraction	45
Table 5.	Copper consumption by end-use in the United States, 1965, 1970 and 1976	66
Table 6.	Lead consumption by end-use in selected industrial countries, 1960 and 1977	68
Table 7.	Zinc consumption by end-use in selected industrial countries, 1960 and 1977	69
Table 8.	Tin consumption by end-use in selected industrial countries, 1960, 1970 and 1977	70
Table 9.	Aluminium consumption by end-use in selected industrial countries, 1960–77	73
Table 10.	The main end-uses of alloying and special metals	75
Table 11.	Per capita Gross National Product (GNP) and consumption of non-ferrous metals in selected countries, 1976	83
Table 12.	Relationship between per capita consumption of non-ferrous metals and per capita income in selected countries, 1976	84
Table 13.	Relationship between per capita consumption of non-ferrous metals and level of industrialization in selected countries, 1976	88
Table 14.	Relationship between per capita consumption of non-ferrous metals, Gross National Product (GNP) and industrial production in the United States, 1870–1975	89
Table 15.	The trend in consumption of non-ferrous metals in West Germany, 1950–77	90
Table 16.	World consumption of non-ferrous metals, 1890–1979	92
Table 17.	World consumption of non-ferrous metals, 1889–1979	95
Table 18.	Per capita consumption of non-ferrous metals in selected industrial countries, 1940–79	97
Table 19.	Consumption of non-ferrous metals by regions, 1890–1979	100
Table 20.	The consumption of non-ferrous metals by countries, 1890–1979	102
Table 21.	World mine production of non-ferrous metals, 1900–79	107

x   *Non-ferrous metals*

		page
Table 22.	World mine production of non-ferrous metals, 1886–1979	109
Table 23.	Mine production of non-ferrous metals by regions, 1900–79	112
Table 24.	Mine production of non-ferrous metals by groups of countries, 1950–79	114
Table 25.	Mine production of non-ferrous metals by countries, 1880–1979	115
Table 26.	Concentration of mine production of non-ferrous metals by countries, 1975, 1976 and 1979	124
Table 27.	World smelter production of non-ferrous metals, 1880–1979	125
Table 28.	Smelter production of non-ferrous metals, 1879–1979	131
Table 29.	Smelter production of non-ferrous metals by regions, 1890–1979	134
Table 30.	Smelter production of copper by regions, 1890–1979	136
Table 31.	Smelter production of non-ferrous metals by groups of countries, 1950–79	137
Table 32.	Smelter production of non-ferrous metals by countries, 1880–1979	139
Table 33.	The foundation of major companies in the non-ferrous metal industry, 1870–1917	148
Table 34.	Total world supplies of non-ferrous metals from mine and smelter production by regions, 1890–1979	160
Table 35.	Supplies of non-ferrous metals from mine and smelter production in selected industrial countries, 1890–1979	161
Table 36.	Proportion of mine production to smelter production of non-ferrous metals by regions, 1920–79	164
Table 37.	Secondary recovery of non-ferrous metals in relation to smelter and mine production, 1950–79	170
Table 38.	Smelter production (S) and secondary recovery (R) of non-ferrous metals in selected industrial countries, 1950–79	171
Table 39.	Share of selected industrial countries in secondary recovery of non-ferrous metals, 1950–79	173
Table 40.	Secondary recovery as a percentage of non-ferrous metal consumption in selected industrial countries, 1950–70	174
Table 41.	Recovery rate for selected industrial countries, 1975	176
Table 42.	Stockpile targets and holdings of non-ferrous metals in the United States, 1970, 1976 and 1980	182
Table 43.	World trade in non-ferrous metals by regions, 1955–76	194
Table 44.	The London Metal Exchange, turnover and stocks, 1970–79	203
Table 45.	Non-ferrous metal prices on the London Metal Exchange, 1881–1979	215
Table 46.	Estimated world reserves and resources of non-ferrous metals, 1950–79	250
Table 47.	The consumption of non-ferrous metals: estimated annual increase and regional distribution, 1971–2000	252
Table 48.	Estimated availability of reserves of selected metallic raw materials	254
Table 49.	Regional distribution of world reserves of non-ferrous metals, 1979	255
Table A1.	Smelter capacities for primary aluminium by groups and companies, at the end of 1979	267

Tables

		page
Table A2.	Smelter capacities for copper by companies, at the end of 1979	270
Table A3.	Smelter capacities for tin by groups and companies, at the end of 1979	271
Table A4.	Mining capacities for nickel by companies, at the end of 1979	272
Table A5.	Smelter capacities for lead by companies, at the end of 1979	273
Table A6.	Smelter capacities for zinc by groups and companies, at the end of 1979	276
Table A7.	Trade in copper by supplier countries and destination countries, 1929–78	278
Table A8.	Trade in lead by supplier countries and destination countries, 1929–78	281
Table A9.	Trade in zinc by supplier countries and destination countries, 1929–78	283
Table A10.	Trade in tin by supplier countries and destination countries, 1929–78	285
Table A11.	Trade in aluminium by supplier countries and destination countries, 1929–78	287
Table A12.	Non-ferrous metal exports as percentage of production, by countries, 1978	289

Figures

		page
Fig. 1.	Periodic table of the elements	6
Fig. 2.	Processes for non-ferrous metals recovery and smelter capacity in West Germany, up to the end of 1980	20
Fig. 3.	Flowchart of copper ore concentration at Bougainville	37
Fig. 4.	Fluidized bed roasting: the LURGI-BASF system with steam generation	39
Fig. 5.	Flowchart of a pressure sintering plant for lead ores	41
Fig. 6.	Double catalysis sulphuric acid plant based on metallurgical SO_2 gases	42
Fig. 7.	The development of stages in pyrometallurgical copper extraction	46
Fig. 8.	Relationship between non-ferrous metal consumption and per capita income, 1976	85
Fig. 9.	World consumption of selected non-ferrous metals, 1890–1979	94
Fig. 10.	World mine production of non-ferrous metals, 1886–1979	110
Fig. 11.	World smelter production of heavy metals, 1880–1979	127
Fig. 12.	World smelter production of light metals, 1890–1979	128
Fig. 13.	World production of alloying and special metals, 1880–1979	130
Fig. 14.	London Metal Exchange quotations, 1881–1979	216
Fig. 15.	Non-ferrous metal prices in New York, 1895–1979	217

Introduction

Non-ferrous metals play a key role in industrial production and our world of technology, both present and future, would be inconceivable without them. Nevertheless, these are not new materials. Some of them have been known to mankind since historic times, others were discovered centuries ago. Non-ferrous metals only became indispensable raw materials, however, at the beginning of the industrial era, when their special properties revolutionized production processes. Use of these metals enabled industry to solve technical problems of ever-increasing complexity in a growing number of fields and progress in technology continually opened up new applications for these metals in various forms. The demand for non-ferrous metals, both in quantity and quality, rapidly rose to unprecedented levels. To meet the escalating demand intensive efforts were needed to explore and open up new deposits where economic extraction would be feasible and also to transform the mining and working of these raw materials. Traditional methods had to give way at all stages of production to more advanced techniques – a process which is still continuing. At the same time it was necessary to gear the market structures to the changing demand arising in consequence of expanding industrialization. A broad field of activity was thus opened up for a free enterprise sector whose salient features were a bold and courageous approach, resourceful planning and willingness to take risks.

The age of technology thus prepared the way for industrial evolution in the non-ferrous metals sector. As consumer and producer countries were usually widely separated geographically, there rapidly developed a worldwide trade network of growing complexity but increasingly closely-knit structure as the numbers of producer countries increased. The potentialities offered by non-ferrous metals for scientific progress and new achievements were a constant source of inspiration for research and technology. The key role of these metals in economic development, however, attracted little attention, because supplies continued to run smoothly to industry with no interruption. Only towards the end of 1973, in the context of the economic and political upheaval in the oil sector, was any particular interest focussed on non-ferrous metals. For the first time the largely unrecorded happenings in the metals economy became a topic of public discussion. In particular, the finite nature of metals resources became apparent, implying a threat to economic growth. There are a great many reasons why it now appears opportune to examine these fears in the perspective of long-term developments in the metals economy, with its natural geological basis and product-specific features, and to take an objective view of the constraints imposed and the prospects offered. The principal aim of this book is to trace the changing structure in the non-ferrous metals economy since the end of the past century, when the industrial process began to gather momentum, and in particular to analyse the reciprocal effects of this process and of the rapid expansion of industrial production.

The introductory remarks on the basic principles of the metals industry (Chapter 1) are designed to give information on the various non-ferrous metals and essential technical data governing their use in industry. This is followed in Chapter 2 by an account of the main features of metals production as a guide to the vertical integration of this sector of industry, from mining to smelting and finally metal fabrication. A survey is then given in Chapter 3 of the different phases in the evolution and growth of this sector during the course of industrialization and of the origins of the world metals economy, showing how technical progress has influenced this development. Of relevance for future trends are the reasons determining the demand for non-ferrous metals. These are analysed and the possibility and implications of substitution processes considered. An attempt is made, with reference to a cross-sectional study, to establish the relationship between the level of development of a country and the consumption of non-ferrous metals (Chapter 4). The subsequent analyses of global and regional consumption trends (Chapter 5) are designed to show the dynamic forces at work in the growth and transformation of mining, smelting and refinery production during the industrialization process. In view of the intense concentration of supplies of non-ferrous metals on the world market, however, the structure of companies and distribution of capacities in this sector of industry are of economic relevance (Chapter 6). An impression of the closely-knit network of the non-ferrous metals economy throughout the world is gained from the study in Chapter 7 of the supply situation of the principal consumer countries in regard to mining products and primary metals. The importance is also discussed of recycling non-ferrous metals and of commercial and strategic stockpiling for countries lacking in raw materials. The following chapter, Chapter 8, analyses the characteristic features of supply and demand obtaining on the international metal markets, the structural changes which have occurred over the years and the current pattern of international trade. The organization of world metal markets (Chapter 9) and price trends during the course of industrialization (Chapter 10) are other subjects covered by our study. In the light of the intensive drive by the developing countries for some years to regulate the pattern of trade in raw materials under their proposed 'Integrated Programme for Commodities', which also includes some metallic raw materials, it appears appropriate to indicate what success has been achieved so far by interventions in this economic field (Chapter 11). The final chapter of the book is directed towards the future. It assesses the medium- and long-term prospects for the supply of essential non-ferrous metals during subsequent progress in industrialization and considers how long resources of non-renewable metallic raw materials may be expected to last. The problems facing us in framing policies to ensure continuity of raw materials supplies for the world metal industries are discussed in this context. In view of the continual progress in industrialization which may be expected and the vast growth in world population, the solution to these problems is now a matter of urgency.

1

The basic principles of the non-ferrous metal industry

1.1 THE MINERALOGICAL RAW MATERIALS AND THEIR METALS

The natural basis for the metal industry consists of the metals present in the earth's crust. Like all materials these may occur in four states, as plasma, gas,[1] liquids and solids; in the narrower sense, however, the term metals is applied to those elements which have the distinctive characteristics of metallic compounds (Hornbogen and Warlimont, 1967, p. 7[2]). The characteristic properties of metals are:

(a) opacity in the solid state;
(b) high reflectivity and lustre (or glance);
(c) high electrical and thermal conductivity;
(d) ductility, i.e., the capacity for plastic deformation by hammering, forging, extrusion, pressing or drawing;
(e) strength, hardness, toughness – properties which can be influenced by alloying or heat treatment.

Of the 105 chemical elements known today 78 are metals, which are classified in the periodic system of different periods and groups (see Fig. 1): some 30 metals have acquired industrial importance.

It is not possible to make a clear-cut distinction between metals and non-metals because there are chemical elements in existence possessing properties common to both.[3] At normal temperature (25°C) – with the exception of liquid mercury – metals are found in the solid state.

---

1 The industrial use of metals in the form of gas or steam has recently assumed greater importance in vacuum steam technology and in the CVD (Chemical Vapour Deposition) process. Two examples only will be mentioned here – the IS (Imperial Smelting) process and zinc refining according to the New Jersey process, which evaporates zinc and condenses it from the vapour phase.
2 For full details of all bibliographical references, see Bibliography, pp. 291–297.
3 The term 'semi-metals', or 'metalloids', is no longer generally used. Of the B-elements germanium (Ge), tin (Sn), antimony (Sb), bismuth (Bi) and polonium (Po) occur both in metallic and non-metallic crystalline forms.

5

Non-ferrous metals

	Ia	IIa		IIIa	IVa	Va	VIa	VIIa		VIIIa		Ib	IIb	IIIb	IVb	Vb	VIb	VIIb	Noble gases
	1 H Hydrogen 1.0080																		2 He Helium 4.003
	3 Li Lithium 6.941	4 Be Beryllium 9.012												5 B Boron 10.81	6 C Carbon 12.011	7 N Nitrogen 14.007	8 O Oxygen 15.994	9 F Fluorine 19.00	10 Ne Neon 20.179
	11 Na Sodium 22.990	12 Mg Magnesium 24.305												13 Al Aluminium 26.98	14 Si Silicon 28.09	15 P Phosphorus 30.97	16 S Sulphur 32.06	17 Cl Chlorine 35.453	18 Ar Argon 39.948
	19 K Potassium 39.102	20 Ca Calcium 40.08	21 Sc Scandium 44.96	22 Ti Titanium 47.90	23 V Vanadium 50.94	24 Cr Chromium 51.996	25 Mn Manganese 54.938	26 Fe Iron 55.85	27 Co Cobalt 58.933	28 Ni Nickel 58.71	29 Cu Copper 63.546	30 Zn Zinc 65.37	31 Ga Gallium 69.72	32 Ge Germanium 72.60	33 As Arsenic 74.92	34 Se Selenium 78.96	35 Br Bromine 79.904	36 Kr Krypton 83.80
	37 Rb Rubidium 85.468	38 Sr Strontium 87.62	39 Y Yttrium 88.91	40 Zr Zirconium 91.22	41 Nb Niobium 92.91	42 Mo Molybdenum 95.94	43 Tc Technetium 98.906	44 Ru Ruthenium 101.1	45 Rh Rhodium 102.91	46 Pd Palladium 106.4	47 Ag Silver 107.868	48 Cd Cadmium 112.40	49 In Indium 114.82	50 Sn Tin 118.69	51 Sb Antimony 121.76	52 Te Tellurium 127.60	53 J Iodine 126.90	54 X Xenon 131.30
	55 Cs Caesium 132.906	56 Ba Barium 137.34	57–71 Lanthanides*	72 Hf Hafnium 178.49	73 Ta Tantalum 180.95	74 W Tungsten 183.85	75 Re Rhenium 186.2	76 Os Osmium 190.2	77 Ir Iridium 192.2	78 Pt Platinum 195.09	79 Au Gold 196.967	80 Hg Mercury 200.59	81 Tl Thallium 204.37	82 Pb Lead 207.21	83 Bi Bismuth 208.981	84 Po Polonium 210	85 At Astatine ~210	86 Ra Radon ~222
	87 Fr Francium 223	88 Ra Radium 226.025	89–103 Actinides**	104 Ku Rutherfordium 262[1]	105 Ha Hahnium 260[1]														

* Lanthanides (Rare earths):

| 57 La
Lanthanum
138.91 | 58 Ce
Cerium
140.12 | 59 Pr
Praseodymium
140.91 | 60 Nd
Neodymium
144.24 | 61 Pm
Promethium
145[1] | 62 Sm
Samarium
150.4 | 63 Eu
Europium
151.96 | 64 Gd
Gadolinium
157.2 | 65 Tb
Terbium
158.93 | 66 Dy
Dysprosium
162.50 | 67 Ho
Holmium
164.93 | 68 Er
Erbium
167.26 | 69 Tm
Thulium
168.93 | 70 Yb
Ytterbium
173.04 | 71 Lu
Lutetium
174.97 |

** Actinides:

| 89 Ac
Actinium
227.05 | 90 Th
Thorium
232.04 | 91 Pa
Protactinium
231.04 | 92 U
Uranium
238.03 | 93 Np
Neptunium
237[1] | 94 Pu
Plutonium
239[1] | 95 Am
Americium
243[1] | 96 Cm
Curium
247[1] | 97 Bk
Berkelium
247[1] | 98 Cf
Californium
251[1] | 99 Es
Einsteinium
254[1] | 100 Fm
Fermium
253[1] | 101 Md
Mendelevium
256[1] | 102 No
Nobelium
254[1] | 103 Lw
Lawrencium
257[1] |

[1] Mass no. of the longest lived of the known isotopes

Fig. 1. Periodic table of the elements
Source: Wincierz, 1973, p. 24.

The lithosphere – the external silicate layer of the earth's crust, approximately 12 kilometres thick – consists mainly of non-metals. Only the outer 1600 metres of this surface crust is at all well known through drilling or from the geological folding of the rock layers. Estimates have been made – from varying, often conflicting, sources – based on numerous analyses, as to the frequency of occurrence of the elements in the earth's solid crust.[1] According to these, the proportion of heavy metals (including iron) amounts to about 6% of the elements making up the earth's crust. The heavy non-ferrous metals, copper, lead, zinc, tin and nickel, together make up only some 0.65%. Light metals on the other hand are present in the earth's crust in considerably higher quantities, accounting for 18%, with aluminium far in excess of the others; the proportion of magnesium is also significantly higher than all other non-ferrous metals, of which the highest proportions occurring are titanium and magnesium. Chromium, nickel, zinc and copper follow some way behind, while smaller amounts of lead and tin are found in the earth's crust (Table 1).

Mining is confined to the outer 2 kilometres of the earth's crust, in which the metals sought occur as principal or secondary components of ore minerals, in considerably higher concentrations, however, than the average values indicated in Table 1. Mining is still largely confined today to the exploitation of terrestrial ore or mineral deposits. Ocean mining of manganese nodules containing copper and nickel (particularly in the Pacific Ocean), as well as the economic utilization of the metal-containing, hot, salt springs on the bed of the Red Sea, are still largely at the research stage (Wincierz, 1973, p. 13 ff.).

Metals rarely occur in nature in the native or almost pure state; among the non-ferrous metals, virtually the only pure copper deposits of importance were those, now largely exhausted, at Lake Superior in the United States. As a rule metals are compounded with non-metallic elements to form ores, usually in mineral combinations with silicic acid, lime, alumina or magnesia. The minerals are denoted as acid ores or basic ores depending on the nature of the surrounding (barren) rock, the gangue. From the metallurgical point of view, a distinction is made between oxide ores, in which the metal is compounded with oxygen – as is the case with the carbonates, silicates and sulphates – or sulphide ores, in which the metal is combined with sulphur.

The metallic minerals are not uniformly distributed in the earth's crust. Processes within the interior of the earth have resulted in formation of primary and secondary masses. The first group, i.e., deposits which have their origins in the magma, include all gangue deposits. In these the ore concentrations in fissures of the enclosing rock are disconformable orebodies, while those in which the ore veins run parallel to the rock strata are known as stratiform or

[1] The content of metal oxides and metal sulphides (particularly of iron) increases considerably in the deeper layers. Owing to the high average density of the earth itself and the composition of meteorites, it is believed that the interior of the earth probably consists mainly of nickel-iron (Wincierz, 1973, p. 13).

Table 1. Technical data on the principal industrial non-ferrous metals

Metal		Density at 20°C g/cm³	Atomic weight[1]	Melting point °C	Boiling point °C	Electrical conductivity $\mu\Omega^{-1}$ cm^{-1}	Frequency ppm
Heavy metals							
Lead	Pb	11.34	207.19	327.4	1,751	0.048	12.5
Copper	Cu	8.96	63.54	1,084	2,595	0.598	55
Zinc	Zn	7.13	65.37	419.6	907	0.177	70
Tin	Sn	7.29	118.69	232	2,270	0.088	2
Light metals							
Aluminium	Al	2.70	26.98	660	2,447	0.382	82,300
Magnesium	Mg	1.74	24.31	649.5	1,107	0.224	23,300
Titanium	Ti	4.51	47.90	1,668	3,260	0.024	5,700
Steel improvers							
Chromium	Cr	7.2	51.99	1,875	2,665	0.078	100
Cobalt	Co	8.9	58.93	1,499	2,900	0.18	25
Manganese	Mn	7.43	54.94	1,244	2,150	0.0054	950
Molybdenum	Mo	10.22	95.94	2,610	4,860	0.19	1.5
Nickel	Ni	8.91	58.71	1,453	2,730	0.16	75.
Vanadium	V	6.12	50.94	1,900	3,380[3]	0.048	135
Tungsten	W	19.27	183.85	3,380	5,900	0.181	1.5
Alloying and special metals							
Antimony	Sb	6.69	121.75	630.5	1,637	0.025	0.2
Cerium	Ce	6.77	140.12	797	3,470	0.013	60
Hafnium	Hf	13.36	178.49	2,222	5,400	0.031	3
Cadmium	Cd	8.64	112.40	321	765	0.135	0.2
Lanthanum	La	6.16	138.91	920	3,470	0.016	30
Lithium	Li	0.53	6.94	180.5	1,326	0.108	20
Niobium	Nb	8.55	92.91	2,468	5,100[3]	0.066	20
Mercury	Hg	13.55	200.59	−38.6[2]	357	0.011	0.08
Rhenium	Re	21.04	186.2	3,180	5,870	0.051	0.0007
Silicon	Si	2.33	28.09	1,410	2,680	10^{-12}[4]	281,500
Tantalum	Ta	16.6	180.95	2,996	5,400[3]	0.081	2
Bismuth	Bi	9.79	208.98	271	1,560	0.009	0.17
Yttrium	Y	4.47	88.91	1,509	3,630	0.019	33
Zirconium	Zr	6.50	91.22	1,852	4,370	0.023	165

1. Reference unit: mass of carbon isotope ^{12}C. 2. Setting point.
3. Estimated. 4. Compensated semi-conductor.
Sources: Wincierz, 1973; *Brockhaus*, 1966.

conformable orebodies. Irregular formations in the surrounding rock are called stockworks, i.e., a mass of interlacing veins, both horizontal and vertical. There may also be metallic minerals in sedimentary structures which have been subjected to various chemical and physical processes and to other agencies, weathering, transportation (rivers, sea currents, ice, wind) with subsequent new formations arising. Non-ferrous ore minerals are frequently found in complex combinations with other minerals (Lüpfert, 1942, p. 18).

According to the criterion of use as industrial materials, the technically most important non-ferrous metals, excluding the precious metals, may be classified as follows:

(a) heavy metals: lead, copper, zinc and tin;
(b) light metals: aluminium, magnesium and titanium;
(c) steel improving agents (as alloying metals) or special metals (as base

metals): chromium, cobalt, manganese, molybdenum, nickel, vanadium and tungsten;
(d) other alloying or special metals: antimony, cerium, hafnium, cadmium, lanthanum, lithium, niobium, mercury, rhenium, silicon, tantalum, bismuth, yttrium and zirconium.

The boundaries between the groups are very fluid: metals preferably used for alloys in the past are now acquiring increasing importance as basic metals for new industrial materials. To meet the continually higher standards imposed by the progress of industrial development some of these special metals, owing to more intensive utilization of their physical and chemical properties, are now taking their place beside the traditional non-ferrous metals in various branches of modern technology.

1.2 OCCURRENCE AND DEPOSITS OF METALLIC RAW MATERIALS

The metallic raw materials are found in a large number of minerals, some of which occur all over the world and others only in specific deposits. Some metals usually occur as compounds and others predominantly or exclusively as by-products in the mining of other metals. Almost all metals in nature are found not in elementary form but as chemical compounds; the occurrence of native metals is the exception and is essentially confined to the nobler metals, i.e., those with less oxygen affinity. The classification of mineral raw materials is generally made today according to the definitions used by the US Bureau of Mines, which have also been adopted by the Federal German Institute for Geophysical Sciences and Raw Materials (BGR) Hanover. The classification is according to:

(a) Resources. A concentration of naturally occurring solid, liquid or gaseous materials in or on the earth's crust in such form that economic extraction of a commodity is currently or potentially feasible.

(b) Reserves. That portion of the identified resources from which a usable mineral or energy commodity can be economically and legally extracted at the time of determination.

The dividing lines between these two categories are, by definition, very elastic. Mineral deposits identified as resources, if successfully prospected under specific economic conditions, become reserves; in the event of a slump in raw materials prices, reserves or deposits for economic or technical reasons may again revert to the category of resources.

The structure and development of the world metal economy is mainly characterized by the type and regional distribution of deposits of the individual non-ferrous metals.

Non-ferrous metals

1.2.1 Heavy metals

Copper

Copper occurs in at least 160 minerals, of which however only a few are of economic importance. The most important sulphide copper ores are copper pyrite (chalcopyrite), variegated purple copper ore (bornite) and copper glance (chalcocite), while the oxide copper ores are malachite, azurite and silicated copper (chrysocolla). Proven deposits of copper glance (chalcocite) are to be found in almost every continent, but deposits of market relevance today are mainly concentrated in the following principal geographical areas:

> In South America the Cordilleras Mountain Range – with the deposits in Chile (Chuquicamata), El Salvador (Antina and El Teniente), Peru (Cerro de Pasco, Atacames and Arequipe), Bolivia (Corocoro), Mexico (La Caridad) and Panama (Cerro Colorado); altogether about 30% of copper deposits in the Western world.
> The west and south-west area of the United States along the Colorado Plateau in the State of Arizona (with the districts of Miami, Globe, Ray, Morenci and Bisbee), Utah (of which Bingham is the largest district), New Mexico, Montana (including the district of Butte) and Nevada (with the deposits of Ely and Chino); about 25% of the copper reserves of the Western World are found in the United States.
> The 'Precambrian Shield' in the Canadian province of Manitoba, Ontario and Quebec, of which the copper-nickel deposits of the Sudbury district and the deposits in Quebec are the most important; some 10% of the mineral reserves of the Western World are located here.
> The Copper Belt in the Province of Shaba, central Africa, which is shared among the states of Zambia, Zaire and Zimbabwe; the African Shield contains just under 20% of the deposits of the Western World.
> In Europe the copper deposits of the Huelva district of Spain and Portugal, those in Ireland and at Rammelsberg in the Federal Republic of Germany; Europe has just under 4% of the Western reserves (Pasdach, 1974, p. 169).
> In the USSR the area comprising the Central and South Urals, the Caucasus and also Kazakhstan, Uzbekistan and Uzokan in the Transbaikal.

During the last few decades the deposits in the Philippines and Oceania, for example in Papua-New Guinea and Fiji, as well as in Australia and in Iran at Sar Chesmeh, have acquired economic significance. Among the many comparatively small deposits in Europe those of Poland should be mentioned in particular.

The main bulk of copper production comes from ores which are primarily mined for their copper content (in the United States around 98%). A large number of by-products – lead, molybdenum, iron and zinc – are also recovered from these ores, however (cf. Table 2), by selective flotation of the ore, while gold, silver, nickel, platinum, palladium, selenium and tellurium occur in the anode slime occurring during the refining of raw copper. Arsenic and sulphur are recovered during copper smelting and rhenium can be obtained by selective processing from molybdenum concentrates produced in the working of certain copper ores. In Canada a great deal of the copper production is from ores which were primarily mined for their nickel content, and a large proportion of world cobalt production is from copper ores in Zaire.

Lead and zinc

These two metals are very closely associated from the geochemical point of view and therefore usually occur together in lead-zinc deposits. The volume ratios vary considerably, however. Some deposits contain predominantly lead or zinc, some approximately the same amount of lead and zinc, of which the latter is by far the most important (about 70% lead mining or 60% zinc mining), and some, in addition, are complex deposits of copper and zinc ores with slight lead contents. As minor metals the following should be mentioned in particular: silver, in lead ores; cadmium, in zinc ores; and, in complex ores, silver, gold, copper, cadmium, antimony, bismuth and arsenic. In this context mention should be made of the particularly interesting Tsumeb deposit in South West Africa which has the highest overall content of non-ferrous metals (copper, lead, zinc, cadmium, selenium, gold and silver). The first jobbing smelters (i.e., those operating on a toll basis) in Europe were originally based on Tsumeb ores.

The most important lead-zinc deposits are found in North America, in the Rocky Mountains (Idaho, Utah, Colorado, New Mexico and Arizona), the Mississippi Valley area (Missouri Lead Belt, Oklahoma, Kansas, etc.) and the Appalachians. These are continued to the north in the districts of the Shield Regions of Canada, while in the south they link up with the deposits in Mexico and Honduras and with the Cordilleras and Andes of Peru towards

Table 2. By-products of copper recovery and copper production from non-cuprous ores in the United States, 1975

By-product	Production (tonnes)	Share of total production of the by-product (%)	By-product	Production (tonnes)	Share of total production of the by-product (%)
		By-products of copper recovery[1]			
Arsenic	–[2]	100	Molybdenum	15,800.0	32.9
Rhenium	0.9	100	Gold	10.3	31.5
Selenium	176.0	100	Sulphur	632,500.0	4.8
Palladium	–[2]	99.9	Zinc	< 500.0	
Tellurium	59.4	100	Lead	< 500.0	
Silver	380.6	35.0	Copper	126,400.0	98.6
		By-products of copper production from non-cuprous ores			
Lead	14,500.0	1.1	Silver	1,800.0	0.1
Zinc	1,800.0	0.1	Tungsten	< 0.5	

1. Other by-products of copper recovery are platinum, nickel and iron. 2. Information from production firms not released for publication.
Source: Schroeder, 1976.

North Bolivia. Africa has lead-zinc deposits in Morocco, Tunisia and Algeria as well as in Zaire, Zambia and South West Africa.

Some of the most extensive deposits in the world, however, are in Australia (Queensland and Broken Hill); in Asia important deposits are found in the USSR (the Urals, Kazakhstan, Uzbekistan) as well as in Iran, China, Burma, Thailand and Japan.

In Europe Yugoslavia, Bulgaria and Rumania dispose of extensive deposits, as does Ireland, where mining started in 1966. Spain, Sweden, Italy, Austria and Poland also belong to the countries with lead-zinc deposits and in the Federal Republic of Germany Bad Grund, Rammelsberg near Goslar (Harz), as well as Meggen, can look back on an ancient tradition of lead and zinc mining (Dumstorff, 1974, p. 195; Weisser, 1977, p. 28).

The main bulk of mine production of lead (over 70%) comes predominantly from works in which zinc and – of secondary importance – silver are the principal profit makers; less than a third come from the actual lead ore mining works in which lead is the main commodity. Up to 80% of lead ores are extracted by deep mining, to which a transition is possible from the original surface mining after a specific ratio of spoil to ore quantity is reached (von der Linden, 1977, pp. 33, 36). Price changes can bring about a marked shift in these relationships, however.

Tin

With tin ores two types may be distinguished, primary ores and secondary ores (alluvial deposits). The only tin ore of importance is cassiterite (tinstone) which as 'mine tin' (or 'pure tin') usually occurs in complex form with other heavy metals; the principal deposits of this kind are found in Bolivia, the USSR (Siberia) and Australia. The alluvial ores occurring in pebble and sand bank deposits in rivers and coastal areas in South East Asia (Malaysia, Indonesia, Thailand), central Africa (Nigeria) and Brazil are considerably easier to work than the complex primary ores. The tin content of the alluvial deposits is certainly small, but when extracted with large floating dredgers they are ready to prepare, with only 0.1% tin content. Cassiterite frequently occurs here in association with tungsten (wolfram). Cassiterite concentrates often contain over 75% tin, those from primary ores about 60% (*Meyers Handbuch*, 1971, p. 251).

1.2.2 Light metals

Aluminium

This does not occur in metallic form in nature but in its compounds, particularly with oxygen or sulphate and as a complex compound with silicic acid, it makes up 8.2% of that part of the earth's crust which is accessible to us. After oxygen and silicon it is the third most frequent element found. Almost three-quarters of all rock-forming minerals are aluminium silicates, with the feldspar group predominant (Wiesinger and Schuchardt, 1974, p. 279).

The primary material for aluminium production, aluminium oxide, is in the main produced from bauxite. In many parts of the globe, however, there are also other extensive, aluminium-rich deposits, from which it would technically be possible to extract aluminium but which are at present not yet competitive with production from bauxite.

The mineralogical composition of the numerous types of bauxite (Cissarz *et al.*, 1973, p. 5 ff.) has an influence on the process technology in the production of aluminium oxide. The majority of the known, high-quality world reserves of bauxite are to be found, approximately one-third each, in Australia and New Guinea. The deposits in Jamaica and Surinam, with 5–7% each, are in comparison only of moderate size, while the entire Eastern Bloc – in which the bauxite deposits of Hungary are especially worth mention – possesses only the same proportion. Twenty-four other countries, including Yugoslavia, France, Greece, the United States and Latin America, also have appreciable reserves.

Magnesium

Magnesium occurs abundantly in the earth's crust and is very widespread. It is found in over 50 minerals, of which, however, only magnesite, dolomite, brucite and olivine (chrysolite) are of importance for extraction. Also major sources of magnesium are all salt deposits, salt lakes and seawater. The largest magnesite deposits are found in the People's Republic of China, North Korea and the USSR. North America and a number of European countries, such as Austria, however, also have supplies of this mineral. Dolomite and the other magnesium-containing ores are likewise found all over the world.

Titanium

The primary material for the extraction of titanium metal is furnished by the two ores ilmenite and rutile, with varying, often high, iron contents; the exploitation of the remaining over 140 known titanium minerals is still at present uneconomic. The most important deposits of rutile are located in eastern Australia. Mining was discontinued in Sierra Leone in 1971 as being uneconomic for the time being (cf. Gocht, 1974, p. 337); of less importance are the deposits in Sri Lanka, India, South Africa and Brazil.

Ilmenite deposits exceed those of rutile many times over, so that the annual world production of titanium from ilmenite concentrates is some 8–10 times greater than that of rutile. Ilmenite is widely found in nature: Australia, the United States, Canada, Norway and the USSR possess the most important deposits, but only four countries in the world at present undertake the necessary raw material preparation for titanium production – the USSR, the United States, the United Kingdom and Japan; a preparation plant is also planned for France.

1.2.3 Steel improvers

Chromium

This does not occur as a metal in nature but is found only in the chemically combined state, mainly as oxides, chromates or silicates. Mining is based exclusively on chromite, which in 1797 was recognized to be a component of red lead ores from which it was first produced as a pure metal in 1854. Chromite is found all over the world, but, compared with the extensive deposits in South Africa and Zimbabwe, the deposits in other countries – including the USSR, Turkey, United States, Finland, the Philippines, Canada and India – are of very secondary importance.

Cobalt

This occurs in the earth's crust almost exclusively in admixture with the ores of other metals, of which the cobalt content is very slight. Only isolated deposits are found with cobalt as the chief component. Cobalt occurs predominantly as a by-product of copper and nickel and the major part of Western production is extracted at copper mines – in particular in Zaire, Zambia and Canada.

Manganese

This metal does not exist as an isolated element in nature. It occurs in many types of ore, often, however, with a very low metal content. The most important minerals for the recovery of manganese are manganese oxides such as pyrolusite and manganite. Owing to the comparatively high solubility of the many minerals contained in the primary rocks, manganese ore deposits are often of a secondary nature, and are indeed usually weathering or marine sedimentary deposits. The most extensive deposits are found in the USSR, Gabon, India, Brazil, South Africa and the People's Republic of China (Wuth, 1974, p. 71 ff.). Manganese-containing deposits are widely distributed in the oceans, and also in rivers and freshwater lakes, but exploration of minerals on the ocean bed is still at the development stage (Kollwentz, 1975, p. 12). The metals primarily of economic interest for the ocean mining of manganese nodules are nickel, copper and cobalt. The potential for the extraction of manganese, molybdenum, vanadium, zinc and titanium is regarded with a certain scepticism, either because of the very slight contents of these metals in the nodules, which makes it questionable whether production could be economic, or because of the high concentration of manganese (25–30%). Artificially accelerated production of this metal could cause far-reaching problems in view of the existing trend towards 'oversaturation' of the market (cf. Boin and Müller, 1975, p. 44).

Molybdenum

By far the most important ore for molybdenum recovery is molybdenum glance (molybdenite), resembling graphite, which can easily be separated even from very low-grade ores by flotation to form concentrates of 75–90%. The principal deposits are situated at Climax (Colorado) in the United States,[1] but molybdenum glance also occurs in many deposits of sulphide copper ores, particularly on the west coasts of North and South America, including El Teniente and El Salvador in Chile.[2] In the United States in 1975 approximately 33% of the total production of molybdenum was mined as a by-product of copper production – in other years this percentage has been even higher (see Table 2).

Nickel

In the case of nickel four types of ore may be distinguished:

(a) sulphidic ores, which usually form numerous ore bodies (Canada, the USSR, South Africa, Australia);

(b) lateritic weathering ores – of considerably lower grade than the sulphidic ores – frequently occurring regionally in ore provinces (New Caledonia, Cuba, the Philippines, Indonesia, Brazil, the United States, Greece);

(c) arsenidic ores, which are today virtually worked out (Schneeberg district of Saxony);

(d) sedimentary ores in the manganese nodules on the ocean floor which, according to tests carried out to date, contain on average approximately 0.99% nickel (Gocht, 1974, p. 101).

In the 1880s the largest nickel deposit in the world was discovered and opened up in the Sudbury district of Ontario, and Canada – which has other significant nickel deposits in Manitoba – even today still supplies about 30–40% of the mine production of nickel. The most important nickel mining areas of the world also include the Pacific island of New Caledonia, where mining began in 1875 and where present output has a nickel content of 2.5–3.0%. The United States has mineable nickel deposits in Oregon and Minnesota. The USSR possesses one of the most extensive nickel deposits in the world on the Kola Peninsula and has also opened up nickel ore mines in Siberia and in the Urals. Since 1966 important nickel deposits have also been discovered in Australia during the course of an exploration campaign. The exploration of these has now put the country in fourth place for nickel mine production. Substantial deposits of nickel ore have likewise been discovered in the Philippines, while in Indonesia there are numerous beds of lateritic ores.

1 The latest drillings in Alaska have shown that possibly the second largest molybdenum deposit in the world is to be found there in an area belonging to a US subsidiary of the Rio Tinto-Zinc Corporation Ltd. However, it also extends partly into the Tongass National Park, which is a Nature Conservancy Area.
2 The Chilean State CODELCO concern started up a new molybdenum extraction plant at Las Cascadas in the spring of 1979. The residues from the copper concentrate plant serve as primary material.

South Africa and Zimbabwe also have substantial nickel ore deposits, of which mining has been greatly expanded during the last ten years. In Europe the nickel deposits in Greece are of some importance and nickel ores are also extracted in Yugoslavia and Finland. Over 95% of nickel is extracted from deposits which are primarily exploited for this raw material. Considerable quantities of by-products occur in the metallurgical working of nickel ores: half (52%) of world production of platinum metals, 30% of cobalt mine production and 4% of copper output in the world (Düsseldorf *Handelsblatt* of 14 August 1978).

The minerals of the ocean bed offer an as yet untapped potential supply of nickel, of which, according to present findings, the manganese nodules in the Pacific and Indian Oceans are of economic interest. The possibilities and problems of opening up marine mineral deposits and their implications for raw materials supplies in the future are examined in detail in Chapter 12.

Vanadium

Vanadium has been identified in nature in 68 minerals containing over 1% V (up to coulsonite with 47.7%), even though it is seldom found in mineable deposits. Recovery is almost exclusively from vanadium-containing intermediate products of iron, copper, zinc and uranium extraction; bauxites as a rule have small vanadium contents. It is of some importance, additionally, as a by-product from petroleum and oil shales. The USSR and (some way behind) South Africa and Australia are estimated to possess the largest vanadium reserves in the world. More extensive vanadium deposits (lead vanadates) are found in the United States and South West Africa as well as in South Africa and Finland, in the form of vanadium-containing titanium/iron-magnetites (*Metalle*, 1965, p. 50).

Tungsten

Tungsten (also known as wolfram) occurs in a great many minerals, of which, however, only wolframite and scheelite are of economic importance. In some deposits tungsten is the only mineral element of value, others also contain tin, molybdenum, antimony, copper, lead and precious metals. The most frequent combination is tungsten with tinstone (cassiterite) as in China, Burma, Malaysia, Thailand, Bolivia, Brazil, Portugal, Spain, Austria (Mittersill) and other countries. In the United States, on the other hand, the most important tungsten deposits are combined with molybdenum (Stevens, 1975, p. 1165).

1.2.4 Other alloying and special metals

Antimony

This metal occurs only in compounds: antimonite (grey antimony or antimony glance) is by far the most important ore and the metal is only recovered as a by-product from a few of the other known 112 antimony-containing minerals (mostly sulphur compounds); it is often found in lead ores, and it is then a component of refined lead. The principal deposits are found in China, South Africa, Bolivia and the USSR. A few European countries also possess minor deposits.

Cadmium

Cadmium does not occur independently – not even in the only important cadmium mineral greenockite – but is found in cadmium-containing zinc ores, from which the metal is recovered by smelting in all major zinc refineries.

Mercury

Mercury is found almost everywhere, despite the fact that, owing to the small amount occurring, it is one of the rarest elements of the earth. Of the 17 known mercury minerals, red cinnabar (cinnabarite or coralline ore) is by far of greatest importance, representing 95% of production; in the United States it is also obtained as a by-product of gold and zinc. The richest deposit in the world is found in the province of Ciudad Real, Spain. The USSR, China, Italy and Yugoslavia also dispose of important mercury reserves, followed at some distance by Mexico, Canada and the United States, whereas deposits in other countries of the Western World, including Turkey and the Philippines, are comparatively slight.

Bismuth

This occurs as a sulphide or is native in southern Bolivia, but, owing to the very slight quantities available, it is only recovered as a by-product of a few ores, e.g., from lead-copper ores in the United States, Peru, Canada and Australia, from tin ores in Bolivia and from nickel-cobalt ores in Mexico, etc.

The numerous other minor metals are usually recovered coupled with or as by-products of other mining activities. They are typically produced as a small adjunct of the main activity of large firms and therefore do not justify a separate branch of industry (Zimmermann, 1972, p. 483). A chart giving the main countries with reserves appears as Table 49, pp. 225–256.

2

The production structure of the non-ferrous metal industry

The production sector of the non-ferrous metal industry displays basically a multi-stage vertical sub-division:

(a) metal ore mining and preparation;
(b) smelting industry and refining;
(c) metal fabrication.

These production stages in the still small production concerns of the early industrial era largely coincided with the organization of the individual works. However, as the domestic raw materials supply base dwindled in the industrial countries and ore mining was increasingly extended to overseas raw materials countries, the mining of metal ores became separated from the smelter industry. The mine workings were henceforth no longer the raw materials suppliers for subsequent production stages within the domain of the company but – under largely autonomous ownership – became market suppliers generally to the primary metal fabrication industry. In theory this has not altered with the setting up of smelters in the raw materials countries, even though, as a rule, the smelters are principally supplied within the concern from their own ore mines.

In the non-ferrous metal industry, in contrast to the steel industry, where subsequent processing to semi-manufactured goods is usually a direct adjunct of smelter operation, the activities of the smelters and of the fabrication works are often widely separated in location, organization and often also company participation (Winterhager, 1955, p. 3).

During the past 20 years, however, there have been signs of a reversal of this trend toward separation of smelter and semi-manufacturing production in the non-ferrous metals industries, with a switch to continuous processing, e.g., in copper with the production of cast rolled wire, in zinc with Ruhrzink-Rheinzink continuous strip casting in mould rolls (Hazelette process) and in the case of aluminium with the introduction of the Properzi process (i.e., large roller mill for strip casting).

2.1 METAL MINING AND ORE DRESSING

Metal mining covers prospecting, exploration, opening up and extraction of the metal contents of the earth's crust by surface mining, deep mining or ocean mining from the sea bed. There are two criteria for evaluating the mineability of raw material deposits.

(a) The natural state of a deposit, i.e., the size and richness, for which the metal content of the ore is of paramount significance. An important part is played here by the accessibility of the deposits (the feasibility of opening them up to mining and also the geographical location and transport facilities).

(b) The other relevant factor is the stage of social development in the area – the comparative wage rates prevailing in the mining district and the social services available (housing, insurance, etc.), the costs of expanding the infrastructure and other specific cost items arising, such as complying with orders relating to environmental protection. A period of six to ten years is generally estimated for the establishment of a mine working from the prospecting stage up to the actual commencement of mining.

As the metal content of the crude ores is usually small, to make smelting worthwhile the ores usually have first to undergo concentration, which involves separation of the metal-containing minerals from the barren rock or gangue and, in the case of complex ores, separation also of the different metallic minerals without bringing about any chemical change in the material. The ore dressing and concentration takes various forms according to the physical properties utilized (see Fig. 2):

(a) the difference in the specific weights of the minerals for gravity concentration;
(b) the surface hydrophobic and hydrophilic properties of the minerals for separation by flotation;
(c) the magnetic conductivity of the metallic minerals for magnetic separation;
(d) the electrical conductivity of the materials for electrostatic separation.

The flotation process is applied today to approximately 90% of copper ores, 60–70% of lead ores and 50% of zinc ores.

The unceasing progress of technology which is a feature of industrialization naturally also has a decisive effect on metal mining. Improvements in prospecting methods have uncovered new reserves and modern techniques have enabled deposits to be mined which were previously regarded as of only marginal importance. Economic mining is now also possible of deposits of increasing complexity with a continually higher metal yield. Improvements in dressing techniques have also permitted the exploitation of low-grade ores and those difficult to open up. Copper mining, for example, has been carried out through the centuries by the selective process of separating the ore from the gangue: for this shaft mining is usually required. Today, however, owing to

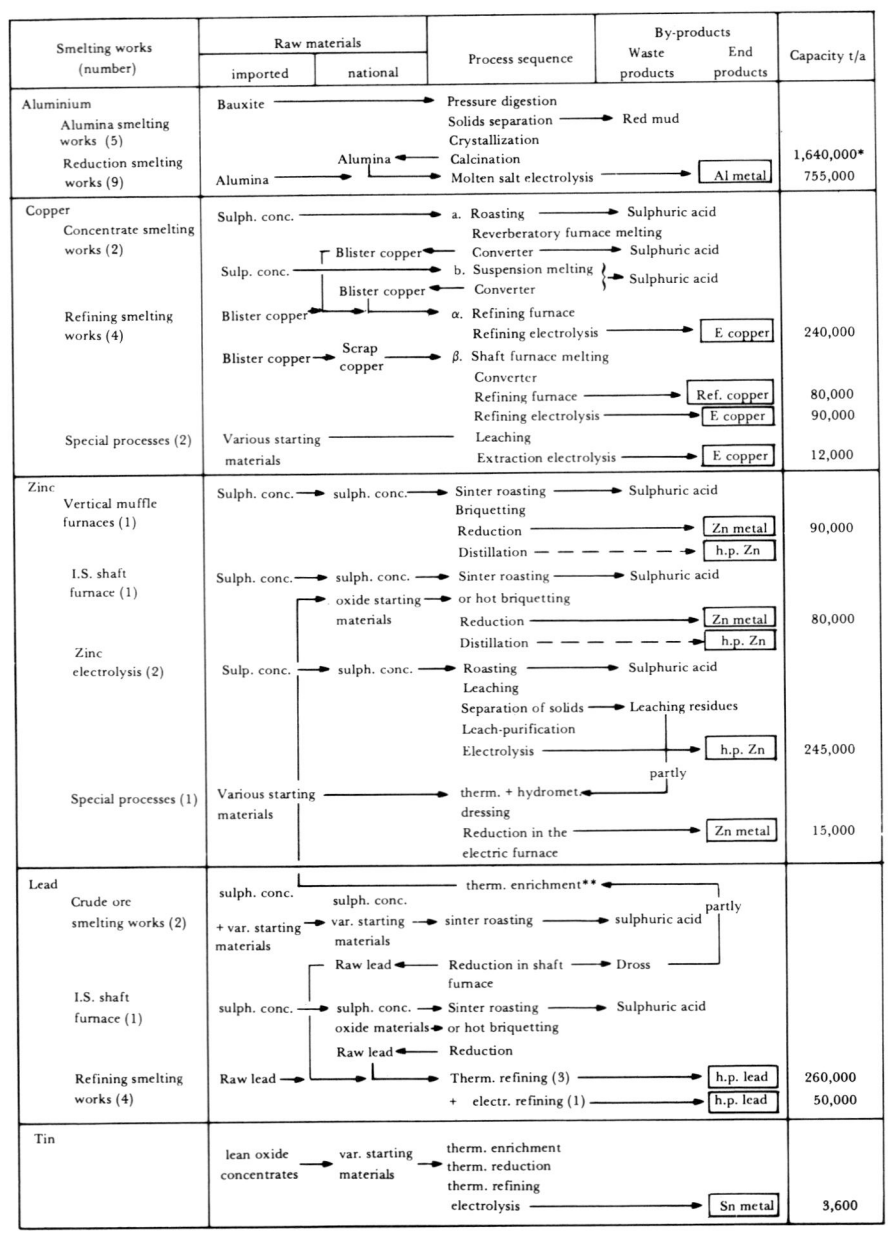

Smelting works (number)	Raw materials — imported	Raw materials — national	Process sequence	By-products — Waste products	By-products — End products	Capacity t/a
Aluminium	Bauxite		Pressure digestion			
Alumina smelting works (5)			Solids separation → Red mud			
			Crystallization			1,640,000*
Reduction smelting works (9)	Alumina →	Alumina ←	Calcination			
			Molten salt electrolysis →		Al metal	755,000
Copper						
Concentrate smelting works (2)	Sulph. conc. →		a. Roasting → Sulphuric acid			
			Reverberatory furnace melting			
		Blister copper ←	Converter → Sulphuric acid			
	Sulp. conc. →		b. Suspension melting } → Sulphuric acid			
		Blister copper ←	Converter			
Refining smelting works (4)	Blister copper →		α. Refining furnace			
			Refining electrolysis →		E copper	240,000
	Blister copper →	Scrap copper	β. Shaft furnace melting			
			Converter			
			Refining furnace →		Ref. copper	80,000
			Refining electrolysis →		E copper	90,000
Special processes (2)	Various starting materials		Leaching			
			Extraction electrolysis →		E copper	12,000
Zinc						
Vertical muffle furnaces (1)	Sulph. conc. →	sulph. conc. →	Sinter roasting → Sulphuric acid			
			Briquetting			
			Reduction →		Zn metal	90,000
			Distillation – – – – – →		h.p. Zn	
I.S. shaft furnace (1)	Sulph. conc. →	sulph. conc. →	Sinter roasting → Sulphuric acid			
		oxide starting materials →	or hot briquetting			
			Reduction →		Zn metal	80,000
			Distillation – – – – – →		h.p. Zn	
Zinc electrolysis (2)	Sulp. conc. →	sulph. conc. →	Roasting → Sulphuric acid			
			Leaching			
			Separation of solids → Leaching residues			
			Leach-purification			
			Electrolysis →		h.p. Zn	245,000
				partly		
Special processes (1)	Various starting materials		therm. + hydromet. dressing			
			Reduction in the electric furnace →		Zn metal	15,000
Lead						
Crude ore smelting works (2)	sulph. conc. →	sulph. conc.	therm. enrichment** ←			
	+ var. starting materials →	var. starting materials →	sinter roasting → sulphuric acid	partly		
		Raw lead ←	Reduction in shaft furnace → Dross			
I.S. shaft furnace (1)	sulph. conc. →	sulph. conc. →	Sinter roasting → Sulphuric acid			
		oxide materials →	or hot briquetting			
		Raw lead ←	Reduction			
Refining smelting works (4)	Raw lead →		Therm. refining (3) →		h.p. lead	260,000
			+ electr. refining (1) →		h.p. lead	50,000
Tin	lean oxide concentrates	var. starting materials	therm. enrichment			
			therm. reduction			
			therm. refining			
			electrolysis →		Sn metal	3,600

* Aluminium oxide
** Rotary process ('Waelz' process)

Fig. 2. Processes for non-ferrous metals recovery and smelter capacity in West Germany, up to the end of 1980
Sources: *Metallurgische Technik, Rohstoffe, Verfahren*, 1975; data from Metallgesellschaft AG, Frankfurt am Main.

Production structure of the industry

Technical terms used in Fig. 2.

Blister copper	Product from the converter; impure copper.
Pressure digestion	Process for digestion of bauxite with the aim of producing alumina (Bayer Process).
Electrolysis	Process for obtaining metals from their aqueous solutions or for refining.
Reverberatory furnace	Unit for melting sulphide concentrates of copper, producing a lean dross and copper matte.
Hot briquetting	Process for sintering fine-grained oxide starting materials prior to use in the IS shaft furnace.
IS shaft furnace	Imperial Smelting shaft furnace for combined production of zinc and lead.
Calcining	Process for production of aluminium oxide (alumina) from the aluminium hydroxide obtained in pressure digestion.
Converter	Unit for blowing copper matte and for producing blister copper.
Copper matte	First enrichment product in the smelting of sulphide-type copper concentrates; mixture of iron sulphide and copper sulphide.
Leach-purification	Refining stage: wet-chemical removal of undesirable impurities before electrolytic production of zinc.
Leaching	Wet-chemical treatment of Zn-containing or Cu-containing materials (calcined material) for production of unpurified Zn (or Cu) solution).
Refining furnace	Unit for melting and pre-refining of crude copper.
Reduction	Conversion of a metal oxide to metal, especially by means of coke or coal.
Calcination	Conversion of a metal sulphide to metal oxide with elimination of SO_2, which is utilized for making sulphuric acid.
Red mud	Waste product from production of alumina from bauxite.
Molten salt electrolysis	Electrolytic production of aluminium from alumina.
Flash smelting	Process for smelting copper matte from sulphide-type copper concentrates (Outucompu Process).
Sinter roasting	Process for desulphurization and agglomeration of fine-grained starting materials in the production of lead and zinc.
Sulphide concentrates	Usual starting materials in the production of copper, zinc and lead.
Alumina	Starting material for aluminium production by molten salt electrolysis.
Rotary process	Process for enrichment of zinc and lead from lean starting materials.

exhaustion of the richer ore deposits, mining is now necessary of porphyry deposits for which the non-selective process is used without separation of the copper-containing components from the gangue. High-capacity modern machinery has rendered this process economic despite the low copper content. Since the mid 1950s the range of surface mining, according to ore content, has been continually extended and at the present time the lower limit for the copper content of the ore is at a level which would not have been considered economic in the past. For copper today this is less than 0.5%. A similar trend is to be noted in the case of other metallic minerals.

2.2 SMELTING AND REFINING

At the smelting works the metals are recovered from crude ores or mined from minerals processed to give ore concentrates (primary metal production).

Because of differing starting materials and the technical properties of the metals, however, the manufacturing process is not so standardized as in iron and steel works. The metallurgical requirements necessitate instead a multiplicity of smelting operations, which not only vary for different metals, but often inevitably diverge considerably even for the same metal. Moreover, smelting works are for the most part mixed operations, because non-ferrous ores generally occur in complex form in the deposits, so that other metals are present as by-products along with the principal metal, and smelting works generally aim to produce by-products (sulphuric acid, salts, etc.).

Despite the great variety in this branch of industry, a basic structure may be discerned in the production of non-ferrous metals (with the exception of aluminium[1]). As a result of advances in concentration techniques in the metal mining industry, especially in the last few decades, a considerable degree of separation of the metallic components from the other minerals can now generally be achieved, but final removal of undesirable accessory materials is still the function of the smelting process.[2]

Thus, the ores or concentrates of the heavy industrial metals copper, lead, zinc and nickel are mainly of a sulphidic nature and for smelting must be converted to the form of oxides in a roasting process involving elimination of the sulphur, so that the concentrates can be reduced with carbon or dissolved in dilute acids. Roasting of ores or concentrates is a heat treatment in an oxidizing atmosphere and leads to metal oxide and sulphur dioxide gas, which is usually converted to sulphuric acid. Ancillary sulphuric acid production is therefore typical of copper, lead, zinc and nickel smelting works, which are thus to some extent also chemical plants and enlarge the scope of the works appreciably.

Depending on the subsequent processing, the roasting process is effected partially, with part of the metal being converted to oxide form and the rest remaining bound to sulphur; in some cases the process is continued until 'dead roasting' is accomplished, when all the metal is present as oxide. Roasting may also lead to extensive formation of the sulphate of the metal, and this is appropriate in the case of copper and zinc ores that are to be further treated by wet processes, as the sulphate is soluble in water. Finally, metal sulphides or oxides can be converted to chlorides by adding chlorine gas or chlorine salts (chloridizing roasting), separation then being possible by leaching or volatilization. From the process engineering standpoint the roasting process is accomplished in various ways; its range extends from heap roasting of lump ore, which takes months, to suspension roasting (flash roasting) of finely-ground concentrates, which only takes seconds. Since the introduction of

1 For the production of primary aluminium, the commonest aluminium ore bauxite is processed to alumina (aluminium oxide, Al_2O_3) and this is then reduced to aluminium by molten salt electrolysis (Gocht, 1974, p. 282).
2 The following description is based in particular on Fischer and Bongers, 1971, p. 227 ff.

fluidized bed technology (around 1950), the traditional roasting equipment – multiple hearth furnaces and rotary kilns – finds less application than fluidized bed furnaces, which have nearly five times greater productivity and are suitable for all kinds of sulphide ores.

Smelting is usually accomplished in three stages:

(a) *concentration*, i.e. enrichment of the metal compounds;
(b) *reduction*, which is conversion to the metallic state;
(c) *refining*, which is the purification or final separation of the metallic substances.

Processing is generally effected in this order, but some other course may be appropriate, and it is also possible to combine two process stages, such as concentration and reduction, in a single metallurgical operation. Recovery of the metal can be achieved by:

(a) pyrometallurgical (dry) process;
(b) hydrometallurgical (wet) process;
(c) electrometallurgical process (molten-salt or aqueous electrolysis).

The metallurgical processing of ores or ore concentrates leads to pure metals, and sometimes to alloys; it only includes the recovering of metals outside laboratory production, however, which now means about 25–30 metals (including those occurring as by-products). Apart from the production of primary metals, the smelting works also undertake the production of secondary metals by metallurgical treatment of recycled material in the form of waste metal and scrap.

2.3 METAL PROCESSING

Further processing of the metals produced in the smelting works begins with melting and casting, and ends with surface treatment of the finished articles.[1] Various processes are applied to the material to give it the shape, surface finish and properties required by the subsequent fabrication. Alternatively, the metals or alloys are cast in smelting works to give ingots, pre-rolling and pre-drawing products, which are further processed in attached or outside works for semi-manufactures, or in foundries, to produce tubes, bars, sections, wire, sheet, strip and other shapes. Conveyance of molten metals to the processing works is also gaining in importance ('hot work' for cast strip and cast wire). Scrap from intermediates, such as process wastes from forging, stamping and rolling operations (process scrap) is also melted down for re-use in the semi-manufacturing works and foundries.

The metalworking processes are based essentially on shaping the metals by

[1] The following description is based in particular on the detailed description given by Eichmeyer (1971).

casting in moulds, by hot or cold deformation or by metal cutting, and joining metals by welding or similar processes. In these operations, heat treatment can produce specific mechanical and technological properties, and surface treatment can provide better resistance to corrosion by atmospheric agents or by various kinds of chemicals.

Depending on the type of metal and its melting and pouring temperature required throughout, intended application, quality required and other technical or economic criteria, various types of furnaces are used in foundries for melting non-ferrous metals. The range includes shaft, hearth, pan, induction or arc furnaces. The current trend is towards use of induction furnaces, as these have the advantage of neutral atmosphere during melting and therefore less risk of oxidation, low furnace temperature etc., and they also offer favourable conditions for alloying, little melting loss and high quality of the molten metals or alloys. Special mention should be made of the latest flame melting process, the Outocompu process, which is suitable in particular for copper and nickel.

Numerous processes have been developed for the casting of non-ferrous metals. The choice of process must first take into account the intended use of the articles. The physical and chemical properties of the metals also play an important part, as the end products have to meet certain mechanical and technological requirements in subsequent processing.

Hot and cold working of metals utilizes their plastic, i.e., permanent, deformability. Such working is accomplished either by non-cutting processes, such as forging, rolling, pressing and drawing, or by cutting operations. Electrical processes may also be employed for metal working; they are mainly used for hard metallic materials by the action of electric current, where the workpiece and the tool form the two electrodes. The most important advantages of electrical processes are the automatic work flow and the avoidance of mechanical stresses, as there is no direct contact between workpiece and tool. Electron beams and ultrasound are also employed for metal forming and removal.

3

The origins of the non-ferrous metal industry

3.1 THE DISCOVERY OF NON-FERROUS METALS AS INDUSTRIAL MATERIALS

To assess the importance of non-ferrous metals in the age of technology and trace the evolution of the metal industry under the influence of world economic industrialization processes we need first to have an idea of the state of knowledge of the metals and their uses in the pre-industrial era.

We know from archaeological discoveries and from tradition that the earliest use of metals extends back to prehistoric times (see Table 3). Probably the first metal was gold, which was found in native form as early as the Stone Age, some 8000 years ago, and later in the same epoch native silver and copper were also found. The first objects made from these metals are thought to be

Table 3. The discovery of the principal non-ferrous metals

Metal		Discovery or first preparation
Copper	4000 BC	Smelted from ores; known as alloy with tin (bronze) since 3000 BC, as alloy with zinc (brass) since 1000 BC.
Lead	3000 BC	Known in Egypt, obtained in Rhodes and Cyprus 550 BC.
Tin	3000 BC	Used in bronze objects as cassiterite (tin-stone) in China and Mesopotamia, and as pure metal 300 BC.
Mercury	300 BC	Amalgam (mercury–gold alloy).
Bismuth	15th century	Mentioned by Valentine, and later by Agricola and Paracelsus.
Cobalt	1735	Discovered by G. Brandt.
Zinc	18th century	Production of pure zinc in Europe; certainly known much earlier in Persia, China and India, and to the Babylonians and Syrians as an alloying component of copper.
Caesium	1746	Prepared as element by P. Platner; in 1860 identified by R. W. Bunsen and G. Kirchhoff by spectrum analysis.
Nickel	1751	Prepared by Alex F. Cronstedt as impure copper nickel; prepared in 1804 by B. Richter as pure metal; used in antiquity as coinage metal in Bactria, Eastern Asia and Southern Europe.
Manganese	1744	Isolated and prepared as metal by Gahn.

Table 3. (cont'd)

Metal		Discovery or first preparation
Antimony	1780	Prepared as metal by T. Bergmann; used in Egypt as early as 4000 BC.
Tellurium	1782	Discovered by F. Müller von Reichenstein in gold ores from Siebenbürgen.
Tungsten	1783	After preliminary work by C. W. Scheele, isolated by J. J. and F. de Elynar in Spain from the minerals wolframite and scheelite; wolframite was described as early as 1574 by Lazarus Becker.
Zirconium	1789	Discovered by H. M. Klaproth as oxide (zirconia); prepared in 1824 by J. J. Berzelius as impure metal.
Molybdenum	1790	Detected by Scheele and Hjelm as an element and molybdenite as its sulphide.
Titanium	1790	Discovered by W. Gregor as oxide in ilmenite sands of Cornwall; prepared as impure metal in 1825 by J. J. Berzelius, and recovered in 1895 by H. Moissan.
Yttrium[1]	1794	Discovered by J. Gadolin.
Chromium	1797	Chromium metal produced by Louis Vauquelin by reduction with carbon; in 1844 by J. J. Berzelius by reduction of chromium chloride with potassium; recovered by R. W. Bunsen in 1854 as electrolytic chromium; Goldschmidt produced aluminothermic chromium in 1893.
Beryllium	1797	Discovered by Vauquelin in the digestion of beryl, and first prepared in metallic form in 1828.
Niobium	1801	Discovered by C. Hatchett.
Vanadium	1801	Discovered by Del Rio in Mexican lead ores and named erythorium – discovery revoked; rediscovered in 1831 by Sefström.
Tantalum	1802	Discovered by G. Ekberg.
Cerium[1]	1803	Discovered by J. J. Berzelius, W. Hisinger and H. M. Klaproth.
Magnesium	1808	First prepared by H. Davy; produced by electrolysis by R. W. Bunsen in 1852.
Selenium	1817	Discovered in lead chamber sludge by J. J. Berzelius.
Lithium	1817	Discovered by J. A. Arfredson during analysis of petalite; metallic lithium prepared electrolytically by R. W. Bunsen and A. Matthiesen in 1855.
Cadmium	1817	Discovered by F. Strohmeyer as impurity in zinc smelter products; first obtained from sphalerite (zinc blende) concentrates in 1827.
Aluminium	1825	Discovered by H. C. Oersted, and by F. Wöhler in Berlin in 1827; first produced industrially in 1854 by H. Saint-Claire Deville.
Lanthanum[1]	1839	Discovered by C. C. Mosander.
Thallium	1861	Isolated by W. G. Crookes from lead chamber sludge.
Indium	1863	Discovered in sphalerite by F. Reich and T. Richter.
Gallium	1875	Prepared from sphalerite by Lecoq de Boisbaudran.
Germanium	1886	Prepared from argyrodite by Clemens Winkler.
Lutetium[1]	1907	Discovered by G. Urbain, 1908 discovered by A. von Welsbach.
Hafnium	1922	Obtained in collaboration between B. Coster and G. de Hevesy.

1. For the discovery of the other rare earths, see Gocht, 1974, p. 357.
Source: *Die Metalle*, 1965; Gocht, 1974; Neumann, 1904; Kieffer *et al.*, 1971.

jewellery, such as rings, arm-bands and brooches, but these were soon followed by utensils such as beakers, dishes and other vessels, as well as nails, simple tools and other articles in daily use. About 4000 BC fundamental progress was made with the discovery that by heating ore-bearing rock molten metal could be extracted from ores. This was obviously first applied to the recovery of copper, followed soon after by silver from lead ores. At first, in fact, no suitable application could be found for the lead which was thus produced. We only know that in ancient Egypt lead and antimony were put to practical use. When it was later discovered – again, apparently by chance – how to separate tin, hitherto known only as a native metal, from its ores, this was smelted together with copper to produce the alloy metal bronze. Owing to its excellent casting properties, the use of this metal came to be preferred, and in course of time an entire cultural era became known as the Bronze Age. Already in the second century BC the Mediterranean peoples knew how to produce brass from copper-zinc alloys. Pure zinc was not produced until about 1745. Pure mercury is believed to have been known in the Far East, in India and China, around 300 BC.

Although important metals were thus already known and used in prehistoric times, the role played by antiquity in the development of metals consisted less in new discoveries than in the application of metals and the diffusion of metallurgical knowledge to northern Europe. The Phoenicians, amongst whom a highly successful bronze industry flourished, handed down their knowledge of the smelting potentialities of metals to the peoples of the ancient civilizations of Asia, and the Greeks developed basic techniques for the recovery and working of copper from the rich ore deposits of the island of Cyprus.

Many centuries then elapsed before further progress was made in the knowledge of metals and their utilization. Pure metallic arsenic was probably not known until the Middle Ages and metallic bismuth is thought to have been in use only since the fifteenth century. Nearly another three centuries passed, however, before the great flood of discoveries began in the field of metals which, even though not put to economic use until much later, served in some measure to pave the way for the forthcoming breakthrough in the fundamental principles governing the industrial process. The large-scale production of elementary zinc and of cobalt dates from about the middle of the eighteenth century. Nickel, too, which had already been used in antiquity for coinage, was only identified as an element at this time and not until 50 years later first recovered as pure metal.

The second half of the eighteenth century saw the discovery of manganese, antimony, tellurium, tungsten (wolfram), molybdenum, zirconium, titanium, yttrium, chromium and beryllium; after the turn of the century niobium and vanadium were found and magnesium produced for the first time in the early 1800s. The discovery of uranium and the most important platinum metals also dates from this period. During the following decades the first recovery of cadmium and lithium and the discovery of the metalloid selenium, of lanthanum and most other metals of the rare earth group were recorded. Among the 'youngest' metals today aluminium is quantitatively the most important; after being prepared in metallic form (1825 or 1827), it was first produced on an industrial scale in 1854.

Finally, the late nineteenth century and early twentieth century marked the discovery and preparation in pure form of thallium, indium and other minor metals, as well as radium, polonium and other radioactive metals (also transuranium).[1]

We may sum up by saying that, after the exploration of the few metals known and used thousands of years ago, a long time was to elapse before the discovery of a great many other non-ferrous metals – metals that were indispensable for the realization of many technical inventions and innovations during the course of industrialization but which only acquired their full significance for the modern economy with the broad-based development of their respective fields of application. This applies also to the 'new' metals, most of which were already known over a century ago. These only became key raw materials, or even vital strategic materials, during the past few decades when their specific suitability for electronics, rocket propulsion, air travel, space flight, construction of satellites and reactors and the development of alternative forms of energy was recognized.

3.2 THE INDUSTRIAL REVOLUTION – THE GENERATIVE FORCE FOR THE NON-FERROUS METAL INDUSTRY

The availability of ores and the capacity for recovering metals from them and working them formed an important basis for handicrafts throughout human history. The growth of commercial production was largely based on the working of metals. Ore mining and metal recovery therefore are among the 'old' economic activities, as opposed to the 'new' branches of industry now being developed on the basis of materials discovered and evolved only by modern technology.

Despite its long history, going back thousands of years, the metal industry has tended until fairly recent times to be essentially a static sector of the economy. Metal requirements were essentially confined to traditional purposes, such as jewellery, coinage, household utensils, simple tools, printer's type and other articles of daily life. The use of metals for bell casting, construction of houses and churches and also the production of weapons and other military equipment has likewise been customary from time immemorial. Little progress was made in the discovery of 'new' metals, principally because

---

1 See Däbritz, 1931, p. 32 ff.; Gocht, 1974, p. 69 ff.; Lüpfert, 1942, p. 7 ff.; *Meyers Enzyklopädisches Lexikon*, 1976, p. 125; Sames, 1971, p. 9 ff.

of ignorance of the legal implications of the development of deposits of usable materials. It also usually takes some time for newly discovered metals to acquire any economic importance due to lack of knowledge of their suitable applications. A basic continuity may therefore be observed in the winning, working and application of metals in the pre-industrial era (Cipolla, 1976, p. 1 ff.). At the beginning of the nineteenth century, therefore, the metal industry, from the standpoint of the consumer and the producer, was still largely at the stage reached in previous centuries, and the world of metals, even on the eve of the industrial era, would have still been fully intelligible to the people of the past.

This continuity ceased towards the end of the eighteenth century. Production techniques based on invention and innovations began to supersede traditional methods and the Industrial Revolution, starting in the United Kingdom and spreading to the European continent and the New World, set in motion a fundamental change in industrial practice. The repercussions were to extend to all walks of life – a metamorphosis which marked the dawn of a new era in the history of mankind. The origins of this development, it is true, are deeply rooted in past centuries, when a new enlightened attitude to intellectual and historical ideas and categories, of thought appeared and the social structure began to crumble in face of powerful uprisings against the prevailing agrarian feudal system. This laid the foundations for a society based on trade and manufacture. A wealth of technical inventions in the early stages of the Industrial Revolution may also be considered to have enormously accelerated a process which had already been under way since the early Middle Ages (Lilley, 1976, p. 119).

First, however, drastic changes were needed in the technical and economic frame of reference – such as the one that began with the invention of the steam engine, which enabled chemical energy from coal to be converted into mechanical force – in order to set in motion the sweeping transformation from custom and tradition to progress and modernization. The intrinsic force of 'creative destruction' continually gathered momentum and finally brought about a radical break with the past. This was to prove a phenomenon with complex repercussions involving social, cultural and political changes extending far beyond the sphere of technology.

The harnessing of these new sources of energy signalled the advent of the Machine Age and the transition from the traditional to the modern industrial scene. Copper from the very beginning occupied a prominent place in the production of steam engines, because of its specific properties, and manufacture of the powered machines rapidly adopted in the different sectors of industry would not have been possible without its use and that of other metallic materials. This paved the way for a far-reaching change in the use of non-ferrous metals. Traditionally devoted to production of articles and utensils in daily use, they were increasingly diverted after the beginning of the nineteenth century to the manufacture of production equipment. There soon arose an unprecedented requirement for metals, both in volume and in quality, with a consequent sudden upsurge in the demands made of the metal industry.

New dimensions in the demand for metals were opened up still further with the use of the steam engine as a means of transport, first for steamships and then increasingly for railway locomotives. The development of the railways, beginning in England and the countries of Western Europe, followed by the United States and the rest of the world, at first brought about a vast increase in the demand for copper for equipping the locomotives with fireboxes, steam pipes, axle bearings, stud bolts, doors and cover plates. Rail waggon construction and the accessories industries also became important fields of application for non-ferrous metals. Modern shipbuilding likewise requires large quantities of copper, bronze and brass for ship's propellors, boilers, steam piping, refrigeration plant, electrical and plumbing installations, wiring and fittings of all kinds. For the development of the metal industry the train and the steamship were of far-reaching importance. This importance extended well beyond their capacity as metal consumers, however, because they now made remote raw materials areas and ore deposits, hitherto confined to local exploitation, accessible to transport, so that these could henceforward be integrated in the world economy. In addition, products of the industry, because of reduced prices as a result of up-to-date means of transport, were now for the first time able to compete on the international market (Treue, 1966, p. 390).

Another landmark in technical progress in the nineteenth century, which created new and rapidly expanding fields of application for non-ferrous metals, is the development of the news services. Telegraphy, with its rapid expansion on a transatlantic scale, created a demand for copper wire as a conductor material, for lead as insulating cable sheathing and for other materials for fittings and equipment. Supply of these commodities by the metal industry was an essential prerequisite for the practical realization of these epoch-making technical innovations. The invention of the telephone and the establishment of a worldwide network of communications, and – a few decades later – the development of radio and television, opened up wide-ranging areas of application for traditional and new metals, the provision of which represented a level of demand hitherto undreamed of by the metal industry.

The widely varying uses of metals, usually dictated by technical considerations, both for machinery and equipment and for transport and telecommunications, confronted the metal industry with new qualitative problems. From the quantitative point of view the decisive impetus in this sector of the economy came from the widespread use of electrical energy in the second half of the nineteenth century. This was first introduced in 1891 with the successful long-distance transmission, without major loss of electrical current, thus enabling electricity to be employed as a source of heat and power unhampered by existing spatial limitations. This revolutionary innovation was rapidly adopted on a wide scale: an electricity grid was set up and developed, electric lighting replaced gas-light, electric trams superseded the old horse-drawn vehicles and other traditional means of transport, and electrical machinery found increasing application in many industrial fields. The immediate outcome of these technical achievements was a rapid growth in the demand for non-ferrous metals, especially copper, which, owing to its high electrical conductivity both for weak and for power current became an indispensable material for electricity distribution and the electrical engineering industry. The result was that consumption of copper, which had hitherto lagged behind that of other heavy metals, by the turn of the century exceeded that of zinc and in the 1920s that of lead as well, even though these metals were also required for the construction of electric motors, batteries and other products of the electrical industry and recorded increasing volumes of consumption (Däbritz, 1931, p. 34 ff.).

A flood of inventions and technical innovations in other developing branches of industry also contributed during these decades to a broad diversification of non-ferrous metal consumption. In the chemical industry, for example, the use of metals was extended not only to modern fittings, piping, tanks (containers) and other equipment, but also to the production of pigments (lead white, zinc white) and solutions (copper vitriol), as requirements for new materials arose for metals in other chemical processes. Similar developments, which continually gave rise to new metallurgical applications to cover refinements or specialized demands, were recorded in the metalworking industries, plant engineering, precision engineering, the optical industry and in the canning and packaging industries. Owing to modernization trends in the traditional fields of manufacture (such as food and drinks manufacture, the textile and leather industry, the wood and paper industry, printing, publishing, the building industry and other fields), new demands were continually being made on the metal industry, and, not least, developments in modern armaments gave impetus to this process, with far-reaching effects in turn on the ranges of application of non-ferrous metals in the civil sector.

Nevertheless, in the 1890s the beginning of the economic use of the combustion engine was to prove one of the most important innovations for the evolution of the metals industry. Motor vehicle construction, in particular, opened up other important fields of application for the traditional metals, both in the construction sector and in the supplier industries. Important incentives to expand the still young aluminium industry and other light metals industries came from the aircraft construction industry, likewise still in its infancy. Quantitatively these innovations only began to exert any strong influence on the metal industry after the First World War, when more rapid headway was made in motorization by land and air. The most striking phenomenon, however, was the rapid advance by light metals in broad areas of application traditionally occupied by heavy non-ferrous metals and in new forms of production, especially as this was accompanied by keener competition of substitute metals vying with one another, triggered off by technical progress and/or prices or other economic reasons. All in all, there was such an enormous increase in consumption of all metals during the few years preceding the world economic slump, that the absolute peak in the history of the metal industry was reached in 1929, headed by copper, which accounted for 60% (Breidenbroich, 1938, p. 12).

The decisive breakthrough from the quantitative point of view in the metals sector dates, however, from the 1950s, in the wake of economic reconstruction after the Second World War and, as industrial development accelerated, of the worldwide boom in car sales, on an unprecedented scale compared with earlier years, in the economically advanced countries. This was also steadily gaining ground in the countries of the Third World, which meant that vehicle production in the world every year reached new record levels. At the same time the aircraft industry profited from the expansion of air transport.

Atomic energy, electronics, rocket technology, space flight and the development of alternative forms of energy characterize the most recent phase of technical development. These represent a new challenge for the metal industry, since the realization of modern technologies has, as well as employing traditional metals, involved the use of metals with exceptional properties, not previously required and hence often inadequately identified. Epoch-making discoveries and developments in the area of metals were necessary in order to unearth these materials from among the hitherto comparatively neglected 'new' metals and to turn them to economic use, and it is as yet impossible to forecast the scope offered by this development, either from the technological or the metallurgical point of view.

In terms of volume, however, the impetus given by these major innovations in the use of non-ferrous metals acquired significance only with the growth of the powerful industrial potential in the world engendered by technological progress and the consequent feedback process. Up to the middle of the twentieth century this development mainly affected the traditional industrial nations, but has since made remarkable progress in the Third World countries in their efforts towards further industrialization. A pointer to the worldwide expansion process is provided by the global index of world industrial production, which indicates the explosive development taking place in the industrial sphere:

(1953 = 100)
1860: 4   1900: 16   1920: 26   1940: 51

1953: 100   1960: 141   1970: 270   1977: 384

An examination of the estimated production figures for the period 1860–1977, which are only able to give a rough indication, particularly for the nineteenth century, shows that, after a relatively moderate increase in industrial activity in the first half of the period, industrial output had increased fourfold by 1900 (starting however from a very low level). From the beginning of the present century up to the outbreak of the Second World War world industrial production – despite setbacks due to events in the First World War and the Great Depression in the early 1930s – substantially increased to over three times the previous level. This already provided advance warning of the mighty industrial expansion which, although interrupted by the Second World War, has continued to gain momentum during the past thirty years. After the immediate backlog and reconstruction needs of the post-war period had been satisfied, by about the mid 1950s, renewed impulses became apparent in the metal industry during the following years as a result of the rapid economic growth taking place in the world, first mainly in the industrialized countries and then emanating from development of the industrial potential of the Eastern Bloc countries, as well as from greater efforts by the Third World to achieve industrialization. The consequent improvement in living standards throughout the world resulted not only in greater metal consumption in the capital goods sector, in transport and other areas of the infrastructure (in the widest interpretation of the word), but also in greater use of metals in housing and a marked increase in metal consumption in the consumer goods sector in new forms and alloys – a development which has proved to be a great incentive to expansion of the metal industry as a whole. This was all the more pronounced as the expansion was continually accompanied, very often in quite spectacular fashion, by progress in technical development. The result was increasing demand, often in new forms, for metallic materials, stimulated recently by economic objectives and the evolution of modern technologies to meet the problem of soaring energy prices.

The automatic feedback which occurred meant that ever-growing and new fields of application were opened up for both traditional and 'new' non-ferrous metals by industrial development, as science and technology, through new inventions and new techniques, established the prerequisites for the metal industry to satisfy continually higher demands for quantity and quality under increasing difficulties in the supply of raw materials. The Industrial Revolution was marked by a flood of momentous inventions and innovations which stimulated industrial progress, with far-reaching effects on the quality and volume of production and consumption. It wrought a profound change in the world of metals. Metals which were previously confined to the fabrication of traditional consumer goods have now become major, frequently key, materials of industrial production for specialized applications, especially in the field of capital goods. After the explosive spurt in recovery of these metals over the past hundred years, the demand for them still shows no signs of flagging and increases yearly, apart from lulls during economic cycles. Because of their importance in the industrial and economic development process, they are frequently included among the strategic commodities in the 'new world economic order' envisaged by the raw materials supplying countries. The impetus given to quality and quantity by the Industrial Revolution was thus a regenerative force for the metal industry. Metal recovery, which was still carried on with traditional methods – often linked with agriculture – now, on the threshold of the technical age, acquired a key position in the economic structure under the pressures of industrialization. This metamorphosis took place in the context of high entrepreneurial commitment and of modern industrial mining and smelting processes which are constantly being refined and updated by science and technology. The non-ferrous metals industry is therefore indissolubly linked with the overall economic trend and with technical progress and its effects on the economy. This association, transcending economic cycles, is a generative force infusing new life into industrialization in its long-term advance throughout the world.

3.3 TECHNICAL PROGRESS

3.3.1 Preparation of the crude ores[1]

The metal content of the vast majority of crude ores is too low for metals to be recovered direct. Preliminary concentration is first required. At the beginning of the industrial period, when the demand for metals was still very low, hand culling of the metal-rich lumps was usually sufficient. Washing in running water was also used to separate the dense, metal-rich lumps from the lighter ballast. The 'Golden Fleece' of classical antiquity was such a process. Manual culling and washing usually leave behind tailings with a comparatively high metal content, so that with improved preparation methods today such deposits (e.g., gold dumps in South Africa) are often re-worked as useful secondary deposits.

Separation

Separation methods relying on visual and hand culling or on gravity concentration (according to specific weight) were no longer adequate to satisfy

[1] An earlier detailed description of the 'state of the art' in mining and smelting was given by Georgius Agricola (1494–1555) in his work *De re metallica*. He describes wet and dry grinding, culling and separation, sizing with screens, classification in running water, hand jigging and ore concentration by sluice-box, tabling and blanket sluicing. Some of these processes continued with very little change up to the nineteenth century.

the increased demands for both quantity and quality. The mining of lean ores, in particular those with fine intergrowth of metallic and gangue components, required suitable separation methods and appropriate plant. The invention of powered machinery and the combustion engine, and the use of electrical energy, made available continually improved equipment for crushing, classification and concentration. Separation based on specific sedimentation (according to specific gravities) in water was enhanced by using a heavier suspension liquid for the particles. From this the sink-float process on the basis of heavy media separation was developed. Other properties of ores were also employed in separation methods which had been developed empirically in the past and were now applied systematically (von Rittinger, 1867).

The behaviour of metallic compounds in a magnetic field has long been known in the case of magnetites, a highly ramified version of iron oxide, abundantly available. Processes based on this principle today supply concentrates with iron contents of up to 70% Fe from crude ores with e.g., 35% Fe. Magnetite and quartz, for example, may be adequately separated by low-intensity magnetic separation. Ores containing haematite with comparatively low magnetic properties can be concentrated by means of high-intensity magnetic separation.

Another physical property of minerals is their behaviour in an electrical field. Because of their differential electrical conductivity, mineral grains in free fall can be deflected to varying degrees and separated into metal-bearing ores and gangue components. Ore separation capacity can be adjusted by previous chemical or thermal treatment which permits improved separation.

Flotation

Even though these processes are all capable of application to the concentration of metal-bearing crude ores, they did not make the decisive breakthrough. The discovery that the properties of ore surfaces could be made hydrophobic or hydrophilic by appropriate treatment led to the development of the flotation process, application of which to sulphide ores, and later to silicate or oxide ores of non-ferrous metals, made possible the large-scale recovery of sufficient quantities of concentrates even from lean ores.

The flotation process is essentially based on the invention of the Bessel brothers of Dresden, for the purification of raw graphite, patented in July 1877 as (Reich) Patent No. 62, Class 22. This invention already showed all the features of flotation, but did not at first find application for ore mining in Germany. In 1860 Haynes, an Englishman, recognized certain affinities between sulphide ores of metals and oily, bituminous substances. In 1885 a process was patented in the United States according to which particles of pulverized ores with high metal content were coated in oil and floated to the surface of oily acidified water. In 1886 the Bessel brothers were the first to produce froth which carried the oily graphite particles to the surface. A wave of international inventions followed all over the United Kingdom, the United States, Australia and Scandinavia. Primarily as a result of the activities of Minerals Separation Ltd, which was established in London in 1901 and obtained the relevant patents throughout the world, applying them mainly in the British Empire, suitable apparatus was developed for achieving separation between the wetted ore particles in suspension and the non-wettable components, as required in the flotation process. Flotation was adopted more quickly and more efficiently in other countries than in Germany, where wet-mill dressing had reached a high technical level. The first flotation plant for dressing the tailings from the lead-zinc mine at Ramsbeck (Sauerland) went into service in 1927. Out of a total of 28, only seven flotation plants were still in operation in 1977, owing to depletion of workable crude ores.

Distillates from the petroleum industry were mainly used for surface treatment during the first few decades. Empiricism was the keynote at that time. Only gradually, beginning around 1920, was the action of certain chemicals more exactly identified and further developed. In addition to *bulk-flotation*, which collects all metallic components in a single concentrate, with the aid of *selective flotation* it now became possible to separate the different metal sulphides from one another out of intergrown ores.

Flotation is by far the most important method for the dressing of metal sulphides. It is now employed for about 95% of all sulphide ores and over a thousand million tonnes of various raw materials are now concentrated each year by flotation. Crude ores from many mines with only low metal contents are now converted by flotation into smeltable concentrates. An example is one of the large modern concentration plants at the Bougainville Copper Mine (Papua-New Guinea), shown in Fig. 3. There is daily concentration of 80,000 tonnes of raw ore with approximately 0.5–0.9% Cu to a concentrate with 25–26% Cu.

The success of flotation and of other mechanical ore-dressing processes depends on whether the metal compounds in the crude ore exist as separate components along with the gangue and can be separated mechanically.

In some cases metal compounds occur as impregnation in the accompanying gangue. These are best extracted by chemical processes, for example by acid or alkaline leaching processes (uranium ores), thermal-alkaline digestion (vanadium ores), chloridizing roasting (calcined pyrites containing copper and lead-zinc) or segregation processes (oxide copper ores). The most important light metal, aluminium, is extracted from its raw material, bauxite, in strongly alkaline solution under pressure. It may be said that existing ore-dressing processes, either alone or in conjunction with others, are able to supply precisely the essential concentrates that are required by the metallurgical industry for the production of important metals.

Origins of the industry

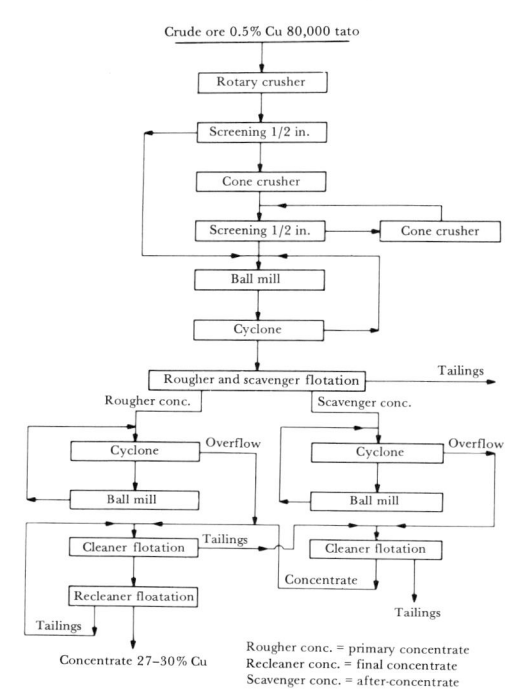

```
                    Crude ore 0.5% Cu 80,000 tato
                              │
                      ┌───────▼────────┐
                      │ Rotary crusher │
                      └───────┬────────┘
                              │
                   ┌──────────▼──────────┐
              ┌───▶│  Screening 1/2 in.  │
              │    └──────────┬──────────┘
              │               │
              │      ┌────────▼────────┐
              │      │  Cone crusher   │
              │      └────────┬────────┘
              │               │
              │    ┌──────────▼──────────┐    ┌──────────────┐
              └────│  Screening 1/2 in.  │───▶│ Cone crusher │
                   └──────────┬──────────┘    └──────────────┘
                              │
                       ┌──────▼──────┐
                       │  Ball mill  │
                       └──────┬──────┘
                              │
                        ┌─────▼─────┐
                        │  Cyclone  │
                        └─────┬─────┘
                              │                             Tailings
               ┌──────────────▼──────────────┐──────────────────▶
               │ Rougher and scavenger flotation │
               └──────┬──────────────────┬────┘
              Rougher conc.        Scavenger conc.
                      │                  │
              ┌───────▼────┐ Overflow  ┌─▼──────┐ Overflow
              │  Cyclone   │──────     │ Cyclone│──────
              └───────┬────┘           └───┬────┘
                      │                    │
              ┌───────▼────┐         ┌─────▼─────┐
              │  Ball mill │         │ Ball mill │
              └───────┬────┘         └─────┬─────┘
                      │     Tailings       │
              ┌───────▼─────────┐    ┌─────▼──────────┐
              │ Cleaner flotation│───▶│Cleaner flotation│
              └───────┬─────────┘    └─────┬──────────┘
                      │              Concentrate
              ┌───────▼──────────┐         │
              │Recleaner floatation│      Tailings
              └───────┬──────────┘
           Tailings   │
                      ▼
             Concentrate 27–30% Cu
```

Rougher conc. = primary concentrate
Recleaner conc. = final concentrate
Scavenger conc. = after-concentrate

Fig. 3. Flowchart of copper ore concentration at Bougainville
Source: LURGI.

Roasting of sulphides

The most important non-ferrous metals occur in nature as sulphides. For further processing they must be converted completely or partially to oxides, or sometimes to sulphates. Oxidation is accomplished at certain temperatures with the oxygen of the air. The process is called 'roasting'. Complete and partial elimination of sulphide sulphur are termed 'dead roasting' and 'partial roasting', respectively. Reaction takes place roughly in accordance with the following overall equation and is exothermic:

$$\text{MeS} + \tfrac{3}{2}\text{O} = \text{MeO} + \text{SO}_2$$

(metal sulphide + oxygen = metal oxide + sulphur dioxide)

Depending on the type of sulphide, a certain amount of heat is released, which previously went unused, but since about 1950 has been used as a source of energy for electricity generation with the aid of new roasting techniques. The equipment and furnaces used, and roasting technology, have undergone fundamental changes during the past 50 years or have been replaced by improved facilities.

To accomplish oxidation, the necessary oxygen is brought into close contact with the surface of the ore or concentrate grains by continuous movement at the particular temperature required, between 500° and 950°C. Originally furnaces were used in which the ore was charged on one side, ignited and transported towards the discharge end by manual shovelling during roasting. Fresh air enters the furnace through inlets. The SO_2-containing roasting gas is discharged from other openings. As early as 1882, under pressure from the German Factory Inspectorate,[1] several different designs of muffle furnace (Maletra type) were constructed and operated in certain roasting works even up to the Second World War.

The costly and unhealthy manual work of the 'shoveller' led to many developments for mechanical movement of the roasting charge. Of the great number of new proposals, various types of furnace found practical application, and many are still in operation today (for special purposes). These include the lined cylindrical furnace, the inside of which is divided by various stages, on which the material being roasted is moved downwards by rake arms. Such furnaces have become known as 'multiple-hearth furnaces'. The first model of such a furnace, proposed by Parker in the United States as early as the middle of the nineteenth century, was not developed further. New designs introduced by Herreshoff and Wedge were also adopted by Metallgesellschaft in 1899 and further developed by LURGI. Despite well-developed designs, controlled air metering and partial recovery of the roasting heat, difficulties arose because fine-grained flotation concentrates, due to excessively dense packing on the individual hearths, did not allow the roasting air sufficient access to the individual ore grains, which led to impaired efficiency and increased costs.

This fine-grained characteristic was deliberately utilized from about 1950 in a completely new type of kiln, the 'fluidized bed furnace'. Both the furnace and the roasting process have essential differences compared with all previous designs. The furnace consists of a cylindrical space with refractory walls, with a grating at the bottom. The product to be roasted is charged above this. After ignition of the sulphide, air is blown through the grating into the hot feed, turbulence is induced and oxidation is a matter of seconds. Depending on grain size, the roasted product is discharged directly from the roasting chamber or with the roasting gases. The heat of the solids and gases is utilized for steam generation. SO_2-rich roasting gases are purified and converted to sulphuric acid. The roasted product, called calcined ore, is in the form of oxides, ready for smelting.

In this furnace hardly any moving parts of the equipment are exposed to intensive heat: transport and movement of the ore in the furnace are accomplished pneumatically. In only a few years all other furnaces have been more or less relegated to marginal positions. The higher efficiency performance of this furnace, compared with the old multiple-hearth furnace, is

[1] Tafel, 1929, p. 300, Table V.

demonstrated by the quantity of sulphur that is roasted off in 24 hours per square metre of roasting area, viz. 9,600 kg in the fluidized bed and 80 kg in the multiple hearth type. The principle was developed around 1950 by BASF and by Dorr-Oliver in the United States for the roasting of pyrites (FeS_2). Today it is also of decisive importance in the roasting of many sulphidic ores such as pyrrhotite (magnetic pyrite), zinc and copper concentrates and other combustible industrial intermediates, and also for endothermic reactions such as the splitting of sulphates, chlorides, pickling solutions and waste acids.

As early as 1951 Metallgesellschaft took over the fluidized bed process (see Fig. 4) from BASF, via LURGI, and brought it up to worldwide importance in conjunction with its own patents and developments. As well as roasting gases with a high percentage of SO_2 and utilizable roasting heat, a fine-grained calcined ore results, and in this form it is particularly suitable for hydrometallurgical preparation. Many pyrometallurgical processes (shaft furnaces) require a roasted product in lump form. Therefore fine-grained calcined ore has to be converted to lumps by briquetting, pelletization or sintering. It is also possible, however, to make use of the heat released during roasting for simultaneous sintering, using additional fuels if necessary. This process, known as 'blast roasting', is still used on an industrial scale. The first units using blast roasting were developed by Bleihütten-Ingenieure, introduced by Metallgesellschaft AG in Germany in 1899, and were employed under the name of Huntington-Heberlein pots until 1914 in almost the entire zinc and lead smelting industry. The considerable manual work, and

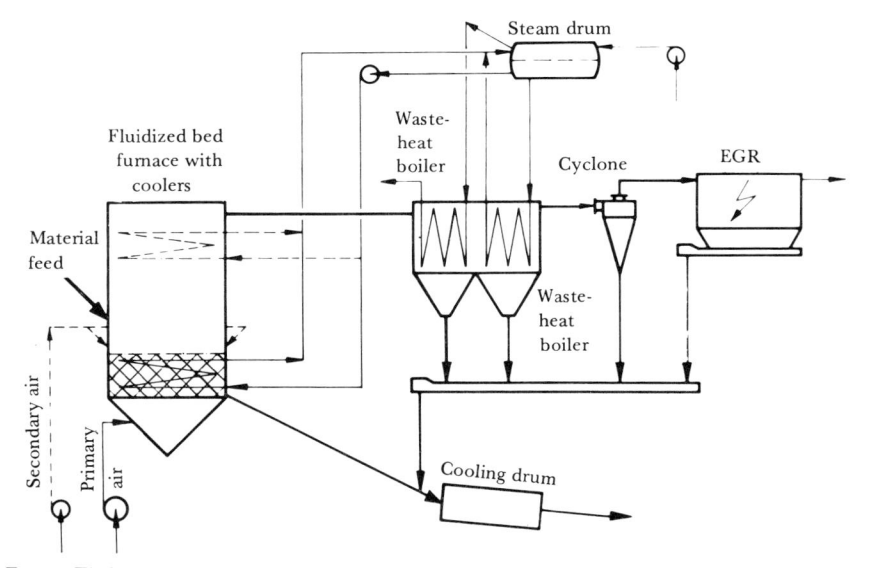

Fig. 4. Fluidized bed roasting: the LURGI-BASF system with steam generation
Source: LURGI.

environmental pollution by roasting gases, soon led to further developments and more intensive mechanization. Around the turn of the century the direct sinter roasting process, invented by the Americans Dwight and Lloyd, gradually came to be adopted in the United States. Another version of roasting, Schlippenbach roasting, was developed within the framework of Metallgesellschaft.

After 1950 the sinter roasting technique underwent yet another decisive change, when the gas flow was reversed from suction-draught to pressure sintering and at the same time the air stream was conducted through the sinter bed repeatedly (see Fig. 5). This development was made simultaneously in Australia (Port Pirie) and in the Federal Republic of Germany. The first European pressure sintering plant went into service in 1956 in Stolberg-Binsfeldhammer. From this time onwards only pressure sintering plants were installed and many existing suction-draught units were converted. This process is an essential preparatory stage for lead and zinc ore smelting by the Imperial Smelting shaft-furnace process.

With the many variants of the fluidized bed roasting process – for the roasting of fine and extremely-fine grained ores, as a preliminary stage of hydrometallurgical extraction processes – and the pressure sintering technique as a preliminary stage of pyrometallurgical processes, roasting technology has reached a high and apparently optimum level of development.

Utilization of roasting gases

In the roasting of sulphide ores, together with the solid calcined ore, a secondary reaction product is gaseous sulphur dioxide (SO_2) at various concentrations in the roasting gas. Economic utilization of the roasting gases and problems of environmental protection are the driving forces behind the policy of ensuring SO_2 utilization by attaching a sulphuric acid plant to practically every roasting unit at a smelting works. Within the production programme of a smelting works, the sulphuric acid (H_2SO_4) produced there represents an unavoidable, if not troublesome, by-product. From the standpoint of net added value, the sulphuric acid is of minor importance relative to the metals produced. The acid from smelting works represents a relatively constant proportion, approximately 24%, of total output of the smelter.

From the historical development of sulphuric acid manufacture, two processes should be mentioned, which have also found application in smelting works during the past 150 years.

> (a) The *lead chamber process*, developed in England around 1750, and alternatives derived from it are based on the oxidation of SO_2 to SO_3 and adsorption in water in the presence of oxygen carriers (catalysts) in the form of nitrogen oxides in aqueous solution. The long oxidation time meant that the efficiency of such plants was low. Furthermore, the acid only contained about 78% H_2SO_4. Such

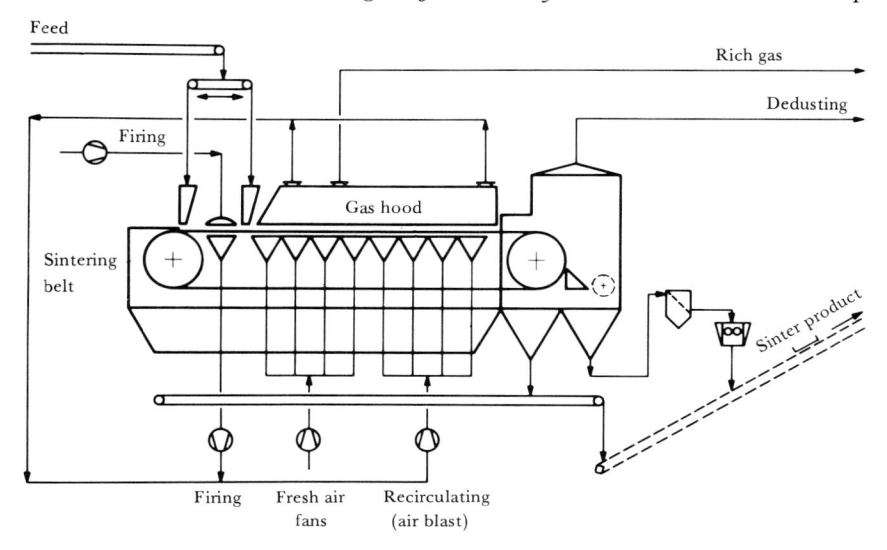

Fig. 5. Flowchart of a pressure sintering plant for lead ores
Source: LURGI.

lead chamber plants were still in operation during the Second World War.
(*b*) In the *contact processes* oxygen transfer is accomplished by means of metal-containing 'contact' catalysts. A corresponding patent for the use of platinum in various forms as catalyst was granted in England as far back as 1831. A decisive breakthrough was the use of the much cheaper and relatively insensitive vanadium pentoxide (V_2O_5) as the catalyst. A patent for a process of this type was granted to BASF in 1913. This process, after several modifications, ousted nearly all other processes within a few years (1960–64) in the *double catalysis* version developed by Bayer-Leverkusen (see Fig. 6). A precondition for high efficiency of this system is dust extraction and conditioning of the gases, which takes place in gas purification systems.

3.3.2 Extraction of metals

Copper

Sulphidic ores of copper in the form of flotation concentrates represent the predominant raw materials for copper extraction. Oxide ores – weathering products of sulphide deposits – oxide-sulphide or silicate mixed ore are of some importance only in certain regions. They represent only a small proportion of world production, however. Sulphide ores are converted primarily by pyrometallurgical processes to unrefined copper; this applies also to new, continuous, variants of the process. The proportion of metal recovered by pyrometallurgical processes in world production is currently about 85%. Hydrometallurgical processing accounts for approx. 15% and is mainly used

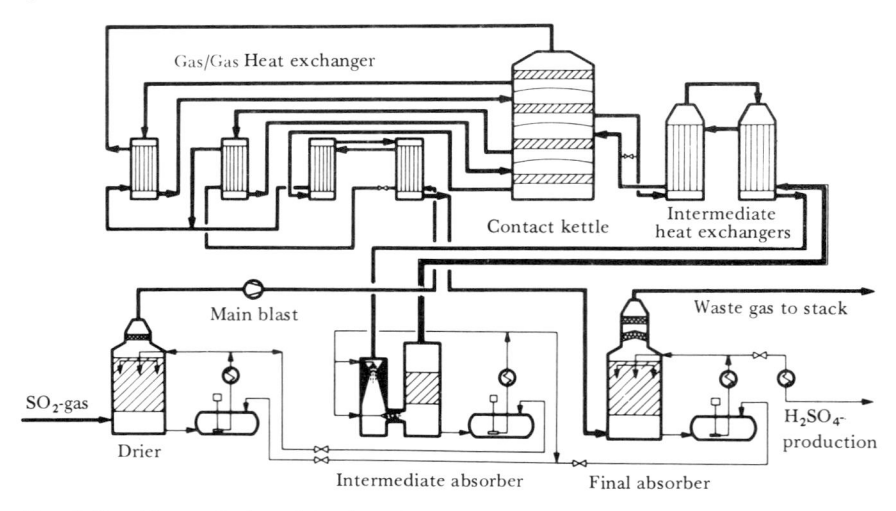

Fig. 6. Double catalysis sulphuric acid plant based on metallurgical SO_2 gases
Source: LURGI.

for poorly concentrating, low-copper oxide, oxide-sulphide mixed ores, dumps at old copper mines and copper-containing calcined pyrites.

Starting from flotation concentrates with about 25% Cu content, generally as chalcopyrite ($CuFeS_2$), a standard process has been developed involving the following stages:

Stage 1: Melting the concentrate (green feed), if necessary after prior roasting with mineral additives or slag, resulting in the following reaction products: copper matte with approximately 30–50% Cu, low-copper slag with less than 0.5% Cu, waste gas with approximately 0.5–2% SO_2.

Stage 2: Blowing of the copper matte (batch process) with air and with addition of mineral materials in two periods with the following reaction products: unrefined or blister copper with 97–99% Cu, high-copper dross, for return or separate processing, waste gas with around 4–9% SO_2 for sulphuric acid production.

Stage 3: Refining of the copper in two steps: oxidation and then casting into anodes with 99.2% Cu and electrolytic refining (since 1910) to cathode copper with 99.99% Cu, anode sludge with noble metals, waste liquor.

Stage 4: Remelting of the copper cathodes to saleable forms.

There has been little change to date in the principle of the process stages. Successful efforts have been made, however, to combine individual stages where possible in one furnace, and furnace designs and systems have undergone some fundamental changes.

For a long time the *shaft furnace* was used for melting down the concentrates, but this required lump or lumped material and additional fuel, preferably coke. Shaft furnaces were replaced by *reverberatory furnaces* around the turn of the century. Even today these are still standard equipment of many copper works throughout the world. Reverberatory furnaces represent an advance over shaft furnaces in their use of fine-grained raw materials, great flexibility in the choice of additional fuels and high melting rate – between 500 and 1,000 tonnes per day of copper matte. Smelters are still even now trying to reduce disadvantages such as high fuel requirement, high incidence of dust and low SO_2 content. Preheated air, additional oxygen and the partial replacement of external fuel by concentrates in specially designed burners have all contributed to improvements such as, for example, higher SO_2 content (varying from 3.5% to 6% or even 10%) in the roasting gas. Where cheap electric power is available and there is a shortage of fossil fuels, *resistance furnaces* (1929) were developed, and these are now in operation all over the world. The smelting capacities are in the range 300–1,650 tonnes per day matte. About 20 furnaces are in service at present.

As a result of efforts to simplify the complete process, partial exothermic and endothermic processes that were previously separated in space and time were combined in a single unit, so that the heat of oxidation evolved during roasting is utilized in order to save fuel. This development work has led to elaboration of the *flash smelting process*, which is operated in three process variants.

(a) The best-known of these is the *Outocumpu Process*. It was developed in Finland in 1946–49 for pyrites, and has found wide application. The reaction furnace consists of the concentrate burner, a vertical reaction shaft in which roasting and melting are accomplished in a few seconds, a horizontal settling chamber, in which copper matte and dross are separated, and a vertical waste-gas stack for the precipitation of molten droplets and dust. The reaction products are: copper matte with 65% Cu in normal operation, up to 80% Cu (concentration matte) with addition of oxygen, copper-rich dross, which requires processing, and SO_2 contents in the roasting gas of 10–18%. Further development work has already led to the production of blister copper. At present about 20 such plants are in operation or under construction, with capacities of more than 50,000 tonnes per annum copper output per unit.

(b) A second variant of the flash smelting process was developed after 1945 by the International Nickel Co. of Canada (Inco) in Sudbury on the basis of commercial grade oxygen (95% O_2) and is known by the name 'OFS' (Oxygen Flash Smelting). In a reaction chamber similar to the reverberatory furnace, dry and hot concentrate is roasted directly with oxygen by concentrate burners, and this has a marked effect on the reaction products: the matte is maintained at 50% Cu, while the dross still contains 0.6–0.7% Cu, and can be further purified by flotation. The waste gas contains 80–85% SO_2 and is used, sometimes liquefied, in the Canadian pulp industry. Because of the small amount of gas, the dust yield is approximately 2% of the charge. The process is autothermic. This Inco plant is the prototype for 'oxygen metallurgy', which is becoming an increasingly interesting proposition, although for the present it has one serious drawback – the high price of oxygen, which accounts for delay in the introduction of this technology on a broader basis. So far plants are to be found only in the Soviet Union.

(c) A third variant of flash smelting has been developed on the principle of cyclone burners in modern coal-fired power stations. The power density for heat generation is much higher in cyclone burners than in flash smelting. The reaction time is less than 0.1 second. When oxygen-enriched air is used, the reactions take place at temperatures up to 1800°C. In the USSR such a process has been developed to operational level – in the first instance for lead concentrates – and presented under the name of the 'Kivcet Process'. The furnace consists of a relatively small smelting cyclone. The melt enters a separating chamber and is further treated by electrothermal reduction in a separate, electrically-heated part of the furnace. At the high reaction temperatures certain metals, such as zinc, evaporate. The reaction products are: copper matte with 50% Cu, dross with 0.35% Cu, waste gas with SO_2 contents of up to 80%, zinc volatilization 75%. It is intended to go beyond copper matte as far as blister copper in one operation.

Conversion (blowing) of the matte to crude copper is the process by which the Cu_2S is converted with the oxygen of the air to SO_2 and unrefined copper. There is also complete drossing of the iron sulphide still present in the matte. The reaction takes place in two phases: in the first there is slagging of iron and formation of white metal (concentration matte) with approximately 80% Cu, and, in the second, reduction to crude copper.

The process is accomplished in batch converters, of which there are various designs. The best-known design is the drum converter of the Peirce-Smith type. The reaction products are: unrefined copper with 97–99% Cu with noble metals and nickel, cobalt, dross containing zinc and nickel, and flue-dust with volatilization products as oxides. Attempts to use concentrates directly in the converter instead of copper matte have not yet resulted in any definite success. Developments at Inco, based on their oxygen technique, have yielded the most interesting results so far. The raw copper has to be refined for many processing purposes.

In order to perform all stages of copper extraction continuously and in a single unit, two alternatives have so far been developed for full-scale industrial use:

(a) The Mitsubishi Process, developed in 1961, has been in operation since 1974 in a production unit with 50,000 tonnes per year blister copper. Separate furnaces are admittedly still used for each stage, but with siphon overflows and launders they have been combined into a single processing unit under computer control. The plant in Japan produces a blister copper with 98.5% Cu and a copper-containing dross, which is returned to the smelting furnace. The waste gases contain up to 15% SO_2. The process is currently being put into service in a second plant with a capacity of 130,000 tonnes per year copper at Texas Gulf in Canada.

(b) Development on the Noranda Process which had been in progress since 1964 was provisionally concluded with the commissioning of a large plant (capacity 70,000 tonnes copper per year). A second plant for the Kennecott Copper Corporation, USA, at Garfield/Iowa with a capacity of 300,000 tonnes copper per year, has now been commissioned. In contrast to the Mitsubishi Process, in the Noranda Process all reactions take place in a single reaction chamber. Air or oxygen-enriched gases are blown into the reactor through nozzles (tuyeres). Movement of metal and dross in the same direction makes it difficult to separate the two phases. The dross (up to 12% Cu) is brought down to less than 0.5% Cu in a separate operation by flotation, and the metal should have the quality of blister copper. With special control of the process it is also possible to produce a matte with approximately 75% Cu, at 8–15% SO_2 in the waste gas.

Further development projects are aimed at fully exploiting the advantages of using oxygen in high concentrations. In existing applications with about 30% O_2 in the reaction gases it has been possible to employ conventional furnace units without special modifications. For better utilization of the advantages of high O_2 concentrations, furnaces and burners should be designed so that the reaction temperatures exceed 1600°C or more without damage to the brickwork. As examples we may consider cyclone burners, such as the Kivcet Cyclone or the FZR reverberatory reactor, which is being developed jointly by LURGI and Norddeutsche Affinerie. Mention should also be made of the Q-S Oxygen Process promoted by Queneau-Schumann. The advantages of oxygen metallurgy are as follows:

(a) the volume of reaction gas is smaller because of absence of nitrogen components (1 vol O_2 corresponds in the case of air to 4 vol N_2);
(b) high density in the reaction space;
(c) high reaction temperatures in excess of 1600°C and rapid reaction time of approximately 0.1 sec;
(d) volatilization of any troublesome elements (such as Zn, As, Pb);
(e) production of blister copper from concentrate in a single unit;
(f) improved process monitoring and control by means of process control computers.

The Outocumpu and Mitsubishi processes represent examples of complete process control by computer. Even individual steps, such as blowing in the

Table 4. The introduction of major stages in copper extraction

Process stages	Process or furnace	Year
Flotation	Flotation	1910
Roasting	Fluidized bed	1950
Roaster gas utilization	Sulphuric-acid double catalysis	1960–1964
Smelting	Reverberatory furnace	1890
	Electric furnace	1930
Roasting and smelting	Flash smelting furnace (Outocumpu)	1960–1970
	Flash smelting process with oxygen (INCO)	1960
Continuous copper extraction:		
roasting, smelting and blowing	Mitsubishi	1961–1974
	Noranda	1964–1973
	Kivcet	Soon to go
	Q.S. (Queneau-Schuhmann)-Oxygen	into operation

Source: Compiled from information from LURGI.

converter, are controlled by computer. It may be assumed that the new methods are being applied increasingly in situations where plants have to be operated with less personnel and with maximum economy.

To summarize, it may be observed that tremendous advances have been made in the pyrometallurgical recovery of copper, especially since the Second World War. Table 4 and Fig. 7 show the sequence in which individual processes were introduced and how the number of process stages has been reduced. With the new processes the specific energy consumption for the extraction of copper concentrates (25% Cu) has also been reduced (Fabian, 1978, p. 504), as the following table shows:

Processes:	Heat consumption (GJ/t Cu)
Reverberatory ore furnace with raw concentrate	21.8
Reverberatory ore furnace with roasted concentrate	13.4
Mitsubishi	10.1
Outocumpu flash smelting	8.4
Electric furnace melting	6.7
Noranda (with 30% oxygen)	6.7
Inco flash smelting (with 95% oxygen)	1.7

The developments discussed so far relate to recovery of copper from primary raw materials. A certain amount of copper also originates from scrap and waste material, such as manufacturing waste (new scrap), scrap copper and alloys, copper-containing oxide wastes and intermediates. The traditional shaft furnaces and converters are used in the melting and separation of these. The metallurgical treatment to adopt depends on which secondary materials are to be processed. Often the air is additionally enriched with oxygen, resulting in an increased melting rate and saving of fuel.

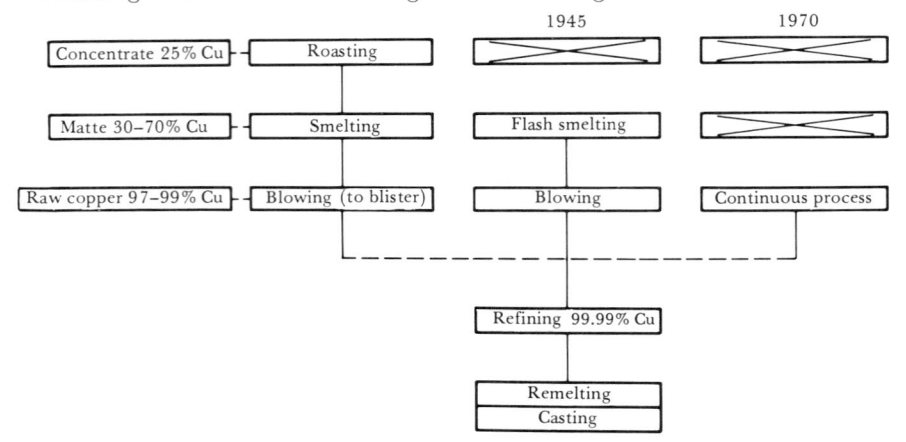

Fig. 7. The development of stages in pyrometallurgical copper extraction
Source: LURGI.

Hydrometallurgical methods have often been tried, but without much success. About 15% of the primary copper produced originates from copper-containing raw materials that are difficult to process by pyrometallurgical techniques. In view of the heterogeneous composition of the raw materials the methods have to be adapted in nearly every individual case. The following are important sources of secondary materials: dissolved copper in mine and processing waste water, low-grade sulphide, oxide-sulphide, oxide and silicate copper ores and many flotation waste products. In the sulphide ores the copper can be made soluble by means of oxidizing agents or partial roasting to sulphates. Lean oxide ores or flotation waste products are leached with sulphuric acid, resulting in copper sulphate ($CuSO_4$). Combined process steps are also employed where expedient. The dissolved metal is mainly separated by two methods:

(a) Cementation (precipitation) of the copper with iron-containing scrap. The precipitate, cement copper or precipitated copper with 80–90% Cu content must invariably undergo subsequent purification. This process, which is mainly used for mine waste water, is gradually losing ground because of the poor quality of the copper, and also because of declining availability of scrap.

(b) In the second method the copper-containing solution is purified to remove undesirable impurities, if necessary by solvent extraction, and the metal is precipitated electrolytically as cathode copper with 99.8% Cu.

Some other interesting processes, in some cases still in the development stage, should be mentioned. The Cymet (Chloride) Process: copper powder, electrolytic iron and elemental sulphur are obtained from cuprous chloride. The Arbiter Process: ammoniacal leaching with oxygen, solvent extraction and extraction electrolysis. Sulphur is precipitated as gypsum. Industrial trials of the process are now in progress at Anaconda. The Sherrit-Gordon Process: ammoniacal pressure digestion. The products are copper and ammonium sulphate. Acid pressure digestion: the end products are cathode copper and elemental sulphur. The LURGI-Mittenberg Process: activating grinding of copper concentrates, acid pressure digestion with oxygen; copper is obtained as cathode copper, and elemental sulphur is also produced. The process was operated for a long time on a semi-industrial scale, but was discontinued for cost reasons.

The various extraction stages provide impure grades of copper, such as blister copper with 96–99.5% Cu, black copper with 90–95% Cu, cement copper with approx. 80–90% Cu or scrap copper, and these have to be refined before final use of the metal. Refining takes place in the following stages: thermal or fire refining or electrolytic refining with remelting of the cathodes and casting of commercial forms. As a rule, fire refining is only a preliminary stage before electrolysis. In some cases the purity of the refined product at about 99.9% Cu is already sufficient.

Before use in electrolysis, anodes are cast from the fire-refined product.

These dissolve in the electrolyte, and the copper is precipitated on the prepared cathode at 99.99% purity. The impurities in the copper anode, such as noble metals, do not dissolve. They remain in the anode sludge and are extracted from it. Less noble metals remain dissolved in the electrolyte. This is drawn off at certain saturation values and processed, e.g., to nickel sulphate.

Lead

Lead is one of the oldest metals known to mankind. Lead mining spread to Germany in the early Middle Ages, in Bohemia around 750 AD, in the Harz area about 970 and in Saxony around 1160. There was a marked surge in lead production after 1900, when there was a steep rise in demand for lead in the chemical and electrical industries and in machine construction. Progress during recent decades has affected not only the extraction of the metal but also its quality. After German and Spanish deposits had been exhausted, the focus of lead extraction shifted more and more overseas, to the United States, Canada and Australia.

The most important lead ore for recovery of the metal is lead glance, galena, PbS (86.6% Pb). The most important concentration process is flotation. This provides concentrates with 50–60% Pb, and in exceptional cases even 70–80% Pb. Grinding processes, flotation, reagents and management of the processes depend on the type of lead ores. As well as zinc and copper, impurities in lead ores frequently include arsenic, tin, antimony, silver, gold and bismuth. If these minerals are not already removed during flotation, they have to be separated in the subsequent smelting or refining process. In particular lead and zinc occur together in many deposits, and in variable proportions. Lead-zinc mixed ores account for 70% of world output of lead ores and 60% of world output of zinc ores. Lead is mainly extracted by one of two variants of a pyrometallurgical process:

(a) The roast reduction process, still the most important, consists of two independent stages: roasting, or sinter roasting, and reduction. Until 1955 sinter roasting was operated as suction-draught sintering in Schlippenbach and Dwight-Lloyd apparatus. Pressure sintering was introduced from 1955 onwards and is now the only method used for lead sulphide roasting. The flow-chart is shown in Fig. 5, p. 41. By circulating gas constituents low in SO_2 repeatedly through the charge, an enriched gas with 4–6% SO_2 is produced for subsequent production of sulphuric acid. Depending on the composition of the charge, the sintered material contains about 42–51% Pb and 1–2% residual sulphur and any mineral additions required (self-fluxing sinter). About 10% of the lead in the sinter is already in the form of metal. The necessary preconditions for smooth operation of the shaft furnace are created in such a sintering plant.

The operation of reduction and smelting is performed in the shaft furnace. The charge consists of self-fluxing sinter, other additives as necessary and metallurgical coke. Because of slight mutual solubility and different densities, the products from smelting can be separated into workable raw lead (bullion) with 90–99% Pb, matte, if copper is present, and dross.

The Imperial Smelting (IS) Process is an improved variant of the shaft furnace process, and is particularly suitable for the processing of lead-zinc concentrates. Sinter roasting is again effected by pressure sintering. The mixed sinter contains about 18–22% Pb and 40–47% Zn. The molten lead collects in the hearth and is tapped as bullion lead. The zinc evaporates and condenses in the molten lead. By controlled cooling it separates as a molten phase from the liquid lead. The process is variable over a wide range in respect of concentrate composition. It found application throughout the world in a short time. Thirteen IS furnaces were in operation in eleven countries in 1980. In the roasting reaction process, lead sulphide (PbS) reacts with lead sulphate (PbSO$_4$) to produce metallic lead and sulphur dioxide. Only high-grade concentrates are used, however. Displacement of the reaction in the direction of metallic lead requires an excess of one or other component, from which a sulphur-excess or oxygen-excess process developed, the first of which is still applied. An additional treatment stage is also required, however. The Boliden Electro Process and the Newman Process are well-known.

(b) Although the shaft furnace process, after a series of improvements, is still dominant in primary lead extraction, more and more competing processes are appearing, in which roasting of the sulphides, reduction and smelting of the charge are accomplished simultaneously in the same reactor. Additional oxygen and prepared lead sulphide concentrates are required.

The Kivcet Process is an example of a direct smelting process of this kind. Sulphide roasting and partial roasting reaction with commercial oxygen are performed in a cyclone and vertical firing shaft at temperatures of up to 1400°C. The oxide melt, with 10–20% metallic lead, flows under a water-cooled partition into an electrically heated furnace where, with addition of coke fines, a lead bullion with approximately 98.2% Pb and 0.1–0.2% S is produced. Flue dust with high zinc content is either recirculated or processed in some other way. This process, already used industrially in the USSR, is also being introduced in Bolivia.

A second direct process has already been presented to the trade, the QSL Process (Queneau-Schuman-LURGI), which is also suitable for nickel and copper recovery. In a long cylindrical reactor equipped with tuyeres for bottom blowing, green pellets consisting of concentrate, additives and flue dust are fed continuously into the oxidation zone of the reactor and oxygen of commercial purity is blown into the bath. The products are lead bullion and a high-lead, low-melting dross, which is deleaded with coke in the reduction zone to about 1%. A demonstration plant is under construction at Berzelius in Duisburg.

Apart from a favourable rating with regard to environmental protection, both processes are expected to have high production output, lower energy consumption and reduced labour costs.

Refining of lead bullion, 90–99% Pb. Molten lead has a certain dissolving power for many elements. Such dissolved impurities are largely removed during refining, on the one hand to achieve the desired purity of the lead, but also for selective extraction of the impurities themselves. The refining process must be variable, and adjustable to the particular impurities. Refining is, therefore, generally a batch process.

Zinc

A systematic zinc industry in Europe dates from the first half of the eighteenth century after the introduction of indirectly fired reduction and suitable condensation vessels. The first zinc smelting works were constructed in Döllach (Carinthia) in 1797, Silesia and Stolberg (Rhineland) in 1808, processing zinc carbonate ($ZnCO_3$, calamine) as raw material. The important zinc ore sphalerite (ZnS), or zinc blende, became dominant when it was discovered how to convert the sulphide to zinc oxide by roasting. The required concentration of the crude ores was for a long time accomplished by the wet concentration method until flotation was introduced in 1926–27, although at first only for the re-use of waste from wet separation. Flotation became the dominant concentration process. The zinc content of the flotation concentrate fluctuated between 50% and 60%, and the iron content as FeS in isomorphic mixture was up to 15%. Apart from lead, the concentrate often also contains copper, vanadium and silver, and in rare cases gold. The zinc oxide resulting from roasting can be reduced to metal either by pyrometallurgical or hydrometallurgical processes, the latter stage via electrolysis now representing the dominant process for zinc extraction.

Depending on subsequent use, two systems are mainly employed today: pressure sinter roasting (Fig. 5, p. 41) gives a calcined product in lump form from sphalerite, and this is now mainly used in the Imperial Smelting shaft furnace.

Since 1960 fluidized bed roasting has largely replaced roasting in the multiple hearth furnace as a preliminary to zinc electrolysis. The fluidized bed furnace (Fig. 4, p. 39), which is now widely used in the non-ferrous metals industry, is very flexible and has throughputs of 100–1,000 tonnes concentrate per day. From the heat of roasting, 0.9–1.2 tonnes steam per tonne of concentrate are obtained. Depending on oxygen addition, the roasting gas contains 10% or more SO_2, and is processed to sulphuric acid. There is a risk of formation of zinc ferrite if the roasting temperature is too high. Zinc ferrite is not soluble in the subsequent leaching stage.

Pyrometallurgical processes. In contrast to other metals, zinc evaporates (at 906°C) during reduction (1250–1300°C) and has to be condensed by cooling, the aim being a high concentration of zinc vapour. To prevent dilution by the heating gases, zinc oxide and carbon are heated indirectly to the reduction temperature. In view of the high affinity for oxygen, back oxidation of the zinc has to be avoided.

Zinc extraction in the horizontal muffle furnace has been practised since about 1800. The system consists of a retort made of refractory clay, closed on one side, which is filled with granular zinc oxide mixed with reducing coal, heated externally, a ceramic condenser in which the gaseous zinc condenses and a separator (allonge) for the zinc dust that arises during cooling of the reaction gas. Low zinc yield (86–90%), low thermal efficiency of approximately 30%, low productivity, environmental problems, and especially the arduous conditions of work for the furnace personnel were reasons why this process was replaced by other methods.

As early as 1910, F. O. Schnelle in Oker and Roitzheim-Remy in the Rhineland were operating vertical muffle furnaces continuously with briquettes of an oxide-coke mixture. This technique can be regarded as the forerunner of the New Jersey Muffle Furnace, several examples of which went into operation in 1929 at the Palmerton works of the New Jersey Zinc Co. The only plant of this kind in Germany was built at Harlingerode (Harz). The advances were considerable compared with horizontal muffle furnaces, such as higher zinc yield, greater purity of the metal with 99.7% Zn, 0.2–0.3% Pb, lower labour costs, improvement of working conditions, larger units, continuous operation, mechanization of nearly all operations, and a more efficient heat economy.

Nevertheless, certain disadvantages have acted against wider application of the process. In particular, the complicated preparation of the furnace charge requires many expensive stages until the briquette ready for the furnace is obtained. Other adverse factors are the expensive refractory material for the retorts (silicon carbide) and poor utilization of the coal residue in the dezinced briquettes.

Electrothermal processes. The first attempts to obtain zinc by electrothermal means were undertaken in Sweden as far back as 1885. The first continuous plant operation by the Trollhättan Process was put into service in 1902. Variants such as the Josephtown Furnace of the St Josephs Lead Co., and the Sterling Process with zinc grades of 99.96%, were developed and are still sometimes used today. The processes based on electricity are important when cheap electric power is available.

The Imperial Smelting (IS) Process. For the first time in the thermal extraction of zinc a shaft furnace is being operated with direct heating. This means that, as well as the reaction gases CO and zinc vapour, the furnace waste gas also contains the heating gases, so that the zinc vapour content in this case drops from around 50% in the muffle furnace process to 4–7%. The furnace is operated with hot lead-zinc containing sinter, preheated coke (600–850°C) and hot blast of 700–750°C and at a dross temperature of 1250–1300°C. Lead oxides are reduced to raw lead and the zinc obtained is vaporized, as are other volatile constituents. The hot furnace flue gas, at about 1000°C, is subjected to sudden cooling to 550–560°C in specially designed spray condensers by means of metallic lead, so that the zinc vapour dissolves in lead. The zinc-containing lead is further cooled to 440°C in special coolers. The zinc separates as a molten layer on the heavier lead and is drawn off. About 400 tonnes of lead are circulated for every tonne of zinc.

The IS Process is suitable for the processing of lead-zinc mixed ores and for the use of imported ores from various sources, although the high expectations for this process have been dampened by the rising costs of coke. Its flexibility also permits the use of lead-zinc containing secondary materials. Products containing zinc and lead that previously had to be dumped can now also be recovered. The product range of an IS plant is illustrated by the example of the Berzelius Metallhütten GmbH, Duisburg,[1] whose production capacities are 32,000 tonnes per year decopperized lead bullion and 85,000 slab zinc with 98.5% Zn and 1.2–1.4% Pb; by-products include 200 tonnes per year cadmium, 1,500 copper and 125,000 sulphuric acid. Eighty per cent of the zinc primaries are imported, and 30% come from secondary materials. This IS plant, which was put into service at the start of the 1960s, replaced a smelting works with horizontal muffle furnaces. The IS Process, as the most important thermal zinc extraction process, also has good chances of survival in the future. The slab zinc produced can be brought to purities of 99.99% Zn by thermal refining in a New Jersey rectifying column.

Hydrometallurgical processes. The main bulk of zinc production is by electrolysis. The concept of electrolytic recovery of zinc was already the subject of a German patent in 1818, which described the essential features of the normal process used today. A pilot plant first went into operation in 1915 at Anaconda (USA), producing 25 tonnes per day. Within a few years industrial plants had been set up in the USA, Canada and Australia (Tasmania). After the loss of the thermal smelters in Upper Silesia the company of Giesches Erben in 1934 started up an electrolysis plant in Magdeburg, with a capacity of 40,000 tonnes of zinc per annum. The method developed was known as the 'Magdeburg Process'. This is still employed today, along with two other methods, the Standard and Tainton Processes. The Magdeburg process comprises three stages: leaching, purification of the leaching solution and electrolysis.

(a) The leaching material used is roasted sphalerite (zinc blende) with over 53% zinc content. Besides the readily soluble zinc oxide it contains sparingly soluble zinc ferrite and other minor constituents in the non-soluble residue. Important developments have been made also in recovering a large part of the zinc still present in the residue (up to 20%), using the wet metallurgical process immediately after leaching. In the interests of environmental protection it is necessary to ensure that the remaining constituents are rendered harmless or, like the iron compounds, to utilize them in steel production. Interesting variants of the residual treatment are the Jarosite (since 1960), Goethite and Haematite processes, which are continually being improved. By efficient leaching and residue purification, a yield of 96–98% of the initial zinc solution can be achieved. The importance of the residue treatment is shown by the fact that, for every 100,000 tonnes electrolytic zinc between 30,000 and 50,000 tonnes iron-containing residues are produced.

(b) Before the zinc-containing solution is subjected to electrolysis, it is first necessary

1 Maczek and von Röpenack, 1980.

to remove undesirable impurities by leaching purification. The selective separation of these elements is performed in up-to-date plant with the aim of recovering them in concentrated form. This purification process has now been perfected to a very high level of economic efficiency and operational safety by refined methods of measurement and in some cases automation.

(c) The most noteworthy advances in electrolysis, however, have been achieved not so much in the electrochemical reactions as in the mechanization and automation of the electrolyte bath facilities. Many years of research have culminated in the automatic stripping machines constructed to detach the zinc coatings mechanically from the basic cathodes in order to re-utilize the latter. Extra-large (Jumbo) cathodes permit the individual bath cells to be drastically reduced in size. The space required, investment and labour costs of these new plants are considerably less than those of conventional plants of the same capacity. The electrolytically deposited zinc, with a purity of 99.995% Zn, is then smelted and refined.

The direct processing of zinc sulphide. Attempts have been made for many years to process zinc sulphide without previous roasting and then to produce elementary sulphur which can be diverted direct to refuse dumps, rather than sulphuric acid. After 20 years' development work, a plant has been erected by Cominco at Trail, Canada, for converting sphalerite with oxygen in sulphuric acid solution under pressure to give zinc sulphate, which is then fed to the existing zinc electrolysis. The first industrial plant is designed for 31,000 tonnes zinc per year and goes on stream in 1981. It is hoped that this will provide greater flexibility in sulphur recovery and problem-free processing of iron-rich concentrates.

Tin

The principal mineral is cassiterite (SnO_2). The most important sources are marine alluvial, mainly in South East Asia. Owing to its high specific gravity, it is possible to produce 0.01% Sn concentrates with 35–75% tin from these alluvial ores. As the metal has high chemical resistance, it is recovered in a two-stage pyrometallurgical process with carbon at 1200–1300°C. The first stage, the ore dressing, obtains a comparatively pure crude tin with 97–99% Sn, so that a tin-rich dross with 8–12% Sn results. This is further reduced in a second dross treatment to a tin of 80% Sn, usually with iron impurities called 'hard-head', which is returned to the reduction furnace (reverberatory or drum-type rotary). Liquation (i.e., crystallizing out of impurities) produces a higher-purity tin, which is further refined by kettle treatment to 99.6% Sn. In Bolivia and Siberia there exist crude ore deposits from which the lean tin ores are volatilized with sulphide and roasted to SnO_2, in which up to 60% Sn is given in the form of flue-dust.

Aluminium

Initial tests by Oerstedt in 1825, and particularly those of Wöhler in 1827 and 1845, led to production of the first metal specimens and to the determination of some properties of aluminium. After Davy and later Bunsen had demonstrated that the metal could be recovered electrolytically, Saint Claire-Deville in 1854 succeeded in isolating the metal in considerable quantities. The application of electrolysis on an industrial scale was made possible after 1866 by the invention of the dynamo. In 1883 the American Bradley made the suggestion that the known solubility of aluminium oxide in molten cryolite should be utilized as the basis for fused salts electrolysis. In 1886 Héroult in France and Hall in the United States both applied independently for patents, which already contained the basic features of the fused salts electrolysis employed today. The raw material for the aluminium oxide was then, as today, almost exclusively bauxite, a weathering product mainly occurring in sub-tropical and tropical countries. Neither the raw material nor the principle of recovery have changed very substantially since the early beginnings. In 1888/89 the first aluminium smelters were established on German soil, close to electricity generating plants wherever possible.

The recovery of aluminium oxide from bauxite. Aluminium hydroxide is recovered from bauxite by hydrothermal decomposition, in which, after calcination at approximately 1250°C, it is produced as anhydrous oxide (Al_2O_3). The alumina content of bauxite fluctuates between 50% and 60% Al_2O_3. The major impurities present are iron oxide (Fe_2O_3), 2–28%, and silicic acid (SiO_2), 1–5%. Apart from bauxite with low SiO_2 content, there are other deposits with higher SiO_2 content, although these are not yet worked on an industrial scale. The bauxite is mixed with caustic soda solution and fused under pressure at temperatures between 160° and 240°C. The concentration of soda solution and the duration and temperature of fusion depend on the type of bauxite. The original intermittent fusion in autoclaves has largely been re-designed as a continuous process. Nevertheless, this system still has drawbacks, such as high energy consumption, high investment costs, liability to breakdown because of the many moving parts in the system, incrustation and fouling of the temperature recorder. A few years ago VAW (Vereinigte Aluminiumwerke AG) introduced a completely continuous system, the 'tubular reactor', up to production stage, with a capacity of approximately 2^6–10^6 tonnes per annum.

The new system permits the use of a wider range of different types of bauxite and high availability of the plant. The fusion products are the aluminium-containing solution, from which the hydrate of alumina is isolated in high-purity form, and an insoluble residue, red mud, the quantity and composition of which varies according to the type of bauxite. Many suggestions have been made for its practical utilization – for instance, as an additive to adjust the composition of cement raw meal or as an aggregate in the building materials industry. Other fusion processes on a pyrogenic basis have been developed industrially but have largely been replaced by the Bayer Process.

In order to safeguard the supply of basic raw materials, especially on political grounds, experiments are constantly being made at considerable cost to explore the use of clays and similar deposits with comparatively high Al contents as raw materials for recovery of the metal. From the technical point of view such possibilities exist, but they are not yet competitive compared with bauxite.

In the purification of the leaching solution vanadium-containing residues with 5–7% vanadium can be isolated. Calcination of the hydroxide ($Al_2O_3 \cdot 3H_2O$) has sometimes been performed exclusively in rotary furnaces at temperatures of 1200–1300°C. Since about 1960 the new process of the circulating fluidized bed has been developed by Alcoa in the USA and independently by VAW/LURGI in Germany. Owing to slower heat consumption it is today almost exclusively installed in new plants and also in the conversion of existing plants. The advantage of the new system, apart from energy conservation, is the lower space requirement and lower maintenance costs. The saving of heat energy is remarkable, as the following breakdown for the calcination of 1 kg Al_2O_3 shows: in conventional rotary furnaces approximately 6,400 kJ; in rotary furnaces with preliminary heat exchangers approximately 3,900–4,200 kJ; in fluidized bed furnaces (circulating fluidized bed) approximately 3,200–3,300 kJ, representing a saving of about 50%.

For a long time the siting of aluminium oxide works was identical with that of the electrolysis plants. To save freight costs, however, they have been transferred to locations more convenient for transport facilities. (For one tonne Al_2O_3, 2–2.5 tonnes bauxite are worked.) In 1970 60% of aluminium was still produced in integral plant complexes but by 1980 this had shrunk to just under 50%. New plants are chiefly being built in Australia and in India, Brazil and other Third World countries.

Electrolysis of the alumina (Al_2O_3). The electrolyte is a molten mass of fused salts (at 950–980°C), comprising cryolite (Na_3AlF_6), aluminium fluoride (AlF_3), calcium fluoride (CaF_2) and aluminium oxide (Al_2O_3, melting point 2000°C). Anodes and cathodes are of carbon. The anode consists of specially manufactured carbon blocks (Söderberg or precalcined anodes). The cathode forms the bottom of the electrolytic cell. The anode is immersed in the molten mass, and the aluminium recovered is deposited at the carbon cathode, from which it is then stripped. One reaction product is the metal; the second is oxygen, which burns at the cathode to CO or CO_2. Of the fluorine lost, 50–70% collects in the anode gas and the remainder passes into the walls of the electrolyte container. The total loss during electrolysis is 25–40 kg fluorine per tonne of aluminium. On ecological grounds and for economic reasons the fluorine has largely to be recovered. The development of electrolytic procedures during the past 80 years has been aimed less at changing the system than improving economic efficiency – to reduce labour requirements, improve heat utilization and economize on fluxes and carbon anodes. These efforts have resulted in a reduction in man-hours between 1950 and 1970 from 30–40 to 3–6 per tonne of aluminium. Electricity consumption declined between 1900 and 1970 by 50% (from 26–28 to 13–16 kWh per tonne Al). New techniques of fluorine recovery by dry gas scrubbing and pyrolysis of fluorine-containing furnace blow-out have been successfully tried out and introduced in recent years.

Magnesium

As the second light metal, magnesium has followed a similar course to aluminium. The most important method of recovery is the fused salt electrolytic procedure, which was adopted for production on a large scale at Hemelingen near Bremen in 1886. The dry (i.e., dewatered) magnesium potassium salt carnallite (KCl · $MgCl_2$ · 6 H_2O) serves as the electrolyte. In 1898 another plant was started up at Bitterfeld, followed by others within the sphere of the IG Farben works at that time. Production increased slowly at first and in 1925 was less than 1,000 tonnes. It was not until magnesium alloys were successfully employed for motor vehicles and aircraft construction that consumption and production soared. In 1944 production in Germany amounted to 34,000 tonnes and in the USA it rose from 2,000 tonnes in 1935 to 145,000 by 1944. At the end of the Second World War total world production was around 250,000 tonnes. It then rapidly declined and has only just regained its former level.

Metal recovery in the fused salt electrolysis is performed in different types of cells, depending on the chemical composition of the electrolyte. The cell developed by the IG Farben Company became a prototype for the entire world. The original electrolyte consisting of natural salts was replaced by IG Farben with magnesium chloride ($MgCl_2$), produced from magnesium oxide (MgO) by chlorination in a reducing atmosphere. The chlorine gas occurring at the electrode is collected and re-used. For the MgO winning magnesite ($MgCO_3$), dolomite ($MgCO_3$·$CaCO_3$) and seawater are used. Some 85% of current world production is derived from electrolysis and 15% from thermal reduction reactions via magnesium oxide (MgO). As reducing agents metals and alloys are used which have a greater affinity with oxygen, such as aluminium, silicon or silicon carbide.

Magnesium is one of the young metals. It plays an important part in the recovery of contemporary metals, such as titanium, as a reducing agent (deoxidant).

Titanium

Titanium is the third and youngest light metal. Although only discovered for industry after the Second World War, it has now acquired decisive importance for highly specialized applications. The most well-known titanium minerals are ilmenite (FeO·TiO_2), 43–65% TiO_2, often with increasing amounts of magnetite (Fe_3O_4) and rutile (90% TiO_2). For metal production only rutile or, if necessary, artificial rutile from ilmenite, is used.

Rutile, mixed with other heavy mineral sands and quartz, mainly occurs in marine alluvial deposits. The wet mechanical preparation process yields high-grade concentrates. The chief producer of rutile is Australia, with a market share of over 90%.

Recovery of metal from the oxide TiO_2 by carbon reduction is impossible because of the formation of titanium carbide and titanium nitride. Following the suggestion made by Kroll in 1938 titanium tetrachloride ($TiCl_4$) is heated with magnesium metal at 850–900°C. The mixture reacts to give titanium metal and magnesium chloride. The product contains up to 65% Ti, 20–35% $MgCl_2$ and unreacted magnesium. Secondary purification then follows, either by hydrochloric acid or by the more important vacuum purification process, in which the magnesium compounds are distilled off at 850–900°C, condensed and returned to the operating circuit. A very high-purity titanium product is thus obtained. Titanium tetrachloride ($TiCl_4$) is produced from the oxide TiO_2 with chlorine gas in a reducing atmosphere at 800–1000°C in the shaft furnace and also recently, because of its higher efficiency, in the fluidized bed furnace. The Kroll process was launched in the USA on a large industrial scale in 1945 and today still forms the basis of production. Sodium metal is often employed in place of magnesium. Some 75% of the production costs of titanium sponge are accounted for by the titanium chloride and magnesium, 2.5% for energy and 5.5% for wages.

Zirconium

This is an interesting metal for nuclear purposes, which – like titanium – can be produced by the Kroll process, by means of $ZrCl_4$.

Nickel

Nickel, one of the most important alloying elements for the production of a number of steels, was mined in over 20 countries in 1978, and is also processed in some of them. Nickel in alloy form was already known in antiquity. Cronstedt (1751) and Richter (1804) isolated the metal. When its effect on the properties of steel became known, there was an enormous increase in its extraction.

The nickel ores of economic interest occur in two different types, sulphide (20%) and oxide (80%), the current ratio worked being 60% sulphide (in 1950 90%) and 40% oxide ores. In this context reference should be made to manganese nodules (not yet commercially available), with contents of 20–25% Mn, 0.5–1.5% Ni, 0.5–15% Cu and 0.2–0.4% Co, found in the Atlantic Ocean, but more particularly in the Pacific. For the metal variations found in the nodules cf. Krüger and Schwarz, 1975, p. 44.

The sulphide crude ores from the deposits of Sudbury (Canada), the largest of their kind, contain 1.5% Ni as pentlandite ((NiFe)$_9$S$_8$), 1.2% Cu as chalcopyrite (CuFeS$_2$) as well as pyrrhotite (Fe$_7$S$_8$) with some nickel. By means of selective flotation concentrates are produced which also contain other metals, so that nickel concentrate, in addition to 9.5% Ni, also has 2.5% Cu, and copper concentrate, in addition to 29% Cu, has 1.25% Ni. The pyrrhotite concentrate also contains 1.1% Ni and 0.11% Cu.

The copper concentrate is then refined in the conventional manner. The copper-containing nickel concentrate is partly roasted, a low-grade matte melted and the principal component separated from the slag. The coarse matte is then bessemerized in a converter to fine matte (with 50% Ni, 30% Cu and 20% S) and subjected to slow, specially controlled cooling, in which the nickel and copper sulphide crystallize out in different ways and are separated by flotation. The nickel concentrate, with 73% Ni and 20% S as well as CO, Cu and Fe, can then be roasted to oxide and pressed to metal ore as sulphate subjected to electrolytic refining. The nickel-containing concentrates may also be refined with oxygen in the flash smelting process. The copper concentrate with 73% Cu and 5% Ni is then processed to give blister copper.

The oxide nickel minerals comprise two types, the limonite type, in which iron oxide minerals are prominent, and the silicate type (garnierite). Unlike the sulphide minerals, the chemical structure of nickel does not permit physio-mechanical preparation, such as flotation.

At the end of the past century silicate nickel ores were predominantly worked. Nickel metallurgy as such did not exist at that time. The recovery processes were therefore modelled on those for iron and steel or copper, so that either ferro-nickel was produced or a matte by means of sulphur carriers. Both processes are still used today for the working of large volumes of oxide minerals. Limonite nickel ores, in particular, are produced both by pyrometallurgical and hydrometallurgical methods, usually under pressure and using ammonia (by the Caron or Sherritt Gordon processes) or with acid (Moa-Bay and Amax processes). Nickel refining is aimed at removing and recovering undesirable impurities if there is a market for them. A number of different refining processes are used, such as electrolysis or carbonyl refining, in which nickel with carbon monoxide reacts with the carbonyl, which at higher temperatures splits into nickel metal and CO. A third alternative is nickel refining by reduction with hydrogen from an aqueous solution.

Cobalt

Virtually all nickel and copper ores contain varying amounts of cobalt as a minor metal. There are no specific standard pyro- or hydrometallurgical processes for its recovery. Depending on the process for the main metal recovery, the cobalt is separated from intermediates or from electrolytic solutions. Cobalt is of particular interest for the production of high-temperature materials, hard-facing alloys and magnetic materials.

Refractory and steel alloying metals

The modern steel industry would be inconceivable without the metals described in the following sections. As alloying constituents they confer special properties on the steels, such as corrosion strength, increased hardness, resistance to wear and high heat resistance. As carbides they are indispensable for the production of hard metals (carbide alloys). They are produced in various compounds according to their intended purpose. As ferro-alloys they are mainly employed in steel working. The pure, usually refractory metals are occasionally used for the production of alloys low in iron. As carbides they are used for the production of hard-facing materials.

Ferro-alloys are produced from ores or concentrates. Depending on their affinity with oxygen and on the temperature, reduction is performed with carbon, silicon or aluminium. On cost grounds reduction with carbon is preferred. For the smelting of ferro-alloys electric arc or resistance furnaces are used almost exclusively; the thermal efficiency is around 50%. For aluminothermic reactions two-stage furnaces are usually employed, with a travelling upper part. The reactive mixture of aluminium grit and metal oxide is then brought into contact with an ignition composition.

Chromium

Chromium is an important alloying constituent for the production of stainless and heat-resistant steels as well as heat-resistant alloys based on nickel and cobalt. It was discovered by Vauquelin in 1797 but only in 1894 was the first metallic chromium produced by Goldschmidt using the aluminothermic process. In 1880 the first ferrochrome was smelted in the blast furnace and in 1900 in the electric arc furnace. The most important mineral is chromite (Fe·Mg) (Cr·Al)$_2$O$_4$. Chromite appears in the form of lumps of rough ore, often as pelletized concentrate with 50–54% Cr$_2$O$_3$.

Ferrochrome

This alloy is normally smelted in an electric reduction furnace, at temperatures of up to 1600°C, from chromite. Owing to its high affinity for carbon, carbides are produced, with up to 10% C, known as ferrochrome carburé. In order to reduce the carbon content the melt is mixed with fresh chromite or pure oxygen is blown through. The alloy containing the least carbon, ferrochrome suraffiné (0.1–0.4%) is produced in a number of complex stages with considerable sacrifice of the metal. A new vacuum process by Union Carbide, the Simplex Process, also produces a low-carbon alloy at 1350°C.

Chromium metal can be produced either by electrolysis or by the aluminothermic process. In electrolysis chromic salt solutions with specific pH values are precipitated either for the chromating of steel surfaces or, in a diaphragm cell on a cathode of stainless steel, to give a metal deposition. There are a number of electrolytic processes.

Vanadium

Vanadium is a comparatively young metal. It was reduced for the first time in 1867 from a chloride solution with hydrogen. Marden and Rich produced ductile vanadium for the first time from pentoxide (V_2O_5) by thermal reduction with calcium metal in 1927.

Pure metal is not in current use. Pentoxide is the most important catalyst in sulphuric acid production and in petrochemistry for the hydration of hydrocarbons. The principal use of vanadium is as an important alloying constituent for a number of steels, also in combination with nickel, chromium, tungsten and molybdenum.

Vanadium compounds are usually in fine dispersion and seldom occur in mineable concentrations. Vanadium is usually recovered as a minor metal or by-product. The chief sources of the raw material are titanomagnetite, from which titanium concentrates and iron are extracted at the same time, as, for example, in Finland. The highveld Steel and Vanadium Corporation Ltd, South Africa, produces a vanadium slag with 25% V_2O_5, from an ore with 55–57% Fe, 12–15% Ti and 1.4–1.9% V_2O_5, in special production stages, while the pig iron is worked to steel. These slags or other V_2O_5-containing ores are decomposed with alkaline salts at around 1200°C, to give soluble vanadate, which with an acid admixture is precipitated as pentoxide. Pentoxide is also the primary product for ferro-vanadium or other alloys recovered by the aluminothermic process.

Tungsten (Wolfram)

In 1781 Scheele in Sweden recovered tungstic oxide (WO_3) for the first time from one of the most well-known minerals, scheelite ($CaWO_4$). Industrial production began in 1847 with a British patent. Owing to its high density, hardness and, in particular, its high melting point of 3380°C, tungsten has found a wide field of application, even in small quantities. Some 20% of world production is used for steel alloys, and 50% for the production of hard-facing alloys, of which tungsten carbide (WC) is the principal component. Tungsten compounds or metal play an important part in space travel and the rocket industry.

The following description of the recovery of tungsten and tungsten carbide from scheelite applies to the mining areas discovered and opened up only a few years ago at Mittersill, Austria, and mainly managed by Metallgesellschaft AG and Voest-Alpine. The crude ore with 0.7% WO_3 is prepared by flotation in two concentrates with 30% or 65% WO_3 according to requirements. The concentrate is calcined in Bergla at 650° with the addition of soda (Na_2CO_3)

and leached under pressure at 220°C, so that the tungsten compounds are water-soluble. The purified solution is processed to WO_3 and this converted with hydrogen to tungsten metal powder (W) and then to tungsten carbide (WC). The Mittersill mine and the smelter at Bergla went on stream in the mid 1970s.

Molybdenum

Substances with a dark irridescent metallic lustre or glance were already known in antiquity. The sulphide (MoS_2) had been isolated by Scheele in 1780. An apparently non-melting metal was recovered in 1790 by carbon reduction. The industrial use of molybdenum began at the turn of the century. Because of its high melting point of 2680°C, molybdenum, like tungsten, was employed in the incandescent lamp industry. Its qualities as an alloying constituent for steels are particularly valuable in combination with chromium and nickel. Alloyed, stainless and tool steels and high-temperature alloys account for almost 90% of molybdenum production.

The most important mineral is molybdenum glance (MoS_2), which can be concentrated by flotation from crude ore to concentrates with 80–90% MoS_2. Molybdenum is often found in association with copper sulphides and is extracted as a minor metal in their working. The molybdenum glance is oxidized in multiple hearth furnaces to oxide (MoO_2) and converted either by hydrometallurgy or by sublimation to pure MoO_2. Ferro-molybdenum (FeMo) is prepared by thermal reduction with silicon and aluminium from iron oxides and MoO_2 (molybdenite) to give 58–63% or 68–75% Mo.

Manganese

Manganese was recovered for the first time in 1774 by Gahm and quite independently by T. Bergmann and was smelted after 1860 in the steel blast furnace as ferromanganese alloy. Its industrial use began in 1895 with the aluminothermic process according to the Goldschmidt patents. Ninety per cent of manganese production is used for deoxidants or as alloying metal in steel production. Many manganese minerals consist of manganese oxides originating in alluvial deposits with iron oxide, water and gangue components, known as wad ores. Large deposits, such as those of Nikopol Tschiaturi in the USSR consist of wad ores. Other primary ore minerals are hollandite, vredenburgite (Mn, Fe_3O_4) and hausmannite (Mn_3O_4). A possible raw material in the future may be manganese nodules, which contain approximately 30% Mn. Manganese metal and manganese alloys can be produced in blast furnaces, electrofurnaces, by thermal reduction or by electrolysis of aqueous solutions. The main product is ferromanganese (FeMn) in various qualities: FeMn with 80–92% Mn, FeMn suraffiné with less than 0.5%, FeMn affiné normal with 75–85% Mn and up to 2% C, and FeMn carburé with

75–80% Mn and 6–8% C. The manufacture of low-carbon types is generally by means of production of silicomanganese in electric furnaces. Commercially available types of manganese metal normally contain 97–98% Mn.

4

Factors determining the demand for non-ferrous metals

4.1 PROPERTIES AND FIELDS OF APPLICATION

Consumption of non-ferrous metals began to expand under the influence of the industrialization process and, as this has gathered momentum and spread over a wider field – despite all economic setbacks due to wars, crises and alternating economic cycles – the expansion has continued unbroken in the long-term trend. Non-ferrous metals, by virtue of their specific properties, or special combinations of properties, which are entirely or partly lacking in other materials, have proved to be an important, and over broad areas even indispensable, raw material for industrial production. This importance is less apparent in volume, however, as is evident from the annual consumption in West Germany, where a total of 2.7 million tonnes of aluminium, copper, lead, zinc, tin and nickel compares with some 46 million tonnes of crude steel (1979). Nevertheless, almost all technical fields are dependent on utilization of the properties of non-ferrous metals, the most important being (see also Table 1, p. 8):

(a) their high thermal and electrical conductivity;
(b) their resistance to high temperatures and thermal shocks, their mechanical strength and capacity for plastic deformation, i.e., ductility;
(c) their capacity for alloying, welding and soldering;
(d) their magnetizability[1] and chemical reactivity (Fischer and Bongers, 1971, p. 226; Rolshoven, 1974, p. 2).

Because of these basic properties an increasing number of potential applications for non-ferrous metals has opened up in the course of the industrialization process, with the advance of technology and its effects on economic growth in the non-ferrous metals sector, both qualitatively and quantitatively. As a result they have now become an integral part of our technical world, which would be unthinkable without them. There is a great

---
1 The magnetizability of non-ferrous metals is confined to nickel and cobalt as pure metals.

spread in the reasons determining their market demand. These primarily relate to the specific properties of the different non-ferrous metals and to the development of their main fields of application. The following survey aims to give general information on these trends in application from the point of view of their economic relevance. It does not extend to technical details, which lie outside the scope of this study.

4.1.1 Heavy metals

Copper

The oldest non-ferrous metal used for technical purposes, this is still today one of the most important primary materials in industry. By the end of the mid 1960s – having overtaken lead and zinc in the 1930s – it was also quantitatively the leading non-ferrous metal. Since then it has dropped to second place in world production and consumption since the light metal aluminium took the lead by volume. The high-ranking position held by copper among other metals in the industrialization process and its unabated technical progress is to be ascribed to the unique combination of specific properties of copper compared with other materials. It is a metal which is comparatively easy to work. It is relatively soft but at the same time tough and ductile, so that it can be drawn into the finest wire and beaten to the thinnest sheet (to a fineness of approximately 0.0025 mm). With a melting point of 1083°C, it is exceptionally weldable. Even though the surface of copper rapidly oxidizes under the combined action of oxygen and the secondary components of the atmosphere to form a patina, it possesses high corrosion resistance, which is vitally important for certain uses of the metal; it is far less susceptible to attack by the atmosphere, water, salts, acids, and other chemicals (with the exception of nitric acid, ammonia and compounds of ammonia) than other non-ferrous metals. The long service life of the material is partly due to this high resistance, which also favours the recycling of scrap, waste and intermediate products with a high copper content. The readiness with which copper can be alloyed with almost every other metal, to enhance its hardness and strength – albeit at the expense of its conductivity – is a great technical asset. As well as the time-honoured addition of tin to produce bronze and the use of zinc-containing copper ores for, e.g., coinage, the variety of alloys today comprises not only brass and the important copper-nickel alloys but also innumerable other copper alloys of widely varying composition which considerably diversify the range of application for this metal. Of all the properties which have contributed to copper's key position in the industrial development process the most important is its outstanding thermal and electrical conductivity. This is only slightly less than that of the precious metal silver, for which industrial large-scale use is ruled out because of its comparative rarity and high price.

As converter or blister copper recovered from copper ores is not sufficiently pure for most purposes, this unrefined copper is still, almost without exception, subjected at the smelter stage to refining processes, after which it will usually have acquired a purity of approximately 99.95%. The copper then goes to the fabrication industry in the forms (sizes and shapes) in which it leaves the smelters and refineries, i.e., as cathodes, wire bars, ingots, cakes, billets and, latterly, rolled wire and continuously cast strip. The subsequent processes are carried out mainly in wire drawing plants (wire mills), rolling mills and pressing plants, as well as foundries, remelting refineries, chemical works, etc. There the bulk of the blanks (up to 90%)[1] are turned into semi-manufactured goods such as sheet, wire, cables, rods, sections, pipes and tubes; approximately two-thirds of these are of unalloyed copper, and the rest of semi-manufactures and of other alloys. A minor percentage (about 9%) is made up by castings from the first processing stage as well as salts, powder and other products.

With the growing diversification of production which marks the industrialization process the specific properties of copper have been found to lend themselves to even more versatile applications. The importance of these for the position of this metal, according to volume and percentage of total consumption, has undergone considerable changes in course of time, depending on the particular technical requirements. Electrical engineering has been by far the most important field of application for copper – particularly for electrolytic copper with a purity grade of 99.95%, as this proved to be the ideal medium for the transmission of electrical current. In other industrial fields, too, technical and economic criteria dictate that there is no substitute for copper for many purposes, so that it has become a highly valued and indispensable material.

Owing to lack of statistical records it is not possible to indicate the trend in the use of copper either globally or according to major consumer countries. An indication of present relationships is afforded by a single study, carried out in 1967 at the instance of the Conseil International pour le Développement du Cuivre (CIDEC), for West Germany, whose consumer structure would appear not to differ significantly from that of other industrial countries of the West.[2]

An indication of structural shifts in copper consumption at the present time may possibly provide a key to the breakdown of copper demand (according to

---

[1] The data relate to the industrial countries of Western Europe; for the major consumer countries, the United States and Japan, no directly comparable statistics are available (Cissarz et al., 1972, p. 61).

[2] The main field of copper consumption at that date was easily electrical engineering, with 56.8%, followed by building, with a 51.4% share. Mechanical engineering in general occupied 14.5% and the transport sector 9.2% (automotive engineering at 6.7% predominating here over shipbuilding, 2.0%, and railway engineering, 0.5%). Precision engineering and optics accounted for 1.4% and the consumer goods sector 2.7% of copper consumed in West Germany (Cissarz et al., 1972, p. 67 ff.).

Table 5. Copper consumption by end-use in the United States, 1965, 1970 and 1976

End-use	1965 thousand tonnes	%	1970 thousand tonnes	%	1976 thousand tonnes	%
Electrical engineering	1,044	48.3	1,119	53.1	1,179	53.8
Building and construction	422	19.5	333	15.8	338	15.4
General mechanical engineering	310	14.4	255	12.1	295	13.5
Transport	231	10.7	176	8.3	234	10.7
Ordnance	46	2.1	121	5.7	36	1.6
Other	108	5.0	106	5.0	110	5.0
Total	2,161	100	2,110	100	2,192	100

Source: Calculated from Schroeder, 1976.

end use), the last available statistics for the United States being for 1976 (see Table 5). The most conspicuous feature is the proportional decline in total consumption in the electrical industry compared with the statistics for West Germany (51.3%). Apart from the conditions peculiar to the country, these would appear to indicate continuing substitution of copper by other materials during the last ten years, in particular by aluminium (also as a conductive material for heavy current and the low voltage range) and by steel, zinc and other metals, as well as plastics.[1]

In mechanical engineering generally the proportion of 14% likewise shows a slight downward tendency in copper consumption in this field. The comparatively high proportion of copper consumption in the building industry (17.4%) in the United States may possibly be due to the fact that copper is more extensively used there for façade cladding and other luxury fittings and finishes. The somewhat higher proportion in the transport sector (11%) may also be due to the consumption habits of a wealthy country, but it possibly indicates that the substitution phase for copper has now come to an end for many applications in this field because of the technical and economic drawbacks entailed.[2] It would also appear that the industrial branches of precision engineering and optics, and in addition the consumer goods industry, have acquired more importance for copper as fields of application (*Mineral Facts and Problems*, 1976, p. 26 ff.). In spite of widespread competition from substitutes such as metals, plastics and other materials, copper for the

1 In automotive engineering, however – after initial Japanese successes – the use of glass fibres in place of conventional copper wire would appear to be a technical possibility.
2 The next step in the progressive expansion of technology may well be the replacement of copper cable in the telecommunications field by a broad-band cable system of coaxial or glass fibre cables. Speech transmission is here performed by light pulses instead of electrical vibrations as hitherto. This system is also suitable not only for traditional telephone, telex and datex use but also for new services such as cable television, video telephones, telecopiers, video conferences etc. This should not seriously affect the volume of copper sales however.

time being is hardly likely to be significantly displaced in its present major fields of application, and for many forms of production should continue to remain a key raw material.

New markets for copper might possibly occur in the area of marine technology, in fields such as seawater desalination, fish culture and energy recovery from the sea. Copper-nickel alloys for seawater pipes are also increasingly used in the offshore industry.

Lead

Up to the second half of the nineteenth century this was an almost universal metal commodity in daily use, because it was simple to recover from readily identifiable ores and easy to work. Among the important properties of lead are its low melting temperature, excellent castability and malleability (plastic deformation), its density and metallic impermeability, as well as its resistance to acids, chlorine and water. Other important qualities include its comparatively low electrical conductivity and its suitability for use in alloys and compounds with specific properties. Although lead was traditionally used in buildings for water and other service pipes, and as a cladding and insulating material, in the closing decades of the last century a growing market also opened up for piping systems, fittings, etc., in the rapidly developing chemical industry, as well as for electro-galvanizing applications. The development of lead-sheathed cable dates from this time and even in the 1960s the sheathing of heavy current and telephone cables in the major industrial countries (with the exception of the United States) still accounted for the largest proportion of lead consumption. This use of lead has considerably declined, however, both absolutely and relatively, as a result of substitution (particularly by aluminium and plastics) and it may be expected that lead in the cable sector will eventually only be used for special fields with very distinctive chemical and physical requirements (Dumstorff, 1974, p. 211 ff.). Even the traditional field of semi-manufactured goods has lost a good deal of importance proportionally in total consumption due to the use of plastics, while the relative development of lead consumption for printer's type and anti-friction bearing metals, alloys and solder metal in the major industrial countries shows a downward trend. In the production of foil, tubes and capsules lead has everywhere increasingly been displaced by aluminium and other materials. One of the most important sectors of consumption for lead was the battery industry which accompanied the development of motor vehicles and the trend towards motorization. In the major industrial countries already some 50% of lead consumption is for starter batteries, traction batteries – as a source of drive for floor conveyors, mine haulage locomotives, tram or trolley cars, etc. – and stationary batteries (Reinert, 1977, p. 67 ff.).

The use of lead as an additive to carburettor fuel (gasoline) in an anti-knock compound, lead tetra-ethyl, necessitated by increasing engine compression,

Table 6. Lead consumption by end-use in selected industrial countries, 1960 and 1977 (%)

End-use	USA 1960	USA 1977	West Germany 1960	West Germany 1977	France 1960	France 1977	UK 1960	UK 1977	Japan 1960	Japan 1977
Cable industry	5.9	1.0	32.5	9.0	26.8	13.4	25.2	10.7	28.9	10.4
Battery industry	34.6	50.3	28.4	46.3	20.2	45.1	19.8	23.3	18.5	50.8
Lead pigments and chemicals[1]	26.0	21.9	16.0	26.5	20.7	20.5	16.4	30.2	10.6	15.4
Semi-manufactures	4.8	1.1	16.4	13.4	19.5	13.5	21.8	16.4	22.1	8.4
Castings	0.7	0.2	1.2	1.6	–	–	–	–	–	–
Type metal, anti-friction metal, lead alloys, solder	19.2	5.6	1.3	2.4	6.1	4.2	9.6	9.4	4.4	5.6
Foil, tubes, capsules	1.2	0.4	1.3	0.7	–	–	1.1	0.5	–	–
Other	7.7	19.7	3.1	–	3.6	3.3	6.1	9.5	15.5	11.8
Total amount (thousand tonnes)	926.4	1,352.4	258.1	346.9[2]	n/a	n/a	384.5	290.4	162.3	325.8

1. Including production of surfaces and powder. Tetra-ethyl is partly included under Lead pigments and chemicals and Other uses. 2. As reported by consumers.
Source: Calculated from *Metal Statistics*, various years.

has likewise contributed to the overriding importance of automotive development for the lead industry. The health hazard associated with the exhaust has, however, given rise to greater efforts to reduce the amount of lead additive.

Lead and lead alloys are also finding increasing application for radiation protection purposes in the medical field. Because of its high toxicity, however, lead is being replaced to some extent by titanium, zinc pigments and other materials in paint manufacture (red lead, white lead). Lead has recently found application for PVC stabilizers produced from litharge.

The wave of substitution of lead by other metals, plastics, metallic compounds and organic materials which swept over industrialized countries in the 1960s in varying degrees may be considered today to have largely come to a halt (Meinberg, 1977, p. 16). Despite the fact that there are many suitable alternative metal combinations for storage batteries, such as nickel-cadmium, nickel-zinc, silver-zinc and mercury-silver, many of these materials are relatively scarce, more expensive than lead or their electrical properties are insufficient to comply with the enormous number of requirements specified by industry (Ryan and Hague, 1977, p. 13 ff.).[1] Because of its widely varied properties lead is also gaining ground in new technologies and applications, so that this traditional metal is also a completely modern material (Sandig and Schmidt, 1977, p. 83).

[1] Recently, however, development of a new type of battery was reported, which looks like being a breakthrough for economical electrically powered vehicles: a zinc-nickel oxide battery which is designed to be smaller, lighter and much more efficient than the traditional batteries. Research is also being carried out on even more efficient batteries of lithium-iron sulphide.

Zinc

Zinc was not discovered until a relatively late date – in spite of the fact that sphalerite (zinc blende), its most important ore, is nearly always found together with lead glance (galena) and blended with sulphur and copper pyrite (chalcopyrite) and other minerals. The process of zinc recovery, however, differs from that of other metals because at the high temperature necessary for its smelting it is not liquid but in gaseous form. Zinc is ductile, with good malleability at 100–150°C, and can be drawn, rolled and pressed. The thin surface coating of zinc oxide or zinc carbonate which forms on it in moist air is insoluble in water and prevents oxidation penetrating to any depth. The ensuing corrosion protection is used especially for electro-galvanizing or hot-dip galvanizing of rolled steel products; traditionally an unrivalled economic method of long-term corrosion protection, this accounts for the largest proportion of zinc consumption (see Table 7). Zinc is also employed for corrosion protection in the building sector, for steelwork, metal doors and windows, street furniture, crash barriers, lamp standards and railings. Another important field of application for zinc is as an alloy with copper to give brass, which, apart from its decorative applications in the furnishing and lighting industries, also has a wide range of functional uses, such as bathroom fittings and central heating. Diecasting offers an extensive field of application for zinc, especially in the automotive industry, which represents two-thirds of the market for zinc diecastings, either for functional parts (carburettors, pumps, etc.) or for fittings and trim. Zinc diecastings are also widely used in the manufacture of household appliances and office machinery, electrical

Table 7. Zinc consumption by end-use in selected industrial countries, 1960 and 1977 (%)

End-use	USA 1960	USA 1977	West Germany 1960	West Germany 1977	UK 1960	UK 1977	Japan 1960	Japan 1977
Galvanising of sheet, strip, tubes, wire	42.3	39.7	32.7	36.0	27.2	25.7	60.2	55.4
Zinc alloys for diecasting	38.5	36.7	10.9	21.9	17.5	19.9	10.7	16.7
Brass products	11.3	12.8	25.9	25.5	34.1	27.8	17.2	13.8
Rolled zinc (semi-manufactures)	4.4	2.7	22.7	14.3	6.9	7.4	4.4	4.5
Zinc oxide and other compounds for chemical purposes	1.8	3.9	1.9	1.7	7.3	10.3	5.0	3.6
Other	1.7	4.2	5.9	0.7	7.0	9.0	2.5	6.0
Total amount (thousand tonnes)	796.4	999.5	318.7	391.1	371.7	315.1	189.3	670.1

Source: Calculated from *Metal Statistics*, various years.

goods and ironmongery. Traditionally the building industry is the principal consumer of zinc semi-finished goods, particularly rolled zinc, for roof drainage systems. Here alloying with smaller quantities of titanium has resulted in a significant improvement in service life.

Zinc consumption is therefore very largely dependent on the development of the automotive industry, on building activity and on the expansion of the infrastructure. It has to face strong competition from other metals as substitutes, since zinc can in theory be replaced in every sphere by other materials (cf. Dumstorff, 1974, p. 222). Aluminium, magnesium and plastics are the most important substitution products in the field of zinc diecasting, especially as these meet the need for reduced weight in automobile construction. However, zinc diecastings are superior to these substitution products in many respects (e.g., exactness of profiling, dimensional accuracy, quality, surface hardness and strength) and so zinc will continue to hold its own in the technology of tomorrow, especially if there is greater concentration on its electrochemical properties in the development of new fields of application (Heubner, 1978, p. iv ff.; Stainer, 1976).

Tin

Tin was also used thousands of years ago for making consumer goods and, in fact, as an admixture to copper for the production of bronze, is the most ancient alloying metal. Its essential physical properties include softness, malleability and good expansion characteristics, which render it suitable for rolling out to fine tinfoil and pressing into tubes, capsules and similar packaging materials. Owing to its high rust and corrosion resistance and also its low surface tension in the molten state, tin finds wide application as surface

Table 8. Tin consumption by end-use in selected industrial countries, 1960, 1970 and 1977 (%)

End-use	USA 1960	USA 1970	USA 1977	UK 1960	UK 1970	UK 1977	France 1960	France 1970	France 1977	West Germany 1960	West Germany 1970	West Germany 1977
Tinplate	70.0	53.0	43.8	51.9	46.1	46.0	61.0	55.4	58.6	11.4	31.6	44.4
Soft solder	14.0	29.3	28.8	9.2	8.9	7.6	22.7	22.6	29.2	3.0	16.1	20.4
Bronze, brass	7.1	7.1	6.7	11.4	12.8	11.4	7.8	6.7	6.6	0.5	1.9	1.0
Tinning	4.2	4.4	5.4	6.6	8.2	8.4	5.3	–	3.3	6.6	7.4	4.2
Anti-friction metal	3.1	2.4	3.6	13.9	17.1	16.1	–	–	–	1.0	2.5	–
Chemicals	1.4	3.5	11.0	7.1	6.9	10.6	3.2	–	–	–	–	–
Other	0.3	0.3	0.7	–	–	–	0.1	15.3	2.3	77.5	40.5	30.0
Total amount (thousand tonnes)	48.2	48.2	42.3	22.1	17.3	13.9	10.0	10.0	9.0	28.2	14.1	11.5

Source: Calculated from data of the International Tin Council, various years.

protection for other metals, especially for the production of tinplate, the principal material used to date in the canning industry. The use of electrolytic tinning, which has largely superseded traditional hot tinning for surface finishing, has reduced tin consumption for this purpose to about a quarter.

A broad field of application for tin is provided by alloying with lead, copper, antimony and other metals. Tin alloys, because of their low melting temperature, represent important soft solders, used especially for precision instrument making, the fabrication of printed circuit boards in electronic engineering and the soldering of tinplate cans, car radiators and so on. Tin is also an essential component of anti-friction metals (i.e., bearing metals) and is used in addition for injection moulded materials in items such as machine components. Tin oxide and other tin compounds are employed in the chemical industry, and finally, pure tin and tin alloys containing antimony and copper are increasingly used in rustic household accessories and consumer goods.

Tinplate manufacture is particularly exposed to competition from aluminium, copper, glass and tin-free steel plate as substitutes and a proportional decline in consumption in this principal field of application has been observable for some years in the United States, the United Kingdom and Japan (but not in West Germany). With the development of new technologies tinplate is attempting to counteract these trends – clearly with some success in the case of deep-drawn tin cans (Forster, 1976, p. 255). Greater demand for tin packaging materials may also be expected as industrialization progresses in the Third World. Although the substitution trend is likely to continue, consumption of tin should still increase as no satisfactory substitutes have yet been found for it in many industrial applications (Gocht, 1974, p. 243; Forster, 1976, p. 254 ff.).

4.1.2 Light metals

Aluminium

This is the most common non-ferrous metal in the earth's crust. It was not discovered, however, until 1827 by Wöhler and was then exhibited in 1855 at the World Exhibition in Paris as a primary metal produced on a laboratory scale. It was not until later after Héroult had developed fused salts electrolysis (based on molten cryolite) that it became a metal of industrial importance. Whereas in 1900 world production of aluminium amounted to only 7,300 tonnes, the metal gained so rapidly in importance that in 1979 this had risen to 5 million tonnes per annum, making it by far the most important non-ferrous metal by volume. Aluminium possesses a specific gravity of 2.7, only a third that of copper, and its thermal and electrical conductivity is approximately 60% that of copper. An aluminium conductor of comparable electrical conductance has only 48.5% the weight of a copper conductor (Wiesinger and Schuchard, 1974, p. 279). When exposed to air, aluminium develops a thin, hard, protective oxide coating and is very largely weatherproof and corrosion-resistant. Aluminium can be hammered, drawn, pressed or rolled and its alloys attain high mechanical strength. It offers considerable scope for refinement. Of the wide range of malleable wrought alloys, duraluminium (Duralumin) is capable of sustaining high stresses, as is Silumin (silicon-aluminium alloy) among the cast alloys. Primary aluminium has a purity grade of 99.0–99.8%, and high-purity aluminium up to 99.99%.

The specific properties of aluminium have opened up a very versatile range of uses for this metal, so that in some cases it has supplanted steel, copper and other materials (see Table 9). In electrical engineering it is used among other things for overhead lines, conductor rails and cable sheathing. In transport it has a wide range of applications: for rail wagon construction, in the automotive industry – where efforts to produce lighter, more fuel-saving and hence more economical vehicles have already resulted in the widespread use of aluminium[1] – for shipbuilding, in the aircraft industry and for space travel. In building, the use of aluminium for façades, roofs, windows and doors has appreciably increased, while in the chemical industry, packaging and the manufacture of household appliances aluminium is now one of the materials most in demand, for both technical and economic reasons. A new field for aluminium should also be opened up by solar engineering, as yet still mainly at the development stage.

As aluminium has hitherto been available fairly cheaply, hardly any effort has been made to find suitable technical substitutes for it. Until the drastic increase in oil prices in 1973, plastics produced on a petroleum base were the strongest competitors for aluminium in many fields. This trend was checked, however, when the price situation became more favourable for aluminium. Surface-treated steel plate and zinc alloys have acquired a certain importance as substitutes for aluminium in the casting sector and, for example, glass fibre-reinforced plastics in the automotive industry. Generally speaking, aluminium is still in a stronger competitive position than other metallic materials (Forster, 1976, p. 101).

Magnesium

This was first produced in 1808 in small quantities as metallic magnesium, but it was not until 1886 that the first industrial production of magnesium by electrolysis of molten carnallite occurred at the Hemelingen aluminium-magnesium factory in Bremen. Although fundamental improvements were

---

1 According to a very rough estimate by the industry, one litre of petrol is saved for every 100 kg weight reduction of a car. Competition from aluminium as a substitute for steel in the automotive industry will probably become much keener, chiefly for aluminium castings for engine blocks, rims, cylinder heads, axle bearings, pistons and radiators. Aluminium components are some 50% lighter than steel products but twice as expensive. In the case of vehicles this extra expense is largely offset by the fuel savings made.

made during the next few decades in the production and processing of magnesium, its widespread industrial use did not begin until the 1920s, when it was employed for the manufacture of printing blocks (clichés), for cast and pressed components in the textile machine industry and in engine construction. In 1941 Germany was still the leading producer of magnesium, the only metal for which it had sufficient raw materials available (as magnesite, dolomite and carnallite), but at the end of the war in 1945 its production was banned and Germany only became a major producer again in the 1960s, and then only for scrap recycling to remelted magnesium.

Magnesium and its alloys have acquired worldwide interest. The chemical, automotive, aircraft and space flight industries are opening up growing markets for a metal that is approximately one-third lighter than aluminium, especially as, apart from its use as construction material, it is an important reducing agent in the recovery of titanium, zirconium, uranium and other metals, as well as a deoxidant for metal melts. The high energy costs involved in its production, however, constitute a deterrent to its use.

Titanium

The industrial use of titanium virtually began only after the Second World War. It is a very 'young' metal, even though it was recovered for the first time

Table 9. Aluminium consumption by end-use in selected industrial countries, 1960–77 (%)

End-use	USA 1961	USA 1977	West Germany 1960	West Germany 1977	France 1960	France 1977	UK 1960	UK 1977	Japan 1963	Japan 1977
Transport	22.0	22.3	24.7	20.5	28.0	25.5	28.0	21.2	17.8	21.7
Mechanical engineering, inc. precision engineering and optics	6.4	5.8	11.2	6.3	8.3	4.6	6.7	5.7	7.7	4.3
Electronics	11.3	9.6	15.4	4.6	12.9	12.3	8.9	10.1	8.0	10.0
Building and construction	23.9	22.5	6.2	14.3	6.4	8.0	7.9	10.2	7.0	32.6
Chemical and food industries, agriculture	0.9	1.3	3.2	1.2	1.8	1.5	1.4	0.7	2.5	1.8
Packaging	7.1	20.8	8.7	7.8	9.1	6.3	7.3	9.3	2.1	5.8
Domestic appliances	10.8	6.8	4.0	6.9	8.7	4.7	9.3	8.7	30.1	6.1
Powder-consuming industries	1.0	0.8	1.1	0.4	2.9	0.3	1.5	2.3	0.7	0.4
Iron and steel industry, aluminothermic industry	3.8	1.8	4.8	4.1	4.3	3.1	4.3	3.8	3.4	2.7
Metal industries	6.1	2.9	11.9	8.5	8.6	9.3	13.0	14.9	11.4	9.7
Export of semi-manufactures	6.6	5.4	8.8	25.5	9.0	24.4	11.8	13.1	9.2	4.9
Total amount (thousand tonnes)	2,235.0	6,057.8	395.9	1,183.4	240.0	686.7	398.5	542.7	322.6	1,908.4

Note: Figures include primary and secondary aluminium.
Source: Calculated from *Metal Statistics*, various years.

in pure form as early as 1825. Industrial production of titanium was first begun in 1948. The highly malleable pure metal combines low specific gravity with high strength. Its strength is five times that of aluminium and on a par with many types of steel, with a weight, however, that is 40% less than that of steel and with good corrosion resistance. These specific properties make titanium a suitable substitute for steel or aluminium in certain fields and it also serves as an alloying metal for steels (ferro-titanium) and aluminium (aluminium-titanium). Due to the energy-dependent, high production costs (by the Kroll process), titanium is a comparatively expensive material, which has so far been the main obstacle to its effective competition with copper. Aircraft construction, to which must be added recently space flight and rocket satellite technology, are by volume the most important fields of application; in Western Europe aircraft and space flight construction account for 75–80% of titanium consumption. Potential fields of application for titanium also exist in shipbuilding, chemical plant engineering, centrifuges, turbines, nuclear energy plant and seawater desalination plants. It is also used for implantation purposes in surgery.

4.1.3 Steel improvers

The increasingly higher technical standards demanded of metals in the course of industrialization have opened up an important and growing field of application for those non-ferrous metals which are suitable as steel improvers, i.e., which form alloys with iron and carbon possessing superior properties. Chromium, cobalt, manganese, molybdenum, nickel, vanadium and tungsten are the most important of these typical alloying metals, which up to the present – with the exception of nickel – have had little application as consumer metals in common use, either alone or in alloys using them as the main constituent. Latterly, however, these metals have also proved to be an important component in non-ferrous metal alloys, although this field of application accounts for a considerably smaller volume. By carefully proportioned additions of these metals, singly or in combination, success has been achieved in improving the properties and quality of steel, as well as of non-ferrous metals, for a wide range of specific purposes. This has permitted the production of special (i.e., hard) steels with high impact or tensile strength and exceptional expansion and spring resistance power, as well as superior refractoriness and a higher fatigue threshold. The improvement in corrosion resistance to air, water, gases, alkalis and acids, culminating in the production of stainless steels, and the achievement of the high magnetizability required for certain purposes, are all attributable to successful steel alloying techniques. These also make an important contribution to the ductility, weldability and high resistance to wear of the steels. Continual refinements in alloying techniques in the non-ferrous metals industry have made it possible to create

Table 10. The main end-uses of alloying and special metals

Metal	Steel industry[1]	Mechanical engineering[2]	Electrical industry[3]	Chemical and petroleum industries[4]	Glass, ceramics, building materials	Foodstuffs and textile industries
Antimony	A	**A**	A	MCA		C
Hafnium		**M**				
Cadmium	A	**MA**	A		C	C
Cobalt	**M**	A		C		
Lithium		C		**CM**	C	
Molybdenum	**M**	A	M	C		
Niobium	**M**		MA			
Mercury		A	**MA**	M		
Rhenium			A	M		
Tantalum	M	M	**MA**		A	
Titanium	M	MA		**CMA**		
Vanadium	**M**	M		C	C	
Bismuth	A		AC	C	C	
Tungsten	**M**	C	M	C	C	
Yttrium		**C**	C			
Zirconium		M	M	M	C	

Key: M = as metal; C = as component; A = as alloying agent; the most important use is printed in **bold**.
1. Including other branches of the metal industry.   2. Including motor vehicles and transport equipment, battery industry, nuclear industry and other metal construction.   3. Including the electronics industry.   4. Including the paint and enamel industry.
Source: Compiled from *Zimmermann's World Resources and Industries*, 1972, p. 481.

materials which, by a feedback process, are able to meet ever more exacting demands on the material or, indeed, to make them possible at all.

Although the importance of these metals, in terms of volume, is predominantly in the alloy sector, their other industrial uses are also of some significance in the pattern of consumption, particularly as prospects for their substitution by other materials are usually very slight, owing to their highly specific nature.

The following brief survey of the most important fields of application for metals of the steel improver group should serve to indicate their relative importance in industrial production (see also Table 10).

Chromium

Chromium is a hard, brittle metal with very high chemical resistance, which is characterized by comparatively high refractoriness. In metallurgy it is quantitatively one of the most important alloying metals. Its main field of application is in the steel industry, but it is also an important component in nickel and copper alloys and for certain purposes serves as an additive to aluminium, cobalt and zirconium. Chromium is especially employed for the production of tool steels and high-speed machining steels; it enhances their compressive and tensile strength and confers on them high resistance to heat and wear, although their weldability declines with an increase in the chromium content. Chromium is equally indispensable for stainless and heat-resistant steels, as it is a polishable coating for the protection of easily corrodible base metals in electro-galvanizing. Such 'chromated' components find particular application in the automotive industry and in the manufacture of consumer goods. The steel industry has a 65–70% share worldwide of the total consumption of chromium. In addition the use of chrome ore is of importance in the refractory industry, for instance refractory chromite for the lining of Siemens-Martin (open-hearth) furnaces, open hearth reverberatory furnaces for the non-ferrous metals industry, and smelters for the glass industry. Chromium is also processed to form numerous chemical compounds (10–15% of consumption) which are employed in the form of pigments, chrome colours, mordant dyes, tanning agents, drilling auxiliaries and abrasives, catalysts, etc., in many branches of industry. There are virtually no substitute products for chromium in its metallic application; only in its chemical use as a pigment can chromium be replaced by other elements, such as molybdenum and cadmium – but not economically at present. No material of equivalent quality to chromate as a tanning agent has so far been found. In its refractory use silicate and other refractories have been employed as substitutes for chromium, as have other substitute materials (e.g. zircon sands) for cost reasons (Grebe *et al.*, 1975, p. 5 ff.; Wuth, 1974, p. 92 ff.).

Cobalt

This found its earliest technical application in the form of salts as a pigment for the blue colouring of glass and pottery, but its utilization was rapidly encouraged by its suitability for the refining of steel and non-ferrous metals. Cobalt is characterized by great hardness and comparatively good corrosion resistance, and also by ferromagnetism, which is further enhanced by alloying with iron, other steel improvers or rare metals. One of the most important fields of application for cobalt (37% of consumption) is now[1] the production of permanent magnetic materials in which high quality has been achieved by alloying with other metals. Another important field (21%) is the production of high-temperature alloys, with chromium, tungsten, nickel and special additions of other metals, which are suitable for withstanding heat, flame and corrosion stresses. These are needed, for instance, in the automotive and oil refining industries and for aerospace requirements (turbines, burners, exhaust systems and thermal shields). Cobalt is also employed in the production of high-strength steels (7%), predominantly employed for tools and machine parts, and finds a wide variety of application in other alloys (28%). The

[1] The breakdown of fields of application for cobalt in the US is according to data for 1972 (Gocht, 1974, p. 121).

utilization of cobalt compounds extends from pigments in the enamelling, glass and ceramic industries to catalysts for the desulphurization of coal and gasoline synthesis. The end consumers of cobalt – for which there is hardly any possible substitute – are the electrical industry, the aircraft and space flight industries, mechanical engineering and machine tool construction, the petroleum and petrochemical industries and the dyeing, glass and ceramic industries. New potential fields for cobalt are offered in its use for Radioisotope 60, which is used, for example, in medicine, materials testing and nuclear engineering.

Manganese

Up to 80% is used in metallic form but it has not yet acquired any technical importance as a pure metal. As an alloy for steel it serves as an oxidation and desulphurizing agent and improves its strength, malleability, weldability and resistance to corrosion and wear. The manganese content varies from about 1% in ordinary low-carbon or rimming steel to 25% in 'specular pig iron' (or 'spiegel iron') and up to 98% in electro-ferromanganese types. The addition of manganese has a similar beneficial effect on non-ferrous alloys. Materials containing manganese are chiefly employed for industrial plant, buildings, bridges, dams and roads; in the transport sector they are applied to railway engineering, automobile construction and shipbuilding. Manganese alloys with nickel, copper or aluminium are particularly suitable for plant engineering in the chemical industry and for numerous applications in the electrical industry, while manganese-magnesium alloys are employed in mechanical engineering, for tanks and containers. Apart from alloying purposes, manganese is also used in chemical compounds for the production of fertilizers, paints, and so on (Wuth, 1974, p. 78 ff.).

Molybdenum

Molybdenum is a very hard metal. It is difficult to smelt, has good ductility when hot and adequate cold working properties. It possesses electrical and thermal conductivity. Molybdenum is the only one of the high-temperature melting point metals (at over 1900°C) which is available in large quantities. It is predominantly used as an alloying element for the improvement of iron and steel, in particular in conjunction with chromium and nickel, but also as an essential component in iron-free super alloys. By far the largest proportion of molybdenum consumption (over 80%) is for iron and steel production; about 5% is used for non-ferrous alloys. Approximately 10% is applied to the construction of heavy-duty plant components, which are especially needed in foundry technology, the electronics industry, reactor construction and space flight technology. Molybdenum compounds are used as lubricants and in chemicals and are also of importance in the fertilizer industry as a vital trace element for atmospheric nitrogen-bonding bacteria. Molybdenum compounds have also proved suitable as catalysts in oil refining and coal hydrogenation (Roethe, 1974, p. 142 ff.).

Nickel

Nickel is a hard, ductile metal which is virtually resistant to corrosion and has extremely high resistance to alkaline solids and solutions. Nickel had at an eary period of history served for the minting of coinage but its employment as a production material dates only from the final decade of the nineteenth century with its particular use for nickel-copper-zinc alloys (nickel silver or 'German silver') and when pure nickel began to be utilized for galvanic coatings on iron and other metals. Steel hardening by addition of nickel alloys began in 1889. The production of non-rusting, i.e. stainless, acid-resisting and refractory and tough, low-temperature steels, with varying nickel contents as well as additions of chromium, manganese, molybdenum and other alloy metals, are today far and away the most important fields of application. The end users are mechanical engineering, building construction and the automotive and consumer goods industries. Low-alloy structural steel and tool steels and high-alloy physical steels represent other important forms of application. In the non-ferrous metals industry, too, nickel is an alloying metal in combination with chromium, molybdenum and zinc, and has great influence on the physical, mechanical, magnetic, electrical and chemical properties of the materials. Such types of non-ferrous metal semi-manufactures are required in chemical plant engineering and in the food and drinks industries, in plant engineering for the petroleum industry and for seawater desalination, in shipbuilding, in the electrotechnical and electronic industries and for the production of consumer goods in daily use (e.g., cutlery and keys).

Pure nickel is used virtually only for nickel-plating (with a share of 10–15% of total consumption), mainly to increase the corrosion resistance of industrial and household goods and for the production of nickel-plated materials. The automotive industry is here the most important purchaser. Nickel compounds are used in the chemical industry as catalysts and nickel chemicals are also useful pigments for glass and ceramics. The breakdown of primary nickel consumption, as pure nickel, ferro-nickel, nickel oxide and nickel salts, for West Germany for 1976 is as follows: steel industry 52.4%, foundries 8.2%, electro-galvanizing 8.4%, semi-manufactures 23.1%, other uses 7.9% (calculated from Kästner *et al.*, 1978, p. 183).

Substitution processes, apart from replacement of stainless steel by aluminium and plastics, extend in some fields to the use of cheaper materials such as chromium and magnesium to reduce the specific nickel contents in the alloys (Forster, 1976, p. 146 ff.).

Vanadium

This is seldom found in mineable deposits (a few are found in Peru and Africa). Extraction of the metal therefore takes place from vanadium-containing intermediates occurring in iron, copper, zinc and uranium recovery. Bauxites, too, usually have fairly small vanadium contents, as do many types of coal and petroleum. Vanadium – apart from numerous applications in the chemical industry – is mainly used in steel production in the form of ferro-vanadium for alloying purposes. Vanadium steels are characterized by hardness and toughness and are therefore particularly employed for tool manufacture. Vanadium is added to non-ferrous alloys based on titanium and aluminium to increase their heat resistance. These metals are used in aircraft construction, rocket construction and for space flight. Despite its specific properties hardly any technical uses have yet been found to date for the unalloyed metal, owing to the costs involved.

Tungsten

Tungsten is one of the heaviest metals and, with the highest melting point of all metals (3380°C), is especially used wherever great strength is still required of the material even at very high temperatures. It is employed in the steel industry for steel alloys. It is also applied to tool surfaces to increase wear resistance, to incandescent lamp filaments and to carbide-cutting tools such as drilling and turning parts. As pure metal it finds application in electronics and, owing to its high resistance to penetration by radioactivity, is an important construction material in nuclear engineering and space technology (*MG-Information* 2/77, p. 2).

4.1.4 Other alloying and special metals

The term 'minor metals' is usually applied to alloying metals with relatively low annual production volumes compared with those of aluminium, copper, lead, zinc, tin and nickel. They comprise a number of metals which, owing to their specific properties, occupy a key position in modern industrial production in certain sectors. Although they were mostly discovered long ago, without exception their development has mainly occurred in the mid twentieth century, prompted in most cases by technical development during the Second World War and the special needs of aircraft construction, armaments and means of communication. This was later accelerated and reinforced by advances in areas of technology which were frequently only possible on the basis of these materials. The minor metals, alone or in alloys, even in very small concentrations, possess properties which produce significant improvements in materials which have to comply with highly specialized requirements in certain contemporary fields. Such materials are in great demand for electronic engineering, air travel, aerospace and satellite technology, reactor construction and alternative methods of energy recovery. Some of these metals are also needed as the main material for highly specialized purposes in which exceptionally high standards of performance are required. Even though many have properties which enable them often to be substituted for each other in certain spheres, a few, such as titanium, zirconium and beryllium, frequently occupy key positions.

4.2 SUBSTITUTION PROCESSES

Although the demand for non-ferrous metals during the course of industrialization has been stimulated by sustained and vigorous expansion and growing diversification of the fields of application, it has also been checked by the emergence simultaneously of substitutes for non-ferrous metals, and within the metals industry itself fluctuating demand has been evident because of temporary or permanent replacement of one metal by another for specific purposes. Both tendencies have always been found side by side in principle ever since metals have been used on an industrial scale. The age of technology, however, with its incessant flow of inventions and innovations, opened the floodgates to an overwhelming number of substitution processes which have influenced the demand for metals.

During the progress of industrialization there have been endless occasions for temporary or permanent substitution of metals: on cost grounds, because of an actual or supposed risk of shortage of a metal, in either the short or long term, for purely technical reasons, such as a possible decline in specific use, or – a factor which has assumed greater importance recently – because of health hazards or on environmental protection grounds. As a rule a combination of these factors is involved. The specific properties of a metal then essentially define the limits of its capacity for substitution in a specific context, with the proviso that in most cases all its properties are not equally indispensable for the purpose concerned. The significance of the widely varying substitution processes for the volume demand for non-ferrous metals during the progress of industrialization is not reflected in the quantitative statistics available. The importance of such processes is apparent, however, from the trends broadly outlined below for large areas of the metal industry.[1]

The potential replacement of metals by each other for reasons of scarcity first became a major factor during the First World War, but in the post-war years it assumed growing technical and economic significance owing to the inroads made in the market by light metals. Aluminium and its alloys increasingly penetrated consumer fields which had previously been supplied by 'old' metals. In particular, the major transport sectors – rail traffic, shipbuilding, heavy goods vehicles and aircraft construction – opened up a

[1] Substitution processes and prospects for individual metals have been discussed in the preceding section.

wide range of potential applications for light metals on account of their technical properties and/or cost advantages. In the electrical industry, too, and in building and other areas, new uses were opened up for this 'young' metal in which it competed with the traditional metals and in many cases supplanted them, probably for ever. Thus aluminium and its alloys captured broad fields of application from copper and brass and rapidly penetrated important fields of application for tin (packaging and tinfoil). Lead also at first sustained considerable market losses in the 1920s due to the decline in the use of lead paints which were replaced by zinc and other metallic paints. However, these and other inroads of one metal into the field of another could be offset or even, as was usually the case, over-compensated for by the overall expansion in the use of all non-ferrous metals. This was accompanied by incessant opening up of new and additional fields of application; for instance, in the case of lead there was a second great boom in consumption after the Second World War, with the enormous growth of the automotive industry, when demand soared for lead starter batteries and anti-knock compounds (tetra-ethyl lead) (Reinert, 1977, p. 67).

Non-metallic materials, such as wood, glass and ceramics, compete with metals in various applications. The most noteworthy, usually permanent, replacement processes affecting the traditional provinces of metals resulted from the widespread development of plastics. Although these had originated in the nineteenth century with the invention of celluloid, several decades were needed for the plastics industry to become established, and it was not until after the Second World War that unprecedented expansion in this field got under way, with far-reaching effects on the metals industry. Admittedly plastics differ fundamentally from metals in the physical and chemical properties of their primary constituents carbon, hydrogen, oxygen and nitrogen, but it is precisely these, available moreover in almost unlimited quantities, which are at the root of their bid to compete with metals. Their inherent capacity to form large organic molecules enables plastics to be pressed, cast or foamed in any form required and they are impact- and crease-resistant as well as proof against acids and corrosion. Plastics do not, however, possess the mechanical strength of metals and they also lack electrical and thermal conductivity, although they are temperature-sensitive (Sames, 1971, p. 78 ff.).

The advantages and disadvantages of plastics materials compared with metals determine the possibilities for their substitution (Forster, 1976, pp. 31, 101, 181 ff., 221 and 255). Plastics were the strongest competitors as a substitute for aluminium up to 1973, when the first drastic increase occurred in the price of oil, their main primary material. Since then prices have shifted relatively in favour of aluminium and this has probably tended to put a brake on further penetration by plastics in the metal industry. Plastics are also replacing copper for some purposes, such as seawater pipes and other piping systems, in house-building, for fittings, and so on. Lead for drain and waste pipes and other building components is increasingly being replaced by plastics, and plastic-sheathed copper pipes are increasingly found instead of galvanized pipes in buildings, particularly as they are lighter and quicker to install and less liable to lime scale.

The development of diecasting techniques has also created an opportunity for substitution of zinc alloys by plastics. Substitution for tin particularly affects tinfoil packaging, especially where modern canning techniques permit the use of plastics.

Substitution processes in the case of the steel improvers, chromium, cobalt, manganese, molybdenum, nickel, tungsten and vanadium, have been described in section 4.1.3 above.

To sum up, it may be observed that during the course of industrialization far-reaching substitution processes have taken place in the metal industry which, in the perspective of the industry as a whole, must be deemed positive if the substitute material is technically more suitable and hence less expensive to produce, thereby serving to lower the costs of the end product or save on raw materials in short supply. The effect of substitution processes on the demand for non-ferrous metals however requires constant monitoring. There are, indeed, processes which – in the foreseeable future at least – should be regarded as irreversible for technical or price reasons. The steady technical progress in metallurgy and the development of substitute materials and their applications, coupled with the impossibility of forecasting price trends in the raw materials market and the energy sector, mean, however, that no definitive statement can be made on the importance of substitution for trends in the absolute or relative demand for non-ferrous metals.

4.3 LEVELS OF DEVELOPMENT AND INDUSTRIALIZATION

The survey of the most important fields of application for non-ferrous metals in section 4.1 has shown quite unmistakably that industrial demand is the determining factor for non-ferrous metals consumption; therefore a probable relationship *a priori* may be assumed to exist between the general level of development of a country – in which the degree of industrialization is a prime influence – and the relative consumption of non-ferrous metals. This supposition is confirmed by an international cross-sectional comparison carried out on the basis of available data from 36 countries (Table 11). The basic indicators taken for the general development level of the countries were the Gross National Product (GNP) per head of the population for the year 1976 and the consumption per head of the population of aluminium, copper, lead, zinc, tin and nickel. 1976 was selected as the year for which the latest statistical data on the Gross National Product and the pattern of non-ferrous metal consumption were available in sufficiently differentiated form for the

Table 11. Per capita Gross National Product (GNP) and consumption of non-ferrous metals in selected countries, 1976

Country	GNP per capita	Primary aluminium	Refined copper	Refined lead	Slab zinc	Primary tin	Nickel
	US$			kg			
Switzerland	9,160	16.47	3.28	2.08	3.17	0.11	0.28
Sweden	9,030	12.35	10.65	2.65	4.66	0.09	2.92
Canada	7,930	13.03	8.96	2.48	6.35	0.21	0.50
USA	7,880	20.87	8.40	4.50	4.78	0.24	0.71
Norway	7,690	28.21	1.59	3.72	4.97	0.27	0.17
Denmark	7,690	1.22	0.97	4.00	2.07	0.08	0.04
West Germany	7,510	15.52	12.10	3.91	5.38	0.26	0.92
Belgium	7,020	24.87	23.23	5.61	12.17	0.31	0.36
France	6,730	9.31	6.94	3.91	5.01	0.20	0.63
Netherlands	6,650	18.08	3.34	2.24	2.59	0.30	0.11
Finland	5,890	4.93	8.52	2.98	4.21	0.04	0.23
Austria	5,620	14.19	4.55	5.38	3.19	0.05	0.56
Japan	5,090	14.27	9.31	2.04	6.17	0.31	1.01
East Germany	4,520	12.51	7.03	5.54	3.87	0.15	0.60
UK	4,180	7.95	8.19	4.40	4.34	2.72	0.55
Italy	3,220	6.50	5.73	3.76	3.63	0.11	0.39
Spain	2,990	6.21	3.64	2.45	3.19	0.11	0.18
Poland	2,880	4.22	5.06	2.68	4.57	0.15	0.23
USSR	2,800	6.58	4.87	2.38	3.62	0.09	0.47
Rep. Ireland	2,620	1.83	0.13	0.73	0.66	–	–
Greece	2,570	5.56	2.18	3.03	1.42	0.03	–
Yugoslavia	1,750	6.98	4.62	3.21	3.00	0.06	0.06
Argentina	1,580	2.20	1.74	1.79	1.52	0.04	–
Brazil	1,300	1.96	1.63	0.48	0.88	0.04	0.04
South Africa	1,290	1.79	2.17	1.33	2.18	0.09	–
Mexico	1,060	0.89	1.33	1.23	0.96	0.03	0.06
Chile	1,050	–	4.46	–	0.15	–	–
Algeria	1,010	–	–	0.30	–	–	–
Peru	840	–	0.57[1]	–	0.60	–	–
Malaysia	830	0.64	–	–	0.72	–	–
Zambia	450	–	0.40[1]	–	–	–	–
Philippines	420	0.40	–	0.12	0.32	–	–
China	370	0.42	0.38	0.23	0.26	0.02	0.02
Indonesia	280	–	–	–	0.22	–	–
India	140	0.27	0.09	0.08	0.15	0.015	0.016
Zaire	130	–	0.04[1]	–	–	–	–

1. Unrefined.
Sources: Calculated from *World Bank Atlas*, 1979; UN *Monthly Bulletin of Statistics*, 1979; *Metal Statistics*, 1978.

major consumer countries at the present time. It is expressly pointed out, however, that the level of per capita income is only *one* determining factor for the non-ferrous metal consumption of a specific country. Other significant variables include:

(a) the degree of industrialization;
(b) the structure of the National Product and of industrial production by sectors;
(c) the infrastructure (in the broadest sense) particular to the country;
(d) absolute and relative prices for non-ferrous metals;
(e) the possibility of substitution of one metal by other metals or materials;

(f) national idiosyncrasies which derive from the raw materials supply position of the country or are the result of statutory decrees relating to environmental protection.

As Fig. 8 and Table 12 below show, an increase in the GNP per capita of the population is usually associated with an increase in the consumption of primary metals. The considerable differences in the metal consumption of countries with approximately the same per capita income leads, however, to the conclusion that, within this basic trend, national peculiarities also exert a considerable influence in the context of the above factors. Such differences may also be explained by the conventional definition of the term 'consumption', which implies the consumption of primary metal volumes available in a country, irrespective of whether the finished products manufactured from them are for domestic use or for export. A country with a relatively high export trade in metal-containing intermediates and finished goods compared with its real domestic consumption per head of metals will, according to this definition, record a higher volume and rate of metal consumption ('consumption-intensity') per unit per head of income, and a higher industrial added value, than a less export-intensive country with the same real domestic consumption.

Table 12. Relationship between per capita consumption of non-ferrous metals and per capita income in selected countries, 1976 (regression estimates)

Metal	Function type $\ln y = a + b \ln x$				Function type $\ln y = a + bx + c \ln x$				
	Constant a	Coefficient lnx	R^2	DV.	Constant a	Coefficients of x	lnx	R^2	DV
Total non-ferrous metals	−8.4407	1.3530 (13.000)	0.833 (168.994)	1.877	−10.7251	−0.0002* (−1.836)	1.7328 (7.533)	0.848 (92.076)	2.099
Aluminium	−7.2342	1.1011 (9.829)	0.775 (96.603)	2.305	−7.8119	−0.0004 (−0.395)	1.1937 (4.584)	0.777 (46.924)	2.329
Copper, refined	−7.0436	1.0120 (7.069)	0.625 (49.977)	1.684	−10.0078	−0.0002* (−1.838)	1.5027 (5.001)	0.664 (28.657)	1.858
Lead, refined	−6.8422	0.9305 (9.339)	0.757 (87.218)	1.373	−10.4756	−0.0002 (−3.327)	1.5119 (7.773)	0.828 (64.830)	1.938
Zinc, slab	−6.6319	0.9270 (10.372)	0.776 (107.587)	1.776	−8.097	−0.0001* (−1.252)	1.1640 (5.571)	0.787 (55.563)	1.865
Tin, primary	−8.1878	0.7314 (4.448)	0.442 (19.787)	1.862	−9.8296	−0.0001* (−0.808)	0.9939 (2.727)	0.457 (10.083)	1.927
Nickel	−9.5738	0.9891 (5.468)	0.576 (29.903)	1.798	−11.1238	−0.0001* (−0.713)	1.2425 (3.108)	0.586 (14.872)	1.859

Notes: Values in brackets: under the coefficients = T-values; under R^2 = F-values. * = not significant at 5% probability of error. Gross domestic product per capita of the population in US$, 1976. 'Total non-ferrous' = aluminium, copper, lead, zinc, tin, nickel, 36 countries. Aluminium = 30 countries. Copper, refined = 32 countries. Lead, refined = 30 countries. Slab zinc = 33 countries. Primary tin = 27 countries. Nickel = 24 countries.
Source: Own calculations, based on Table 11.

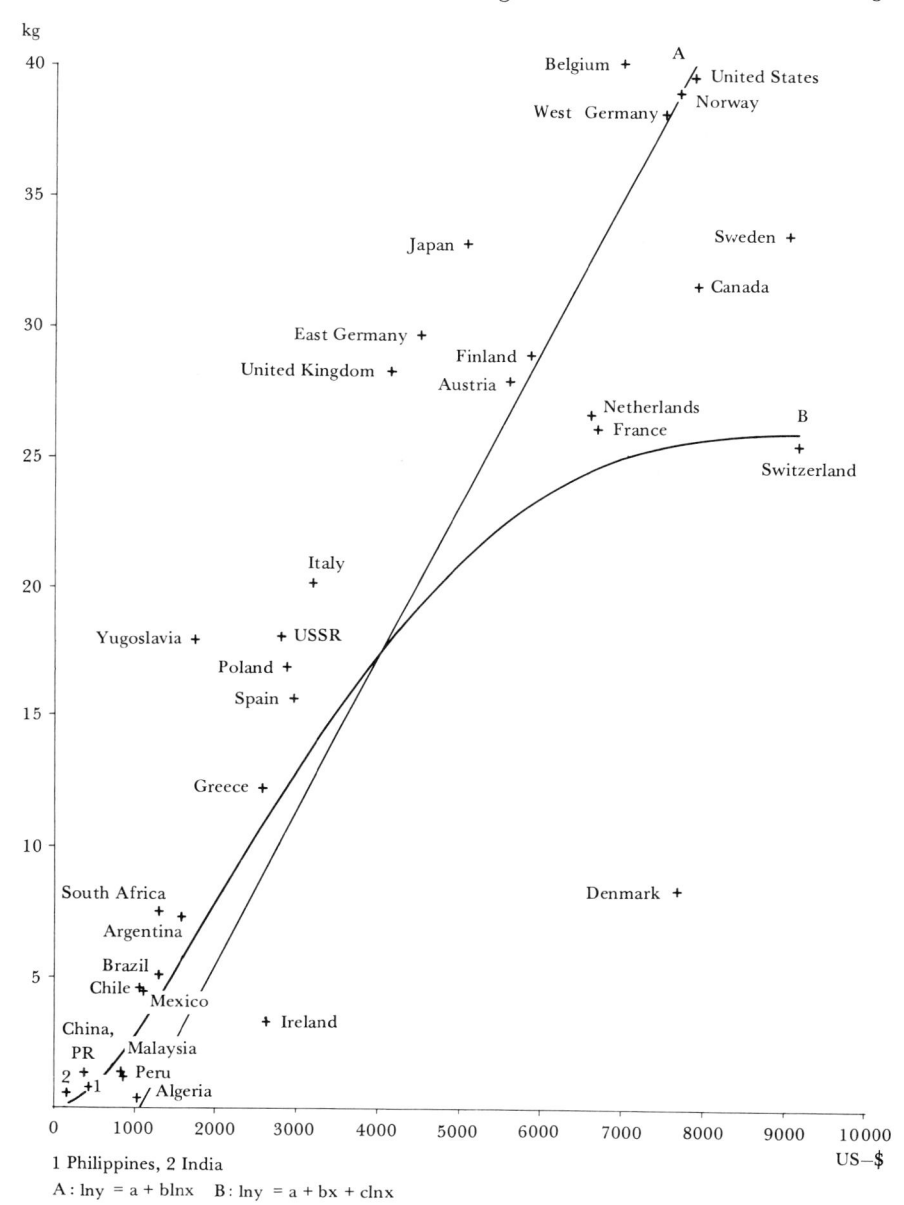

Fig. 8. Relationship between non-ferrous metal consumption and per capita income, 1976
Sources: *World Bank Atlas*, 1979; UN *Monthly Bulletin*, 1979; *Metal Statistics*, 1978.

A: $\ln y = a + b \ln x$ B: $\ln y = a + bx + c \ln x$

In order to check on how close an association exists between the level of consumption of non-ferrous metal smelter production, i.e. primary metals (y) and per capita income (x) as an indicator of the general level of development of a country, regression estimates were made for the total of the most important metals quantitatively and also for each individual metal of this group for 24–36 countries on the basis of the variables available, with the help of the following function types:

(1) $y = a + bx$ (4) $lny = a + blnx$
(2) $y = a + blnx$ (5) $y = a + bx + clnx$
(3) $lny = a + bx$ (6) $lny = a + bx + clnx$

The results and also the statistical corroboration for regressions (4) and (6) in which the maximum determining factors resulted are given in Table 12. These two regression curves have also been entered in Fig. 8. The ascending curve A ($lny = a + blnx$) gives the approximate relationship observed between the increase in per capita GNP and the increase in metal consumption. According to this both the total consumption of the quantitatively most important non-ferrous metals – aluminium, copper, lead, zinc, tin and nickel – and also the consumption of the individual metals show a positive correlation with the development of the GNP per head of the population. The different coefficients of lnx clearly show that the elasticity of consumption of the different metals varies according to the development of per capita income. In fact values of over one are obtained for aluminium and copper and – in consequence of the high share of these two metals – also for the total consumption of the non-ferrous metals included in the estimates, whereas the coefficients for nickel, lead, zinc and tin (in which the latter is a considerable way behind) are quite definitely less than one.[1]

For the regression line B (function type $lny = a + bx + clnx$) somewhat higher determinant quantities were found. The path described by this curve records an expansion, which, with increasing and already comparatively high incomes, leads to at first still positive but, towards the end of the curve, negative consumption elasticities. According to this, the connection between the two values would then be 'severed', from a specific income level upwards, not indeed in the functional sense but as a reflection of the fact that income elasticity of the demand for primary metals tends to approach zero, and may in fact pass into the negative range.[2] Even if the results of the cross-sectional analyses are not unequivocal, they suggest that a decrease in consumption elasticity and increasing severance of the growth rates of the National Product

[1] A corresponding study excluding Belgium, the Netherlands and Norway, which give extreme values due to the conventional concept of 'consumption' in metal statistics, produced only insignificant deviations from the estimated results and hardly any better determinant quantities.
[2] Estimates of the relationship between the pattern of primary energy consumption and per capita income produced the same results in the trend (Hoffmeyer and Neu, 1979, p. 160 ff.).

and of non-ferrous metal consumption would appear to be at least conceivable. This could be explained by the fact that the necessary structural change associated with economic growth, which results in a change in the contributions made by the industrial sectors to the production of the GNP, have resulted in a decreasing intensity (i.e., rate + volume) of metal consumption. This may well explain, for instance, the increase to be observed in the contribution made by the service industries to the National Product as a concomitant of progressive economic growth, and the change in the structure of industry with comparative losses on the part of the fabrication industries in favour of less metal-intensive branches of individual production and of branches of industry which are based on other materials.

The regression analyses so far are essentially confirmed by our estimate of the relationship between the level of consumption of non-ferrous metals (smelter products), y, and the degree of industrialization of a country measured as a share of the fabrication industries in the Gross National Product, x. In the survey also carried out for the year 1976 with the above six function types, the function $lny = a + blnx$ again shows approximately the observed relationship between the relative development of these two variables during the course of industrialization. The values of the coefficients however are appreciably higher than the estimate of the relationship between per capita consumption of non-ferrous metals and the level of the Gross National Product. In the study related to the degree of industrialization, slightly better determinant quantities were found for function type (6), which describes an expansion path with decreasing consumption elasticities and increasing severance of the relative growth of the metal fabrication industries and non-ferrous metal consumption (see Table 13).

The results of the estimates are also supported by the outcome of time theory analyses on the relationships between the per capita consumption of non-ferrous metals (y) and the development of the GNP per head of the population (x_1) and of industrial production (x_2), for the United States for the years 1870–1975 (aluminium 1915–1975, nickel 1880–1975), which can be taken as representative for the development of a country from the commencement of its industrial activity up to a high level of industrialization today (see Table 14). A multiple correlation must be excluded, owing to the intensive mutual interdependence between the explanatory factors. Only with the help of simple regressions could one expect to obtain a reference pointer to the influence of an exogenous factor (x) on the variable (y) to be explained, although even with a simple regression the individual influences are not clearly identifiable because of the strong parallelism in the direction taken by the trend. The regression was carried out for the quantitatively most important metals – aluminium, copper, lead, zinc, tin and nickel respectively – for the sectional periods 1870–1950 and 1950–1977, in which the estimates displayed the best correlation with the function type $lny = a + blnx$.

Table 13. Relationship between per capita consumption of non-ferrous metals and level of industrialization in selected countries, 1976 (regression estimates)

Metal	Function type lny = a + blnx				Function type lny = a + bx + clnx				
	Constant a	Coefficient lnx	R^2	DV	Constant a	Coefficients of x	lnx	R^2	DV
Total non-ferrous metals	−7.5335	2.9067 (6.052)	0.526 (36.624)	0.958	−18.0194	−0.1907 (−3.771)	7.7917 (5.740)	0.672 (32.760)	1.181
Aluminium	−7.1099	2.6379 (3.027)	0.285 (9.166)	1.250	−19.6267	−0.2211* (−1.335)	8.3069* (1.917)	0.338 (5.629)	1.496
Copper, refined	−6.0216	2.0763 (3.528)	0.300 (12.447)	1.193	−15.9730	−0.1594 (−2.543)	6.5053 (3.567)	0.432 (10.629)	1.563
Lead, refined	−4.3844	1.4753 (2.760)	0.2200 (7.617)	0.557	−13.7376	−0.1310 (−2.104)	5.4562 (2.787)	0.334 (6.505)	1.002
Zinc, slab	−4.2153	1.4535 (2.969)	0.227 (8.816)	0.944	−9.9737	−0.0901* (−1.624)	3.9946 (2.442)	0.292 (5.967)	1.133
Tin, primary	−4.7814	0.7393 (1.090)	0.047 (1.188)	1.266	−15.9934	−0.1401* (−1.634)	5.3418* (1.847)	0.146 (1.970)	1.203
Nickel	−5.8742	1.2804 (1.499)	0.097 (2.248)	0.721	−16.0066	−0.1249* (−1.175)	5.4231* (1.496)	0.155 (1.834)	0.804

Notes: Values in brackets: under the coefficients = T-values; under R^2 = F-values. * = not significant at 5% probability of error. Level of industrialization measured as share of manufacturing industry in GNP. 'Total non-ferrous' = aluminium, copper, lead, zinc, tin and nickel, 35 countries. Aluminium = 25 countries. Copper, refined = 31 countries. Lead, refined = 29 countries. Slab zinc = 32 countries. Primary tin = 26 countries. Nickel = 23 countries.
Source: Own calculations, based on Table 11.

The most important results to be noted are as follows:

(a) Consumption of aluminium, copper, lead, zinc, tin and nickel over the whole period and in both sectional periods is positively correlated with the development of the per capita income and industrial production; only consumption of tin in the two estimates shows negative coefficients for the sectional period 1950–1977.

(b) In the correlation of consumption with per capita income, in the case of all heavy metals, the coefficients for the whole period were exceeded by the coefficients for the first sectional period up to 1950. In the case of aluminium, however, higher values were shown for the whole period under observation, 1950–1975. The lowest coefficients for the sectional period 1950–1975 are found in particular for copper, zinc, tin and lead, whereas the values for aluminium and nickel are comparatively high.

(c) The correlation between consumption of non-ferrous metals and the development of industrial production for the whole period under review gave higher values for aluminium, nickel and copper than for zinc, lead and tin. The maximum values were without exception for the first sectional period up to 1950 and showed for all metals a marked levelling off in the sectional period 1950–1975, in which the highest coefficient recorded was for aluminium, with a clear lead over nickel, lead, copper, zinc and tin.

The empirical values also appear to indicate, therefore, a decreasing elasticity in metal consumption in the United States in relation to per capita income and degree of industrialization, which – as shown in the coefficients – is comparatively much more pronounced for heavy metals, although to varying degrees, than for aluminium.

Table 14. Relationship between per capita consumption of non-ferrous metals, Gross National Product (GNP) and industrial production in the United States, 1870–1975 (regression estimates)

Metal	Constant	lnx_1	R^2	DV	Constant	lnx_2	R^2	DV
Aluminium								
1915–1975	4.8621	3.8698 (40.717)	0.966	0.768	0.4264	2.0107 (49.011)	0.976	0.740
1915–1950	4.9652	3.5120 (21.903)	0.934	1.513	0.1753	2.0826 (25.127)	0.949	1.499
1950–1975	6.2842	2.6584 (10.346)	0.817	0.390	3.1833	1.3849 (14.282)	0.895	0.296
Copper								
1870–1975	4.6900	2.6443 (24.760)	0.855	0.122	2.5444	1.1536 (31.450)	0.905	0.231
1870–1950	4.6438	3.6908 (30.703)	0.923	0.327	1.9143	1.4868 (42.402)	0.958	0.819
1950–1975	6.4048	0.6957 (6.167)	0.613	1.141	5.7874	0.3177 (5.059)	0.516	0.903
Lead								
1870–1975	5.3317	1.3535 (23.705)	0.844	0.171	4.2357	0.5897 (29.105)	0.891	0.250
1870–1950	5.3113	1.8968 (27.970)	0.908	0.362	3.9101	0.7634 (35.597)	0.941	0.595
1950–1975	5.8076	0.7129 (5.323)	0.541	0.108	5.1904	0.3220 (4.394)	0.446	0.686
Zinc								
1870–1975	4.6569	2.3973 (23.942)	0.846	0.087	2.7016	1.0495 (30.961)	0.902	0.140
1870–1950	4.6156	3.3114 (26.977)	0.902	0.220	2.1435	1.3442 (39.142)	0.951	0.456
1950–1975	6.2329	0.6230 (4.384)	0.445	0.983	5.7228	0.2747 (3.586)	0.349	0.884
Tin								
1870–1975	3.0403	1.2415 (12.147)	0.587	0.434	1.9749	0.5626 (14.527)	0.670	0.284
1870–1950	3.0036	2.1655 (16.604)	0.777	0.434	1.3480	0.8962 (21.298)	0.852	0.712
1950–1975	4.0248	−0.0080* (−0.061)	0.0002	0.949	4.0882	−0.0166* (−0.253)	0.003	0.956
Nickel								
1880–1975	0.4733	4.3442 (19.683)	0.805	0.303	−3.2501	1.9514 (24.820)	0.868	0.479
1880–1950	0.1823	6.1321 (17.369)	0.814	0.474	−4.5641	2.5478 (22.814)	0.883	0.855
1950–1975	3.2900	3.2899* (13.510)	0.736	1.551	1.7692	0.6911 (9.150)	0.777	1.571

Notes: The regressions were calculated on the basis of function type ln$y$ = a + $b$ln$x$, where y = per capita consumption; x_1 = Gross National Product per head of the population; x_2 = Index of Industrial Production. Figures in brackets = tonnages. * = not significant at 5% probability of error.
Source: Own calculations from data of the US Bureau of the Census, 1975.

Our study also leads to the conclusion that there is a decrease in metal consumption elasticities in relation to the growth of the National Product and of industrial production in West Germany (Table 15):

(a) Consumption of copper, lead, zinc and tin from 1950 to 1977 showed a decrease in the trend per billion Net Social Product (at 1962 prices) and only rose in the case of aluminium and nickel.
(b) For the Net Social Product (at 1962 prices) over the same period an annual average increase of 5.2% is found, so that for the first-named metals respectively a marked severance is to be observed therefore between growth of the National Product and/or of industrial production and the increase in metal consumption.
(c) The consumption of non-ferrous metals between 1950 and 1977 for industrial production as a whole also decreased for the metal fabrication industry per unit produced in the case of copper, zinc, lead and tin, whereas for aluminium and nickel to date this has continued to increase.

Table 15. The trend in consumption of non-ferrous metals in West Germany, 1950–77

Metal	Consumption (thousand tonnes) Total	Per billion Net National Product	Consumption per unit produced Industrial production total	Processing industry (1962 = 100)
Aluminium				
1950	49.8	0.38	36.4	48.7
1955	174.2	0.84	64.1	92.8
1960	313.0	1.04	90.2	115.2
1965	387.4	1.03	118.2	107.7
1970	669.8	1.43	157.2	138.3
1975	703.7	1.07	162.9	140.6
1977	912.3	1.28	179.1	164.6
Copper				
1950	181.8	1.39	137.9	148.1
1955	353.6	1.70	152.4	157.4
1960	389.2	1.30	119.2	119.4
1965	403.8	1.07	94.3	93.6
1970	499.5	1.07	87.7	85.9
1975	634.6	0.97	107.6	105.7
1977	724.9	1.02	111.8	109.0
Lead				
1950	100.4	0.77	113.2	121.5
1955	193.6	0.93	123.9	127.7
1960	239.5	0.79	108.9	109.1
1965	272.9	0.72	94.7	94.0
1970	308.9	0.66	80.6	78.9
1975	224.5	0.34	56.5	55.5
1977	282.9	0.40	64.8	63.2

Table 15. (cont'd)

Metal	Consumption (thousand tonnes) Total	Consumption (thousand tonnes) Per billion Net National Product	Consumption per unit produced Industrial production total	Consumption per unit produced Processing industry (1962 = 100)
Zinc				
1950	131.7	1.01	124.5	133.6
1955	219.5	1.06	117.6	121.2
1960	296.7	0.99	113.1	113.3
1965	330.0	0.88	95.9	95.2
1970	395.7	0.85	86.5	84.7
1975	297.4	0.45	62.7	61.6
1977	329.5	0.46	63.2	61.7
Tin				
1950	7.9	0.06	165.7	177.9
1955	9.3	0.05	110.8	114.1
1960	14.5	0.05	122.7	123.0
1965	13.0	0.04	83.9	83.3
1970	15.1	0.03	73.3	71.8
1975	13.0	0.02	60.9	59.8
1977	14.9	0.02	63.5	61.9
Nickel				
1950	6.2	0.05	88.7	95.3
1955	11.2	0.05	91.0	93.7
1960	23.0	0.08	132.8	133.1
1965	30.7	0.08	135.3	134.3
1970	40.9	0.09	135.5	132.7
1975	42.8	0.07	141.1	138.7
1977	54.2	0.08	157.6	153.8

Notes: 1950–1970: Net National Product constant prices for 1962; 1975 and 1977: Gross Domestic Product (GDP) in constant prices for 1970. The deviation in the pattern of values is probably at least partly influenced by the necessary linking of the Indices of Industrial Production 1962 = 100 with 1970 = 100; changes in stocks may also have been a factor in the calculation on the basis of sample years – because of the usual definition of consumption in the statistics.

Sources: Author's own calculations from *Bevölkerung und Wirtschaft 1872–1972*, Statistiches Bundesamt, Wiesbaden, Stuttgart and Mainz, 1972; *Statistisches Jahrbuch für die Bundesrepublik Deutschland*, Wiesbaden, 1978.

5

The pattern of consumption of non-ferrous metals

5.1 THE PRODUCT STRUCTURE OF WORLD CONSUMPTION[1]

From the wealth of traditions handed down it is known that metals were already used thousands of years before our present era, and we know that the exploitation of metals was largely an important economic factor before the Industrial Revolution and the beginning of the age of technology. Up to the nineteenth century, however, consumption of non-ferrous metals was still very slight. Indeed, it is estimated that over the past several thousand years the total amount of metal recovered and utilized was less than during the first ten years following the Second World War. Even in 1800 total world consumption for the major metals by volume – copper, lead, zinc and tin – is estimated at only 47,000 tonnes, and it was not until 1860 that it increased to some 300,000 tonnes per annum.

As non-ferrous metals, by virtue of their special properties, prove to be key raw materials from the very beginning of industrial development, the

Table 16. World consumption of non-ferrous metals, 1890–1979

Year or period	Aluminium	Copper[1]	Lead[2]	Zinc	Tin	Nickel	Total
		Consumption (thousand tonnes)					
1890		288.5	566.6[3]	347.2	55.7		1,258.0
1900	7.3	512.7	871.3[3]	474.8	81.6		1,947.7
1910	44.2	921.8	1,122.8[3]	824.9	118.8		3,032.5
1920	131.9	929.0	973.5[3]	688.5	127.0		2,849.9
1930	205.9	1,639.4	1,522.9[3]	1,232.6	161.1		4,761.9
1940	822.8	2,711.1	1,653.1[3]	1,740.6	166.6		7,094.2
1950	1,583.6	3,009.3	1,867.6[3]	2,075.2	170.2	182.3[4]	8,888.2
1960	4,177.3	4,755.8	2,617.0	3,081.8	200.6	292.7	15,125.2
1970	10,027.9	7,291.3	3,914.2	5,041.8	225.5	576.6	27,077.3
1979	16,017.2	9,882.5	5,480.9	6,332.2	234.4	776.6	38,724.8

1 For a definition of 'consumption' see the introductory remarks in the Appendix.

Table 16. (cont'd)

Year or period	Aluminium	Copper[1]	Lead[2]	Zinc	Tin	Nickel	Total
			Annual average change[3]				
1890–1900		5.5	3.7[3]	3.5	3.5		4.5
1900–1910	19.9	6.1	2.8[3]	5.5	3.6		4.5
1910–1920	10.9	−1.3	−0.9[3]	−3.1	−0.8		−0.6
1920–1930	6.3	6.7	4.0[3]	7.1	4.1		5.3
1930–1940	14.1	5.3	1.4[3]	3.4	0.9		4.1
1940–1950	6.4	0.4	−0.3[3]	1.2	−1.4		2.3
1950–1960	10.7	4.9	5.4	4.7	2.6	7.0[4]	5.5
1960–1970	9.6	4.7	4.3	5.5	1.7	7.8	6.0
1970–1979	5.4	3.4	4.0	2.4	0.6	3.4	4.1
			Index 1950 = 100				
1890		9.6	30.3	16.7	32.7		14.2
1900	0.5	17.0	46.7	22.9	47.9		22.0
1910	2.8	30.6	60.1	39.8	69.8		34.1
1920	8.3	30.9	52.1	33.2	74.6		32.1
1930	13.0	54.5	81.5	59.4	94.7		53.6
1940	52.0	90.1	88.5	83.9	97.9		79.8
1950	100	100	100	100	100	100	100
1960	263.9	158.0	140.1	148.5	117.9	160.6	170.2
1970	632.8	242.1	209.4	243.0	132.5	316.3	306.0
1979	1,010.7	328.1	293.2	305.2	137.7	426.0	437.6
			Share of world consumption (%)				
1890		22.9	45.0	27.6	4.4		100
1900	0.4	26.3	44.7	24.4	4.2		100
1910	1.5	30.4	37.0	27.2	3.9		100
1920	4.6	32.6	34.2	24.2	4.5		100
1930	4.3	34.4	32.0	25.9	3.3		100
1940	11.6	38.2	23.3	24.5	2.4		100
1950	17.8	33.9	21.0	23.4	1.9	2.0	100
1960	27.6	31.5	17.3	20.4	1.3	1.9	100
1970	37.1	26.9	14.5	18.6	0.8	2.1	100
1979	41.3	25.5	14.2	16.4	0.6	2.0	100
			Per capita consumption (kg)				
1890		0.19	0.38	0.23	0.04		0.83
1900	0.01	0.32	0.54	0.30	0.05		1.22
1910	0.03	0.54	0.65	0.48	0.07		1.76
1920	0.07	0.50	0.52	0.37	0.07		1.53
1930	0.10	0.79	0.74	0.60	0.08		2.30
1940	0.36	1.18	0.72	0.76	0.07		3.09
1950	0.63	1.20	0.75	0.83	0.07	0.07	3.55
1960	1.40	1.59	0.88	1.03	0.07	0.10	5.07
1970	2.78	2.02	1.08	1.40	0.06	0.16	7.50
1979	3.69	2.28	1.26	1.46	0.05	0.18	8.93

1. 1890–1920 unrefined copper; 1930 onwards refined copper. 2. 1890–1950 pig lead; 1960 onwards refined lead. 3. Calculated on the basis of three-year average. 4. 1953.
Source: Calculated from *Metal Statistics*, various years.

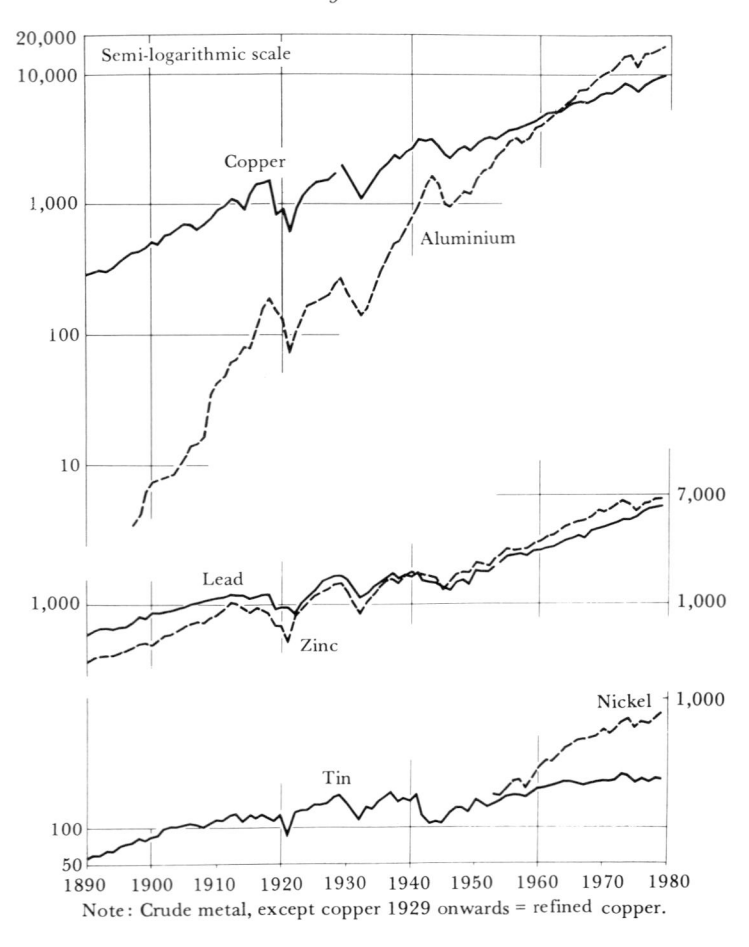

Fig. 9. World consumption of selected non-ferrous metals, 1890–1979 (thousand tonnes)
Source: *Metal Statistics*, various years.

following decades ushered in a massive expansion in their use. At the turn of the century a total consumption of 1.95 million tonnes was recorded (including aluminium, which was then quantitatively still insignificant), and by the outbreak of the First World War there was an enormous escalation in annual consumption to over 3 million tonnes. After the decline due to the war a new expansion phase for metal consumption arose in the 1920s and 1930s, and by 1940 world consumption of aluminium, copper, lead, zinc and tin had risen to over 7 million tonnes. After the hiatus of the Second World War a third period of rapidly accelerating metal consumption began around 1950 – with intermittent weaker phases due to economic cycles. This continued till the early seventies, when there was a marked slowing down of consumption growth. In 1979 total consumption of the quantitatively most important non-ferrous metals, aluminium, copper, lead, zinc, tin and nickel, at 38.7 million tonnes, was five times as high as before the outbreak of the Second World War.

The pattern of growth in consumption – corresponding to the different requirements arising during the industrialization process – varied considerably in the case of individual metals over the course of time. Copper displayed the most marked expansion in consumption from 1890 to 1940, at a rate which outstripped even the considerable increase in consumption of the other heavy non-ferrous metals lead, zinc and tin during the same period. Consumption of the light metal aluminium in these decades expanded at an uneven pace, however, although it started at a low level. From 1950 to 1977 the pace of consumption growth for all non-ferrous metals, at an annual average increase of 5.2% – compared with 3% for 1900–1950 – was still markedly higher than in the early phase of the industrialization period. Although this tempo was given marked impetus by the consumption pattern for aluminium, copper, lead and zinc nevertheless also recorded a greater upswing in consumption after 1950 than in the first half of the twentieth century.

Table 17. World consumption of non-ferrous metals, 1889–1979 (regression estimates)

	World consumption a	World consumption b	R^2		World consumption a	World consumption b	R^2
Aluminium, primary				Zinc			
1897–1979	2.164	0.098	0.97	1889–1979	5.857	0.031	0.96
1897–1950	1.940	0.108	0.93	1889–1950	5.964	0.027	0.88
1950–1979	7.525	0.081	0.98	1950–1979	7.615	0.043	0.96
Copper, unrefined				Tin			
1889–1975	5.853	0.034	0.95	1889–1979	4.321	0.013	0.82
1889–1950	5.859	0.034	0.89	1889–1950	4.206	0.015	0.65
1950–1975	7.807	0.045	0.97	1950–1979	5.074	0.016	0.80
Copper, refined				Nickel			
1929–1979	7.285	0.038	0.94	1953–1979	5.248	0.057	0.95
1929–1950	7.312	0.037	0.58	Cadmium			
1950–1979	8.023	0.042	0.98	1966–1979	2.751	0.047	0.06
Pig lead				Magnesium			
1889–1955	6.533	0.015	0.83	1966–1979	5.227	0.035	0.85
Refined lead							
1953–1979	7.619	0.038	0.99				

Notes: All calculations were performed on the basis of a logarithmic trend. The coefficients of all variables were significant to a 5% probability of error.
Source: Own calculations from consumption data given in *Metal Statistics*, various years.

Since 1950 a more pronounced slowing up in the growth of consumption cannot be ignored, however. This is reflected in a drop in the annual average increase of total consumption of the six quantitatively most important non-ferrous metals, aluminium, copper, lead, zinc, tin and nickel, which fell on average from 5.5% in 1950–1960 to 4.1% in 1970–1979. Following this trend, remarkable shifts have occurred in the product structure of world consumption of non-ferrous metals since the turn of the century. In 1900 lead was still dominant in metal consumption and, with a 45% share, was considerably ahead of copper (26%), zinc (24%), tin (4%) and aluminium (0.4%). By the First World War copper consumption had advanced, under the influence of electrification, to take a 30% share of non-ferrous metal consumption in the world; zinc consumption also increased its share to 27%, but lead, despite a relative decline to 36%, still took first place in world consumption. This situation continued even into the 1920s. Only from 1930 onwards did copper register the maximum consumption figure in the world, with almost 35%, until in the 1960s it was relegated to second place by aluminium, the position it still occupies today with 26% (1979), accompanied by a marked rise in aluminium consumption (41%) and relative losses in zinc (16%) and lead (14%).[1]

Metal consumption, therefore, displays during the course of time great vicissitudes, reflecting the current stage of industrialization and the pace of industrial development and also providing an indication as to which sectors of the economy were of predominant influence on the consumption of metal in a specific period. For instance, the increase in copper consumption reveals the upswing in the electricity industry after 1960 and the rise in aluminium consumption is a pointer to the development of the automotive and aircraft industries and to the increasing use of this metal as a packaging material and in building. Shifts in the pattern of metal consumption, however, are quite unmistakable.

Although generally the consumption of metals per head rapidly increased in the earliest countries to be industrialized during the initial decades of growth, different trends have become apparent in the statistics of metals by countries

---

[1] In a comparison of absolute volumes of consumption it should of course be noted that the specific weight of aluminium is much less than that of copper, lead, zinc, tin and nickel (see Table 1, p. 8). With corresponding conversion to volumetric figures – expressed in m^3 – which to a certain extent show the quantity of material available for fabrication, the 1977 values (in 1,000 m^3) – aluminium (5,317), copper (1,010), zinc (806), lead (392), nickel (73), tin (72) – show that there was in fact no change in the order of consumption of these metals by volume but that the gap between aluminium and the other metals had widened considerably. Because of the varied nature of the metals such estimates should be treated with reservation, because the volume of material necessary for the manufacture of a production unit varies according to the metal (*Metal Statistics*, 1937, p. vi). The quantitative values still underline the overriding importance of aluminium in the consumption of non-ferrous metals, which, according to volume, was already 130% higher in 1977 than that of the other metals.

Table 18. Per capita consumption of non-ferrous metals in selected industrial countries, 1940–79 (kg)

	EEC	West Germany	France	UK	USA	Japan	USSR
Aluminium							
1940		3.46	1.71	2.15	1.56	0.70	0.31
1950		1.04	1.32	3.65	5.41	0.23	
1960	4.65	5.88	4.66	6.82	8.53	1.61	2.95
1970	10.57	11.03	8.14	7.29	17.03	8.73	5.48
1979	19.28	17.41	11.14	7.64	22.76	15.55	7.06
Annual average change, 1950–79 (%)	7.77[1]	10.20	7.63	2.58	5.08	15.64	4.70[1]
Copper, refined							
1940		3.29	2.51	14.51	6.59	3.38	1.15
1950		3.80	2.64	10.63	8.57	0.77	
1960	7.09	9.70	5.18	10.70	6.78	3.26	3.04
1970	8.13	11.49	6.51	9.99	9.08	7.86	3.91
1979	11.40	12.95	6.70	8.92	10.16	11.48	5.14[1]
Annual average change, 1950–79 (%)	2.53[1]	4.32	3.26	−0.60	0.59	9.76	2.80[1]
Lead							
1940		2.68	1.42	7.22	4.26	1.59	0.44
1950		2.10	1.77	4.69	5.27	0.30	
1960	3.89	4.50	3.53	5.47	3.58	1.07	1.49
1970	4.26	5.09	3.79	4.72	4.60	2.02	2.02
1979	6.40	5.89	3.95	5.96	6.09	2.31	2.95[1]
Annual average change, 1950–79 (%)	2.66	3.62	2.81	0.83	0.50	7.29	3.66[1]
Zinc							
1940		4.35	1.60	5.49	4.92	1.18	0.44
1950		2.75	2.29	4.78	6.01	0.62	
1960	4.25	5.57	3.77	5.27	4.37	2.03	1.73
1970	4.98	6.52	4.34	5.01	5.24	5.97	2.80
1979	6.75	6.80	5.36	4.27	4.53	6.72	3.79
Annual average change, 1950–79 (%)	2.46[1]	3.17	2.98	−0.39	−0.97	8.56	4.21[1]
Tin							
1940		0.14	0.11	0.62	0.56	0.14	0.05
1950		0.17	0.18	0.47	0.47	0.06	
1960	0.27	0.27	0.25	0.44	0.29	0.16	0.12
1970	0.24	0.25	0.21	0.34	0.26	0.27	0.07
1979	0.25	0.25	0.18	0.24	0.22	0.27	0.09
Annual average change, 1950–79 (%)	−0.40	1.34	0	−2.29	−2.58	5.32	−1.50[1]
Nickel							
1953		0.14	0.15	0.35	0.60	0.02	
1960	0.35	0.43	0.42	0.50	0.54	0.19	0.35
1970	0.55	0.67	0.71	0.68	0.73	0.95	0.41
1979	0.90	1.26	0.72	0.63	0.81	1.14	0.49
Annual average change, 1953–79 (%)	5.10[1]	8.82	6.22	2.29	1.16	16.82	1.79[1]

Table 18. (cont'd)

	EEC	West Germany	France	UK	USA	Japan	USSR
Magnesium							
1966	0.23	0.71	0.09	0.15	0.38	0.06	0.11
1970	0.27	0.82	0.13	0.12	0.41	0.11	0.12
1979	0.27	0.53	0.16	0.11	0.45	0.18	0.22
Annual average change, 1966–79 (%)	1.24[1]	−2.22	4.53	−2.36	1.31	8.82	5.48
Cadmium							
1966	0.02	0.02	0.02	0.03	0.03	0.01	0.01
1970	0.02	0.03	0.02	0.02	0.02	0.01	0.01
1979	0.03	0.03	0.02	0.03	0.02	0.01	0.01
Annual average change, 1966–79 (%)	3.17	3.17	0	0	−3.07	0	0

1. Annual average change for period 1960–79.
Source: *Metal Statistics*, various years.

during the most recent period (1950–1979) which may be symptomatic of future consumption trends in general:

(a) The regional differences in per capita consumption[1] are particularly marked in the case of aluminium and nickel. Japan recorded an average annual increase of 16% and next came West Germany, with rates of 9–10%, and France (6–7.8%), while the remaining countries recorded rates for aluminium of between 5% (United States, USSR) and 2.6% (United Kingdom) and for nickel of about 1–2%; the low starting level of the first-mentioned countries should of course be noted.

(b) In the case of refined copper the range of increase extends from 10% in Japan, through increases of 3–5% in certain European countries, to a reduction (−0.6%) in per capita consumption in the United Kingdom.

(c) Japan leads in the case of lead and zinc with an average annual increase of around 8–9%, ahead of the principal European industrial countries. Here the most marked cases of decline in consumption per head are found in the United States (increase in lead of only 0.5% and decrease in zinc of approximately 1%).

(d) The decline in consumption of tin is even greater in the United States (−2.7%) and in the United Kingdom, whereas Japan again displays the maximum increase in consumption per head, taking precedence over West Germany and France.

Details of the level of consumption per head of the quantitatively most important non-ferrous metals have already been given for 36 countries in Table 11. The detailed figures given there show that, although the major industrial countries together account for the principal share of consumption of

1 Reference should again be made in this context to the definition of 'consumption' basically employed in the statistics used (see Appendix 1), according to which the rates sometimes tend rather to provide indications of the structure of the metal fabrication industry than the 'real' per capita consumption by consumers.

non-ferrous metals, in relation to population the smaller individual countries in Western Europe have a considerably higher proportion. Even though this is partly to be ascribed to the statistical definition of 'consumption' (see Appendix 1) and derives from circumstances peculiar to the countries, it also reflects the relatively high level of development and advanced state of industrialization in these countries.

5.2 REGIONAL AND NATIONAL TRENDS IN CONSUMPTION

In the initial phase of industrial development and in the following decades the main emphasis of metal consumption in Europe was centred clearly in the United Kingdom, followed by Germany, France and the other countries. Even in 1910 the non-ferrous metal consumption of these three European countries exceeded that of the entire North American continent and Europe accounted for 60% of world consumption of raw copper and lead, 69% of zinc and 50% of tin. North America, however, occupied first place in the consumption of aluminium, although then at a low level, with almost 50%. After the First World War (1920) it then overtook Europe in the consumption of raw copper, lead and tin, and lagged behind only in zinc consumption. In the two decades up to the Second World War, however, Europe again recorded a higher consumption of the above metals (with the exception of tin) than America; but at the end of the war, North America was the main consuming region for all the most important non-ferrous metals by volume – including nickel, which had only then acquired any major industrial importance. The United States has maintained this position in the consumption of aluminium up to the present day, but since the 1960s Europe's consumption of the other metals has been greater than the total for both North and South America. Latin America has pushed up its shares of world consumption only during the last ten years to around 5% for unrefined copper and 4% for lead, zinc and tin, while its share of aluminium has remained under 3% and of nickel under 2%.

These alternating positions of Europe and America, extending up to the first decade after the Second World War did not alter the basic regional pattern of metal consumption observable in the world since the beginning of the age of technology. This shows that the United States and Western European countries, the leading industrialized countries, were the principal consumers of metals. It was inevitable that the major industrial regions of the world became the chief consumers of non-ferrous metals, as it was their principal industries, particularly the capital goods and transport industries, which were responsible for the massive demand for copper, lead, zinc, aluminium and other metals. Although at times this demand underwent fluctuations in response to changing economic cycles, thanks to the progressive development of technical improvements and innovations the strong upward trend was maintained (Breidenbroich, 1938, p. 12).

Table 19. Consumption of non-ferrous metals by regions, 1890–1979 (% of world total)

Year	Europe	EEC	North America	Latin America	Africa	Asia	Australia and Oceania	Eastern Bloc countries[1]	World total* (thousand tonnes)
				Aluminium					
1900	17.8		39.7						7.3[2]
1910	20.4		49.1						44.2[3]
1920	40.4		58.0	–	–	1.5	–	–	131.9
1930	48.4		46.1	–	–	5.3	0.2	–	205.9
1940	58.5		27.0	0.2	0.0	6.1	0.2	7.9	822.9
1950	25.2		34.2	22.9	0.1	1.7	0.4	15.5	1,583.6
1960	31.4	17.4	39.8	1.3	0.3	5.0	9.0	21.3	5,157.1
1970	26.8	16.3	37.4	1.9	0.6	12.0	1.3	20.0	12,503.5
1979	24.9	19.4	34.5	3.1	0.8	14.8	1.3	20.5	20,338.5
				Copper, refined					
1930	48.4		46.0	0.3	0.2	4.8	0.3	–	1,639.4
1940	44.3		35.7	0.4	0.3	9.7	0.9	8.7	2,711.1
1950	33.5		46.0	2.0	0.8	3.3	1.1	13.3	3,018.2
1960	40.6	34.2	28.0	1.9	0.7	8.1	1.5	19.2	4,755.8
1970	34.1	28.1	28.6	2.5	0.6	12.6	1.6	20.0	7,293.6
1979	28.9	23.6	25.1	4.7	1.0	16.1	1.3	23.2	9,882.5
				Lead					
1890	64.5		27.3	–	–	–	–	3.3	566.7[4]
1900	65.7		32.0	–	–	1.0	0.9	–	871.3[5]
1910	59.9		35.3	–	–	1.5	0.6	–	1,122.8[6]
1920	39.7		54.9	1.2	0.2	2.9	1.1	–	973.5
1930	55.9		36.0	1.6	0.3	5.2	1.0	–	1,524.9
1940	45.2		36.1	1.7	0.5	7.9	2.0	6.6	1,653.1
1950	34.9		45.7	4.0	0.9	1.9	2.5	10.1	1,867.6
1960	40.6	34.1	26.1	3.3	0.9	5.2	2.0	21.9	2,617.0
1970	34.7	27.4	25.5	4.3	1.1	7.5	1.7	25.1	3,914.2
1979	30.4	23.9	26.7	5.3	1.5	8.4	1.5	26.3	5,480.9
				Zinc					
1890	79.4		17.8	–	–	–	–	–	347.2[7]
1900	72.6		25.7	–	–	–	–	–	474.8[8]
1910	69.1		29.4	–	–	–	–	–	824.9[9]
1920	53.8		43.1	0.7	0.1	1.8	0.5	–	688.5
1930	60.6		32.5	1.1	0.2	4.6	1.0	–	1,232.6
1940	44.3		39.3	0.8	0.5	6.4	2.4	6.3	1,740.6
1950	33.1		46.5	1.5	0.7	3.7	2.5	12.0	2,075.2
1960	36.6	31.6	27.3	2.5	1.0	8.8	3.1	20.7	3,081.8
1970	30.1	24.8	23.4	3.3	1.5	16.4	2.4	22.8	5,041.7
1979	27.0	22.8	18.2	5.3	1.9	19.3	1.9	26.4	6,332.2
				Tin					
1890	69.0		27.1	–	–	–	–	–	55.7[19]
1900	58.6		38.7	1.0	0.3	0.4	0.7	–	81.6[11]
1910	50.0		42.0	1.8	0.4	–	0.8	–	118.8[12]
1920	35.0		54.7	1.6	0.4	7.1	1.2	–	127.0
1930	44.1		45.6	1.6	1.1	6.8	0.8	–	161.1
1940	33.1		46.2	1.9	1.0	8.7	1.8	7.3	166.6
1950	32.3		45.2	2.5	1.5	7.0	1.5	10.0	170.2
1960	34.6	31.4	48.1	2.7	1.6	10.6	2.1	20.3	200.6
1970	30.5	27.0	26.7	2.2	1.7	17.7	1.9	20.0	225.5
1979	21.1	10.2	5.6	4.2	1.9	2.6	1.6	5.5	234.4

Table 19. (cont'd)

Year	Europe	EEC	North America	Latin America	Africa	Asia	Australia and Oceania	Eastern Bloc countries[1]	World total* (thousand tonnes)
					Nickel				
1953	21.1		54.9	0.2	–	1.1	0.3	22.5	182.3
1960	32.4	27.3	35.0	0.2	0.1	6.3	0.8	25.3	292.7
1970	30.4	24.1	28.5	0.5	0.6	17.6	0.7	21.7	576.6
1979	30.1	23.7	24.5	1.6	0.7	18.4	0.7	24.2	777.6

1. Where no figures given, amounts are included in European and Asian totals.
*Unspecified: 2. – 42.5; 3. – 30.5; 4. – 4.9; 5. – 0.4; 6. – 2.7; 7. – 2.8; 8. – 1.7; 9. – 1.5; 10. – 3.9; 11. – 0.3; 12. – 5.0.
Source: Calculated from *Metal Statistics*, various years.

Europe and North America were still dominant in world metal consumption in 1950, with 70–80%; since then, however, development trends in metal consumption in these two focal areas of industrial production have been characterized by continually decreasing shares of world consumption. It is true that these two regions have so far continued every year to reach new peak levels in the overall total consumption of metals and still continue to account for some 50–60% of world metal consumption, but it cannot be overlooked that the expansion of consumption in these two 'old' industrial regions is tending to slow up, more and more, both absolutely and relatively. A counter-trend is taking place – without interruption to date – in the countries of the Eastern Bloc and Asia. The strongest growth is to be observed in the latter during the past ten years, Japan still taking up the lion's share of world consumption among the Asian countries. The Eastern Bloc countries succeeded in doubling their world share between 1950 and 1977 and today occupy third place after Euope and America. Metal consumption in Africa and Australia has increased many times over, but, with a share of less than 2%, it still takes an extremely modest place according to world standards.

In the breakdown of world consumption of non-ferrous metals by countries two distinct phases with very different features may be discerned in the course of industrialization (see Table 20).

(a) The last 30 years of the nineteenth century and the following two decades up to the outbreak of the First World War were marked by a progressive concentration of rapidly increasing consumption in the industrialization of the leading countries, especially the United States, Germany, the United Kingdom and France.

(b) Between the two world wars the former leading consumer countries, with further expansion in consumption, recorded continually decreasing shares of world consumption in favour of the countries who were catching up on industrialization, including especially the USSR, Japan and some European countries.

(c) Since 1950, with sustained expansion of consumption, further decreases are constantly apparent in the shares of the 'old' industrial countries and vigorous increases in the shares taken by countries where industrialization only began during recent decades and where it is now forging ahead. At the same time, with the efforts of the Third World to become industrialized, the circle of consumer countries is seen to have grown.

Table 20. The consumption of non-ferrous metals by countries, 1890–1979 (% of world total)

Country	1890	1900	1910	1920	1930	1940	1950	1960	1970	1979
				Aluminium						
USA		39.7	49.0	58.0	43.2	25.0	52.0	36.9	34.8	31.3
USSR					4.9	7.3	13.6	15.1	13.3	11.6
Japan					5.3	6.1	1.2	3.6	9.1	11.3
West Germany				12.7	11.7	29.4	3.1	7.5	6.7	6.7
France		9.6	12.2	11.0	9.7	8.3	3.5	5.1	4.1	3.7
China		*	*	*	*	*	*	2.2	2.2	3.6
Italy		*	2.0	1.5	4.0	5.2	3.0	2.4	2.8	2.8
UK		8.2	6.1	5.3	11.7	12.6	11.6	8.6	4.1	2.6
Canada		*	*	*	*	2.0	3.7	2.4	2.2	2.2
Belgium and Luxembourg		*	*	*	0.5	*	*	*	1.8	1.5
Hungary		*	*	*	*	0.5	0.4	*	*	*
Spain		*	*	*	*	0.2	*	*	*	*
Australia		*	*	0.1	0.1	*	0.4	*	*	*
East Germany		*	*	*	*	*	*	1.8	*	*
Total		57.5	69.4	88.6	91.1	96.4	92.5	85.5	80.9	77.3
World consumption (thousand tonnes)		7.3	44.2	131.9	205.9	822.8	1,583.6	4,177.3	10,027.9	16,017.2
				Copper, unrefined						
USA	35.5	34.0	36.9	53.4	42.4	34.1	44.0	24.5	23.6	17.4
USSR	2.8	4.0	3.1	0.5	3.8	7.9	9.4	13.8	13.6	14.7
Japan	0.8	*	*	9.0	4.8	10.9	0.7	6.2	11.9	11.8
West Germany	16.4	21.2	23.1	7.8	13.8	6.8	3.1	9.9	8.3	7.3
UK	26.5	21.2	15.8	11.4	10.5	20.4	14.0	11.8	6.6	6.0
France	9.5	10.1	9.3	7.4	9.2	4.3	4.4	5.4	5.2	5.6
China	*	*	*	*	*	*	*	*	3.2	4.6
Italy	1.4	1.6	0.3	1.6	3.5	2.9	2.8	4.3	4.3	4.5
Canada	*	*	*	*	1.4	4.4	4.0	2.7	3.8	3.1
Belgium and Luxembourg	1.4	1.2	1.4	0.8	2.1	*	2.3	1.9	2.1	2.2
Australia	*	*	*	0.9	*	1.1	*	*	*	*
Sweden	*	*	*	*	2.0	1.7	2.2	2.0	*	*
Total	94.2	93.3	91.0	92.8	93.3	94.5	90.0	82.5	82.4	77.3
World consumption (thousand tonnes)	288.5	512.7	921.8	929.0	1,439.9	2,219.0	2,437.6	3,926.0	6,041.2	6,287.0

Table 20. (cont'd)

Country	1890	1900	1910	1920	1930	1940	1950	1960	1970	1979
				Copper, refined						
USA					44.8	32.1	42.9	25.8	25.5	22.6
USSR					4.1	8.1	10.3	13.7	13.0	13.8
Japan					4.2	8.9	2.0	6.4	11.3	13.5
West Germany					14.5	8.5	6.0	10.9	9.6	8.0
UK					10.4	25.8	13.6	11.8	7.6	5.0
China					*	*	*	*	2.5	3.6
Italy					3.1	2.4	2.4	3.9	3.8	3.6
France					8.2	3.7	4.1	5.0	4.5	3.6
Belgium and Luxembourg					1.8	*	1.9	1.9	2.0	3.1
Canada					1.2	3.6	3.2	2.2	3.1	2.5
Sweden					*	1.4	2.1	1.9	*	*
Total					92.4	94.6	88.6	83.5	82.8	79.3
World consumption (thousand tonnes)					1,639.4	2,711.1	3,009.3	4,755.8	7,293.6	9,882.5
				Lead						
USA	27.3	30.6	31.0	52.3	34.2	34.1	43.0	24.7	24.2	24.5
USSR	3.3	2.3	4.0	*	3.8	5.1	6.4	12.2	12.5	14.2
West Germany	14.5	19.8	17.1	6.9	10.8	11.3	5.4	9.2	7.9	6.6
UK	28.0	23.4	17.0	16.6	17.1	21.1	12.6	11.0	6.7	6.1
Japan	*	1.0	1.3	2.6	3.9	6.9	1.3	3.8	5.4	4.9
Italy	3.5	2.6	2.3	1.4	2.5	3.0	2.5	3.0	4.3	4.7
France	11.0	11.1	7.3	6.9	9.5	3.4	4.0	6.2	4.9	3.9
China	*	*	*	*	*	*	*	2.7	4.1	3.8
Canada	*	1.4	1.5	2.6	1.8	2.1	2.7	*	*	2.2
Spain	*	*	*	1.5	1.6	1.8	*	*	*	2.1
Belgium and Luxembourg	3.5	3.3	2.6	3.6	3.2	*	2.4	2.1	*	*
Australia	*	0.9	0.6	1.1	*	2.0	2.5	*	*	*
Total	91.1	96.2	73.8	95.6	88.4	90.8	82.7	75.1	74.5	79.3
World consumption (thousand tonnes)	566.6	871.3	1,122.8	973.5	1,524.9	1,653.1	1,867.6	2,617.0	3,906.3	5,480.1

Table 20. (cont'd)

Country	1890	1900	1910	1920	1930	1940	1950	1960	1970	1979
					Zinc					
USA	17.4	19.6	29.4	43.1	31.3	37.3	44.1	25.7	21.3	15.8
USSR	2.4	3.3	3.0	*	3.4	4.9	8.0	12.0	13.5	15.8
Japan	*	*	*	1.4	3.8	4.8	2.5	6.1	12.4	12.3
West Germany	26.0	26.5	22.4	10.4	15.5	17.5	6.4	9.6	7.9	6.6
France	11.3	13.1	6.8	6.7	10.4	3.7	4.6	5.6	4.4	4.5
UK	22.6	19.5	21.6	17.1	12.0	15.2	11.6	9.0	5.5	3.8
Italy	0.5	0.7	1.0	0.7	1.8	2.2	1.6	2.8	3.5	3.6
China	*	*	*	*	*	*	*	*	3.0	3.0
Poland	*	*	*	*	*	*	*	3.0	2.6	2.8
Canada	*	*	*	0.7	1.2	1.9	2.4	*	*	2.5
Belgium and Luxembourg	10.5	9.1	9.3	11.6	9.6	2.6	3.6	3.4	2.5	*
Spain	1.1	0.8	0.5	1.2	*	*	*	*	*	*
Australia	*	*	*	0.6	1.1	2.4	2.5	3.1	*	*
Total	96.1	97.5	98.0	93.5	90.1	92.5	87.3	80.3	82.5	76.1
World consumption (thousand tonnes)	347.2	474.8	824.9	688.5	1,232.6	1,740.6	2,075.2	3,081.8	5,041.8	6,332.2
					Tin					
USA	27.1	38.7	42.0	54.7	44.1	44.1	42.5	26.1	23.9	21.1
Japan	*	*	*	*	2.5	6.0	2.8	7.3	12.7	13.3
USSR	3.1	2.3	1.7	0.1	3.1	6.0	6.5	13.1	7.5	10.2
West Germany	15.3	15.8	15.3	5.8	9.6	6.0	4.6	7.2	6.7	6.5
UK	32.3	19.7	17.8	15.1	12.2	17.8	13.9	11.6	8.3	5.6
China	*	*	*	*	2.0	*	*	4.0	5.8	5.5
France	9.7	8.2	6.1	4.2	7.3	2.7	4.4	5.7	4.7	4.2
Brazil	*	*	*	*	*	*	*	*	*	3.4
Italy	1.4	1.8	2.2	1.7	2.7	2.4	2.5	2.5	3.2	2.6
Canada	*	*	*	*	1.5	2.1	2.7	1.9	2.3	2.3
Poland	*	*	*	*	*	*	1.2	*	*	*
Spain	1.1	1.4	1.0	0.9	1.2	0.7	*	*	*	*
Belgium and Luxembourg	*	1.5	1.3	1.5	*	*	*	*	*	*
Australia	*	0.7	0.9	1.2	*	1.8	1.5	2.1	1.7	*
Total	90.0	90.2	88.3	85.2	86.3	89.6	82.6	81.6	76.6	79.9
World consumption (thousand tonnes)	55.7	81.6	118.8	127.0	161.1	166.6	170.2	200.6	225.5	234.4

Table 20.   (cont'd)

Country	1953	1960	1970	1979
		Nickel		
USA	52.6	33.5	25.9	22.9
Japan	1.0	6.0	17.2	17.0
USSR	22.5	25.3	17.3	16.7
West Germany	3.7	7.9	7.1	10.0
France	3.5	6.6	6.3	5.0
UK	9.6	9.5	6.5	4.5
Italy	0.9	2.3	3.4	3.4
Sweden	*	3.0	4.0	2.9
China	*	*	3.5	2.4
Canada	2.3	1.5	2.6	1.5
Australia	0.3	0.8	*	*
Belgium and Luxembourg	0.3	*	*	*
Total	95.7	96.4	93.8	89.1
World consumption (thousand tonnes)	182.3	292.7	576.5	777.6

Note: The ten most important countries for each metal in order of importance in 1979 are included. Countries which, in a given year, did not yet belong or no longer belonged to this group are marked * for that year.
Source: Calculated from *Metal Statistics*, various years.

On the whole, as industrialization progresses, an increasing spread is found in world consumption of all metals, which is also reflected in the fact that the cumulative shares of the respective ten major consumer countries, without exception, have substantially declined since reaching their respective peak by 1979. At the same time the increasing residual quota in the case of all metals during the course of time has been distributed in predominantly very small shares over an increasing number of consumer countries.

Despite this progressive scatter in world consumption, however, the composition of the leading group of consumer countries for the quantitatively most important non-ferrous metals, aluminium, copper, lead, zinc, tin and nickel – with sometimes alternating order of importance – has been identical since the onset of the industrialization process. The United States took the lead (except for aluminium) in 1940 due to the war, followed by the major industrialized nations of the Western world – Japan, West Germany, the United Kingdom and France – and the USSR, which nevertheless (with the exception of zinc) now ranks second in the world.

6

Growth and change in the pattern of non-ferrous metal production

6.1 WORLD MINING

6.1.1 Development and product structure

Mining of non-ferrous metals in the world a century ago, compared with today, was still quantitatively quite insignificant. The total worldwide mining of crude ores of the heavy non-ferrous metals, copper, lead, zinc and tin, only amounted to 350,000 tonnes.[1] Under the pressure of growing demand, recovery of these metals from ores had already increased fivefold to 1.9 million tonnes by the turn of the century and after that increased tenfold to 18.9 million tonnes by 1979 (see Table 21).

An even greater upturn occurred in the expansion of bauxite, the most important primary material for the production of aluminium, which only began to any appreciable extent at the turn of the century (88,000 tonnes in 1900). It increased tenfold up to 1920 and by one hundred times after that, to reach nearly 88 million tonnes in 1979 (corresponding to an aluminium content of around 22 million tonnes[2]). This means that in just under 80 years the volume of production is now almost a thousand times greater.

This enormous growth in world mining took place at a varying pace, which was primarily determined by the demands made on the metal industry during the progress of industrialization, but was also influenced by economic cycles and other internal events, as well as technological and metallurgical advances. The first phase of expansion on a modern scale was recorded in world mining in the last third of the nineteenth century, under the influence of the rapidly escalating industrialization of the United States. At the beginning of the 1890s a widespread economic recession affected the industrialized countries, which put a brake on the development of mining. This was due in no small part to the

---

1 All quantitative data for mine production – with the exception of bauxite – relate to the metal content of the ores extracted.
2 Four tonnes of bauxite yield about 2 tonnes Al_2O_3, from which 1 tonne Al is obtained with a purity grade of 99.5–99.9% (*Meyers Handbuch über die Technik*, 1971, p. 253).

Table 21. World mine production of non-ferrous metals, 1900–79

Year or period	Bauxite	Copper[1]	Lead	Zinc	Tin	Nickel	Total
		Mine production (thousand tonnes metal content)					
1900	22.0	494.2	873.0	471.0	80.0	8.0	1,948.2
1910	89.0	860.1	1,198.0[2]	1,055.0[2]	119.0	24.0	3,345.0
1920	225.3	956.6	860.0	845.1	123.6	32.9	3,043.5
1930	426.4	1,595.9	1,603.1	1,509.0	178.3	59.5	5,372.2
1940	1,086.4	2,396.5	1,761.6	1,973.6	238.7	137.6	7,594.4
1950	2,112.8	2,524.5	1,677.6	2,187.2	176.9	148.2	8,827.2
1960	6,905.0	4,241.9	2,375.9	3,350.5	188.8	341.8	17,043.9
1970	15,125.6	6,402.6	3,462.7	5,561.2	217.1	663.4	31,432.6
1979	21,979.5	7,953.9	3,619.6	6,324.0	273.2	696.3	40,810.5
		Annual average change[3] (%)					
1900–1910	15.0	6.0	3.2	8.4	4.05	11.6	5.6
1910–1920	9.7	0.3	−3.3	−2.7	−0.03	0.4	−0.9
1920–1930	6.6	6.8	6.2	6.7	4.0	8.3	5.8
1930–1940	9.8	3.6	1.1	3.2	2.3	10.3	3.5
1940–1950	6.9	0.6	−0.4	0.9	−2.2	0.9	1.5
1950–1960	12.6	5.2	3.7	4.2	−0.2	8.1	7.0
1960–1970	8.5	4.6	3.4	5.3	2.4	7.2	6.6
1970–1979	5.2	3.2	1.2	2.0	0.9	2.4	3.8
		Index (1950 = 100)					
1900	1.0	19.6	52.0	21.5	45.2	5.4	22.0
1910	4.2	34.1	71.4[2]	48.2[2]	67.3	16.2	37.9
1920	10.7	37.9	51.3	38.6	69.9	22.3	34.5
1930	20.2	63.2	95.6	69.0	100.8	40.5	60.9
1940	51.4	94.9	105.0	90.2	134.9	93.2	86.0
1950	100	100	100	100	100	100	100
1960	326.8	168.0	141.6	153.2	106.7	231.1	197.2
1970	715.4	253.5	206.4	254.1	122.7	447.7	355.2
1979	1,039.6	315.0	215.7	289.0	134.1	469.9	461.2
		Share of world mine production (%)					
1900	1.1	25.4	44.8	24.2	4.1	0.4	100
1910	2.7	25.7	35.8	31.5	3.6	0.7	100
1920	7.4	31.4	28.3	27.8	4.1	1.1	100
1930	7.9	29.7	29.9	28.1	3.3	1.1	100
1940	14.3	31.6	23.2	26.0	3.1	1.8	100
1950	23.9	28.6	19.0	24.8	2.0	1.7	100
1960	39.7	24.4	13.6	19.2	1.1	2.0	100
1970	48.1	20.4	11.0	17.7	0.7	2.1	100
1979	53.8	19.5	8.9	15.5	0.6	1.7	100
		Mine production per capita (kg)					
1900	0.04	0.31	0.55	0.29	0.05	0.01	0.12
1910	0.05	0.50	0.70	0.61	0.07	0.01	1.94
1920	0.12	0.51	0.46	0.45	0.07	0.02	1.64
1930	0.21	0.77	0.78	0.73	0.09	0.03	2.60
1940	0.47	1.04	0.77	0.86	0.10	0.06	3.31
1950	0.84	1.01	0.67	0.87	0.07	0.06	3.53
1960	2.31	1.42	0.80	1.12	0.06	0.11	5.83
1970	4.19	1.77	0.96	1.54	0.06	0.18	8.71
1979	5.07	1.83	0.84	1.46	0.05	0.16	9.41

1. 1880 figures: 156,400 tonnes extracted, index 6.2 (for 1886), 0.11 kg per head. 1890 figures: 273,800 tonnes extracted, index 10.8, 0.18 kg per head. 2. Figures are for 1911. 3. Calculated on the basis of three-yearly averages.
Sources: Calculated from *Metal Statistics*, various years; Friedensburg, 1965a, p. 65.

strong speculative element of industrial activity, which had now taken on new dimensions, sometimes involving spectacular failures of firms. In the wake of the world economic boom which set in soon after the turn of the century, world mining attained high growth rates in output up to the outbreak of the First World War, admittedly starting from a very low level. The aftermath of production setbacks due to the war – exacerbated by the high volumes of scrap available from surplus munitions stocks – resulted in an absolute slump in copper, lead, zinc and tin and severe cutbacks in production growth of bauxite and nickel. In 1923, however, the best pre-war results were again exceeded and during the subsequent years of that decade considerably higher outputs were reached. The world economic crisis then dealt a severe blow to the metal industry, which was heavily involved. Its expansion was sharply curtailed in the early 1930s and, even after the economy had begun to revive, the previous vigorous growth in world mining was not reached again up to the outbreak of the Second World War. During the early years of the war the enormous demand for metals unleashed by munitions production gave a considerable boost to mining output, but, owing to the adverse effects of the war on the world economy, there was soon a perceptible slackening and eventually an abrupt recession in mining output set in.

After the end of the war the demand for metals for reconstruction and expansion of production potential rose to an unprecedented scale – at first in the 'old' industrial countries – despite the vast amount of scrap available from surplus armament stocks, and this became a powerful driving force in world mining. At the beginning of the 1950s previous peak results were already exceeded and – stimulated too by the spurt in demand due to the Korean War – all sectors of mining again underwent marked expansion. When this conflict ceased the boom slackened off as market conditions returned to normal and an incipient upturn was checked by the recession of 1966–67. After this had been successfully overcome under the impetus of an auspicious period in the world economy, mining then again entered on a new healthy growth phase, which was encouraged by new and more exacting demands on mining capacity arising from the realization of technical innovations and more vigorous expansion and diversification of industrial production in the world. The distinct deterioration in the world economic situation which began in the middle of 1974 and bottomed out in 1975 then gave rise to considerable strains in the sales and profit position of world mining, as a result of the expansion of capacities during the boom, and this was reflected in a marked levelling off of growth rates for the period 1974–1979.

The new records established should not indeed conceal the fact that the pace of expansion in world mining, with the exception of bauxite, which still showed somewhat stronger trends between 1950 and 1979 than in the first half of the century, has continually slowed down since 1950. No doubt a great many factors are responsible for this. Among these the continual improvement in

Table 22. World mine production of non-ferrous metals, 1886–1979 (regression estimates)

	World production a	World production b	R²		World production a	World production b	R²
Bauxite				Zinc			
1900–1979	4.814	0.088	0.981	1911–1979	6.673	0.030	0.917
1900–1950	4.804	0.088	0.935	1911–1950	6.835	0.021	0.602
1950–1979	9.337	0.078	0.978	1950–1979	7.772	0.038	0.972
Copper				Tin			
1886–1979	5.686	0.036	0.961	1900–1979	4.624	0.010	0.634
1886–1950	5.672	0.037	0.900	1900–1950	4.641	0.009	0.285
1950–1979	7.855	0.043	0.983	1950–1979	5.146	0.010	0.667
Lead				Nickel			
1911–1979	6.841	0.019	0.844	1900–1979	2.368	0.056	0.949
1911–1950	7.004	0.010	0.302	1900–1950	2.382	0.055	0.832
1950–1979	7.509	0.027	0.957	1950–1979	5.181	0.056	0.947

Note: All calculations performed on the basis of a logarithmic trend. The coefficients of all variables were significant to a 5% probability of error.
Source: Own calculations from production data given in *Metal Statistics*, various years.

output rates is only a minor consideration. Greater importance attaches to the constant substitution of other materials, particularly plastics, for non-ferrous metals and to competition from 'above-ground mining', due to improved recycling processes. Factors of greater consequence for profitability, however, would appear to be the continual improvement in material quality and technological successes in efforts to reduce the unit metal consumption per manufactured product.

Thus, annual growth rates in world mining have tended increasingly to lag behind those for industrial production. Whereas for the period 1950–1960 the ratio of increase in mine production to industrial production of the heavy metals copper, lead, zinc, tin and nickel was still 1:1, from 1960 to 1970 this ratio averaged only 0.65:1 and between 1970 and 1977 it declined to 0.58:1.[1]

The powerful expansion process in world mining in the past hundred years took place under the influence of the demands imposed on the metal industry, with varying shares being taken by the non-ferrous metals. The regression estimates for trends in the pattern of mining production (see Table 22 and Fig. 10) show that bauxite production expanded at much the highest rate and, of the heavy metals, copper over the long term displayed the most marked growth, followed by zinc, lead and tin. In this trend only the values for the

[1] Author's own calculation according to production data in *Metal Statistics*, various years, and the Index for Industrial Production (World) for the UN *Monthly Bulletin of Statistics*, various years. The results present a relative assessment of the estimates of Friedensburg from the year 1965, according to which the increase in total mining production of the world to industrial production was roughly in the ratio 0.76:1 (Friedensburg, 1965, p. 65).

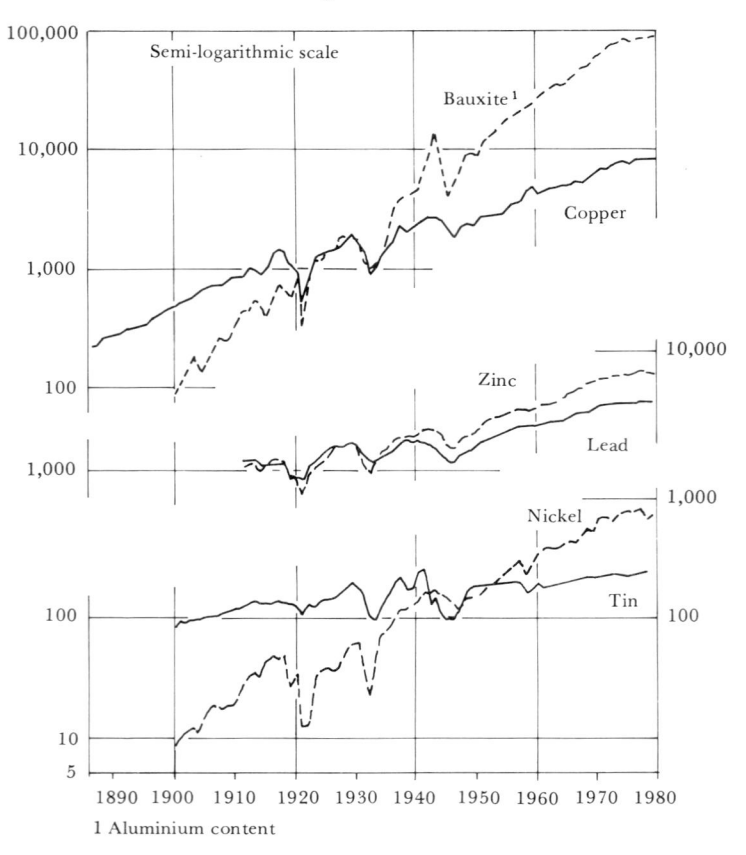

Fig. 10. World mine production of non-ferrous metals, 1886–1979 (thousand tonnes)
Source: *Metal Statistics*, various years.

quantitative less important nickel were somewhat higher. Almost without exception the trend for all heavy metals in the period 1950–1977 showed a somewhat sharper increase than in the first half of the century, whereas in the case of bauxite the more vigorous expansion trend showed a slackening off after 1950.

The result of this variable pattern of development is a clearly changing product structure of world mine production during the course of industrialization. A profound transformation took place due to comparative losses for the heavy metals in favour of light metals production. Bauxite production, which calculated according to its aluminium content still only accounted for 1% of world mining production at the turn of the century, had already risen in two decades to over 7%, by the outbreak of the Second World War had reached nearly 15% and in 1950 made up a quarter of world production of the six quantitatively most important non-ferrous metals. Since 1960 (at 40%) it has occupied first place among these and has to date been able to extend its peak position to a share of 54% of world mining production (see Table 21, p. 107).

The product structure of world mining has also undergone a considerable transformation in the case of the heavy metals. In the nineteenth century and in the years up to the First World War lead and zinc had higher shares of world mine production (around 32–36%) than copper (26%) and from then up to the middle of the 1930s these three metals were more or less equal at around 30% respectively. Since that time, however, copper has steadily been gaining ground, up to a maximum to date of some 42% in 1979. Lead and zinc also exchanged their traditional places, with considerable losses by lead (some 19%) accompanied by an increase in the zinc share to just under 34%. Finally, during these years (1930–1977) tin also declined in importance, with a downturn in its share of world mine production of heavy non-ferrous metals from 3.6% to 1.3%, and today it has been overtaken by nickel, whose share has risen from 1.2% to 3.7%.[1]

6.1.2 The international structure of mining output

The industrialization process has influenced not only the product structure but also the regional pattern of world mining. Up to the latter part of the nineteenth century ore mining was centred in Europe: Great Britain with its abundant metal resources, already known to the Romans in Cornwall, was the chief mining country and the deposits in the Pyrenean peninsula had made Spain an important ore producer as well. In Germany lead mining in the Harz Mountains and Erzgebirge ('Ore Mountains') and copper mining from the Mansfield shales can be traced back to the Middle Ages. The winning of smithsonite (hemimorphite) in Germany likewise dates back to this time and has been identifiable in Upper Silesia since the sixteenth century. France and Belgium are other European countries with an ancient mining tradition. When the European countries became industrialized, however, with rapid growth in their metal consumption, their own ore resources were no longer adequate to cover their needs. Encouraged by the progressive improvement in transport and communications facilities which were a concomitant of industrialization, moves were gradually made to discover, open up and mine ore deposits in overseas territories, especially as the exploitation of European deposits in comparison with these was considerably less economic (Avieny, 1941, p. 11).

[1] Author's own calculations according to production data appearing in *Metal Statistics*, various years. Attention is particularly drawn to the difficulty of making such quantitative comparisons of different types of metal. In an evaluation of mining according to unit values (based on the $ values given by the US Bureau of Mines) copper since 1880 has far outpaced lead, zinc, tin and nickel. In this process lead and zinc as well as tin and nickel have changed places since 1960 (Friedensburg, 1956, p. 65).

Table 23. Mine production of non-ferrous metals by regions, 1900–79 (% of world total)

Year	Europe	EEC	North America	Latin America	Africa	Asia	Australia and Oceania	Eastern Bloc countries[1]	World total* (thousand tonnes)
				Bauxite					
1960	15.7	8.6	7.4	46.9	5.7	5.6	0.3	18.4	27,620.1
1970	12.6	5.4	3.5	40.7	5.4	6.3	15.3	16.3	60,710.0
1979	9.0	2.3	2.0	25.4	14.9	4.1	31.4	13.2	87,918.0
				Copper					
1900	18.5		57.8	11.9	1.4	5.8	4.6		494.2
1910	14.0		59.9	14.6	0.6	5.7	5.2		860.1
1920	5.1		61.0	21.2	2.8	7.0	2.9		959.6
1930	10.9		48.7	22.7	10.6	6.3	0.8		1,595.9
1940	5.2		45.7	19.8	18.0	4.6	0.8	5.9	2,396.5
1950	4.5		42.2	18.9	20.6	3.7	0.6	9.5	2,524.5
1960	3.1	0.3	32.5	18.8	23.2	5.1	2.6	14.7	4,241.9
1970	3.2	0.1	33.9	15.5	20.2	5.5	2.5	19.2	6,402.6
1979	3.5	0.1	26.2	19.8	16.2	6.3	5.0	22.9	7,953.9
				Lead					
1920	23.2		53.7	10.4	6.6	3.9	1.6		860.0[2]
1930	18.7		41.0	17.7	2.9	7.1	12.6		1,603.1
1940	15.7		35.7	18.1	2.5	6.2	16.6	5.2	1,761.6
1950	15.4		32.1	21.9	7.1	1.0	13.2	8.8	1,685.5[3]
1960	15.3	5.1	17.3	16.9	9.1	3.5	13.2	24.8	2,375.9
1970	13.9	3.3	26.4	12.5	5.9	3.5	13.2	24.7	3,462.7
1979	13.2	2.0	24.3	13.1	5.2	3.5	11.5	29.2	3,619.6
				Zinc					
1920	29.6		66.2	1.7	1.0	1.6	–		845.0
1930	30.0		43.8	11.0	1.9	5.2	8.1		1,509.0
1940	23.6		40.3	12.5	1.7	4.5	12.7	4.7	1,973.6
1950	16.1		38.9	15.7	6.9	2.4	9.2	10.7	2,210.0[4]
1960	16.6	7.9	22.8	14.7	8.0	5.7	9.6	22.6	3,350.5
1970	13.9	5.2	31.3	12.3	4.4	6.7	8.8	22.6	5,561.2
1979	15.4	6.8	23.7	15.8	3.4	6.5	8.4	26.8	6,324.0
				Tin					
1920	2.6		–	24.4	6.6	63.0	3.4		123.6
1930	1.9		–	22.0	5.9	69.4	0.8		178.0
1940	1.6		–	17.0	11.3	63.6	1.5	5.0	239.0
1950	1.5		–	18.7	13.2	58.5	1.1	7.0	177.0
1960	1.2	0.6	–	11.7	11.0	47.9	1.2	27.1	189.0
1970	1.3	0.1	–	16.5	9.1	53.6	4.1	15.4	217.1
1979	1.4	1.0	–	15.5	5.3	57.5	4.8	15.5	237.1
				Nickel					
1920	4.3		85.4				10.3		33.0
1930	3.7		79.2	0.5		1.7	14.9		60.0
1940	1.8		81.0	0.4	0.3	2.7	7.6	6.2	138.0
1950	0.3		75.7	0.5	0.6		2.9	20.0	148.0
1960	0.6		60.3	4.3	0.9	0.2	15.7	18.0	342.0
1970	2.1		44.0	0.4	3.1	1.6	25.4	23.4	663.4
1979	3.2		20.5	5.0	8.7	10.1	22.4	30.0	696.3

1. Where no figures given, amounts are included in European and Asian total. * Unspecified: 2. – 0.6; 3. – 0.5; 4. – 1.0.
Source: Calculated from *Metal Statistics*, various years.

The first phase of this transformation in the regional pattern of world mining began in the second half of the nineteenth century when North America moved up to become the principal region, first for copper mining and a little later for lead and zinc extraction. The peak period of this trend – in terms of share of world production – occurred before the outbreak of the First World War, when North America recorded a 60% share of global mine production for copper, 66% for zinc and over 50% for lead.

A feature of the second phase, beginning in the 1920s, was that mining which originally profited in the former production areas from the strong upswing in world consumption of non-ferrous metals, now encountered a growing demand for metallic raw materials in the countries embarked on industrialization in the more remote areas. This certainly contributed to the economic opening up of overseas territories without the countries concerned in fact deriving the financial benefits of this or having any opportunity to do so. Although it has progressively lost ground, North America still remains the leading region for world mining of non-ferrous metals, whereas Europe's importance in this field continues to decline. South America and – some distance behind – Africa are steadily gaining in importance as mining regions and increasing shares of world output are now recorded in Australia and Oceania.

The third phase, beginning with the Second World War, is marked unmistakably by the rapid advance of the Eastern Bloc countries in world mining of non-ferrous metals. In 1979 these countries predominated over other regions with their shares of lead (29%) and zinc (27%) and already made a considerable contribution to world output of copper (23%), nickel (30%), tin (18%) and bauxite (13%). Another remarkable phenomenon is the steady emergence of Australia and Oceania as important mining areas of the world. This particularly applies to bauxite recovery, in which this previously insignificant area has within a span of less than twenty years taken a leading place, with a 31% share of world production and, in the case of nickel, a fifth of global mining output.

Of interest in this context is how the position of the developing countries has progressed in the mining of non-ferrous metals in the world during the past 30 years, a period of decolonization and political independence for important raw materials producers in the non-ferrous metals field (see also Table 24):

Copper. The share of the developing countries from 1950 to 1979 in the mine production of copper in the Western world rose from 40.4 to 43.7%. The share taken by the developing countries in world production – excluding the Eastern Bloc – for 1979 is 53.4%, compared with 44.6% in 1950.
Lead. The developing countries, with a 23.5% share of world mine production, play a less important role as producer regions than in 1950. The Western industrial countries in 1979 still accounted for almost half the total mine production of the world, although their share has declined since 1950 owing to vigorous expansion of lead in the Eastern Bloc countries.

Table 24. Mine production of non-ferrous metals by groups of countries, 1950–79

	Total world production (thousand tonnes)	Western industrialized countries	Developing countries	Eastern Bloc countries
		(% of world total)		
Bauxite				
1950	8,418.1	32.7	51.4	15.8
1960	27,620.1	29.0	52.5	18.6
1970	60,710.0	31.3	52.4	16.3
1979	87,918.0	42.4	44.4	13.2
Copper				
1950	2,524.7	50.2	40.4	9.4
1960	4,241.9	41.4	43.8	14.7
1970	6,402.1	36.9	41.9	21.3
1979	7,953.9	33.4	43.7	22.9
Lead				
1950	1,685.5	61.3	29.1	9.5
1960	2,375.9	47.4	27.8	24.8
1970	3,462.7	55.4	19.9	24.7
1979	3,619.6	50.3	23.5	39.2
Zinc				
1950	2,209.9	66.4	21.9	11.7
1960	3,350.5	54.5	23.0	22.6
1970	5,561.2	59.0	18.4	22.6
1979	6,324.0	52.1	21.0	26.9
Tin				
1950	176.9	21.9	71.1	7.0
1960	188.8	15.2	57.7	27.1
1970	217.1	6.6	78.0	15.4
1979	237.2	7.7	76.8	15.5

Source: Calculated from *Metal Statistics*, various years.

Zinc. The developing countries have managed to maintain their position as producers and suppliers (their share of world production in 1979 was 21%). In the Western industrial countries mining recovery of zinc expanded at a slower pace than in the Eastern Bloc countries.

Bauxite. In bauxite mining the developing countries have been unable to keep pace with production in the industrial countries. Their share of world mining production amounted in 1979 to 44.4%, compared with 52.4% in 1970. This is to be attributed mainly to the massive upswing of production in Australia.

Tin. The developing countries, because of the rich deposits in South East Asia and Bolivia, have recorded an overwhelming growth in production. Today they account for around 75% of world production of tin.

The reasons for this extremely unsatisfactory trend in the countries of the Third World and their failure to achieve a stronger position in world mining despite the wealth of raw materials they possess are doubtless due to very complex factors and differ completely from one metal to another. It may be regarded as a serious drawback generally that a feature of state takeovers or nationalization measures in the developing countries has been mining expropriations without adequate compensation, so that the international mining concerns have now become more wary in pursuing their activities in countries of the Third World. An additional deterrent is that living conditions there, combined with political factors, have often become more difficult for experts at managerial level from industrial countries. As a result there is frequently higher mobility of technical experts, or they tend to leave the country. The investment of the international companies is therefore again being concentrated more heavily in the developed countries (Sies, 1976, p. 11; 1977, p. 1009). Although in these countries the most profitable deposits have been severely depleted during the course of industrialization, developments in preparation and smelter techniques have now made possible the exploitation of increasingly complex deposits so that it is a worthwhile proposition to mine lower-grade ores. Examples which may be quoted here, apart from Canada and Australia, are the newly opened Polish copper mines and the current attempts in the United Kingdom to exploit projects with low-grade lead-, zinc- and tin-bearing ores.

These shifts in the regional structure of world mining output during the

Table 25. Mine production of non-ferrous metals by countries, 1880–1979 (% of world total)

Country	1880	1890	1900	1910	1920	1930	1940	1950	1960	1970	1979
					Bauxite						
Australia					*	0.1	*	*	.	15.3	31.4
Guinea					*	*	*	*	5.0	4.1	13.9
Jamaica					*	*	*	*	21.1	19.8	13.1
USSR					*	*	6.9	8.9	12.7	10.7	7.4
Surinam[1]					*	15.5	14.2	24.2	12.5	9.9	5.4
Guyana					3.5	7.2	14.0	19.7	9.1	7.3	3.8
Yugoslavia					3.1	5.6	6.5	2.4	3.7	3.5	3.4
Hungary					*	6.3	12.9	7.3	4.3	*	3.4
Greece					*	0.1	1.7	0.9	3.2	3.8	3.3
France					29.6	35.7	11.3	9.6	7.5	5.0	2.2
USA					58.8	19.7	10.3	16.0	7.4	3.5	*
Germany					1.5	*	*	*	*	*	*
Italy					1.5	9.5	13.1	1.8	*	*	*
Rep. Ireland					1.2	0.1	*	*	*	*	*
Burma					0.7	*	*	*	*	*	*
Indonesia					*	*	6.3	6.3	*	*	*
Total					99.1	99.7	97.2	97.2	86.4	85.9	87.3
World production (thousand tonnes)					901.3	1,705.5	4,345.4	8,451.1	27,620.1	60,710.0	87,918.0

Table 25. (cont'd)

Country	1880	1890	1900	1910	1920	1930	1940	1950	1960	1970	1979
					Copper						
USA	16.2	43.1	55.7	57.0	57.2	40.1	33.2	32.7	23.1	24.4	18.1
USSR	2.2	1.8	1.4	2.6	*	2.1	5.6	8.6	11.8	14.5	14.5
Chile	27.9	9.7	5.3	4.4	0.3	13.8	15.2	14.4	12.5	10.8	13.3
Canada	0.1	*	1.7	2.9	3.9	8.6	12.4	9.5	9.4	9.5	8.1
Zambia[2]	*	*	*	*	*	*	11.1	11.8	13.6	10.7	7.4
Zaire[3]	*	*	*	*	2.0	8.7	6.2	7.0	7.1	6.1	5.0
Peru	0.4	*	1.7	3.2	3.6	3.0	1.8	1.2	4.4	3.4	5.0
Poland	*	*	*	*	*	*	*	*	*	*	4.3
Philippines	*	*	*	*	*	*	*	*	*	2.5	3.7
Australia	6.3	2.8	4.7	5.2	2.8	*	*	*	2.6	2.5	2.9
Spain	23.6[4]	19.2[4]	10.9[4]	5.6	2.4	3.7	*	*	*	*	*
Germany	7.0	6.6	4.2	2.7	1.6	*	*	*	*	*	*
South Africa	3.3	*	*	*	*	*	*	*	*	2.3	*
Japan	2.6	5.6	5.7	5.7	5.3	4.5	2.9	1.6	2.1	*	*
Venezuela	*	2.1	*	*	*	*	*	*	*	*	*
Mexico	*	1.6	4.6	6.2	*	4.6	1.6	2.4	1.4	*	*
Bolivia	*	*	*	*	1.1	*	*	*	*	*	*
Yugoslavia	*	*	*	*	*	1.5	1.8	1.7	*	*	*
Total	89.6	95.0	95.8	95.5	90.1	98.3	91.8	90.9	88.0	85.7	82.8
World production (thousand tonnes)	156.4	273.8	494.2	860.1	959.6	1,595.9	2,396.5	2,524.5	4,241.9	6,402.6	7,953.9

Country	1880	1890	1900	1910	1920	1930	1940	1950	1960	1970	1979
					Lead						
USSR					0.8	4.5	6.6	12.6	13.6	16.3
USA					52.4	31.6	23.6	23.3	9.4	15.0	14.9
Australia					1.6	12.5	16.6	13.3	13.2	13.2	11.5
Canada					1.9	9.4	12.2	9.0	7.9	11.4	9.4
Peru					*	1.2	2.9	3.9	5.5	4.5	5.1
Mexico					9.8	14.5	11.1	14.2	8.0	5.1	4.8
China					*	*	*	*	3.4	3.1	4.3
Yugoslavia					*	1.3	3.9	5.1	3.8	3.7	3.6
Morocco					*	*	*	2.9	4.0	*	3.2
Bulgaria					*	*	*	*	4.0	2.8	3.2
North Korea					*	*	*	*	*	2.0	*
Spain					12.6	6.8	2.1	2.4	*	*	*
Germany					4.5	3.8	5.4	*	*	*	*
Burma					3.1	5.5	4.6	*	*	*	*
Italy					2.5	*	*	2.3	*	*	*
Tunisia					1.7	*	*	*	*	*	*
Rhodesia					1.7	*	*	*	*	*	*
Total					91.9	87.6	86.9	82.8	71.8	74.2	76.3
World production (thousand tonnes)					860.0	1,603.1	1,761.6	1,677.6	2,375.9	3,462.7	3,619.6

Table 25. (cont'd)

Country	1880	1890	1900	1910	1920	1930	1940	1950	1960	1970	1979
					Zinc						
Canada					2.3	8.1	9.7	13.0	11.0	22.5	19.0
USSR					*	*	4.3	5.9	11.2	12.6	16.1
Australia					*	8.1	12.7	9.2	9.6	8.8	8.4
Peru					*	*	*	4.0	4.7	5.4	7.8
USA					63.9	35.8	30.6	25.9	11.8	8.7	4.7
Mexico					1.6	8.2	5.8	10.2	8.0	4.8	3.9
Japan					0.5	*	2.2	*	4.7	5.0	3.9
Poland					1.0	6.6	*	4.3	4.3	3.4	3.8
Rep. Ireland					*	*	*	*	*	*	3.4
China					*	*	*	*	*	*	2.5
North Korea					*	*	*	*	*	2.3	*
Germany					17.8	10.5	13.3	4.5	3.4	2.9	*
Italy					4.6	5.3	4.7	4.0	3.9	*	*
Spain					3.4	3.3	2.3	*	*	*	*
Sweden					2.0	2.0	*	*	*	*	*
Algeria					1.0	*	*	*	*	*	*
Burma					*	2.0	*	*	*	*	*
Newfoundland					*	*	3.3	*	*	*	*
Congo					*	*	*	3.5	*	*	*
Total					98.0	89.9	88.9	84.5	72.7	76.4	73.5
World production (thousand tonnes)					845.1	1,509.0	1,973.0	2,187.2	3,350.5	5,561.2	6,324.0
					Tin						
Malaysia					32.4	36.5	35.4	33.7	28.0	34.0	26.6
Thailand					6.5	6.6	7.3	6.0	6.6	10.0	14.3
Indonesia					12.9	19.4	17.6	18.4	12.2	8.8	12.4
Bolivia					23.9	21.8	16.1	17.9	10.4	13.9	11.6
USSR					*	*	*	4.5	10.6	4.6	7.5
China					9.7	4.0	4.8	2.3	15.9	10.1	7.2
Australia					3.5	0.8	1.5	1.1	1.2	4.1	4.8
Brazil					*	*	*	*	*	1.8	3.0
Zaire[2]					*	*	5.2	7.7	4.8	3.0	1.5
Nigeria					*	4.8	5.1	4.8	4.1	3.7	1.2
Burma					*	1.7	1.9	*	*	*	*
Japan					*	0.7	0.8	*	*	*	*
Total					88.9	96.3	95.7	95.8	93.7	94.0	90.2
World production (thousand tonnes					123.6	178.3	238.7	176.9	188.8	217.1	237.2

Table 25. (cont'd)

Country	1880	1890	1900	1910	1920	1930	1940	1950	1960	1970	1979
					Nickel						
USSR					*	*	6.3	19.6	17.0	16.6	21.5
Canada					84.5	79.2	81.0	75.7	57.0	41.8	18.9
New Caledonia					10.3	15.0	7.6	2.9	15.7	20.9	11.9
Australia					*	*	*	*	*	4.5	10.5
Indonesia					*	*	1.6	*	0.1	1.6	5.3
Cuba					*	*	*	*	4.2	5.6	5.0
Philippines					*	*	*	*	*	*	4.8
South Africa					*	*	*	0.5	0.9	1.8	4.2
Dominican Republic					*	*	*	*	*	*	3.6
Botswana					*	*	*	*	*	*	2.3
USA					0.9	*	*	0.5	3.3	2.1	*
Norway					1.2	1.5	0.7	*	*	*	*
Burma					*	1.7	0.5	*	–	*	*
Greece					*	0.8	0.4	*	*	1.3	*
Germany					*	*	* 0.6	*	*	*	*
Japan					*	*	* 0.6	*	*	*	*
Finland					*	*	*	0.3	0.6	0.8	*
Poland					*	*	*	*	0.4	*	*
Total					97.0	98.2	99.3	99.5	99.2	97.0	88.0
World production (thousand tonnes)					32.9	59.5	137.6	148.2	341.8	663.4	696.3

Note: The ten most important countries for each metal, in order of importance in 1979, are included. Countries which, in a given year, did not yet belong or no longer belonged to this group are marked * for that year.
1. Dutch West Indies until 1975. 2. Northern Rhodesia until 1964. 3. Belgian Congo to 1960. Republic of the Congo 1960–64. Democratic Republic of the Congo 1964–71. 4. Includes Portugal.
Source: Calculated from *Metal Statistics*, various years.

course of industrialization have been accompanied by very significant changes in the shares taken by the different countries and changes in the order of precedence. This explains why, for example, only very few of the ten leading producer countries of mining production by volume in 1979 already belonged to this group at the turn of the century, or even earlier, and why many countries even in 1950 did not yet belong to this major group. It also throws light on the position held by the traditional mining countries which, measured by their own shares of world mining output during this impressive growth period in ore mining, has in some cases considerably weakened.

Copper

The classical example of a regional change of structure in world mining is provided among the heavy non-ferrous metals by copper mining. Although this was first carried on in Europe with the most important areas, even at the beginning of the nineteenth century, still being in the United Kingdom

(Cornwall and Devon), copper production in Chile benefited from the increasing demand from Europe a few decades later. Already in the seventeenth century copper mining had begun there at the rich deposits of El Teniente in the Cordilleras, and Chuquicamata and Coquimbo in the Andes, but it was not until the building of the railways and the development of transport facilities that it was possible for this mining region to be integrated into the world mining economy. This meant that in 1840 Chile for the first time became the leading copper ore producer in the world and in 1876 with 62% reached its maximum share of output. Chile was unable to maintain this position for very long however, as, owing to the high freight charges for shipping, its ores (which at first were smelted at Swansea in the United Kingdom, and later on by the comparatively more expensive domestic smelting) failed to remain competitive internationally (Hess, 1955, p. 14). Thus the United States outstripped it with mining of copper deposits in Michigan, Arizona and Montana – where the yield exceeded Devon, Cornwall, Spain, Cyprus and all the smaller European finds – and for the first time in 1883 overtook Chilean production to become the leading copper producer in the world. However, its share of mining of copper ores had declined from the peak of 57% in 1920 to 18% by 1979, although production today is still quantitatively about two-and-a-half times higher than it was then. The increase in mining production of copper, which in relative shares is decelerating considerably in the United States, is due to the fact that the high-grade ores there were largely depleted after a few decades and since then they have had to fall back on increasingly inferior ore deposits. Today copper ore mining in the United States is predominantly surface mining (up to 80%). Although employment of large-scale machinery makes this relatively inexpensive, it is now becoming more difficult and costs are rising because of the comparatively low metal content of the deposits and the strict regulations on environmental protection, regulating permissible levels of air and water pollution. The average metal content of the American copper ore mining output declined from 16% to 0.6% Cu between 1940 and the early 1970s. Winning of copper by leaching, which makes it possible to recover less than 0.4% Cu, increased proportionately (10% in 1972) (Ramms, 1959, p. 151; Grunwald and Musgrove, 1970, p. 156; Friedensburg and Dorstewitz, 1976, p. 48).

The 'old' copper country Chile, after losing its top position in the world, sank almost into obscurity during the following decades and did not regain second place in world production until the 1920s under the aegis of the American mining companies. After that, as mining output increased, it was able to maintain its 1930 share of 13% at a fairly constant level. Due to the heavy expansion of copper mining in the USSR after the Second World War Chile slid to third place in world production, followed by Canada, another important producer with an 8% share of world production in 1979 (Table 17).

By contrast with the United States, 80% of Canadian copper production has to be extracted by deep mining, partly from deposits in which the main product is nickel and others where lead and zinc are important secondary products. The main emphasis of copper mining will probably be displaced to a greater extent to the Province of British Columbia, where copper can be partly recovered by surface mining (Friedensburg and Dorstewitz, 1976, p. 231).

Other members of the group of ten major copper mining countries, which together account for almost 82% of world production today, are Zambia and Zaire, whose rich copper deposits, with contents of between 2% and 16% are found especially in the 800 km long Copper Belt extending from Zimbabwe into the Shaba Province (Katanga).[1] Peru has also contrived to achieve remarkable expansion of its copper mining even though its development, owing to the frequently inadequate infrastructure and the large volumes of overburden, necessitates high investment (Friedensburg and Dorstewitz, 1976, p. 319 ff.). The expansion of copper ore mining in Poland is based primarily on extraction from the numerous deposits with contents of 1.3% Cu at Glogów, Lubín and Legnica (Friedensburg and Dorstewitz, 1976, p. 331). For the Philippines copper is by far the most important mining product. Two-thirds comes from surface mines and the deep mining is economic because of the gold and silver content of up to 0.5% of the copper content (Friedensburg and Dorstewitz, 1976, p. 324 ff.). Finally, Australia, following the discovery and commencement of exploitation of other deposits in the past 20 years, is today again one of the ten leading copper producers in the world, a position it previously held from before the turn of the century up to 1920.

The remaining world production (approximately 20%) is shared among over 50 other countries,[2] including Spain, Portugal and Germany[3] and countries of minor importance whose copper mining was of world importance in the early phase of industrial development.

Lead and zinc

The changes in the national pattern of lead and zinc mining – they are usually extracted together as mixed ores – are similar to those in copper mining:

(*a*) The structure of production has fanned out considerably during the last century to include a larger number of mining countries.
(*b*) The main emphasis of world mining had already shifted before the turn of the

1 The production trend in both these countries however has been declining since the mid-1970s: political unrest and growing uncertainty for foreign workers, destruction of plant and of transport routes, deterioration of equipment, a growing shortage of technicians and skilled technical staff and other production problems partly associated with nationalization measures in the copper industry there have resulted up to 1977 in ever-growing losses of production.
2 The *Minerals Yearbook* in 1974 named altogether 65 copper mining countries (*Minerals Yearbook, 1974*, 1976, Vol. I, p. 534 ff.).
3 In West Germany the only copper ore mine closed down in 1955, but relatively small quantities of copper ores are also present in the lead/zinc production of the Rammelsberg Mine of Preussag AG (e.g., 1,700 tonnes of copper content in 1979) (Forster, 1976, p. 34).

century from Europe to the United States, which in 1920 was already in first position, with 52% lead and 64% zinc.
(c) The United States lost its leading position in the 1950s and took second place after the USSR for lead with just under 15%, while for zinc with 5% they were in fifth place after Canada, the USSR, Australia and Peru.
(d) The USSR managed increasingly to boost its position as producer of both ores in recent years to 16% for each, so that for lead it now takes first place in world mining and is only slightly outdistanced by Canada in zinc.

The ten principal mining countries today, which together in 1979 produced 76% of world lead and 74% of world zinc, are virtually the same for both metals. Japan, Poland and the Republic of Ireland are missing from the ten leading producers of lead and Yugoslavia, Morocco and Bulgaria, important lead producers, are absent from the leading ten for zinc. The previously quite important mine production of zinc and lead in Germany (which in 1920 still represented some 5–18% of the world total, and in 1940 with lead and latterly in 1970 with zinc, albeit with only small shares, was still included among the ten leading world producers of these ores) has declined so severely that at present only three mines are still extracting lead and zinc ores (Annual Report 1979 of the Fachvereinigung Metallerzbergbau – Association of Metal Ore Mining – Düsseldorf).

Tin

The pattern of ore production by countries, within the limits imposed by the deposits themselves, has changed the least among all metals. By far the most important production area is the Malayan peninsula, which probably also played a part in this capacity in prehistoric times and in antiquity, and around the turn of the last century was responsible for about 60% of world production (Friedensburg and Dorstewitz, 1976, p. 265). As a result of the upswing in tin mining in Bolivia, the Dutch East Indies (now Indonesia, with the Island of Bangka as the most important mining area), Siam (Thailand), China and Australia, the Malayan share up to the end of the 1920s declined to about one-third and in 1979 – although still the principal mining country – it accounted for only a quarter of world production. With an only slightly different order of importance since then, the traditional producer countries of Malaysia, Bolivia, Indonesia and Thailand combined are today responsible for just under two-thirds of world production. Indonesia might possibly move up during the next few years above Bolivia,[1] as its tin production in the form of

---

[1] Bolivian tin mining is at present facing its biggest ever crisis. The main obstacle to raising production in tin mining is considered to be the taxation system with its over 50 (!) different mining taxes, the assessment basis of which is deemed unjust. This would be a disincentive to productive investments, even though less and less tin would be recovered from the ores with existing equipment. The necessary tax reform is being delayed because the State is afraid of losing its income (22.9% of total State income in 1978). Reform is, however, of the utmost urgency in view of the importance of tin exports as currency earners (in 1978 some half of export earnings derived from tin).

concentrates could be increased by about 20% to over 30,000 tonnes per annum by putting into operation offshore excavators (Metallgesellschaft *Tägliche Nachrichten* (Daily News) of 9 May 1979).

Nickel

In nickel production Canada is traditionally the world leader. Its share, however, declined during the past 50 years from over 80% to 42% in 1970; in 1979 it accounted for only just under 20%. Although arising from previous overproduction, this nevertheless still reflects the increasing competition on the world market due to the widespread opening up of lateritic deposits. After Canada the French overseas territory of New Caledonia in the south west Pacific – in which about half of the proven nickel reserves of the world are to be found – has belonged for very many years to the top group of producer countries. During recent decades the USSR has caught up with it in volume of mining output and latterly even overtaken it, but in New Caledonia also a further increase in mining output is to be anticipated, especially as mining is planned of recently proved nickel deposits. Australia, where appreciable expansion of nickel ore production dates only from the late 1960s, after a feverish exploration drive stands today in fourth place for world production, ahead of Indonesia, Cuba and the Philippines – some distance behind – where large-scale mining of nickel ores only began quite recently.

Bauxite

The most important primary material today for the production of aluminium, bauxite has twice undergone a fundamental regional change in its pattern of mining during the relatively short time span in which this light metal has taken the lead by volume in production and consumption among the non-ferrous metals. Its extraction was at first mainly confined to Europe and the United States. In 1930 Europe was still responsible for altogether 57% of bauxite mining in the world, with France as the most important producer country (36%), and the United States for 20%. During subsequent decades the north of South America, the present-day Surinam and Guyana, acquired greater importance. The same applies to the USSR. After the discovery of extensive, rich deposits there, Jamaica, with a share of one-fifth, became after 1960 the main producer country in the world.[1] It lost this position at the beginning of the 1970s to Australia where exploitation had begun of the rich silicatic bauxite beds discovered there, which are estimated at around a third of the assured and probable world reserves (Friedensburg and Dorstewitz, 1976, p. 44). Already in the 1970s Australia, with approximately a quarter of world production, had

---

1 The five foreign firms involved in bauxite exploitation (Alcan, Alpart, Reynolds, Kaiser Aluminium & Chemical Corporation and Alcoa) are obliged to pay taxes on the basis of a calculated formula serving to guarantee the income of the Government and to increase production.

become the largest bauxite supplier and it further increased its share by 1979 to 31%. Bauxite production in the Republic of Guinea has also undergone rapid expansion and its production is of the same order as that of Jamaica. Even though bauxite is abundantly available all over the world, in 1979 75% of mining was concentrated in only six countries, Australia, the Republic of Guinea, Jamaica, the USSR, Surinam and Guyana. The European countries, among which the main producers are Yugoslavia, Hungary, Greece and France, and the United States, all with shares of around 2–3%, were still of very minor importance for bauxite mining by world standards.

Summing up, it is to be observed that the mining of non-ferrous metals during the progress of industrialization has undergone an expansion inconceivable by traditional standards, which has been accompanied by a profound change in its product structure. The long-familiar heavy metals, despite an enormous and sustained increase in their extraction, have forfeited considerable importance compared with the light metals, and the growth in steel-improving metals and minor metals spotlights their increasing specific importance in the general field of technology, with advances in industrialization and diversification of the commodities offered on the market often resulting in key positions for certain forms of production. Another remarkable feature, however, is the striking change taking place, normally in several phases, in the regional structure of mine production and in the pattern of world consumption of non-ferrous metals by countries. This change is reflected in the worldwide expansion and considerably greater geographical spread of mining products on the market.

It must still be said, however, that the mine production of non-ferrous metals in the world continues to be relatively concentrated geographically (see Table 26). Even in the case of the earliest known heavy non-ferrous metals copper, lead and zinc, of which deposits are found all over the world, only six countries combine to produce 60–66% of world supplies; for tin, which is of comparatively rare occurrence, 80% of mining output comes from only six countries. The extraction of raw materials for the production of light metals is even more concentrated than for heavy metals, even though bauxite and magnesium are among the minerals most frequently occurring in the earth's crust. Of world production of bauxite in 1979 74% was provided by six countries and of magnesium raw materials 91% by only four countries, while 94% of world titanium production based on rutile was concentrated in 1976 in just two countries. Of the non-ferrous metals used for steel-improving – manganese, nickel, chromium, molybdenum, cobalt and vanadium – 83–95% was mined in 1979 by four to seven countries. Only tungsten and nickel production have a wider scatter, with 75–83% shared among eight countries. In the case of the minor metals the picture is very similar: niobium and tellurium are almost exclusively produced by four countries; in 1979 bismuth, selenium and beryllium – where statistics are published – between 73 and

Table 26. Concentration of mine production of non-ferrous metals by countries, 1975, 1976 and 1979

Metal/ore	Year	Total producer countries	Major producers Number	Share of world output (%)
Heavy metals				
Copper	1979	66	6	USA (18), USSR (15), Chile (13), Canada (8), Zambia (7), Zaire (5)
Lead	1979	62	6	USSR (16), USA (15), Australia (12), Canada (9), Peru (5), Mexico (5)
Zinc	1979	60	6	Canada (19), USSR (16), Australia (8), Peru (8), USA (5), Japan (4)
Tin	1979	80	6	Malaysia (27), Thailand (14), Bolivia (12), Indonesia (12), USSR (8), China (7)
Light metals				
Bauxite	1979	74	6	Australia (31), Guinea (14), Jamaica (13), USSR (7), Surinam (5), Guyana (4)
Magnesium[1]	1979	91	4	USA (47), USSR (24), Norway (14), Japan (6)
Titanium[2]				
Ilmenite	1976	96	6	Australia (32), Norway (24), USA (19), USSR (12), Malaysia (6), Finland (4); also Canada from titanium-bearing iron ores.
Rutile[2]	1976	93	2	Australia (93), USSR (0.9)
Steel improvers				
Chromium	1976	84	7	South Africa (28), USSR (25), Albania (9), Rhodesia (7), Philippines (5), Finland (5), India (5)
Cobalt	1976	87	5	Zaire (56), Zambia (13), USSR (9), Finland (5), France (4)
Manganese	1976	83	5	USSR (34), South Africa (22), Australia (9), Brazil (9), Gabon (9)
Molybdenum	1976	90	4	USA (59), Canada (17), Chile (13), USSR (11)
Nickel	1979	83	8	USSR (22), Canada (19), New Caledonia (12), Australia (11), Indonesia (5), Cuba (5), Philippines (5), South Africa (4)
Vanadium	1976	95	5	South Africa (42), USA (28), USSR (14), Finland (6), Chile (5)
Tungsten	1976	75	8	China (22), USSR (19), Bolivia (7), USA (6), South Korea (6), Australia (6), North Korea (5), Canada (4)
Other alloying and special metals				
Antimony	1979	85	8	Argentina (20), South Africa (18), China (16), USSR (12), Canada (5), Thailand (5), Mexico (5), Yugoslavia (5)
Beryllium	1976	73	3	USSR (60), Brazil (26), Argentina (7)
Cadmium[1]	1979	80	9	USSR (16), Japan (14), USA (11), Canada (8), Belgium–Luxembourg (8), West Germany (7), Australia (4), France (4), Poland (4), Mexico (4)
Niobium	1976	97	4	Brazil (75), Canada (12), USSR (7), Nigeria (3)
Mercury	1979	92	5	USSR (32), Spain (18), USA (16), Algeria (16), China (10)
Bismuth	1976	91	7	Australia (21), Japan (16), Peru (15), Bolivia (15), Mexico (14), China (6), Canada (4)
Selenium[3]	1976	93	6	Japan (37), Canada (27), USA (14), Belgium–Luxembourg (6), Mexico (5), Sweden (4)
Tellurium[3]	1975	99	4	USA (40), Canada (24), Peru (21), Japan (14)

Note: Calculated on metal content of production (except for bauxite).
1. Smelter production. 2. Production of concentrates. 3. Refinery production.
Sources: Calculated from *Metal Statistics*, 1980; US Department of the Interior, 1977.

93% were mined in seven, six and three countries respectively; over 90% of mercury and 85% of antimony are recovered by eight countries; and nine countries together account for 80% of cadmium production. It should be noted that the countries of the leading group often have individually very high shares of mine production (see Table 26).

6.2 SMELTING AND REFINERY PRODUCTION

6.2.1 Development and product structure

In the wake of the expansion of demand for non-ferrous metals in the last part of the nineteenth century there was a rapid increase in the market range of smelter and refinery products in the world – a development which has persisted up to the present day at a varying pace. Up to the outbreak of the First World War smelter production of the then quantitatively most important metals, copper, lead, zinc and tin, as well as of aluminium (then only on the threshold of its development), have increased nearly fourfold. After the setbacks caused by the war expansion accelerated with new vigour and even though the metal industry was soon severely affected by the world recession, it succeeded in the subsequent buoyant phase of recovery in achieving expansion of smelter production, which eventually by 1940 – i.e., in 30 years of by no means steady economic development – had more than doubled.

During the Second World War there was again a slowing down of growth, but afterwards, stimulated by the efforts of the countries towards reconstruction and the development of their economic potential, a period of marked expansion began in the metal industry, during the course of which the volume of smelter production almost quadrupled from 1950 to 1979.

Table 27. World smelter production of non-ferrous metals, 1880–1979

Year or period	Aluminium	Copper[1]	Lead[2]	Zinc	Tin	Nickel	Total
	Smelter production (thousand tonnes)						
1880		161.5	354.0	218.0	40.1		773.6
1890	0.2	280.9	539.5	348.6	56.6	2.5	1,228.3
1900	7.3	499.2	871.3	478.5	81.3	7.6	1,945.2
1910	43.8	895.1	1,127.0	810.2	118.8	19.0	3,013.9
1920	127.7	948.8	872.6	707.6	121.3	24.0	2,802.0
1930	269.7	1,800.4	1,658.1	1,400.1	161.1		5,289.4
1940	782.9	2,581.6	1,735.6	1,668.7	166.6		6,935.4
1950	1,506.9	3,186.7	1,849.9	2,059.6	170.2	147.8	8,921.1
1960	4,543.2	4,997.9	2,716.8	3,150.9	200.6	325.5	15,934.9
1970	10,302.0	7,951.6	3,987.8	5,217.7	221.3	585.4	27,905.8
1979	15,217.3	9,354.0	5,547.7	6,437.3	242.9	674.0	37,473.2

Table 27. (cont'd)

Year or period	Aluminium	Copper[1]	Lead[2]	Zinc	Tin	Nickel	Total
		Annual average change[3]					
1880–1890		5.7					4.7
1890–1900	42.4	6.1	4.2	3.5	3.8	10.4	4.7
1900–1910	20.3	5.8	2.8	5.4	3.3	9.4	4.5
1910–1920	10.6	−0.7	−2.5	−3.2	0.1	3.7[4]	−0.7
1920–1930	8.6	6.9	6.3	8.0	4.3		6.6
1930–1940	12.5	4.0	0.8	2.9	1.7		2.7
1940–1950	6.2	1.3	0.4	1.8	−1.5		2.6
1950–1960	11.2	4.7	4.2	4.4	0.2	7.9	6.0
1960–1970	8.8	4.8	3.7	5.4	2.6	6.4	5.8
1970–1979	5.1	2.9	4.0	2.1	0.6	2.8	3.3
		Index (1950 = 100)					
1880		5.1	19.2	10.6	23.6		8.7
1890	0.01	8.8	29.2	16.9	33.3	1.6	13.8
1900	0.5	15.7	47.1	23.2	47.8	5.1	21.8
1910	2.9	28.1	60.9	39.3	69.8	12.9	33.8
1920	8.5	29.8	47.2	34.4	71.3	16.2	31.4
1930	17.9	56.5	89.7	68.0	94.7		59.3
1940	52.0	81.0	93.8	81.0	97.9		77.7
1950	100	100	100	100	100	100	100
1960	301.5	156.8	146.9	153.0	117.9	220.2	178.6
1970	684.1	238.4	215.7	253.6	130.0	396.1	312.5
1979	1,010.4	293.7	300.1	312.9	142.7	456.0	419.7
		Share of world smelter production (%)					
1880		20.9	45.7	28.2	5.2		100
1890	0.01	22.9	49.8	28.4	4.6	0.2	100
1900	0.4	25.7	44.8	24.5	4.2	0.4	100
1910	1.5	29.7	37.4	26.9	3.9	0.6	100
1920	4.6	33.8	31.1	25.3	4.3	0.9	100
1930	5.1	34.0	31.3	26.6	3.0		100
1940	11.3	37.3	25.0	24.0	2.4		100
1950	16.9	35.7	20.7	23.1	1.9	1.7	100
1960	28.5	31.4	17.0	19.8	1.3	2.0	100
1970	36.9	27.2	14.4	18.7	0.8	2.1	100
1979	40.6	24.9	14.8	17.2	0.7	1.8	100
		Smelter production per head of population (kg)					
1880		0.11	0.25	0.15	0.03		0.55
1890		0.19	0.35	0.23	0.04	0.002	0.82
1900	0.05	0.31	0.54	0.30	0.05	0.005	1.22
1910	0.03	0.52	0.65	0.47	0.07	0.01	1.75
1920	0.07	0.51	0.47	0.38	0.07	0.01	1.51
1930	0.13	0.87	0.80	0.68	0.08		2.56
1940	0.34	1.12	0.76	0.73	0.07		3.02
1950	0.60	1.27	0.74	0.82	0.07	0.06	3.57
1960	1.52	1.67	0.91	1.06	0.07	0.11	5.34
1970	2.85	2.10	1.10	1.45	0.06	0.16	7.73
1979	3.51	2.16	1.28	1.48	0.06	0.16	8.64

1. 1880–1920 unrefined copper, 1930 onwards refined copper. 2. Refined lead. 3. Calculated on the basis of three-year averages. 4. 1910–19.
Source: Calculated from *Metal Statistics*, various years.

With a total of 37.5 million tonnes the production volume in 1979 was nearly 19 times higher than at the turn of the century. Nevertheless, an increasing tendency for growth to slow down in smelter production over the past 30 years cannot be ignored. In the 1970s only refined lead production has tended to accelerate once more.

Accompanying the powerful expansion of the metal industry under the pressure of industrial development, a profound change is to be noted in the structure of the metal market range. In 1900 world production of non-ferrous metals still consisted almost exclusively of heavy metals – the share of aluminium was less than 1% – but by 1950 the share of light metals had already risen to 17% and in 1979 it had risen to over 40% of the total. Aluminium in the 1960s for the first time overtook copper in its share of world production of non-ferrous metals, which since 1920 quantitatively had been leading smelter production in the heavy metal sector. Today world aluminium

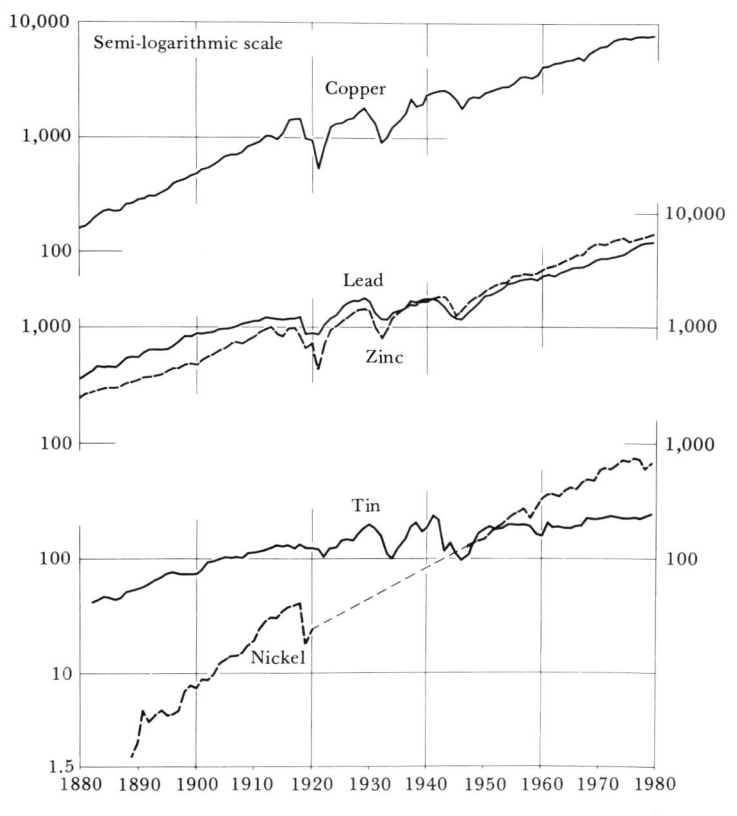

Fig. 11. World smelter production of heavy metals, 1880–1979 (thousand tonnes)
Source: *Metal Statistics*, various years.

production is at 15 million tonnes, one-and-a-half times as high as copper production with 9.4 million tonnes (1979 figures); the latter has displayed declining shares of world smelter production since 1940.

In the smelter production of heavy metals, following shifts in demand during the course of industrialization, a remarkable change in structure has also taken place which is still not yet completed. Up to the First World War lead was the non-ferrous metal in the greatest absolute demand, with a share of 40% of the production of heavy metals, but it then lost this advantage to copper, whose share rose from 30% to 42%. The importance of lead compared with zinc in smelter production also declined in course of time, and after 1950 it was overtaken by zinc, which in 1979, with almost 29%, represented a considerably higher share of world smelter production of heavy metals than lead, with 25%. During the same period tin and nickel likewise underwent a

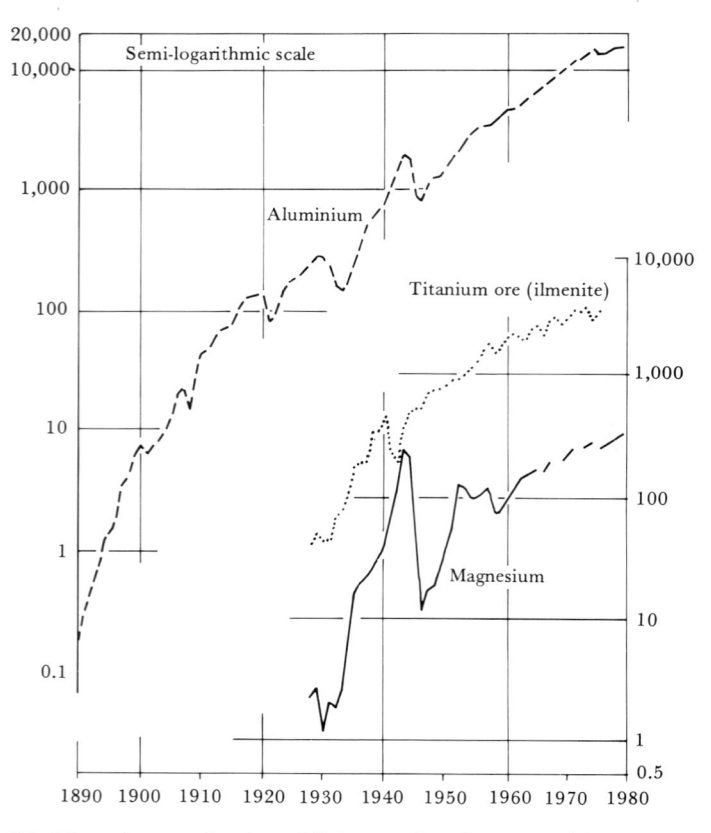

Fig. 12. World smelter production of light metals, 1890–1979 (thousand tonnes)
Sources: *Metal Statistics*, various years; *Minerals Yearbook*, Vol. 1, various years.

change in their relative positions; the share of nickel in 1979, at 3% of world production of heavy metals, was some three times as high as that of tin.

There follows a brief survey of trends in the production of the major industrial metals.

Aluminium

Production of aluminium during the first decades of industrialization was something of a rarity: in 1886 it amounted to only 12 tonnes, but it rose in 1900 to 7,300 tonnes and by the outbreak of the First World War had risen to 70,000 tonnes (Peach and Constantin, 1972, p. 472 ff.). Even with a fourteenfold increase by 1940 to 783,000 tonnes, world production of aluminium still remained absolutely and relatively small, but at the end of the Second World War there was a burst of expansion. From 1.5 million tonnes in 1950, production in 1970 for the first time exceeded the 10 million tonne mark and rose in 1979 to 14.2 million tonnes, which put the share of aluminium at some 40% of world metal production. In terms of growth rate this expansion during the past 30 years has given aluminium a clear lead over all other metals, with the exception of titanium (rutile) and vanadium, whose comparatively low production increased rather more rapidly – even if an increasing slackening was also discernible in the expansion of aluminium.

Copper

The second most important non-ferrous metal today, copper, in comparison with aluminium, displayed a much slower but steadier growth rate. The annual average increase of 6% was interrupted only during the two world war periods. Since the beginning of the 1960s, however, the production of both unrefined and refined copper – in line with the trend in aluminium – has shown a continually decreasing growth rate, even though world production in 1979 (9.4 million tonnes) had more than trebled since 1950. It rose considerably more rapidly than mine production of copper and outstripped this also respectively on an annual basis with an upward tendency. This is clearly apparent in the increased importance of the recycling of waste and remelted materials and scrap, which today accounts for one-sixth of the production of refined copper.

Lead and zinc

The production of lead and zinc reveals a roughly similar trend, although zinc, from the turn of the century onwards, showed a greater increase. Although zinc lagged behind refined lead in the 1970s, zinc production in 1979 at 6.4 million tonnes exceeded that of lead by a fifth and the gap between the two metals since 1950 has continued steadily to widen.

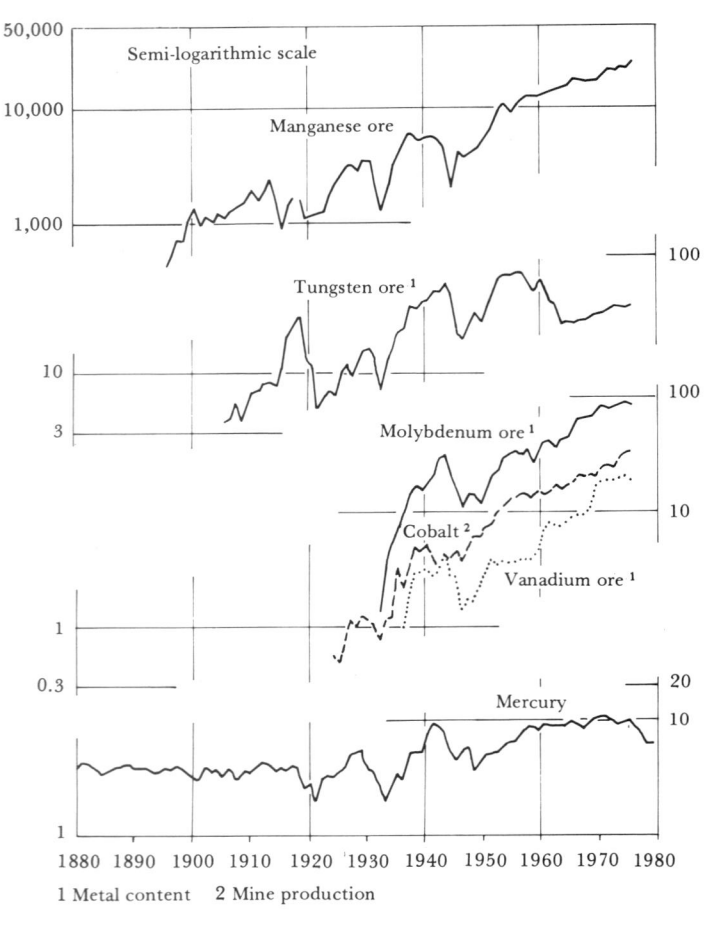

Fig. 13. World production of alloying and special metals, 1880–1979 (thousand tonnes)
Source: *Minerals Yearbook*, Vol. 1, various years.

Nickel and tin

Nickel production expanded relatively even more strongly than zinc, lead and copper, and in 1976 was nearly 100 times as great as at the turn of the century, when admittedly production was extremely low. Since 1950 alone production has increased fivefold. In comparison the increase in tin production has been very slight. Up to 1950 it was twice that at the turn of the century and since 1950 has risen very little.

The variable growth in smelter production of the different non-ferrous metals, which led to changes in the global production structure, is shown particularly clearly in the results obtained in our regression estimates for

Table 28. Smelter production of non-ferrous metals, 1879–1979 (regression estimates)

	World production a	World production b	R²		World production a	World production b	R²
Heavy metals				**Steel improvers (cont'd)**			
Copper, unrefined				Manganese			
1879–1979	5.362	0.037	0.965	1895–1975	6.450	0.044	0.915
1879–1950	5.316	0.039	0.923	1895–1950	6.628	0.036	0.750
1950–1979	7.853	0.042	0.981	1950–1975	8.993	0.045	0.904
Copper, refined				Molybdenum			
1931–1979	7.326	0.395	0.952	1932–1975	1.870	0.064	0.796
Lead				1932–1950	1.720	0.082	0.361
1883–1979	6.132	0.023	0.929	1950–1975	2.984	0.064	0.924
1880–1950	6.224	0.019	0.818	Nickel			
1950–1979	7.558	0.036	0.985	1889–1920	1.050	0.088	0.920
Zinc				1947–1979	4.946	0.056	0.964
1880–1979	5.551	0.032	0.966	Tungsten			
1880–1950	5.635	0.029	0.912	1905–1975	1.937	0.032	0.609
1950–1979	7.685	0.040	0.977	1905–1950	1.611	0.048	0.635
Tin				1950–1975	4.137	−0.030	0.451
1884–1979	4.175	0.015	0.801	Vanadium			
1880–1950	3.981	0.019	0.744	1936–1975	0.534	0.058	0.615
1950–1979	5.164	0.010	0.620	1936–1950	1.040	−0.005	0.001
Light metals				1950–1975	0.943	0.086	0.946
Aluminium				**Other alloying and special metals**			
1885–1979	−0.537	0.122	0.908	Antimony			
1885–1950	−1.278	0.150	0.068	1965–1977	3.627	−0.010	0.380
1950–1979	7.568	0.078	0.979	Cadmium			
Magnesium				1928–1979	0.609	0.052	0.917
1928–1979	1.742	0.089	0.731	1928–1950	0.381	0.071	0.743
1928–1950	0.925	0.163	0.521	1950–1979	1.930	0.040	0.913
1950–1979	4.168	0.057	0.843	Mercury			
Titanium (ilmenite)				1890–1979	7.965	0.011	0.550
1928–1975	4.341	0.093	0.929	1890–1950	8.137	0.004	0.989
1928–1950	3.502	0.207	0.965	1950–1979	8.800	0.013	0.239
1950–1975	6.853	0.057	0.919	Bismuth			
Titanium (rutile)				1938–1975	0.041	0.039	0.889
1928–1975	−1.509	0.190	0.872	1938–1950	0.226	0.003	0.004
1928–1950	−3.638	0.423	0.912	1950–1975	0.515	0.039	0.894
1950–1975	3.703	0.103	0.907	Beryllium			
Steel improvers				1935–1975	0.417	0.047	0.373
Chromium				1935–1950	−0.497	0.139	0.515
1897–1975	−10.463	0.311	0.107	1950–1975	0.262	−0.031	0.375
1897–1950	−13.696	0.462	0.078	Niobium			
1950–1975	7.969	0.035	0.877	1951–1975	1.262	0.067	0.536
Cobalt				Selenium			
1924–1975	−0.1708	0.077	0.935	1951–1975	0.252	−0.011	0.083
1924–1950	−0.430	0.096	0.842				
1950–1975	2.184	0.050	0.928				

Note: All calculations performed on the basis of a logarithmic trend. The coefficients of all variables were significant to a 5% probability of error.
Source: Calculated from *Metal Statistics*, various years.

development trends in the production of 23 non-ferrous metals during the past 100 years, in which as well as the basic metals, the most important light metals, steel improvers and other alloying and special metals are included (Table 28). An especially conspicuous feature is the sharp rise in the growth trend of light metals compared with the heavy metals during the whole period under review, in addition to which a stronger upswing was apparent also in the steel improvers and the other alloying and special metals. The trend for heavy metals from 1950 to 1977 showed more rapid expansion than that of the period 1879–1950 (the only exception is tin, with declining production over the long-term trend), whereas for the light metals, without exception, a stronger growth trend was evident in the decades up to 1950 than from 1950 to the present day (the lower starting level of the initial period should be noted, however). The growth of aluminium, magnesium and titanium during recent decades was below the long-term trend, but even so all light metals, without exception, showed an upswing in production growth during these most recent decades that was considerably more rapid than that of the heavy metals.

6.2.2 The international structure of smelter and refinery production

With the rapid growth of world smelter production of non-ferrous metals in the course of industrialization, profound changes occurred in its international structure. Up to the second half of the nineteenth century the countries of Europe accounted for the main bulk of smelter output, with the smelting works established on the ore deposits supplying them. With the rapid expansion of ore mining in North America the smelting industry developed there for processing the domestic raw materials gained in importance. The opening up of ore deposits in overseas countries further strengthened the supremacy of the industrial regions in smelter production. Although the new mining regions were generally a long distance away, the ores or concentrates obtained there had to be shipped to the industrial countries for smelting, because the mines, which were operated predominantly by foreign companies or with the aid of foreign capital, did not as a rule have smelting works attached to them. This may be attributed not merely to the undeniable efforts of the industrial countries to consolidate their strong economic and political position, but also in many cases could frequently be ascribed to purely technical and economic factors: the new mining countries still largely lacked an infrastructure, there was a shortage of suitable skilled technicians and procurement of capital goods, equipment and energy supplies was often difficult. The appreciable capital requirement added to financial risks and political imponderables may also have played a part. The mining countries of the Third World thus had no opportunity, in the early phase of industrialization, to build processing capacities based on their domestic raw materials.

Smelting and processing of ores and concentrates therefore expanded for many decades mainly in the industrially advanced regions. Additional reasons for this included links with existing traditional activities and the existence of the necessary know-how and of an entrepreneurial far-sightedness and initiative which was ready to take risks and accept the challenge of entering the new fields of technology. In addition to the traditional smelters at the pit, usually with their own ore base, jobbing smelting works were set up on a toll basis for processing foreign concentrates. The processing of imported ores meant that smelting works formerly oriented towards processing their own raw materials were still able to maintain their position even when the domestic ore base became exhausted, especially as the rate of market growth kept pace with increasing industrialization. In this way they increasingly became 'smelters at the market', not as a result of careful consideration of factors connected with location, but because of a change in procurement and sales conditions long after the choice of location had been made – a process of adjustment which is still continuing today (Ebeling *et al.*, 1977, p. 56). (In contrast to the heavy metals, the location of the aluminium smelters was originally oriented more strongly to the availability of cheap energy, which is the decisive cost factor in the production of aluminium. In many countries with workable bauxite deposits, neither electrical nor thermal energy is available even now in sufficient quantities for economical production.) Since the turn of the century, however, there has been a tendency not only to concentrate the heavy metal ores in the country of extraction, but also to smelt them there as well, in order to make use of production advantages (cheaper labour, lower investment costs, etc.) and achieve a more favourable transport/cost relationship by shipping higher-grade products. This process has made decisive strides, nevertheless, only during the last few decades, under the impulse given by more and more countries with raw material resources obtaining political autonomy and then intensifying their industrialization, in which they have increasingly geared their efforts towards refining their own raw materials production. Endeavours towards co-ordinating the location of mining works and smelters recognize the fact that the extraction of heavy metals is based on well-known empirical experience that has been tested over the centuries, and less developed countries are as a rule more capable of following advances in the smelting processes than rapid development in many other forms of industrial production with comparatively higher technical requirements (*Metal Statistics*, 1953, p. ix).

In the regional structure of world smelter production, this development process is reflected in an initially increasing share by Europe, which reached maximum values as early as 1890 for unrefined copper (45%), lead (64%) and zinc (83%), though it lost its position of supremacy in copper to North America towards the end of the nineteenth century, and in lead and zinc after the First World War. The highest share of world output of aluminium was at first in Europe but then shifted to North America where, since 1970, development has grown more rapidly. The leading position of these two industrial regions in the field of world smelter output lost ground increasingly after the turn of the century, and in 1950 amounted to 84% for aluminium, 51% for unrefined copper, 70% for refined copper, 61% for lead, 78% for zinc, 52% for tin and 80% for nickel.

In the most recent phase of industrial development (since 1950) the regional structure of world smelter production has changed at an even more rapid pace, to the detriment of the 'old' industrial regions (see Table 29):

Table 29. Smelter production of non-ferrous metals by regions, 1890–1979 (% of world total)

Year	Europe	EEC	North America	Latin America	Africa	Asia	Australia and Oceania	Eastern Bloc countries[1]	World total* (thousand tonnes)
				Aluminium					
1900	56.2		43.8	–	–	–	–	–	7.3
1910	55.3		44.7	–	–	–	–	–	43.8
1920	41.3		58.7	–	–	–	–	–	127.1
1930	48.5		51.5	–	–	–	–	–	270.0
1940	50.1		36.5	–	–	4.5	–	8.9	782.9
1950	16.3		67.2	–	–	2.0	–	14.5	1,506.9
1960	19.1	10.8	55.6	0.4	1.0	3.5	0.3	20.1	4,528.0
1970	19.6	8.9	44.4	1.6	1.6	9.1	2.0	21.4	10,302.0
1979	23.7	13.3	35.6	4.4	2.6	9.6	2.8	21.3	15,217.3
				Copper, refined					
1930	19.0		63.8	9.8	2.0	4.7	0.8		1,800.4
1940	17.4		58.2	9.7	4.3	4.1	0.7	5.6	2,582.0
1950	20.5		49.0	10.6	5.9	3.0	0.9	10.2	3,187.0
1960	19.5	11.3	40.4	5.8	11.2	5.5	1.7	16.0	4,998.0
1970	17.2	10.4	33.3	7.6	11.6	9.8	1.9	18.7	7,591.6
1979	14.7	10.0	25.4	12.2	9.1	11.9	1.9	24.8	9,354.0
				Lead					
1890	64.4		24.0	4.1	–	–	7.5		539.5
1900	46.1		34.2	9.2	–	0.2	10.0		871.0[2]
1910	44.7		34.1	10.7	–	0.3	8.8		1,127.0[3]
1920	29.0		53.8	10.1	3.0	3.7	0.4		873.0
1930	24.8		42.3	15.4	1.3	5.9	10.3		1,659.0
1940	20.4		39.1	14.0	1.5	6.0	13.9	5.1	1,736.0
1950	27.5		33.8	15.0	2.7	0.9	10.8	9.3	1,849.9
1960	31.8	17.5	23.0	10.3	2.1	3.6	7.7	21.5	2,716.1
1970	25.4	14.3	24.5	9.2	4.4	6.0	5.5	25.0	3,266.5
1979	21.5	14.8	22.4	10.1	3.1	5.9	6.3	30.7	3,407.2
				Zinc					
1890	82.5		17.5	–	–	–	–		343.1
1900	76.5		23.5	–	–	–	–		479.0
1910	69.8		30.1	–	–	–	0.1		810.0
1920	36.2		61.8	–	–	0.7	1.3		718.0
1930	50.3		40.1	2.1	1.3	2.2	4.0		1,400.0
1940	34.0		49.5	2.0	0.8	3.9	4.6	5.2	1,669.0
1950	28.4		49.8	2.1	1.1	2.4	4.1	12.1	2,060.0
1960	29.3	22.5	32.5	3.2	2.7	5.9	3.8	22.6	3,150.9
1970	26.3	18.1	24.6	3.7	2.8	13.5	4.9	24.3	5,217.7
1979	28.3	20.1	17.2	5.1	2.9	14.8	4.7	27.0	6,437.3

Table 29. (cont'd)

Year	Europe	EEC	North America	Latin America	Africa	Asia	Australia and Oceania	Eastern Bloc countries[1]	World total* (thousand tonnes)
				Tin					
1900	12.3		–	–	–	82.9	4.7	–	80.3[4]
1910	25.6		–	–	–	69.6	4.8	–	114.8
1920	19.9		10.8	–	–	65.8	3.4	–	122.2[4]
1930	31.7		–	–	–	67.4	0.9	–	180.7
1940	23.1		0.6	0.5	3.4	65.7	1.6	5.1	233.0
1950	33.5		18.2	0.7	2.2	37.8	1.1	6.5	187.1
1960	24.8	10.5	6.9	1.4	1.8	39.2	1.1	24.8	206.7
1970	19.1	5.8	2.0	2.4	5.5	53.7	2.4	15.0	221.3
1979	10.4	7.8	1.9	10.8	2.5	57.1	2.2	15.1	244.5
				Nickel					
1950	23.7		56.0	–	–	–	0.3	20.0	148.0
1960	24.0	14.5	42.9	4.5	0.4	5.8	3.5	19.0	326.0
1970	17.0	2.0	34.7	0.4	2.4	15.3	4.8	25.3	585.4
1979	11.8	3.3	19.1	4.1	5.1	19.1	9.9	31.0	674.0

1. Where no figures are given, amounts are included in European and Asian totals. *Unspecified: 2. – 0.3; 3. – 1.4; 4. – 0.1.
Source: Calculated from *Metal Statistics*, various years.

(a) In Europe smelter production expansion was slightly below global scale. This applies particularly to refined copper, lead and tin. In aluminium production, however, the European share had increased to 25% by 1979.

(b) North America is characterized by a severely declining share in world output for all metals. It was still the leader in 1979, however, in the production of aluminium (36%) and unrefined copper (22%), was roughly on par with the Eastern Bloc countries in the case of refined copper (25%) and had dropped back behind Europe and the Eastern Bloc countries in the production of lead (22%) and zinc (17%). Smelter production of tin, depending on raw materials available, is relatively insignificant.

(c) Latin America in 1979 accounted for an output of 18% of world copper (17% in 1950), but fell back in lead production (10%). This region however strongly increased its share of tin production to nearly 10% (1.5% in 1950), doubled it for zinc to 11% in 1979 and increased its aluminium production to a share of some 4%.

(d) In Africa production of unrefined and refined copper expanded at a slightly slower rate than other regions. The share of world production fell to 16%. There was a slight increase in the shares of aluminium, lead, zinc and tin to about 3%.

(e) In Asia – led by Japan – the growth rate of smelter production was faster than the global average, so that the shares increased for all metals.

(f) Australia and Oceania also acquired greater importance as producers of non-ferrous metals, though in 1979 at about 2.6% world market shares were still relatively small. Only in nickel production was a share of 10% achieved.

(g) The Eastern Bloc countries in the period 1950–1979 displayed by far the greatest expansion of the metallurgical industry during the past 30 years. Their shares in world production rose accordingly and in 1979 had advanced for unrefined copper to 24%, zinc to 27%, lead to 31% and aluminium to 21%.

Although the expansion of mining operations in the developing countries has been unsatisfactory in view of their wealth of raw materials resources, this applies even more strongly to their smelter production, although it varies with the metals concerned. The data for the period 1950–1978 show that:

(a) the share of the developing countries in world production increased
    for aluminium   from 0.4% to 10.4%
    for zinc   from 3.9% to 9.3%
    for tin   from 40.5% to 69.3%
(b) the share of the developing countries in world production decreased
    for copper   from 35.7% to 32.6%
    for lead   from 17.7% to 11.8%.

Thus, smelting of the ores after they have been concentrated is still performed predominantly in the industrial countries. Only about 30% of ores extracted in the developing countries are also smelted there, chiefly in Zambia and Zaire, which refine their entire output of copper ore themselves. The share quota has remained relatively constant since 1950 and shows that expansion of smelting capacities in these countries has only just kept pace with the increase in mining capacity. In contrast, the industrial countries increased their smelting capacities, overwhelmingly in the case of Japan. Exceptions are Australia and South Africa, which expanded their mining capacity very much more than their smelting capacity, so that there was a sharp increase in exports of ore from these countries. In the Eastern Bloc countries the expansion of the smelting stage was parallel to the increase in mining output.

The degree of processing in the mining countries exhibits considerable variation according to ores; the relevant factors in this are the degree of vertical

Table 30. Smelter production of copper by regions, 1890–1979 (% of world total)

Region	1890	1900	1910	1920	1930	1940	1950	1960	1970	1979
Europe	44.5	26.4	19.9	7.6	11.7	6.1	6.7	4.9	5.4	6.2
EEC	–	–	–	–	–	–	–	1.9	1.5	2.0
North America	36.4	57.5	58.7	63.3	52.7	48.9	44.7	34.5	30.7	22.2
Latin America	11.5	6.9	11.5	17.1	19.5	17.2	16.9	16.8	14.1	17.9
Africa	–	–	0.1	2.4	9.6	17.1	19.4	22.0	20.3	15.6
Asia	5.4	4.9	5.6	7.0	5.5	4.9	2.2	5.3	8.5	12.3
Australia and Oceania	2.2	4.3	4.2	2.6	1.0	0.8	0.6	1.7	1.8	2.2
Eastern Bloc countries[1]							5.0	9.5	14.8	19.2	923.5
World production (thousand tonnes)	280.8	499.2	895.1	949.0	1,578.9	2,413.0	2,518.6	4,287.0	6,320.0	7,818.7

1. Where no figures are given, amounts are included in European and Asian totals.
Source: Calculated from *Metal Statistics*, various years.

integration in the various branches of industry, the technology required and the energy demand, and also the distance between the supplying countries and the markets. For instance, no more than 10% of bauxite is smelted to aluminium actually in the countries of extraction, whereas more than 75% of copper ores are processed to metal in the mining countries. There has also been an increasing shift to the construction of capacities for smelting tin ore in the developing countries, so that a level of smelting of over 75% is now recorded in this sector.

Expansion of smelting capacities in the mining countries would improve their potential net added value and provide them with an important source of income. It would therefore appear to be necessary, according to criteria of development policy. Whether, at what rate and to what extent this can be

Table 31. Smelter production of non-ferrous metals by groups of countries, 1950–79

	Total world production (thousand tonnes)	Western industrialized countries	Developing countries	Eastern Bloc countries
		(% of world total)		
Aluminium				
1950	1,506.9	85.1	0.4	14.5
1960	4,543.2	77.6	2.0	20.4
1970	10,257.0	73.3	5.2	21.5
1979	15,217.3	68.3	10.4	21.3
Copper				
1950	2,518.6	54.8	35.7	9.5
1960	4,287.3	46.6	38.6	14.8
1970	6,307.7	48.2	32.7	19.1
1979	7,818.7	43.9	32.6	23.5
Lead				
1950	1,849.9	73.0	17.7	9.3
1960	2,716.8	65.2	13.6	21.2
1970	3,987.8	65.0	11.8	23.2
1979	5,547.7[1]	64.2	11.8	24.0
Zinc				
1950	2,059.6	84.0	3.9	12.1
1960	3,150.9	71.5	5.9	22.6
1970	5,217.7	69.4	6.4	24.2
1979	6,437.3	63.6	9.3	27.0
Tin				
1950	187.1	52.9	40.5	6.6
1960	206.7	33.6	41.6	24.8
1970	220.8	24.8	60.2	15.0
1979	244.5	15.7	69.3	15.0

1. Refined lead, including secondary lead.
Source: Calculated from *Metal Statistics*, various years.

accomplished is still a problem, in view of the prevailing scarcity of capital for tangible assets and for training purposes, and the question arises as to how a partnership will be realized between producer and consumer countries, especially in regard to the necessary capital and technology transfer. The Customs policies, and possibly other import restrictions, on the part of the consumer countries should also be reviewed, since in all industrial countries the duties payable on ores and concentrates are insignificant, but these rise – generally very appreciably – with the degree of processing. Admittedly such practices are primarily directed towards protection against competition from other industrial countries, but they also cause difficulties in the establishment and expansion of processing industries in developing countries. Generally, however, the limited access to equipment and technology for processing raw materials – whether for financial reasons or because of difficulty in practical application through lack of specialist knowledge – is an even greater obstacle to expansion of the smelting stage in the developing countries with mining works than the great variety of restrictive import practices of the consumer countries.[1]

With the expansion of the processes of industrialization in the former raw materials countries, which has resulted in their increasing demand for non-ferrous metals, the change of structure in favour of the less-developed countries with their own raw materials base will undoubtedly accelerate, even though the high capital requirements for equipment and training represent a considerable obstacle. Nevertheless, the competitive position of the smelters in developing countries will improve compared with the situation in the industrial countries, because of the stricter regulations on environmental protection in the latter. Construction of a new smelting works – in particular a lead smelter – requires considerable expenditure to comply with the regulations in densely populated areas, whereas developing countries with more sparse population can adopt less strict protection specifications. In future, therefore, it may be economically feasible to erect smelters 'where the market isn't at the factory gate' (Sies, 1977, p. 1010).

The changes in the regional structure of world smelter production derive from a profound change in the development of the supply of metallurgical products in the various countries. Its essential feature is an increasing spreading out of production and therefore of supply to more and more countries as industrialization progresses, and this has accelerated even more rapidly in the most recent phase, since 1950. Around the turn of the century only a few countries still supplied the world with metallurgical products, and even in 1940 the ten most important producer countries were responsible for

---

[1] A brief survey of technological and financial factors influencing the location of processing facilities is given in: UN Interregional Workshop on Negotiation and Drafting of Mining Development Agreements, *Processing*, prepared by the United Nations Secretariat (ESA/RT/AC.7/12), New York, October 1973 (quoted by Bosson and Varon, 1977, p. 87).

over 90% of metal supply. In 1979 this share was still substantial: 70% for lead and zinc, 77–81% for aluminium and raw copper and some 80% for unrefined copper, nickel and tin. The leading group of countries at a given time is largely identical over the entire period. In general, we can see a certain levelling tendency in production, with the effect that the leading producer countries of the early years of industrialization have seen their share of world output continuously decreasing, after an initial, still substantial, relative increase as output continued to expand. Only those producer countries which started to establish and develop their own metallurgical industry later, in the main not until after 1950, are generally expanding at above the global average rate.

Table 32. Smelter production of non-ferrous metals by countries, 1880–1979 (% of world total)

Country	1880	1890	1900	1910	1920	1930	1940	1950	1960	1970	1979[2]
					Aluminium						
USA			43.8	36.7	49.0	38.5	23.9	43.3	40.2	35.1	30.0
USSR			*	*	*	*	7.2	13.9	15.4	16.5	15.8
Japan			*	*	*	*	3.4	1.7	2.9	7.1	6.6
Canada			*	8.0	9.4	12.9	12.7	23.9	15.2	9.3	5.7
Germany			34.3[1]	18.3[1]	9.4	11.4	26.1	1.8	3.7	3.0	4.9
Norway			*	2.1	4.4	10.2	3.6	3.1	3.8	5.1	4.4
France			13.7	21.7	9.6	9.6	7.9	4.0	5.2	3.7	2.6
UK			8.2	11.4	6.3	5.2	2.5	2.0	*	*	2.4
China			*	*	*	*	*	*	1.5	1.8	2.4
Australia			*	*	*	*	*	*	*	2.0	1.8
Italy			*	1.8	0.9	3.0	4.9	2.5	1.8	*	*
Austria			*	*	1.6	1.1	*	*	1.5	*	*
Switzerland			*	*	9.4	7.6	3.6	1.3	*	*	*
Spain			*	*	*	0.4	*	*	*	*	*
India			*	*	*	*	*	*	*	1.6	*
Total			100.0	100.0	100.0	100.0	96.2	95.8	91.3	85.2	76.6
World production (thousand tonnes)			7.3	43.8	127.7	269.7	782.9	1,506.9	4,543.2	10,302.0	15,217.3
					Copper, unrefined						
USA		36.4	57.5	58.7	63.3	46.2	38.2	36.6	26.1	23.6	17.1
USSR		1.7	1.6	2.5	0.2	2.2	4.8	8.7	11.7	14.6	15.0
Chile		12.6	5.2	4.0	10.4	13.2	14.4	13.7	11.8	10.2	12.1
Japan		5.5	4.9	5.6	*	*	3.7	1.5	4.4	7.9	10.9
Zambia		*	*	*	*	*	11.1	11.2	13.4	10.8	7.6
Canada		1.1	1.7	2.9	3.9	6.4	10.6	8.3	8.4	7.1	5.1
Peru		*	1.7	3.0	3.6	3.0	*	*	3.8	2.8	4.8
Zaire		*	*	*	*	8.6	5.5	6.8	7.0	6.1	4.7
Poland		*	*	*	*	*	*	*	*	*	4.4
Germany		8.7	6.2	4.2	2.2	2.8	2.1	1.9	1.5	*	2.4
UK		31.8	16.0	7.9	2.7	1.1	*	*	*	*	*
Australia		2.1	4.4	4.2	2.6	*	*	*	1.7	1.8	*
France		0.9	*	*	*	*	*	*	*	*	*
Yugoslavia		*	*	*	0.3	1.6	1.8	1.6	*	*	*
Mexico		0.6	4.5	7.0	5.3	3.4	1.4	2.2	*	*	*
Total		99.6	99.5	100.0	95.5	89.5	93.5	92.2	89.8	87.3	84.0
World production (thousand tonnes)		280.9	499.2	895.1	948.8	1,578.0	2,413.0	2,518.6	4,287.3	6,320.0	7,789.2

Table 32. (cont'd)

Country	1880	1890	1900	1910	1920	1930	1940	1950	1960	1970	1979
					Copper, refined						
USA						66.2	49.0	42.2	32.9	26.8	21.2
USSR						2.6	5.2	8.8	12.2	14.2	15.8
Japan						4.4	3.9	2.7	5.0	9.3	10.5
Chile						9.8	9.7	9.4	4.5	6.1	8.3
Zambia						*	*	*	8.1	7.7	6.0
Canada						1.6	9.2	6.8	7.6	6.5	4.3
Germany						7.4	7.3[2]	6.2	6.2	5.4	4.1
Belgium and Luxembourg						4.5	1.3	4.3	4.0	4.5	3.9
Poland						*	*	*	*	*	3.6
China						*	*	*	*	*	3.0
UK						2.5	6.8	6.1	4.3	2.7	*
Zaire						*	2.6[2]	3.0[3]	*	2.5	*
France						0.9	*	*	*	*	*
Australia						0.8	*	*	*	*	*
Rhodesia						*	1.4	2.5	*	*	*
Total						96.8	96.4	91.9	89.3	85.7	80.7
World production (thousand tonnes)						1,800.4	2,581.6	3,186.7	4,997.9	7,591.6	9,354.0
					Lead[4]						
USSR	*	*	*	*	*	*	4.6	6.0	12.9	15.3	18.2
USA	25.1	24.0	30.9	32.8	52.3	34.0	27.6	25.5	17.7	18.8	17.0
Australia	*	7.5	10.0	8.8	*	10.3	13.9	10.8	7.7	5.5	6.3
Canada	*	*	3.3	*	1.5	8.3	11.5	8.3	5.3	5.7	5.4
Japan	0.1	*	*	*	*	*	*	*	*	5.5	5.2
Mexico	*	4.1	9.2	10.7	9.4	13.9	11.5	11.9	6.1	5.4	5.1
Germany	24.3	18.7	13.9	14.1	6.8	7.5	10.1[2]	7.6	7.6	6.5	4.7
China	*	*	*	*	*	*	*	*	*	3.1	4.4
UK	16.4	9.0	3.1	2.6	*	*	*	4.0	5.4	4.3	3.6
France	1.7	*	2.0	1.8	1.7	*	*	2.7	4.0	3.7	3.5
Spain	22.6	26.0	17.7	17.0	13.8	7.3	2.7	*	*	*	*
Italy	3.1	3.3	2.7	*	1.8	1.5	2.1	*	*	*	*
Belgium	2.3	1.8	*	3.6	1.8	3.6	*	3.2	3.4	*	*
Greece	*	2.6	1.9	1.5	*	*	*	*	*	*	*
Austria	*	1.8	*	1.6	*	*	*	*	*	*	*
Burma	*	*	*	*	3.1	4.9	4.7	*	*	*	*
Rhodesia	*	*	*	*	1.6	*	*	*	*	*	*
Poland	*	*	*	*	*	1.8	*	*	*	*	*
Peru	*	*	*	*	*	*	1.8	*	*	*	*
Yugoslavia	*	*	*	*	*	*	*	3.1	3.3	*	*
Total	95.6	98.9	95.7	94.5	93.8	93.1	90.5	83.3	73.5	73.8	73.4
World production (thousand tonnes)	354.0	539.5	871.3[1]	127.0	872.6	1,658.1	1,735.6	1,849.9	2,716.8	3,266.5	3,407.2

Table 32. (cont'd)

Country	1880	1890	1900	1910	1920	1930	1940	1950	1960	1970	1979
					Tin						
Malaysia		49.3	60.6	50.1	56.8[5]	54.7	55.4	37.4	37.5	40.8	30.1
Thailand		*	*	*	*	*	*	*	*	9.9	13.6
Indonesia		18.9	22.3	13.8		8.1	9.5	*	1.0	2.4	11.4
USSR		*	*	*	*	*	*	4.3	9.7	4.5	7.4
China		*	*	5.7	8.8	4.0	4.9	2.2	14.5	9.9	7.0
Bolivia		*	*	*	*	*	*	*	*	*	6.5
Brazil		*	*	*	*	*	*	*	*	*	4.2
UK		20.3	9.8	16.5	17.4	27.2	20.3	15.5	13.9	11.1	4.0
Spain		*	*	*	*	*	*	0.8	*	*	2.5
Australia		11.5	4.7	4.8	3.4	0.9	1.6	1.1	1.1	2.4	2.2
USA		*	*	*	10.8	*	0.6	18.0	6.9	2.0	*
Nigeria		*	*	*	*	*	*	*	*	5.7	3.7
Netherlands		—	—	—	*	1.1	*	11.4	*	2.9	*
Germany		*	2.5	9.1	2.5	2.8	1.3	*	*	*	*
Belgium		*	*	*	*	0.3	0.6	5.2	3.9	*	*
Japan		*	*	*	0.2	0.5	0.7	*	*	*	*
Zaire		*	*	*	*	*	3.4	1.8	1.2	*	*
Total		100.0	99.9	100.0	99.9	99.6	98.3	97.7	95.4	89.6	88.9
World production (thousand tonnes)		56.6	80.3	114.8	122.2	180.7	233.0	187.1	206.7	221.3	242.9
					Zinc						
USSR	1.8	1.1	1.3	1.1	*	*	5.1	6.3	12.7	13.9	16.9
Japan	*	*	*	*	*	*	3.6	2.4	5.9	13.1	12.3
Canada	*	*	*	*	2.4	7.9	10.1	9.0	7.5	8.0	9.0
USA	9.6	17.5	23.5	30.1	59.4	32.3	39.4	40.1	25.0	16.6	8.2
Germany	45.4	25.5	32.3	28.1	14.0	7.0	19.0	6.6	6.1	5.8	5.5
Australia	*	*	*	0.1	1.4	4.0	4.6	4.1	3.8	4.9	4.7
Belgium and Luxembourg	27.5	*	24.9	21.3	11.9	12.6	4.2	8.5	7.9	4.4	3.9
France	7.3	5.3	8.8	7.3	2.8	6.5	2.5	*	4.7	4.3	3.9
Poland	*	*	*	*	0.7	12.5	*	5.5	5.6	4.0	3.3
Italy	*	*	1.5	1.6	*	*	2.4	*	2.7	*	3.2
UK	3.2	8.5	6.3	7.8	3.2	3.5	3.6	3.5	2.4	2.8	*
Spain	3.2	*	*	*	1.4	*	*	*	*	*	*
Netherlands	*	40.1	1.5	2.6	*	*	*	*	*	*	*
Austria	*	2.1	*	*	*	*	*	*	*	*	*
Sweden	*	*	*	*	0.8	*	*	*	*	*	*
Norway	*	*	*	*	*	2.5	*	*	1.4	*	*
Mexico	*	*	*	*	*	2.1	*	2.4	1.7	*	*
Total	98.0	100.0	100.0	100.0	98.0	90.9	94.5	88.2	87.4	77.8	70.9
World production (thousand tonnes)	218.0	348.6	478.5	810.2	707.6	1,400.1	1,668.7	2,059.6	3,150.9	5,217.7	6,437.3

Table 32. (cont'd)

Country	1880	1890	1900	1910	1920	1930	1940	1950	1960	1970	1979
					Nickel						
USSR	0.2	0.2	0.1	*	*	*	*	*	19.6	17.8	21.2	25.2
Japan	*	*	*	*	*	*	*	*	*	5.8	15.3	15.7
Canada	19.5	*	*	*	*	*	43.3	64.3	43.2	39.2	32.3	13.2
USA	19.5	16.7	32.0	43.2	49.5	58.0	21.3	11.8	12.7	3.8	2.4	6.0
Australia	*	*	*	*	*	*	*	*	*	*	*	5.4
Norway	58.7	16.7	4.0	0.1	0.5	1.6	2.4	*	6.8	9.3	6.6	4.6
New Caledonia	*	*	*	*	*	*	*	*	0.3	3.5	4.7	4.5
Dominican Rep.	*	*	*	*	*	*	*	*	*	*	*	3.7
South Africa	*	*	*	*	*	*	*	*	*	*	1.5	3.0
UK	*	*	6.0	18.5	17.3	12.8	31.2	*	14.3	10.5	6.3	2.8
Cuba	*	*	*	*	*	*	*	*	*	4.5	3.1	*
France	2.0	5.0	38.0	21.0	7.4	4.4	*	*	2.3	3.1	1.9	*
Germany	*	33.3	18.0	17.2	22.3	*	*	*	0.3	0.8	*	*
Total	100.0	71.9	98.1	100.0	97.0	76.8	98.2	76.1	99.5	98.3	95.3	84.1
World production[6] (thousand tonnes)	0.5	0.5	2.5	8.1	20.2	25.0	45.0	140.0	147.8	325.5	585.4	674.0

Note: The ten most important countries for each metal, in order of importance in 1979, are included. Countries which, in a given year, did not yet belong or no longer belonged to this group are marked * for that year.
1. Including Austria and Switzerland. 2. Including Austria. 3. Belgian Congo. 4. 1970 and 1979 pig lead from ores and unrefined lead. 5. Including Indonesia. 6. 1870–1900 totals, own calculations (lower in statistics).
Sources: Calculated from *Metal Statistics*, various years; Berg and Friedensburg, 1941.

Aluminium

In the case of aluminium, German and other European concerns at first took the lead, but the United States had already become the most important producer around the turn of the century (see Table 32). In 1940 Germany still ranked first in world output of aluminium, with a 26% share. The world market share of the United States, however, which had already been at its maximum in 1920, with nearly 50%, and then reached a new peak in 1950 with a substantial 43% share, had fallen to 30% by 1979, despite further strong increases. In the past two decades the USSR has moved up to second place with approximately 16%, and aluminium production in Japan has also increased out of all proportion during this period, so that it is in third place with some 7% of world output, ahead of Canada. West Germany and Norway follow, each with about 5%, ahead of France, the United Kingdom, China and Australia, each with 2–3%. It is worth noting that the aluminium production of the United States is some eight times higher than its domestic output of bauxite (calculated on the basis of aluminium content): Jamaica, Surinam and Australia are the largest suppliers of bauxite primary raw material. The USSR has to import about a third of its bauxite, mainly from Yugoslavia and Greece.

The next most important producer countries, namely Japan, Canada, West Germany, Norway and the United Kingdom, are entirely or largely dependent on imports of aluminium-containing primary materials (bauxite and/or aluminium oxide) for supplying their smelting works, as are Austria and Switzerland (Cissarz et al., 1973, p. 43), whereas France has recourse to its own deposits and is of some importance as an exporter of aluminium. For West Germany the most important bauxite supplying countries are Australia, Yugoslavia and Sierra Leone, whereas aluminium oxide is mainly imported from Surinam and Guinea (Cissarz et al., 1973, p. 159 ff.).

Copper

World smelter output of copper is still concentrated relatively strongly in the leading group, despite diversification of its structure by country as the process of industrialization continues: in 1977 just five countries accounted together for about 60% of production of unrefined and refined copper. The 'old' European metallurgical producers were superseded by the United States even before the turn of the century. With shares of around two-thirds of world output of raw and refined copper, Europe and the United States supplied only 17% and 21% respectively of the output of unrefined copper in 1979. The large American copper concerns Kennecott, Anaconda, Phelps Dodge, Asarco, Amax, Duval, etc., are generally fully integrated from mining to smelting operations and refining, and sometimes as far as secondary processing, or they have at their disposal – as in the case of Asarco and Amax – capacities whose utilization requires extensive purchasing of concentrates. American metallurgical output up to 1970 was traditionally 10–15% above domestic mine production, although subsequently it fell to some 5% lower. A major reason for this may be the reduced supplies of ore from the now nationalized mines in Chile and Peru. Even then the output of refined copper was still about a quarter higher than mine production of unrefined copper, because a higher proportion of scrap was used.

Since the 1960s the USSR has taken second place in the world metallurgical production of unrefined and refined copper, with a share of about 15% in each case, as a result of intensive expansion of its capacities, which have nearly doubled in just three decades.

In unrefined copper production, Chile follows in third place with a 12% share, although expansion of its output temporarily lagged behind development as a result of political developments and measures to nationalize the copper industry. In other countries production of refined copper was able to pick up again. In recent years about 85% of domestic ore has been smelted inside the country, whereas Chile had been characterized by a proportion of about 95% even in the 1930s, and also from 1950 to 1970. The ratio of output of refined to unrefined copper again increased to 75% in the past decade.

Japan's deposits of copper ores are only very slight, but, by building up its metallurgical industry, it has moved up to fourth place in unrefined copper output in the last decade, and today it is actually the third largest producer of refined copper in the world. Japan's imports of copper ores – more heavily diversified than Western Europe, which also has little ore of its own – are mainly from the Philippines and Canada.

Zambia and Zaire, which as copper-exporting countries joined with Chile and Peru in the CIPEC (Conseil Intergouvernemental des Pays Exportateurs de Cuivre) in 1967,[1] are now numbered among the world's leading countries in the smelter production of copper, occupying fifth and eighth place respectively,[2] as a result of expansion of their metallurgical capacities. In Zambia practically the entire output of copper ore is now smelted within the country, and in Zaire 94%, so that export of ore is now relatively limited. Output of refined copper, however, is certainly still capable of expansion. The copper trade was greatly hampered by the closure of the Benguela railway after the civil war in Angola in 1975, as this links the African Copper Belt with the West African seaport of Lobito in Angola. Admittedly operation had largely been resumed at the end of 1978, but in the Zaire section and also in Angola extensive repairs were still needed for the transport of heavy loads – quite apart from the fact that the rail link in Angola is controlled by forces of the political opposition, and is disputed because of the transport of foreign troops. Some measure of relief for Zambia was provided by the resumption, at the beginning of 1979, of the rail link through Zimbabwe to the South African port of East London, though its capacity is limited by the long reloading time required in Zambia. Copper is again being exported via Mozambique and also the Chinese-built Tazara railway, which links the Zambian copper district to the East African port of Dar es Salaam in Tanzania – although its maintenance represents a heavy economic burden for Zambia. The railway is also used for part of the goods traffic of the mining province of Shaba in Zaire, whereas otherwise the country is dependent on time-consuming transport to its port of Matadi on the West African coast, or to East London.

Although Canada occupies fifth place in unrefined copper output, its metallurgical output could be further expanded, as its share is 64% of its ore output, whereas Peru and Poland, which follow in the next two places, already smelt more than 90% of their mining output themselves.

West Germany, together with Belgium-Luxembourg, Spain, the United Kingdom, France, Sweden and other European countries, as well as Japan, are suppliers of refined copper. They do not have any noteworthy ore base of

---

1 At the end of 1975 Indonesia was accepted as a full member of CIPEC, and Australia and Papua New Guinea, followed by Yugoslavia, became associate members (without voting rights).
2 However, African copper output has shown a declining trend in recent years, for which there are political and economic causes.

their own, but are largely dependent on imported primaries: only Belgium-Luxembourg, however, is a net importer.

Lead

Although the principal countries for smelter production before the turn of the century were Germany, Spain and the United Kingdom, the United States has occupied first place without a break from 1900 up to the present day. Its peak share was recorded in 1920, with some 52%, but after a continuous decline, the leading share – with a record figure for production, however – is only about 18%. As the trend in lead demand, apart from other industrial applications, is very closely linked with motorization, i.e. with car stocks and their utilization, it is not surprising that – after the USSR, which has occupied first place in world production since 1977 – the principal industrial nations of the Western world, Canada, Australia, West Germany, the United Kingdom, Japan and Mexico, were also principal lead producers in the smelter hierarchy. The ore deposits of the older industrial countries have, however, become largely depleted during the course of industrialization so that these countries for many years now have been operating their primary smelter production mainly on the basis of imported ores. A further sales outlet is opening here for ores from Australia, Canada, Latin America and other overseas areas, wherever their own smelter capacities are insufficient for concentration of their domestic ores.

Zinc

Here the trend is similar to that for lead. The smelting industry, which in the nineteenth century was mainly centred on the ore production in the European continent, was largely carried on in Germany and Belgium. At first only European ores were processed there, but later on imported ores and concentrates were also used, as is still the case today in these and other European countries, and in Japan. Since the turn of the century the United States, which can largely fall back on its own raw materials, has rapidly gained in importance: lead, which acquired a leading position in 1910, had doubled by 1920 with a production share of almost 60%, and in 1950 still accounted for 40%. In the 1970s, however, the United States, with a share of only 8%, was in fourth position in the world after the USSR, Japan and Canada, chiefly because of the obsolescence of the American smelting industry, which led to widespread shutdowns of production capacities.

Tin

The tin smelting industry even before the turn of the century was concentrated in the South East Asian ore countries, with a share of 70–80% of global production. The main bulk of the Malaysian, Thai, and Burmese, and part of the Dutch East Indian, ores were sent to the Straits Settlements (Malaysia) for smelting. Besides this the smelting industry in the United Kingdom, in which ores chiefly from Nigeria and Bolivia were smelted, was of special importance. Even at the end of the 1950s this structure had hardly changed, notwithstanding a decrease in the share held by these traditional producer countries. Belgium had also become a smelter for ores from the Congo, and at the German Berzelius smelter at Duisburg Bolivian ores, in particular, were concentrated (cf. Ahlfeld, 1958, p. 26 ff.).

During the past 20 years the importance of the traditional South East Asian countries has been challenged by the development of the smelting industry in Indonesia and Thailand, which now take some 50% of world production. They are followed by the USSR and China, which have become the next largest tin processors before Bolivia, Brazil, the United Kingdom, Spain, the United States and Australia. Bolivia, standing in second place after Malaysia for mine production of tin, has been for some years one of the ten leading countries for tin smelting, which may possibly be explained by the fact that the complex primary ores found there (as also in the USSR and in Australia) are considerably more difficult to smelt than the soap ores in South East Asia.[1] The smelter production of Zaire continues to decline in importance, especially owing to the low tin content of the ores, but also for reasons of shortage of skilled workers and difficulties in transport.

Nickel

The smelter production of nickel in the Western world, up to the exploitation of the deposits in New Caledonia (1874), was confined to the working of relatively small ore deposits in Germany, Greece, Italy, Norway and Sweden; the smelting of the soon considerable volume of Caledonian nickel ores was also first carried out in Europe. Since the turn of the century, however, after the discovery of deposits in the Sudbury district of Ontario, Canada has acquired a dominant position in ore mining. It was only in 1917 that, under pressure from the British Government, it started itself processing nickel matte, which up to then had mainly been sent to the United States for refining. It was soon producing almost exclusively, through the International Nickel Company of Canada Ltd and its British subsidiary Mond Nickel Company, over half the smelter production of nickel in the world. Since 1950, however, the international concentration of crude nickel production has considerably decreased. At that time only ten countries accounted for virtually the entire smelter production, but in 1977 the share had fallen to 86% and of this Canada's share, with increasing production, had decreased from 43% to 22%, and, with strikes, this had declined by 1979 to 13%. This change in structure

[1] The tin smelting capacity of Bolivia will soon rise by 10,000–30,000 tonnes per annum, because the new tin smelters equipped with German technology for concentrates with a low metal content have made it possible to produce tin with a purity grade of 99.0%; nevertheless, the supply of the plant with primary material is not yet assured (Metallgesellschaft AG, *Technische Nachrichten*, 23 August 1979).

was strongly influenced by powerful expansion of nickel production in the USSR, which today, despite its much lower mine production, by importing Cuban primary ores is now ahead of Canada in smelter production. The development of nickel production in Japan, which has no domestic ore mining but now takes third place in world smelter production through the import of primary materials from Australia, Canada and New Caledonia (nickel production began in Australia in 1970), as well as the commencement of smelting production in other countries, such as the Dominican Republic and the Philippines, have also contributed to diversify the world pattern of smelter production. Important smelter producers with comparatively small mine production are the United States, Norway and Great Britain, which, with no basic ore of their own, for the most part smelt Canadian and African nickel ores, and France, which obtains the primary material almost exclusively from New Caledonia. West Germany, which like Spain and Italy produces no crude nickel, is completely dependent on imports to cover its requirements and imports not only nickel matte and nickel speise from Canada but recently, in addition, supplies from Australia (Kästner *et al.*, 1978, p. 135 ff.).

6.3 THE COMMERCIAL STRUCTURE OF THE MINING AND SMELTING INDUSTRIES IN THE WESTERN WORLD

Although the company structure in the international mining and smelting industry did not, of course, assume its present form until the process of industrialization was under way, its specific characteristics had already become evident with the onset of the massive demand for non-ferrous metals, as a result of the particular production and market conditions in this sector of the economy. Its essential feature is the overwhelming proportion of large concerns, whose activities generally extend beyond national boundaries. The metals industry offers comparatively little scope to small and medium-sized businesses, because generally they are in no position to meet the technical and financial requirements associated with the recovery, processing and marketing of minerals. Prospecting, opening up and working of ore deposits, and the construction of metallurgical plant, impose high demands on the economic soundness and financial resources of companies – especially as the physical remoteness of the ore deposits, often located in developing countries with an inadequate infrastructure and far from the industrial countries which form the most important consumer areas, inevitably means regional scatter in production and processing. To invest and produce under such conditions and open up worldwide marketing channels requires special entrepreneurial qualities and involves exceptional economic and financial risk, which is often exacerbated by political imponderables.

The dawn of the age of technology offered a new challenge, an opportunity for the metal industry to operate on a hitherto unknown scale. This stimulated a 'promoterist' period of expansion in the late nineteenth century, as it did in other industries. Many international mining and metallurgical concerns were established then which are still of worldwide importance today (see Table 33). The wave of industrial expansion continued after the First World War with enterprises such as Selection Trust, Rio Tinto Zinc and Charter Consolidated, and many Australian and Canadian mining companies (Sames, 1971, p. 100).

There are historical reasons for the Anglo-American predominance in this phase of emergence: the United Kingdom, the oldest industrial country, was also initially the leader, during the second half of last century, in the mining of iron ore, coal and ores of copper, lead and zinc, and on the basis of this experience developed mining in its colonial empire in order to supply raw materials to the British smelting and processing industry. As the United States caught up in industrialization, its mining and metals industries gained rapidly

Table 33. The foundation of major companies in the non-ferrous metal industry, 1870–1917

Year	Original name	Present name	Country
1870	St Joseph Lead Co.	St Joe Minerals Corp.	USA
1873	Rio Tinto Co.	Rio Tinto Zinc Corp Ltd	UK
1880	Société Le Nickel	Société Le Nickel	France
1881	Metallgesellschaft	Metallgesellschaft AG	Germany
1881	Soc. Minière et Métallurgique de Penarroya	Penarroya SA	France
1883	North Broken Hill Ltd	North Broken Hill Holdings Ltd	Australia
1885	Copper Queen Consolidated Mining Co.	Phelps Dodge Corp.	USA
1887	Union de Desargentation Hoboken	Metallurgie Hoboken-Overpelt	Belgium
1887	Straits Trading Co. Ltd	Straits Trading Co. Ltd	Malaysia
1887	American Metal Co. Ltd	Amax Inc.	USA
1888	Aluminium Industrie AG, Chippis	Alusuisse	Switzerland
1885	Pittsburgh Reduction Co.	Aluminium Co. of America	USA
1888	De Beers Mining Co. Ltd	De Beers Consolidated Mines Ltd	South Africa
1889	Rand Selection Corp. Ltd	Rand Selection Corp. Ltd	South Africa
1889	Johannesburg Cons. Investment Co. Ltd	Johannesburg Cons. Investment Co. Ltd	South Africa
1882	Consolidated Gold Fields of South Africa Ltd	Consolidated Gold Fields Ltd	South Africa
1895	Anaconda Copper Corp.	Atlantic Richfield Co.	USA
1895	General Mining & Finance Corp.	General Mining & Union Corp.	South Africa
1897	Union Corp.		
1899	American Smelting & Refining Co.	Asarco Inc.	USA
1900	Aluminum Co. of Canada Ltd	Alcan Aluminium Ltd	Canada
1905	Zinc Corporation	Rio Tinto Zinc Corp.	Australia
1906	Union Minière du Haut Katanga	Union Minière	Belgium
1906	Consolidated Mining & Smelting Co. Ltd	Cominco Ltd	Canada
1915	Kennecott Copper Corp.	Kennecott Corp.	USA
1915	Broken Hill Ass. Smelters Pty Ltd	Broken Hill Ass. Smelters Pty Ltd	Australia
1915	Cerro de Pasco Corp.	Centromin	Peru
1916	Electrolytic Zinc Co. of Australasia	EZ Industries Ltd	Australia
1916	International Nickel Company of Canada Ltd	Inco Ltd	Canada
1917	Anglo American Corp. of South Africa Ltd	Anglo American Corp. of South Africa Ltd	South Africa

Note: Older companies still trading today include the Belgian firms Vieille Montagne (founded 1837) and Asturienne (1853).

in importance, and American mining activities were increasingly extended to other countries, especially in Latin America. The result was that the United Kingdom was overtaken in mining output by the United States even before the First World War and the American concerns soon gained a position of supremacy in the world market.

In the wake of industrialization came a tendency towards concentration in the business sector – hand in hand with the actual establishment of new companies. In the early phase this was for the most part a horizontal process, involving the affiliation of smaller companies in a financially weak position to more powerful competitors, which was often favoured by the fact that the mining companies operated in the same geographical areas. Although at first efforts towards concentration on the part of the concerns were primarily motivated by the desire to monopolize the markets (in the case of copper, for example), later on there were economic and technical reasons aimed at creating by means of large-scale enterprises the necessary conditions for economic mining of generally low-grade ores. The resultant large mining concerns are in general still able, even today, to supply beyond the needs of their own metal works and provide a proportion of the basic raw materials required for metallurgical and processing industries which are operating without their own resources. In recent years there has been a decisive change in this respect in some developing countries due to nationalization of their mines and metallurgical works.

In addition to concentration at a horizontal level, concerns were also soon expanded in the sense of vertical integration: more and more stages of production came under centralized control from the mine to the smelter and refinery right up to the manufacture of semi-finished goods, either by mine works incorporating later stages of production in order to secure sales outlets or by metallurgical works and manufacturers of intermediates bringing mining operations under their control in order to safeguard their supplies of raw materials. Although of course the processes of horizontal and vertical concentration were often taking place at the same time, they were also observed to alternate.[1] The fact that in Europe mergers in the metals industry mainly took place between refineries and manufacturers of intermediates is due to the shortage of raw materials there.

Important efforts were also made towards concentration in metal trading: as early as 1887 the American Metal Co. was established by Metallgesellschaft AG in association with the firm of Henry R. Merton, an important English metal dealing company, which itself had close links with Metallgesellschaft. Even before the First World War, Metallgesellschaft AG in Frankfurt had acquired a controlling interest in the Norddeutsche Affinerie, Hamburg, and the Vereinigte Deutsche Metallwerke AG was also included among its

[1] Concentration processes in the development of American copper concerns are described by Knoblich (1962, p. 63 ff.).

concerns in the copper processing sector. Another example is the firm Aron Hirsch und Sohn, which took over the Ilsenburg copper works and the Eberswalde brass works so that it would have an industrial base for its trading products (Knoblich, 1962, p. 81 ff.). A similar process in the United States was the establishment of the Phelps-Dodge copper concern on the part of the New York trading establishment of the same name.

As the pattern of companies in the international metals economy is an important factor in determining the structure of the supply and hence of pricing in metal markets, this is described in outline below for the most important branches of the metal industry.

Aluminium

Development of the aluminium industry and especially the explosive growth in output since the middle of the 1930s were accompanied by considerable concentration in the business sector. The rapidly increasing consumption of this metal in the leading industrial countries prepared the ground for the establishment of large concerns, the activities of which were broad-based from the very beginning. The leading concerns generally unite all production stages from extraction of the raw material bauxite – primarily in developing countries – via alumina production for the enrichment of aluminium oxide and production of the metal in the metalworks, to further processing of the metal in plants for manufacture of intermediates, including foundries, foil-rolling mills and remelting works. It may be observed that integration operates more effectively from the bauxite mine to the aluminium electrolysis than from the latter stage up to the manufacture of intermediates.

Among the large concerns the lead was easily taken for many decades by the Aluminium Company of America (Alcoa) which, like its predecessor the Pittsburgh Reduction Company, had a virtual monopoly of production in the United States and, by controlling the largest proportion of world output by cartel agreements, was able to determine the price of aluminium. This monopoly position, lasting practically from 1890 to the Second World War, and unique in the history of American industry, was ended by a judgment of the US Supreme Court,[1] following which a number of new aluminium producing companies were organized with government assistance (Brubaker, 1967, p. 100).

Twelve companies are currently engaged in aluminium production in the USA, among which Alcoa, with approximately one-third of domestic capacity, still takes the lead. Alcoa and the next largest concerns, Reynolds Metal Company and Kaiser Aluminium and Chemical Corporation, together

[1] Already in the 1930s the US anti-trust authorities imposed restrictions on Alcoa enforcing the disincorporation of their assets abroad. These companies were combined in Aluminium Ltd (Alcan) with headquarters in Canada. Alcoa and Alcan for many years were not permitted to have joint shareholders.

produce almost two-thirds of American output of primary aluminium. Among the major aluminium producers worldwide, some way behind these three American concerns, are Alcan Aluminium (Canada), Pechiney Ugine Kuhlmann SA (France) and Alusuisse-Schweizerische Aluminium AG (Switzerland). These six concerns and their subsidiaries and shareholdings in 1979 accounted for some 45% of bauxite and 64% of alumina production capacities and 52% of smelter capacity for primary aluminium compared with 65%, 72% and 59% in 1974. The loosening of the structure to be observed during the post-war years is still continuing but the large concerns mentioned – mainly as consortia – are today involved in virtually all the most important aluminium projects in the Western world (Stamper and Kurtz, 1978).

Apart from these six principal companies, a further fifty firms together produce around one-quarter of world production of bauxite, alumina and aluminium. Most of these firms are not integrated and some are State enterprises – including the West German government-owned Vereinigte Aluminiumwerke AG – or are operated with the State as a major shareholder – for example in Jamaica, which has nationalized 51% of its bauxite mining (Sies, 1978, p. 23). Such firms are associated with the major aluminium concerns in the form of a partnership (see Appendix, Table A1).

Copper

As demand for this key raw material expanded with the progress of industrialization, the structure of companies in the industry was characterized by the fact that a comparatively small group of mining concerns was able to secure control over a large part of ore mining and metal production, in an effort to dominate the international copper market. Mine and smelter production in the United States was first concentrated in the hands of a few producers, among which the Anaconda, Kennecott and Phelps Dodge Groups already had a considerable lead before the First World War. At the end of the war the American firms became active in the copper mining sector in Chile, Mexico, Canada and Peru. By 1926 American mining concerns already controlled 75% of world mine production and 48% of copper mining outside the United States. Belgian and British group interests, such as Union Minière du Haut-Katanga, Société Générale Metallurgique de Hoboken, British Metal Corporation and Rio Tinto Corporation, encouraged by the political ties existing at that time between the industrialized countries and the overseas territories, established the copper deposits in the Belgian Congo, Katanga and Rhodesia, and also Canada, as their preferred zones of influence, in some cases with the participation of American capital. In 1926 these groups controlled 12% of world mine production of copper and 27% of copper mining outside the United States. Up to 1937 the ratio of strength, under the influence of the economic recession, was still in favour of the British, Belgian and Canadian concerns. The American firms, however, with 62%, compared with the 24% of the other groups, still dominated world mining production and with 43%, compared with 36%, also exercised major control over copper mining outside the United States. The collective share of the two groups from 1926 to 1937 was between 81% and 90% of world copper mining (Glebsattel, p. 73 ff.).

The high concentration in the company structure of the copper industry under the dominance of the major Anglo-American companies was maintained even after the Second World War. In 1959 the 12 major firms with 2.8 million tonnes were responsible for 75% of mine production of copper and together produced 3.8 million tonnes, approximately 80% of refinery capacity. After 1968, they accounted for approximately 66% of mine production with 2.98 million tonnes and, with 5.1 million tonnes, around 77% of refinery capacity for copper. The opening up of new mines all over the world in response to the growing demand for copper increased the number of copper-producing countries, and led to increasing nationalization measures in the most important copper-producing countries, Chile, Zaire, Zambia and Peru. These were accompanied by a distinct change in the company structure of the world copper industry. At the end of 1978 the 12 major mining producers at 3.8 million tonnes still disposed of 42% of mining capacity and with 3.7 million tonnes of 40% refinery capacity in the Western world. Apart from a reduction in the sphere of influence of the top group of copper-producing concerns, these figures also clearly reveal that the vertical concentration in these has considerably diminished. This especially applies to the wholly or partly nationalized copper concerns in Chile, Zaire and Zambia, whose refining capacity at 75.5% or 90% (particularly in the two first-named countries) is still considerably above their mining capacity. In contrast Japan and West Germany, in particular, dispose of surplus refinery capacity.

The structure of ownership in the world copper industry and hence also the balance of power in the copper market have changed especially by the nationalization of foreign ownership in copper mines, copper smelters and refineries. The wave of nationalization moves began in 1966 in Congo-Kinshasa, the present-day Zaire, with the taking over of all works and other assets of the Union Minière du Haut-Katanga (UMHK) by the state-owned company La Générale des Congolais de Minerais (GECOMIN), which since 1973 has been trading under the name La Générale des Carrières et des Mines (GECAMIN). The payment initially agreed for 15 years for the remaining management and compensation was discharged in 1975 with a payment of 4 billion Belgian francs. Marketing from now on is in the hands of the state export company Sté. Zaroise de Commercialisation des Minerais (SOZACOM). The nationalization of US property in Chile began in 1967 with the taking over by the Chilean Government of 51% of the capital of the El Tiente Mine of the Braden Copper Company, which up to then had been completely in the possession of the American Kennecott Copper Corporation. The same procedure occurred in 1970 with the Chuquicamata and El Salvador plants of the American Anaconda Company. Compensation payments are being made for these under long-term agreements. Marketing continued to be in the hands of the American companies who had to guarantee the Chilean industry a share of production. Nationalization was completed in 1971, when compensation payments were set against failure to re-invest and 'excess profits' of previous years. The marketing company is now the government-owned Corporación del Cobre (CODELCO) (Forster, 1976, p. 73 ff.).[1] Recently it became known, however, that the Chilean Government were restricting their commitments in the copper sector to the large-state-owned mines and that they aim to restore the remaining property to private ownership. This policy of opening the door to foreign investment and private investment is intended to be a cornerstone of the Chilean programme for freeing the economy from political control and introducing a free market system.[2]

In Zambia the Government took over at the beginning of 1970 51% of the foreign capital invested in the copper industry, the rest remaining the property of the Anglo-American Corporation and of the Roan Selection Trust Ltd (RST) – 80% of whose capital had previously been in American hands – which combined their works in Roan Consolidated Mines Ltd (RCM) or Nchanga Consolidated Mines Ltd (NCCM) and maintained the most important copper mines of the country in operation on the basis of ten-year contracts. The final nationalization began in 1973, and in 1975 ownership of the most important mines was transferred to the State. The state holding company Zambia International and Mining Corporation (Zimco) via sub-holding companies controls over 90 firms and marketing is carried on by the state trading company Metal Marketing Corporation of Zambia (MEMACO). In Peru the Government in 1973–74 resorted to measures which virtually implied nationalization of the leading company for mining, smelting and refining, the Cerro de Pasco Corporation, whose works were transferred to the state-owned company Cetromice Peru. The Southern Peru Copper Corporation, however, still remained in the hands of American firms (Schroeder, 1977, p. 4).

Apart from full nationalization in the above countries, a form of government influence has also been established, under which foreign private capital is only permitted under certain official conditions with a minority shareholding of the state. Other copper-producing countries are also adopting such measures,

---

1 The smaller and medium-sized copper mining works were merged into the state-owned Chilean company ENAMI.
2 The Anaconda Company USA has therefore succeeded with a $20 million bid for the copper deposits at Los Pelambres, which with proven ore reserves of some 428 million tonnes is over three times as large as those of the four major copper mines currently in operation in the country, though the ores are admittedly of considerably lower Cu content.

such as the Philippines, Papua-New Guinea, Botswana and, not least, Iran, where state control over the exploitation of raw material resources will no doubt increase (Gebhardt and Knördl, 1977, p. 26).

Even after the changes in ownership conditions described above, the structure of companies in the world copper industry at the end of 1979 still displays a remarkable concentration in all areas (see Appendix, Table A2). A large portion of refinery capacity is still quite clearly with the large American concerns but the developing countries have gained considerable ground. In this connection should also be mentioned the activity of the Conseil Intergouvernemental des Pays Exporteurs de Cuivre (CIPEC) set up by Chile, Zambia, Zaire and Peru in 1967.

Lead

The scattered distribution of lead deposits over the earth has helped to determine the features of company structure in this field of the metal industry. There is a top group of leading firms, divided among many countries, among which none is dominant worldwide. Nevertheless, there is still a certain amount of concentration in the lead industry, as the ten leading concerns combined at present together account for some 45% of smelter capacity of refined lead in the Western world and the 15 largest firms bring it up to some 50% altogether (see Appendix, Table A5). A decentralization tendency however cannot be overlooked in this field, as even as late as 1969 five firms had possessed control of over 41% of the total smelting capacity for lead in the Western world and the ten largest firms were able to control almost two-thirds of the production potential of lead smelters in this region.

The major concerns, without exception, are integrated from the mine up to the final processing, but in the lead and zinc industries, to a greater degree than in the copper industry, there are also independent mineworkings, smelters and refineries. As a rule jobbing smelters and refineries obtain their materials supplies from imported ores and concentrates and frequently dispose of primary material from their own mines as well. Smelters of large concerns also sometimes carry out jobbing contracts in order to extend the utilization of their capacities (Cissarz *et al.*, 1971, p. 22 ff.).

Apart from Australia, where the Rio Tinto concern accounts almost exclusively for the entire smelter production of lead, the regional concentration in this industrial sector is most pronounced in North America. In the United States in 1979 five integrated mining and smelter concerns – Asarco Inc., St Joe Minerals Corporation, Amax-Homestake Lead Tollers, Gould Inc. and the Bunker Hill Co. – produced two-thirds of domestic mine output. The other mine production is accounted for chiefly by three other large companies, which, like those previously mentioned (with the exception of Amax-Homestake), at the same time control zinc production as well. On the other hand there are a large number of firms in America (over 200 in 1971) engaged in secondary lead recovery. In Canada two major integrated concerns – Cominco Ltd and Brunswick Mining and Smelting Corporation – are dominant; the Canadian firms produce around 15% of lead exports in the world. In the lead industry – to a greater extent than that of copper – European firms also belong to the top group of world producers. By refinery capacity, the leading concerns include Société Minière et Metallurgique de Penarroya (France), Metallgesellschaft AG with Berzelius Metallhütten GmbH, and their central shareholdings in Blei- und Silberhütte Braubach and Norddeutsche Affinerie and the Preussag Group (West Germany), Refined Metals and the Associated Lead Manufacturers Ltd (United Kingdom), Metallurgie Hoboken-Overpelt (Belgium) and SAMIM SpA and the Tonolli Group (Italy): these are among the fifteen leading companies which today combine to produce about a quarter of world output. These are for the most part firms which already existed before the turn of the century; they represent a traditional branch of the metals industry in Europe, which, when industrial development began towards the end of the nineteenth century, were competing to supply over two-thirds of world production. Since the advances made by the large American concerns and the start of lead production in many other countries, including a number of developing countries – Peru nationalized the mining companies and Mexico 'Mexicanized' them – the world market share of these companies continued to shrink, without their being ousted, however, from the top group.

In recent decades it may be observed that the market shares of worldwide leading concerns in the lead industry have undergone only slight fluctuation. This is a clear indication that outsiders have hardly any chance of penetrating the lead market today, certainly not unless they co-operate with an established concern (Althaus and Baack, 1977, p. 8).

Zinc

The structure of the zinc industry has always been similar to that of lead, as these two metals largely occur in the same deposits and usually in association. The concentration of firms in the mining of zinc ores in the Western world is however lower: 15 firms together supplied some 50% of total mine production in 1973, and in some countries production is restricted to one or two firms (Forster, 1976, p. 210). The major concerns, which are usually multinationals, have without exception a vertical integration structure from the mine to the smelter stage. However, some companies do not possess smelter capacities adequate to process their mining production (Canadian Electrolytic Zinc Ltd, Texasgulf Inc., Asarco Inc., Centromin Peru), while others have a mine production which has lagged behind demand, so that they have to rely on supplies from other domestic mines or on imported concentrates for the utilization of their production plant (Mitsui Mining & Smelting Company Ltd (Japan), Electrolytic Zinc Company (Australia), Outocumpu Oy (Finland),

Metallgesellschaft AG and Preussag (West Germany) and also the zinc smelters in Yugoslavia).

In this production sector, too, however, the increasing rate of breakdown of the traditional structures is unmistakable, as already by 1979 the ten major companies accounted for only 46% of total capacity (see Appendix, Table A6). The concentration in Europe is here higher than in the United States: the capacities of the eight principal companies in Europe are sufficient to cover 90% of zinc consumption in this region, whereas in the United States the five major concerns cater for only half of the domestic zinc requirements. A noteworthy feature is the extent to which the Japanese zinc producers have forged ahead: in 1979 the four largest Japanese firms already accounted for some 25% of the smelter capacity of the 15 leading concerns in the Western world.

Tin

Whereas up to the Second World War there was a very closely knit association between the recovery and smelting of tin, a marked loosening of vertical links subsequently occurred (Stodiek, 1970, p. 27), while mergers of suppliers of tin concentrates tended to increase. Thus, Bolivia carried out nationalization of the three major mining concerns and the transfer of exports of the still private mines to the Banco Minero (between 1952 and 1956) for the complete pooling of supplies, and in recent years the State has still remained the largest supplier. In Indonesia tin mining at Bangka, Billiton and Singapore is likewise run by the State and tin ore mining is also nationalized in Zaire. Ownership of the mines is more widely dispersed in Malaysia, Thailand and Nigeria but there, too, a few large firms predominate. The fifteen leading mining companies have approximately a 50% share of total capacity. In the smelter sector of industry, in which the major mining companies are hardly represented, the principal firms in Malaysia, the United Kingdom, the United States and the Netherlands, even in the post-war period, were together responsible for about 90% of production in the Western world. Since then the distribution of supplier companies has fanned out, owing to the erection of tin smelters in Thailand, Nigeria, Australia, Zaire and Brazil, but even today the five largest concerns dispose of two-thirds of smelter capacity for crude tin in the world (see Appendix, Table A3).

The competitive behaviour of the suppliers has been influenced by the seven producer countries combining in the International Tin Agreement (ITA) for the purpose of price stabilization. As a supplier group their market hegemony is modified relatively by the participation of the most important consumer countries in the Agreement.

Nickel

The heaviest concentration among the quantitatively most important metals is displayed by the nickel industry. In 1979 up to 67% of mine extraction of nickel was in the hands of the four concerns Inco (Canada), Falconbridge Nickel Mines Ltd (Canada), Le Nickel SLN (France) and Western Mining (Australia), who jointly share 57% of total production capacities (refineries and smelters) for nickel commodities.[1] During the past 30 years the number of suppliers has increased from three (in the early 1950s) to over 20. The London Metal Exchange, with the introduction of a nickel contract on 3 April 1979, has now permitted 11 relatively large nickel producers whose metal meets the stipulated requirements access to trading at the Exchange. Symptomatic of this structural loosening process is the fact that in 1969 91% of Western production of crude nickel was still accounted for by the five leading producer countries, whereas in 1977 this figure was only 68%. At the same time the market share of Inco (Canada), the largest supplier to the Western market, was pushed down from 37% in 1970 to 14% in 1979 (Forster, 1976, p. 172 ff.).

The loosening structure of the market supply of nickel is attributable to a number of reasons. It is partly associated with the recent discovery and exploitation of new deposits, including those in Australia, but it may also possibly be due to the fact that the ore-winning countries are now making greater efforts to smelt their ores and concentrates domestically rather than exporting them. A certain part may be played by the fact that the location of crude nickel production was traditionally mainly determined by the prevailing economic circumstances from the mining point of view and by the availability of a cheap power supply, whereas today sales orientation is gaining influence as a factor for the choice of smelter location. In this, however, the prevailing environmental control legislation again has an inhibiting effect (Kästner, 1978, p. 135 ff.).

Steel improvers and alloying and special metals (minor metals)

The structure of companies in the production of steel improvers and alloying and special metals is similar to that for the basic metals, as the former are also extracted as by-products at the main workings of the mining concerns. The large copper producers are therefore at the same time the leading producers of arsenic, selenium, rhenium, and tellurium and supply the biggest proportion of molybdenum on the market, of which Amax Inco. (USA), supported by the molybdenum deposits in Colorado, has the maximum world share with 60%. The leading firms in lead and zinc extraction also produce the highest proportion of cadmium, germanium, antimony, bismuth, indium, thallium and gallium. In the mining of rare earths the Molybdenum Corporation of America – which is the strongest vertically integrated company – leads with a

1 Ferro-nickel, nickel powder, nickel oxides, nickel sulphides and nickel metal.

share of around 60% of world production and jointly with a subsidiary of the American chemical giant Du Pont de Nemours controls approximately two-thirds of world production. The famous names among the production companies also include Earth Ltd (India) and Nuclebras (Brazil), which likewise have a fairly extensive vertical integration structure (Sames, 1971, p. 173).

7

The supply situation of the principal consumer countries

7.1 THE SUPPLY OF MINING PRODUCTS AND PRIMARY METALS

The trend in international metal consumption during the course of industrialization and the simultaneous change observable in the regional structure of world mining and smelter production indicate a growing discrepancy in volume between the demand and supply of non-ferrous metal ores and of the metals. In regard to the supply situation it may also be observed that over a similar period surpluses and deficits in international ore mining had been for many years much more pronounced than those in metal production. The share taken by mine production (according to metal content) in the consumption of smelter products is shown in the regional breakdown of supplies of mine products (Table 34).

During the course of industrialization Europe has become increasingly dependent on imports and by 1979 this had reached the following scale of magnitude: for aluminium 60%, copper 90%, lead 70%, zinc 40%, tin 95% and nickel 90%. In the countries of the EEC the deficiency quota to be imported amounts to 87% for aluminium, 99.7% copper, 85% lead, 52% zinc and 100% nickel. North America, after a previously fairly balanced position of supplies for aluminium, has become increasingly dependent on imports since 1930 (94% in 1979). The supply of copper ores – after production had considerably pushed up domestic requirements at the turn of the century – has increasingly lagged behind domestic consumption since 1950 (16% in 1979). Dependence on lead imports has increased to 40%. The supply quota for zinc diminished between 1920 and 1979 by some 60 percentage points to 130%, whereas for nickel, from the surplus position recorded in 1950, an import share of 25% had developed by 1979. For tin, North America, owing to a lack of its own mineable deposits, has always been completely dependent on the import of primary raw materials.

Latin America, owing to increasing industrialization and hence growing consumption, has reduced its surplus of all important metals substantially but

Table 34. Total world supplies of non-ferrous metals from mine and smelter production by regions, 1890–1979

Metal and year	Western Europe	EEC	North America	Latin America	Asia	Africa	Australia and Oceania	Eastern Bloc countries	World
\multicolumn{10}{c}{Proportion of mine production[1] to consumption of smelter products (%)}
Aluminium									
1930	254.9		88.4		5.5		66.7		207.1
1950	79.0	69.8[3]	38.4	4,260.7	540.6	1,690.0	14.3	136.4	132.9
1979	39.2	12.7	6.2	872.3	29.6	1,965.6	2,549.4	69.6	108.1
Copper									
1900	27.9		162.5	714.2[2]	←	573.5	→		96.4
1950	14.4	8.0[3]	91.0	776.3	186.2	2,231.3	45.4	76.9	103.6
1979[4]	9.8	0.3	84.1	342.4	31.7	1,364.1	312.6	79.4	80.5
Lead									
1920	51.7		87.4	796.4	117.2	2,855.0	128.6		88.3
1950	39.7	13.6[3]	63.5	491.3	48.6	712.5	478.9	78.8	90.3
1979[5]	28.8	14.9	60.1	165.8	27.5	222.5	509.7	73.3	66.0
Zinc									
1920	67.5		188.8	284.0	106.4	2,000.0	0		122.7
1950	51.3	27.1[3]	88.1	1,096.2	68.5	995.4	387.3	104.6	106.5
1979	57.0	37.6	129.7	298.8	33.8	177.8	444.9	101.5	99.9
Tin									
1920	7.2		0	1,505.0	865.6	1,620.6	286.7		97.3
1950	4.9	3.2[3]	0	769.8	869.8	896.2	73.1	72.9	104.0
1979	5.5	4.6	0	287.5	314.8	304.9	308.1	68.2	101.2
Nickel									
1950	1.2	2.2[3]	119.9	400.0	0	1,066.7[3]	860.0	98.7	93.6
1979	9.7	0	74.8	286.1	49.3	1,125.9	2,947.2	111.1	89.5
\multicolumn{10}{c}{Proportion of smelter production to consumption of smelter products (%)}
Aluminium									
1900	315.4		110.3	0					95.2
1950	61.5	48.5[3]	111.9	0	109.8	0	0	89.6	82.1
1979	71.2	51.3	77.3	104.2	48.5	239.9	156.6	77.8	74.8
Copper									
1890	68.0		163.3[6]	584.1[2]	695.5[7]	← 213.7[6] →			97.3
1950	22.3	6.5[3]	96.1	686.4	111.6	2,091.8	47.1	77.6	103.6
1979[4]	17.2	6.8	70.0	304.1	60.5	1,294.5	134.3	80.3	79.1
Lead									
1890	93.5		106.8[6]	808.0[9]	111.9[9]	876.7[9]	1,146.1[6]		94.8
1950	77.3	70.7[3]	73.4	369.7	48.0	294.6	429.7	85.6	98.3
1979	95.2	95.2	101.1	160.5	64.9	158.3	310.5	92.6	101.2
Zinc									
1890	103.9		100.8[6]	0[9]	40.0[9]	0[9]	245.0[9]		100.4
1950	85.1	80.9[3]	104.9	184.4	63.3	153.3	162.2	100.6[10]	99.3
1979	106.8	93.5	95.9	98.4	78.1	150.2	255.5	103.9	101.7
Tin									
1910	74.6		0	47.6	890.0[9]	0	550.0		101.6
1950	114.0	79.2[3]	44.2	30.2	594.1	157.5	76.9	72.9[10]	109.9
1979	38.8	33.9	8.6	207.0	322.6	146.3	146.0	68.0	103.6

1. Metal content. 2. 1910. 3. 1960. 4. Consumption of refined copper, since unrefined copper given only to 1975. 5. Consumption of refined lead. 6. 1900. 7. Japan only. 8. Consumption and production of refined lead. 9. 1920. 10. USSR only.
Source: Calculated from *Metal Statistics*, various years.

The supply situation of principal consumers 161

it is still one of the main regions for supplying the principal metals to countries dependent on imports.

The development of mine production in Asia, owing to deliberate acceleration of industrialization in the region, particularly in Japan, has failed to keep pace with the boom in consumption. Apart from tin, therefore, which has continued appreciably to exceed demand, the dependence of the region on imported copper, lead and zinc enormously increased between 1950 and 1979.

Africa, despite a decrease in mine production by regions owing to a rise in its own consumption needs, is still one of the most important surplus areas in the world for bauxite, copper, lead, zinc, tin and nickel.

Australia and Oceania during recent decades have become an important surplus producer region (for, e.g., bauxite) and exports of cobalt, lead, zinc and nickel have increased considerably. The ratio of smelter production to consumption of smelter products is shown in the supply of primary metals. This is much higher than in mine production (Table 35), because of considerable expansion of smelter capacities. No account is taken here of dependence on ores and concentrates.

The principal consumer countries vary in the extent to which they are able to cover their requirements for primary aluminium from their own production;

Table 35. The supply of non-ferrous metals from mine and smelter production in selected industrial countries, 1890–1979

	USA	Japan	West Germany	France	Italy	UK
	Proportion of mine production[1] to consumption of smelter products (%)					
Aluminium						
1920	173.1	–	19.9	459.8	163.8	0
1950	41.2	0	2.1	365.8	80.7	0
1979	8.7	0	0	82.7	1.5	0
Copper[2]						
1890	115.4	660.9	38.0	0	53.5	1.3
1950	63.8	65.2	0.9	0.5	0.6	0
1979	64.5	4.4	0.1	0.1	0.1	0
Lead						
1920	88.5	15.9	57.2	3.4	158.0	6.9
1950	40.7	44.3	46.7	16.8	63.9	1.4
1979	40.1	17.6	9.1	14.0	10.6	0.7
Zinc						
1920	182.1	46.5	208.9	3.7	798.0	1.5
1950	61.8	101.2	74.7	12.8	263.9	0
1979	29.4	31.3	28.1	12.8	29.1	0
Tin						
1920	0	–	0	0	0	0
1950	0	6.4	0	0	0	3.8
1979	0	2.2	0	0	0	17.4

Table 35. (cont'd)

	USA	Japan	West Germany	France	Italy	UK
Proportion of smelter production to consumption of smelter products (%)
Aluminium						
1900	110.3	0[3]	71.4[4]	142.9	88.9[5]	185.2[5]
1950	79.2	130.5	55.8	109.8	77.9	16.3
1979	91.0	56.1	69.5	66.3	60.1	86.1
Copper[2]						
1890	107.2[6]	665.2	51.5	0.5	0	117.0
1950	104.0	132.3	109.2	17.9	15.2	47.1
1979	88.6	74.0	48.2	12.6	4.4	24.4
Lead						
1890	83.5	0[6]	122.6	17.7[6]	89.8	30.6
1950	58.8	0[6]	140.9	68.6	82.7	31.3
1979	91.4	82.8	103.3	103.9	48.9	110.5
Zinc						
1890	98.7	0[4]	122.9[6]	46.4	212.1[6]	38.0
1950	90.3	95.1	103.3	70.9	112.8	28.2
1979	52.7	101.4	85.2	86.9	90.1	32.1
Tin						
1890	0	22.0[3]	0	0	0	54.4
1950	46.5	8.5	10.1	0	0	122.9
1979	9.5	4.2	27.0	0	0	86.4
Nickel						
1953	32.7	152.6	17.6	50.8	0	138.9
1960	34.7	106.3	10.9	51.5	0	123.4
1979	21.9	80.2	1.2	6.7	0	54.0

1. Metal content. 2. From 1950: refined copper. 3. 1930. 4. 1920. 5. 1910. 6. 1900.
Source: Compiled and calculated from *Metal Statistics*, various years.

import dependence in 1979 ranged from 44% for Japan, 40% for Italy, 27% for France, 30% for West Germany to 14% for the United Kingdom and 9% for the United States.

For raw copper production (unrefined copper cake) the United States in 1975 recorded a surplus of around 20% over consumption, Japan showed an even balance in supply and demand, while West Germany still had a supply deficit of 58% and France, Italy and the United Kingdom have had to rely on imports of primary materials to cover their requirements. The trend in refined copper shows that the supply quotas of the major consumer countries of the Western world have declined during the course of industrialization. In the United States in 1979 a figure of 89% was recorded (1970 109%), in Japan 74% (1970 86%) and in West Germany some 48% (1970 58%). In contrast the United Kingdom with only 24% (1970 37%), France with 13% (1970 10%) and Italy with 4% (1970 6%) continued to be heavily dependent on imports. In these countries the expansion of refinery capacities has lagged considerably behind the increase in consumption.

The supply situation of principal consumers

In the case of lead the United States recorded a deficiency quota in smelter production compared with consumption of 9% in 1979, and Japan recorded 17%. France, on the other hand, was largely able to cover its supply requirements from domestic production. West Germany was still able to maintain its traditional surplus position and the United Kingdom in 1979, under the influence of a comparative downturn in consumption, was likewise an exporting country. Italy, however, chiefly because of the high share of consumption of its automotive industry, displayed a comparatively high import requirement of some 50%.

In zinc Japan recorded a 1979 smelter production in excess of domestic consumption and France and Italy also achieved more favourable results than in 1950, as they were able to cover some 90% of their demands from their own supplies. In the United Kingdom the situation remained almost unchanged with an import quota of 68%. West Germany, which like Japan and Italy has the advantage of some ore deposits of its own, slipped from a surplus position in 1950 to a deficit of some 15% in 1979. The United States, with a 47% import quota, showed an even more adverse supply balance in 1979.

In the case of tin, among the leading consumer countries of the Western world only the United Kingdom and West Germany have any appreciable smelter plants at their disposal. These countries were able in 1979 to meet up to 86% and 27% respectively of their consumption from domestic production but have to rely on imports of primary materials. The United States with 10% and Japan with 4% produce only a very small part of their smelter production requirements themselves, while France and Italy are completely dependent on imports.

The supply situation for nickel in the principal Western consumer countries is largely in deficit as Japan and the EEC countries completely lack an ore base, and in the United States is only very slight. In the countries mentioned (with the exception of Italy) smelter capacities do exist, however, on the basis of imported primary raw materials, so that in 1979 the following supply quotas were recorded: United States 22%, Japan 80%, West Germany 1%, France 27% and the United Kingdom 54%.

In the regional breakdown of non-ferrous smelter products supply in the Western world, dependence on imports is increasing, to varying degrees, in the major industrial zones North America and Europe for aluminium, copper, lead, zinc (except North America) and tin (see Table 34, p. 160). The supplier countries continued to be those with abundant raw materials – Latin America, Africa, Australia and Oceania – which have achieved very substantial progress in the expansion of their smelter production over the past ten years, even though, with decreasing surpluses as a result of progressive industrialization in these regions, an increasing domestic need must be anticipated.

The regional analysis of the supply structure for non-ferrous metals has

Table 36. Proportion of mine production to smelter production of non-ferrous metals by regions, 1920–79

	1920	1950	1960	1979		1920	1950	1960	1979
	Western Europe					EEC			
Aluminium	38.3	128.4	124.9	55.1	Aluminium			115.4	24.7
Copper	77.8	66.9	61.5	57.3	Copper			7.1	4.1
Lead	81.3	50.9	41.9	30.2	Lead			24.9	15.7
Zinc	98.3	60.3	60.3	53.4	Zinc			16.1	40.2
Tin	12.7	4.3	4.3	12.9	Tin				12.0
	North America					Latin America			
Aluminium	56.9[1]	134.0	30.9	8.1	Aluminium			17,800.1	836.3
Copper	107.0	95.4	93.9	120.2	Copper	90.3	113.5	110.2	112.6
Lead	102.7	104.1	75.9	59.4	Lead	98.6	45.5	184.1	103.3
Zinc	128.0	101.2	72.9	192.8	Zinc		1,371.6	487.6	151.4
Tin					Tin		2,546.2	762.1	138.9
	Asia					Africa			
Aluminium	245.9[1]	1,969.0	239.9	61.2	Aluminium			10,107.7	819.2
Copper	102.0	165.4	95.6	52.4	Copper	118.8	106.7	104.3	105.4
Lead	104.7	101.2	86.0	42.4	Lead	203.8	241.8	331.1	140.5
Zinc	266.0	108.7	102.0	43.4	Zinc		650.0	319.0	118.7
Tin	97.3	147.0	110.5	97.6	Tin		568.3	559.5	208.3
	Australia and Oceania					Eastern Bloc countries			
Aluminium			149.2	1,627.6	Aluminium		608.7	138.5	89.5
Copper	110.6	96.2	154.0	232.8	Copper		99.3	98.6	98.8
Lead	329.3	111.7	150.1	160.8	Lead		93.4	102.2	79.2
Zinc		238.7	270.1	174.1	Zinc		104.0	106.1	97.7
Tin	102.4	95.0	95.7	218.5	Tin		100.0	100.0	100.3

1. 1940.
Source: Calculated from *Metal Statistics*, various years.

already furnished indications that both the major industrial regions of the Western world are heavily reliant on imports of primary raw materials and, despite their considerable expansion of smelter production, almost without exception have a deficiency requirement of smelter products, compared with the comparatively slight one in mine products. This is shown even more clearly by the supply situation of the leading Western consumer countries (Table 35, p. 161).

It is in aluminium that the leading consumer countries of the West display the largest supply deficit of primary raw materials – which in the United States, still one of the surplus countries in 1920, had risen by 1979 to 91%. Japan, West Germany and the United Kingdom import the primary material for aluminium production because they lack their own mineable bauxite deposits.

The import requirements for mining products of copper have also increased in all the countries mentioned. Although the United States was able to meet two-thirds of its requirements for raw material products from its own ore resources, West Germany, France, Italy and the United Kingdom today have virtually no mineable deposits, so that they have to obtain their supplies of primary raw materials from imports. This is also largely true of Japan (Gebhard and Knörndel, 1977, p. 32).

In the case of lead and zinc the supply deficits in all the countries mentioned have continually risen during the course of industrialization. They are, however, less pronounced than those of the two metals mentioned above. The United Kingdom has traditionally the greatest supply deficit in lead, because of the essential lack of a domestic basis – not even 1% of its consumption of primary lead could be met from its own ore production. This was followed by West Germany with a deficit of 91%, France 86%, Italy 89% and Japan 82%, whereas the United States was still able to cover some 40% of its domestic consumption from its own ore basis. In the case of zinc – with declining supply quotas – the United States, Japan, West Germany and Italy in 1978 were able to cover about a third of consumption from their domestic primary materials, whereas France imported up to 87% and the United Kingdom up to 100%.

The most marked difference in this structure of demand and supply is in the case of tin ores: the United States, West Germany, France and Italy have to rely on imports to cover their requirements and in 1979 only the United Kingdom drew on 17% from its own supplies.

7.2 THE IMPORTANCE OF SECONDARY RECOVERY

As well as mine production – the primary production – the recycling of remelted metals and scrap, forming the so-called secondary production, also plays an important part in the supply of non-ferrous metals to industry. This applies especially in the consumer countries which are lacking in their own primary resources or only have inadequate mineable deposits of non-ferrous metals. This is because remelted metals are generally not waste materials but raw materials which can lend themselves to recycling any number of times and can again be incorporated in production. Non-ferrous metals are in this respect non-polluting materials and, on the contrary, their potential recycling clears the environment of the waste materials that occur directly or indirectly in consumption and by the use of recovered materials serves to conserve natural resources. Recycling, in view of the ever-increasing volume of 'waste products' to be observed as industrialization progresses, therefore represents an anti-pollution factor of increasing relevance as a source of raw materials and as an energy conservation expedient for the economic use of resources and a means of spreading the use of these vital materials over a longer time span.

Waste materials and residues occurring in the processing of metals to intermediates and finished products are usually termed 'new scrap', whereas used metals recovered from industry, transport, building structures, infrastructure facilities, household wastes and other fields are designated as 'old scrap'. The utilization of new scrap reduces the quota of materials during processing while the re-utilization of old scrap represents an additional metal supply supplementing primary production. The scrap metal trade is concerned with the collection of old metal for re-use, often via direct suppliers to the smelters operated as subsidiaries, which provide large sorted consignments. Other firms, however, are also engaged in collecting scrap from widely scattered sources. In the metal smelter field some medium-sized and small smelters are exclusively engaged in recovering slab metal from non-ferrous metal scrap and manufacturing waste, by sorting and separation of the material occurring, refining processes, blending with primary metals and so on (Winterhagen, 1955, p. 3).

The possibility of recycling varies widely in the case of different metals. Separation of metal production by primary and secondary raw materials in the statistics is also not possible in the same way for different metals.

Aluminium

Aluminium does not corrode and products which have been scrapped can be re-used in production by way of recycling, so that virtually none of the energy input is lost: less than 5% of the energy used for initial production of the material is required for the comparatively easy recovery of aluminium from waste materials (Heilmann, 1978, p. 3). Eighty per cent of the aluminium scrap used comes from production wastes – i.e., new scrap – of which the composition is usually known. The rest is obtained from old scrap – mainly from discarded vehicles and shredded bulk refuse. In spite of improvements in recovery processes no high-grade material has yet been produced from this, as small impurities of zinc or steel have to be removed (*Die Weltmetallindustrie*, 1969, p. 8). The recycling of pure aluminium sheet by electrodynamic separation is still in process of development. The problems arising in recovery of old scrap – as well as the rapidly growing production of primary aluminium, which has reduced its urgency – are responsible for the lower recycling quota for aluminium compared with copper or lead. Nevertheless, 20% of the total requirement for aluminium, especially for aluminium casting, is already covered by remelting or secondary metal (Gocht, 1974, p. 287), and in 1978 the recovery share in the production of smelter aluminium was 30%. The market for secondary aluminium (for remelted aluminium and its alloys, including jobbing contracts from waste materials for the initial processing stage) is determined by the level of activity of the foundries and consequently the demand for aluminium alloys. In the statistics a separation between production from primary and secondary raw materials is fully possible because the latter are not used in the extraction of the metal from alumina by means of molten salt electrolysis: this is used only for the production of high-purity (99.99%) aluminium. Here the production result cannot be separated according to primary material, but the recovery volumes are relatively insignificant in quantity.

Copper

Similarly, remelted material and scrap from copper and brass, because of the resistance of these metals to corrosion, have continued to represent valuable raw materials from scrap; they can be re-introduced into the production/consumption cycle with less wastage than in the case of aluminium. With conductor copper, which is an almost chemically pure electrolytic copper, the regenerated material can be smelted by suitable processes to high-grade refined copper. In the case of plastic-sheathed wire and cables, the separation of the copper is fairly simple from the technical point of view. Heavy cables with lead sheathing and bitumen insulation yield only coarse black copper, however. In the case of electric motors and dynamos with compact units of iron, steel and copper, recovery of black copper was also until quite recently only possible – apart from stripping by hand – by oxidation of iron (in which iron and steel were lost). This can now be prevented by a new cryogenic process. Of the copper alloys, mainly new scrap from the processing plant is reclaimed. Mixed scrap must be sorted by hand (Jetter, 1975, p. 88 ff.).

It is difficult to separate copper production according to 'primary raw materials' and 'remelted and scrap materials', because a considerable amount of recycled material in smelters and refineries which chiefly process primary raw materials is immediately returned to the production flow. 'Unrefined copper production' in this book generally relates only to recovery from primary materials, whereas 'refinery production' is taken to include recovery from copper scrap.

Lead

Recovery from lead is in comparison much simpler; almost 90% of used batteries, which today represent the main field of consumption for lead, are recycled by the lead smelters. Cable lead can be separated by hand or melted off and recovery of lead is also possible when chemical plants are scrapped. A distinction is made in the case of lead scrap between battery lead, old soft lead (from lead cables and chemical plants) and antimonial lead (from printer's type, antifriction or bearing metal and other lead alloys) as well as mixed lead batches (Jetter, 1975, p. 89 ff.).

The greatest proportion of lead scrap, like that of copper, is processed in smelters and refineries which are mainly engaged on production of primary raw materials. The reclaimed lead from scrap is estimated at around 60% of the production from ores, and the main bulk of this (85–90%) is from old lead scrap, primarily due to the extensive use of lead for batteries, which have a very limited service life, so that the lead soon becomes available again as recycling material.

Zinc

Recovery of zinc is possible from steel scrap and zinc diecastings are usually re-utilized. The zinc contained in brass is collected during recovery of the valuable copper metal (Jetter, 1975, p. 91). In the case of zinc it is difficult to determine the extent of secondary production, as zinc scrap, due to the reaction of the metal with oxygen, occurs mainly in oxidized form. On the other hand, zinc oxide is recovered from primary raw materials. Only the production of remelted zinc is comparatively easy to record but it makes up a mere 10% of the total volume of secondary zinc, which itself amounts to about 35% of zinc smelter production from ores.

Tin

The recovery of tin for use in the production of tinplate has become very difficult since the changeover to electrolytic tinning and hence production of a very thin top coating, as the tin is fused on to the steel plate in stoving and can no longer be separated from it. Up to the present time only 10% of metal is recovered and processed from canning scrap, as low-grade, tin-containing steel scrap and the recycling of the tin contained in used tinplate cans will continue to be a very difficult problem both technically and from the economic point of view (Jetter, 1975, p. 82).

On the other hand, the tin contents of alloys, if present in adequate quantities in the end product, are remelted when the goods are scrapped. Secondary tin from alloys is therefore of greater importance than secondary tin metal (in the United States from 1950 to 1967 the latter accounted for only 12.8% of total production of secondary tin). But the proportion of tin in various alloys has been reduced over the years and tin-containing alloys have partly been replaced by cheaper materials. Both trends have tended to reduce recovery from secondary tin (Stodieck, 1970, p. 71). The quantification of tin recovery from remelted and scrap materials is therefore becoming more difficult because the main proportion is recovered from scrap in the form of alloys.

Chromium and nickel

The recovery material from chromium and nickel is reclaimed today by the scrap trade from the low- and high-alloy steels and recycled in the stainless steel smelters. Where galvanized coatings have been applied, however (for example, as corrosion protection), economic recovery of these heavy metals is still very difficult (Jetter, 1975, p. 91).

The total volume of metal recovered from scrap has substantially increased in recent decades – running parallel to the trend of primary production of metals. For the five most important metals by volume, aluminium, copper, lead, zinc and tin, there was an almost threefold increase in the annual output

The supply situation of principal consumers

of secondary metals in the Western world between 1950 (3.8 million tonnes) and 1979 (over 10 million tonnes).[1] Even compared with 1960 – when the recycling of ex-munitions metals had long ceased – the annual metal production from secondary materials had still doubled in 1979. At the same time the composition of this production has altered in such a way that the share of aluminium recovered today has also risen in volume from 11% (1950) to 36% (1979) to take first place among the metals mentioned and, both absolutely and relatively, it now exceeds the traditional peak in the yield of secondary refined copper, which declined in the period from 44% to 35%. The recovery of lead expanded over the same period to a much smaller extent and increased proportionally from 17% (1950) to 25% (1978). The same applied to zinc, with 18% (1979) compared to 12%. For tin, after an absolute increase since the beginning of the 1960s, a relative and absolute decrease in the production of secondary materials can be observed, which, as a proportion of secondary production of all metals, amounted in 1979 to just under 0.5%.

The importance of recycling – 'mining above ground' – also throws light on the ratio of metals recovered to new extraction by mine production. For the most important non-ferrous metals by volume there are considerable quantitative differences, whereas the long-term trend (1950–77) is marked by declining recovery quotas, common to all these metals, as may be seen in Table 37.

The proportion of secondary metals in smelter production differs considerably, both absolutely and also over the long-term trend. From 1950 to 1979 the following trend may be observed in the Western world. In 1950 the recovery quota was highest in the case of copper at 74%, followed by lead 53%, zinc 34%, tin 27% and aluminium 29%. By 1979 it had declined for copper to 62%, zinc 26% and tin 22% and risen for lead to 56% and for aluminium to 31%, so that today the recovery quota for lead is relatively the highest, followed by copper, aluminium, tin and zinc. The share of secondary metals in world production varies, however, according to countries and among these often differs considerably with time, which means that there are also discrepancies in the accuracy of the actual data. This share is relatively low as a rule in regions with low metal consumption – such as Africa and Latin America – and displays higher quotas in the industrial countries with high consumption. In the latter, however, differences can be observed – apart from varying levels of intensity of recycling measures – attributable to the following factors:

(a) the provision of a country with primary raw materials, because recovery of secondary metals is also relatively greater when the recycled material is the predominant or sole domestic raw material;
(b) the national pattern of end consumption for the metal in question,

---
1 Excluding the quantities of scrap already included in refined lead production

Table 37. Secondary recovery of non-ferrous metals in relation to smelter and mine production, world total, 1959–79 (thousand tonnes)

Metal	1950	1955	1960	1965	1970	1975	1979
Aluminium							
Smelter production	1,287.9	2,590.5	3,617.6	5,095.2	8,055.9	9,896.2	11,970.4
Secondary recovery	429.8	611.1	754.5	1,511.0	2,182.6	2,599.9	3,751.9
as % of smelter production	33.4	23.6	20.9	30.0	27.1	26.3	31.3
as % of mine production	24.3		10.9		17.2		19.7
Copper							
Smelter production	2,278.6	2,706.7	3,653.3	4,135.9	5,102.5	5,624.2	5,979.2
Secondary recovery	1,696.2	2,135.4	2,148.4	3,007.4	3,292.8	2,720.2	3,699.7
as % of smelter production	74.4	78.9	58.8	72.7	64.5	48.4	61.9
as % of mine production	74.2		59.4		63.6		60.3
Lead, refined							
Production	1,678.2	2,047.1	2,140.7	2,427.5	3,061.1	2,890.3	3,132.8[2]
inc. estimated scrap	255.0	370.0	340.0	428.0	555.0	616.0	737.0
Secondary recovery[1]	970.8	982.1	930.2	1,177.5	1,295.0	1,413.3	1,742.8[2]
as % of smelter production	57.9	48.0	43.5	48.5	42.3	48.9	55.6
as % of mine production	63.7		52.1		51.1		68.5[2]
Zinc							
Production	1,810.1	2,301.0	2,438.4	3,127.5	3,954.6	3,743.6	4,697.3
Secondary recovery	699.4	731.1	716.2	829.0	997.1	913.9	1,231.6
as % of smelter production	38.6	31.8	29.4	26.5	25.2	24.4	26.2
as % of mine production	35.9		27.6		25.2		26.6
Tin							
Production	174.7	174.5	155.5	153.3	188.2	183.8	207.8
Secondary recovery	50.2	52.7	57.3	54.6	42.5	37.0	45.0
as % of smelter production	28.7	30.2	36.9	35.6	22.6	20.1	21.7
as % of mine production	30.5		41.6		24.6		23.4[3]

1. Excluding scrap already included in refinery production. 2. 1978. 3. Including secondary recovery of pure tin in Mexico.
Source: Calculated from *Metal Statistics*, various years.

because secondary metals are not complete substitutes for the primary metal in all applications;

(c) deviations in growth rates of consumption of non-ferrous metals.

The fluctuations found in the rate of secondary to primary production in a country over the course of time derive principally, however, from price factors, bottlenecks in supplies or surplus conditions, as well as the fact that the secondary smelters can adapt more readily to alternating economic cycles than is possible with the primary smelters (see Table 38).

The share of secondary recovery and of direct use of scrap in primary materials is therefore not a constant figure but fluctuates – apart from external influences such as an excessive incidence of scrap after wars – according to the market conditions, in which experience has shown that rising and high prices for a metal mean a rising and relatively high scrap output, and the reverse applies when the market tends to decline. Invariably the scrap yield exerts a market influence quite independent of the policies of the primary producers.

Table 38. Smelter production (S) and secondary recovery (R) of non-ferrous metals in selected industrial countries, 1950–79

		1950	1960	1970	1979[1]	1950	1960	1970	1979[1]
		(thousand tonnes)				(%)			
Aluminium									
USA	S	651.9	1,827.5	3,607.1	4,556.9	74.7	85.9	89.4	74.7
	R	221.1	298.9	937.1	1,542.2	25.3	14.1	20.6	25.3
Japan	S	24.8	133.2	727.9	1,010.4	87.4	72.9	69.3	57.5
	R	3.6	49.5	322.1	746.5	12.6	27.1	30.7	42.5
West Germany	S	27.8	168.9	309.3	741.9	33.2	55.4	54.6	63.7
	R	56.0	135.7	258.5	423.6	66.8	44.6	45.5	36.3
France	S	60.6	235.2	381.1	395.1	71.9	84.2	81.3	70.4
	R	23.7	44.0	87.4	165.7	28.1	15.8	18.7	29.6
UK	S	29.9	29.4	39.6	395.5	26.9	18.6	18.4	63.8
	R	81.1	128.6	220.9	203.6	73.1	81.4	84.8	36.2
Italy	S	37.0	83.6	146.7	269.1	71.2	66.6	48.8	52.3
	R	15.0	42.0	154.0	245.0	28.8	33.4	51.2	47.7
Copper, refined									
USA	S	1,344.2	1,642.6	2,034.5	1,981.3	58.2	66.5	62.0	44.9
	R	965.2	905.7	1,244.3	2,433.5	41.8	35.5	38.0	55.1
Japan	S	84.7	248.1	705.3	983.7	40.8	48.8	60.3	63.9
	R	122.9	260.8	464.2	555.0	59.2	51.2	39.7	36.1
West Germany	S	198.3	309.1	405.8	382.5	51.5	53.8	53.3	44.9
	R	186.7	265.6	355.6	403.2	48.5	46.2	46.7	55.1
France	S	22.0	40.2	33.6	45.3	38.6	28.2	17.6	24.3
	R	35.0	102.3	157.3	141.3	61.4	71.8	82.4	75.7
UK	S	193.2	213.1	206.2	121.7	49.5	43.7	42.7	46.3
	R	197.0	274.3	276.7	141.3	50.5	56.3	57.3	53.7
Italy	S	11.1	15.5	15.5	15.6	32.4	19.2	7.5	7.0
	R	23.2	65.0	190.0	206.6	67.6	80.8	92.5	93.0
Lead, refined									
USA	S	471.8	481.2	748.3	773.7	51.9	62.1	64.7	58.7
	R	437.5	294.2	409.0	545.0	48.1	37.9	35.3	41.3
Japan	S	16.0	74.2	209.0	228.4	51.6	54.3	76.1	78.5
	R	15.0	62.4	65.6	62.7	48.4	45.7	23.9	21.5
West Germany	S	141.5	206.8	305.4	305.0	78.1	84.4	81.7	76.4
	R	39.6	38.1	68.6	94.4	21.9	15.6	18.3	23.6
France	S	50.6	109.8	170.0	208.2	48.5	75.8	81.1	92.8
	R	53.8	35.0	39.5	16.2	51.5	24.2	18.9	7.2
UK	S	73.9	147.5	287.0	247.4	26.1	61.7	76.4	80.8
	R	97.5	91.4	88.5	58.9	56.9	38.3	23.5	19.2
Italy	S	37.8	53.6	79.3	55.8	70.0	64.1	75.3	44.9
	R	16.2	30.0	26.0	68.6	30.0	35.9	24.7	55.1
Zinc									
USA	S	825.9	787.1	866.3	525.7	73.6	76.5	73.8	58.7
	R	295.8	241.2	308.0	370.0	26.4	23.5	26.2	41.3
Japan	S	49.0	186.6	680.7	789.4	63.3	78.6	91.4	75.2
	R	26.0	50.7	64.4	260.1	34.7	21.4	8.6	24.8

Table 38. (cont'd)

		1950	1960	1970	1979[1]	1950	1960	1970	1979[1]
		(thousand tonnes)				(%)			
West Germany	S	136.1	191.9	301.2	355.5	52.2	87.1	70.7	72.2
	R	124.7	28.5	125.0	136.9	47.8	12.9	29.3	27.8
France	S	67.8	149.1	223.7	249.0	79.6	82.5	89.3	94.7
	R	17.4	31.7	27.0	13.8	20.4	17.5	10.8	5.3
UK	S	71.4	75.5	146.6	76.7	43.0	45.2	61.3	51.3
	R	94.7	91.8	92.5	72.9	57.0	54.8	38.7	48.7
Italy	S	37.9	85.3	142.1	202.8	92.7	90.6	90.5	96.1
	R	3.0	8.9	15.0	8.3	7.3	9.5	9.6	3.9
Tin									
USA	S	33.6	14.3	4.5	4.7	51.1	39.0	18.1	17.9
	R	32.2	22.4	20.3	21.5	48.9	61.0	81.9	82.1
Japan	S	0.4	1.7	1.4	27.7	25.0	32.1	23.0	82.7
	R	1.2	3.6	4.7	5.8	75.0	67.9	77.0	17.3
West Germany	S	0.8	1.9	2.2	4.1	24.2	20.9	19.8	51.9
	R	2.5	7.2	8.9	3.8	75.8	79.1	80.2	48.1
France[2]	R	5.0	6.2	1.5	0.2	–	–	–	–
UK	S	29.0	28.1	24.5	9.8	80.6	80.1	77.8	66.2
	R	7.0	7.0	7.0	5.0	19.4	19.9	22.2	33.8
Italy[2]	R	0.6	1.0	3.0	3.8	–	–	–	–

1. Lead: 1978.   2. No smelter production.
Source: Calculated from *Metal Statistics*, various years.

This was shown clearly in the attempt to stabilize copper producer prices in 1963–64, which largely foundered because it was possible for processing firms to fall back on copper scrap (Sies, 1976, pp. 5 and 14).

The countries with the highest metal consumption – apart from temporal fluctuations – and which record the largest amount of scrap are naturally the leading recyclers (see Table 39). A noteworthy feature is that the national share taken by the United States – which in 1950 was still some way ahead in recovery of all metals except lead – has declined with steadily rising production during the last 30 years. The United Kingdom also recorded comparatively high losses. On the other hand, Japan in particular, and also West Germany, managed to increase their secondary recovery of non-ferrous metals both absolutely and relatively. Generally speaking, a widening distribution, as in the production of primary metals, can be seen in the international breakdown of figures for the yields of secondary metal in the Western world.

The latest known (1977) share of secondary recovery in the consumption of

Table 39. Share of selected industrial countries in secondary recovery of non-ferrous metals, 1950–79 (% of world total)

Country	1950	1960	1970	1979	1950	1960	1970	1979
	\multicolumn{4}{c}{Aluminium}	\multicolumn{4}{c}{Copper}
USA	51.4	46.9	42.9	41.1	56.9	41.1	37.8	39.2
Japan	0.8	5.8	14.8	19.9	7.3	10.5	14.1	15.0
West Germany	13.0	15.9	11.8	11.3	11.0	12.1	10.8	10.9
France	5.5	5.1	4.0	4.4	2.1	4.6	4.8	3.8
UK	18.9	15.0	9.2	4.7	11.6	12.5	8.4	5.2
Italy	3.5	4.9	7.1	6.5	1.4	3.0	5.6	5.6
Total	93.1	93.6	89.8	87.9	90.3	83.8	81.5	79.7
World total (thousand tonnes)	429.8	856.4	2,182.6	3,751.9	1,696.2	2,202.7	3,292.8	3,699.7
	\multicolumn{4}{c}{Lead}	\multicolumn{4}{c}{Zinc}
USA	45.1	31.6	31.6	31.1	42.2	33.7	30.9	30.0
Japan	1.6	6.7	5.1	3.6	3.4	8.3	14.5	21.1
West Germany	4.1	4.1	5.3	5.4	17.8	4.0	12.5	11.1
France	5.5	3.8	0.4	0.9	2.5	4.4	2.7	1.1
UK	10.0	10.1	6.8	3.4	13.5	12.8	9.3	5.9
Italy	2.7	3.2	2.0	3.9	0.4	1.2	1.5	0.7
Total	69.0	59.5	51.2	48.5	79.8	64.4	71.4	69.9
World total (thousand tonnes)	970.8	930.2	1,295.0	1,742.8	699.4	716.2	997.1	1,231.6
	\multicolumn{4}{c}{Tin}				
USA	64.1	39.0	47.8	47.8				
Japan	2.4	6.3	11.1	12.9				
West Germany	5.0	12.5	–	8.4				
France	10.0	10.8	3.5	0.4				
UK	13.9	12.2	16.5	11.1				
Italy	1.2	1.7	7.1	8.4				
Total	96.6	82.5	86.0	89.0				
World total (thousand tonnes)	50.2	57.5	42.5	45.0				

Note: World totals do not include Eastern Bloc.
Source: Calculated from *Metal Statistics*, various years.

the most important non-ferrous metals[1] is shown in Table 40. It can be seen that:

(a) In the case of aluminium, those countries lacking raw materials, i.e., Italy, the United Kingdom, West Germany and Japan, record the

[1] It should be noted that in the quotas for the year 1950, on the one hand recycling of scrap from discarded war stock was not yet completed and, on the other, the rebuilding of smelter capacities and their expansion in the countries affected by post-war factors were still only beginning.

Table 40. Secondary recovery as a percentage of non-ferrous metal consumption in selected industrial countries, 1950–70

	1950	1960	1970	1977	1979[1]
Aluminium					
USA	26.9	26.0	26.9	28.0	30.8
Japan	19.0	32.9	35.3	40.4	41.4
West Germany	112.5	43.4	38.6	42.8	39.7
France	42.9	20.7	21.2	28.6	27.8
UK	44.1	36.0	49.8	48.0	48.8
Italy	31.6	42.4	55.2	58.9	54.7
Copper					
USA	75.2	74.0	66.9	60.9	108.9
Japan	192.0	75.9	56.6	37.9	41.7
West Germany	102.8	51.5	51.0	42.0	50.8
France	32.6	43.2	47.6	43.7	39.4
UK	36.8	49.0	50.0	40.4	28.3
Italy	36.3	35.1	69.3	70.0	58.7
Lead					
USA	54.5	45.5	43.4	48.2	55.9
Japan	61.0	62.7	31.2	27.0	23.5
West Germany	39.4	15.9	22.2	32.3	34.7
France	72.9	21.7	20.5	17.3	15.3
UK	41.3	32.8	33.8	20.5	24.3
Italy	57.3	38.5	15.5	30.9	36.0
Zinc					
USA	33.4	30.5	28.7	28.5	37.1
Japan	46.6	31.4	14.9	9.0	33.4
West Germany	94.7	9.6	31.6	40.1	32.8
France	18.2	18.4	12.3	11.1	4.8
UK	39.4	33.3	31.1	28.7	30.5
Italy	9.1	10.5	8.4	10.7	3.7
Tin					
USA	44.5	42.8	37.7	32.4	43.4
Japan	25.5	24.7	16.4	16.8	18.6
West Germany	31.7	49.7	58.9	19.5	25.0
France	66.7	54.4	14.3	9.2	2.0
UK	29.7	30.2	37.6	47.0	37.9
Italy	14.0	19.6	41.7	72.6	63.3

1. 1978 for lead.
Source: Calculated from *Metal Statistics*, various years.

greatest shares of secondary recovery whereas the countries with their own bauxite deposits (France) or with relatively easy possibilities of procurement of primary materials (the United States) record much lower consumption quotas for recovery.

(b) In the consumption of refined copper and lead a much higher value is attached to the secondary material in the United States and Italy – probably because of their comparatively more intensive recycling – than in the other industrial countries.

(c) In the case of zinc the United States, Japan and West Germany, owing to their special efforts and successes in the recovery of this material, show far greater consumption quotas from recycled material.
(d) Re-utilization of tin by recycling is highest in Italy, the United States and the United Kingdom.

The secondary quotas indicated so far give ratio of volume of production of secondary material to volume of primary material produced (or the corresponding consumption relationship), which can be taken as an index of the demand for secondary metals. A more comprehensive measurement concept is offered by the 'recovery rate', which gives the secondary metal recovered from the total quantity available for recovery. This can be evaluated as an index of the supply of secondary metal. For the calculation of the recovery rate the following formula has been developed (Grace, 1978, p. 253 ff.):

$$R_R = \frac{P_s + X_{ss} - M_{ss} + DUS}{P_P + M_P - X_P + P_s + M_s - X_s + S_p + S_s + DUS}$$

where
P_s = production of secondary metal
DUS = direct scrap use
P_P = production of primary metal
M_P = import of primary metal
M_s = import of secondary metal
X_P = export of primary metal
X_s = export of secondary metal
M_{ss} = import of scrap (secondary scrap)
X_{ss} = export of scrap
S_p = changes in stocks of primary metal
S_s = changes of stocks of secondary metal.

This recovery rate, which can only be calculated for a few metals, because the necessary data are not complete, diverges considerably from the approximate calculation, for those metals (aluminium, copper and lead), of the share of secondary material in the total production of the metals in all countries, as Table 41 clearly indicates. In the case of aluminium (except for the United Kingdom) and copper (except for the United States) it is therefore usually considerably lower, but in the case of lead (except for Italy) it is markedly higher. In the case of aluminium the recycling quota in the industrial countries for the period 1965–75 is very consistent, with the exception of Italy, which has considerably intensified its recycling activities during this period. West Germany, Japan and the United Kingdom, with remarkably consistent recycling quotas, support the belief that a level of 25–30% generally is feasible. The lower quotas of France and the United States, on the other hand, indicate that their recycling potential has not been fully exploited.

Table 41. Recovery rate for selected industrial countries, 1975 (%)

	Aluminium	Copper	Lead
USA	23.5	53.5	57.4
Japan	25.6	4.7	23.7
West Germany	28.8	30.5	25.6
France	20.6	39.5	20.7
Italy	22.2	25.2	20.3
UK	37.2	38.8	60.6

The recycling quotas for copper are generally higher than those for aluminium, which may be a result on the one hand of the higher value of copper and on the other of the narrower scope offered for substitution of primary copper by the secondary material. However – as in the case of aluminium – there appears to be no general trend in the recycling quotas. It is noteworthy moreover that France and the United States are obviously being more successful in their efforts to recycle copper – in contrast to aluminium – than West Germany and the United Kingdom. The recycling quotas for lead show wide differences among the countries under review. The reason for this in the case of West Germany and Japan (with lower quotas) may be that in the latter the direct scrap use is not taken into account and for the former the data on recovery for scrap are incomplete. The high recycling quota for the United Kingdom would lead one to suppose – provided that the price relationships between metals and scrap are similar – that in the other countries a substantial recycling potential is still not being utilized (Grace, 1978, p. 253 ff.).

Summing up, it may be observed that the contribution made to world supplies of raw materials by reclaimed non-ferrous metals, particularly for high-consumer countries without an adequate basis of primary raw materials, has steadily increased during the course of industrialization and today plays a major part. As the metal contents of the known deposits become depleted and hence new production of metals becomes more difficult and more expensive, there is no doubt that recycling will acquire greater importance and possibilities in this field should in no way be regarded as exhausted. It must also be recognized however that a growing total consumption of metals – which is to be expected with increasing industrialization, even in countries of the Third World – can ultimately only be satisfied if additional volumes of primary materials are made available in adequate quantities.

7.3 THE ROLE OF STOCKPILE HOLDING

Stockpiling of non-ferrous metals ensures continuity of supplies of raw materials to industry. A distinction must be made here between commercial stocks of private industry and strategic reserves which are usually laid down on the initiative of the state, which finances them and administers them by government institutions. The importance of stocks for the market economy varies according to the particular purpose for which they are to be used. Because of the continual build-up or cut-back, depending on production and/or price conditions, commerical stocks are a permanent variable in market business, and, owing to the speculative element involved, largely unpredictable. Stocks held for strategic reasons (generally on a long-term basis), on the other hand, have an influence on the market in the expansion phase of the increased demand they entail and, in the case of occasional releases, due to the correspondingly increased supply.

Commercial stocks have always existed from the very beginning of the metal industry, although they unquestionably acquired their importance as a market factor with progress in industrialization. The laying down of strategic reserves on the part of the state, however, dates back only to the First World War.

7.3.1 Commercial stocks

In the metals sector stocks are held at all stages of production and trading. On the one hand, they are supplies necessary for business operations and, on the other, they may be stocks either accumulated unintentionally, because forecasts of metal demand were too high and production was expanded excessively, or laid down, maintained, increased or reduced by a company for speculative reasons. The most important factors determining the extent of these commercial stocks are the absolute level and the expected trend in consumption and prices, as well as the procurement risks for the different metals. Commercial stockpiling, therefore, requires a temporal market equilibrium. Stocks at different production levels and for trading purposes increase when the volume of production within a specific period is not fully consumed and they fall as soon as more raw materials of various categories are consumed than produced. On the whole the result is a balance of stocks in hand arising from the positive or negative balances of production and consumption in past periods, which producers, traders and consumers maintain up to a specific point of time.

Commercial stockholding in the metals sector is essentially made up of the following items:

(a) concentrates at mineworkings and en route to the smelters;
(b) concentrates at the smelters;
(c) metals at smelters and refineries;
(d) metals at various stages of metal trading operations;
(e) metals at works producing semi-manufactures (intermediates);
(f) metals in the subsequent processing industries;
(g) metals in licensed warehouses of the metal exchanges.

The compilation of a complete statistical record of this wide variety of stocks scattered all over the world and their constant changes is beset by exceptional problems and hence their short-term effects on the market are difficult to predict. The trend in current stocks indicated in the licensed warehouses of the London Metal Exchange (LME) and the New York Commodity Exchange (COMEX), therefore, are of key importance for the assessment of the market situation at any time in the case of individual metals, particularly – as the price analysis later on demonstrates – as these are liable to have market repercussions and are sensitive in their reaction to the market.

At the mining works stockpiling ensures that the production concerned can only be delivered in the volumes required by the smelters. Holding of stocks at the smelters, traders and subsequent processing works, however, is deliberately planned according to criteria of supply policy, which naturally also contains a speculative element. It is primarily a question here of minimizing purchasing risk to maintain production and also of providing a cushion for the company itself against the usual, very often pronounced short-term price fluctuations in the non-ferrous metal markets. A number of factors combine to influence the purchasing or procurement risk, including in particular:

(a) the physical distance between the producer and consumer countries, the speed of transport, safety of transport routes and also the political stability in the producer countries;

(b) the degree of vertical concentration in the individual metal markets, because control of levels of production which already hold stocks usually reduces the procurement risk;

(c) the respective 'statistical' position, because production surpluses tend to reduce the procurement risk while production deficits serve to increase stocks held;

(d) the short-term range of manoeuvre of mine and smelter production in adapting to increasing demand.

Within the entire stockpiling process the most vital component is the procurement of necessary reserves to safeguard continuity of production – i.e., the consumer-dependent part of the reserves. Allowing for economic cycles, this is even more accentuated. In the upswing phase, the entrepreneurs are forced to fall back on their stocks to increase production but at the same time they will attempt to replenish these quickly in order to provide a cushion against expected price increases – and also to make up the now higher level of production and cater for the improved sales prospects. In a period of economic slump in which total demand, under the influence of the stock cycle, inevitably declines more rapidly than consumption, stocks held will prove to be excessive as production falls. A forward quotation under the spot price will then result in a cutback in the stocks previously considered necessary for the business and as reserves. When stocks are held for price reasons it has then proved advantageous to release them on the spot market in order to buy them back on the forward market. There have also been cases, however, where in a recession no appreciable reduction occurred in the stockpile volumes held by the consumers. For example, in the marked recession in the United States in 1957/58 stocks of tin rose even higher in relation to consumption. The reason for this was that the interventions of the ITC largely cut out the price risk of stockpile holding and, as the producer countries began to impose export restrictions on tin, the risk in a continuous raw material supply was even greater (Stodieck, 1970, p. 104 ff.).

The absolute extent of the stockpile volumes is not only relevant for the supply situation but also has repercussions on price trends. A price-stabilizing effect is exercised by the build-up and cutback in stocks when these contribute to reciprocal adaptation of supply and demand. The influence of stocks has a destabilizing effect, though, if gluts in consumption or production are occasioned or intensified by changes in stocks held. Changes in stockholdings can be the cause of price movements but they are themselves often consequent upon them. An absolute clear-cut relationship between changes in stocks and prices cannot be established. A potential buyer of raw materials may possibly cut back on stocks with rising prices because, owing to an increase in the interest rate, by purchasing the necessary materials his production would become more expensive and his profit per unit product would be narrowed. Possibly, however, a potential purchaser will build up his stocks even with an upward price trend, so long as the calculated profits plus the anticipated future price increases will still exceed the costs of holding stocks, or at least cover them. With falling prices the producer will generally still maintain his stocks because the interest rate falls and the ratio of calculated earnings to costs of stockholding becomes more favourable. Whether and to what extent such considerations determine the behaviour of the entrepreneur in making changes in his stocks depends in every case in principle on the scale of the price changes anticipated – either upward or downward (Stodieck, 1970, p. 99).

Potential purchasers of mine products, metals or semi-manufactures (intermediates) have more freedom of disposal, but only over those stocks which are in excess of the minimum to be held for technical reasons in order to insure against possible difficulties in the supply of essential materials, so that the stockpile is influenced over the short term partly by the price trend. Such stockpiling by the producers can therefore largely offset fluctuations and discrepancies in metal recovery and consumption.

Commercial stockpiling in this general context cannot therefore be definitely described as a price-stabilizing feature, and in fact may operate to the contrary. The trend here is so difficult to estimate that stocks and their changes can have unforeseen effects as price-determining mechanisms in the markets. The uncertainty provoked by this among producers and consumers may in turn influence production or consumption decisions on their part and thus affect the price trend indirectly.

7.3.2 Strategic reserves and other measures to safeguard supplies

In order to ensure supplies of vital raw materials – including non-ferrous metals – for industry in time of crisis, over a relatively long period, strategic reserves of 'sensitive' materials (i.e., those for which a particular country is relatively dependent on imports) are held by some major consumer countries.

The additional demand arising from stocking up on strategic reserves – in the same way as the accumulation of commercial stocks – tends to trigger off an upward movement in prices, with the difference, however, that there may be special repercussions on the market, depending on the extent and timing of purchase. Such purchases have the effect of stabilizing prices during a phase of prevailing production surpluses, when commodities are acquired for strategic reserves which would otherwise come on the market with a falling price trend, as happened with tin in the years 1950–56 (Stodieck, 1970, p. 82). Releases of strategic reserves, however, can depress price movements because of the increased market supply. This is very unwelcome to the producer countries when it results in an increase in supply at a time of weak or sluggish demand. On the other hand, price increases tend to be damped down by sales of strategic reserves when these contribute to replenishing an inadequate market supply, although this is of mainly theoretical importance, because a country which has laid down reserves for strategic purposes is hardly likely to run these down when market bottlenecks occur, unless it intends to profit from their sale.

The United States

The need for a national strategic stockpile policy was earnestly expressed for the first time in the United States towards the end of the First World War, when dependence on foreign supplies for certain raw materials and supply problems due to the war had become clearly evident. Practical steps however were not taken until 1938, when stocks were laid down of indispensable raw materials obtained from overseas for the Navy. The first Stockpiling Law was then passed in 1939. In the non-ferrous metals sector the Treasury Department was under an obligation to build up reserves of chromite and tin, which are among the 'sensitive' raw materials for the United States. In 1940, because of difficulties in procurement due to the escalation of the Second World War, the Reconstruction Finance Corporation assumed additional responsibilities for the acquisition of raw materials. The Surplus Property Act of 1944 was a further step in the direction of guaranteeing supplies of raw materials and in 1946 the First Strategic and Critical Materials Stockpile Act was passed, which laid the foundations of the national stockpile system practised today (International Economic Studies Institute, 1976, p. 259).

The strategic reserves considered necessary at that time in the United States were fully accumulated at the end of the 1950s. At the beginning of Kennedy's Presidency the level was checked and, with an equivalent value then of $7.7 billion, found to be twice as high as necessary. The stockpile policy was then marked by a phase of comparative restraint on the part of the United States during the next few years. From 1959 onwards no supplementary purchases of importance were made until the Vietnam War, when substantial procurements were again undertaken.

The national stockpile system was primarily introduced in the United States for strategic reasons but economic aims were soon also involved. As well as safeguarding raw materials for emergencies or crises, the stockpile system was occasionally instrumental in promoting domestic mining industries and other purposes. An outstanding example is provided by the massive purchase of lead and zinc during and after the settlement of the Korean conflict. Despite the opportunity provided at that time of being able to rely at any time on Canadian and Mexican imports should other resources of supply fail, substantial increases were made in domestic purchases in order to support the domestic lead and zinc industries. From time to time stockpiling operations were instituted for other purposes, e.g., to ease the national budget.

In 1973 the stockpile functions were transferred to the Federal Preparedness Agency of the General Services Administration and a thorough review was made of planning, with the result that drastic reductions were made in stockpile targets (from $4.8 billion to $700 million at 1973 prices); surpluses were retained, however, of a few raw materials, especially tin. Proceeds from the sale of stockpile materials contributed to balancing the national budget and counteracting further inflationary tendencies. In December 1975 the reserves had an estimated market value of altogether $6.9 billion, of which, however, only $1.1 billion was applied to the declared targets. Between 1958 and 1975 a total of $6 billion was used for the creation of the stockpile, whereas the Treasury Department during the same period obtained $7 billion from sales of stockpile materials.

In October 1976 it was announced that henceforth – after being based on a one-year period – a strategic stockpile policy would be geared to a three-year requirement, in which for the first time a distinction would be made between civilian and military needs. A necessary updating and also an examination of the political foundations at least every four years is planned. The new stockpile targets meant a fundamental change in the surplus situation prevailing hitherto in the holding of reserves: for 72 materials the targets were raised above the appropriations provided for in 1973, for 12 materials they were reduced and for eight materials the existing appropriations were raised, with the result that for only 18 of the non-ferrous metals were higher stocks permitted than stockpile appropriations, while in the case of 29 minerals considerable deficits existed. A similar situation is found even in the inventory of stocks presented for the end of 1978 (Table 42).

Non-ferrous metals

Table 42. Stockpile targets and holdings of non-ferrous metals in the United States, 1970, 1976 and 1980 (thousand tonnes)

	Stockpile targets			Stockpile holdings		
	End 1970	End Sept. 1976	End March 1980	End 1970	End Sept. 1976	End March 1980
Lead	480.8	59.1	784.7	1,031.2	545.3	545.3
Copper	703.1	0	1,178.5	229.9	0	26.4
Zinc	508.0	340.0	1,191.2	1,016.1	340.0	341.1
Tin	235.7	41.1	33.0	256.7	207.0	203.7
Aluminium[1]			5,530.2			3,124.5
Bauxite[2]	10,464.8	4,712.2	531.4	16,891.3	14,385.4	14,385.0
Titanium[3]	30.4	29.3	119.3	31.8	29.3	29.3
Cobalt	17.3	5.4	38.7	35.5	18.5	18.5
Manganese[4]	124.2	9.7	28.9	299.8	242.8	234.1
Molybdenum[5]	16.6	0	0	19.3	0	0
Nickel	49.9	0	185.4	45.4	0	0
Vanadium[6]	0.5	0	11.5	3.0	0.5	0.5
Tungsten[7]	27.2	1.9	18.8	59.3	51.3	37.4
Antimony	36.9	0	18.3	42.4	36.9	37.0
Cadmium	0.3	2.0	11.2	4.6	2.9	2.9
Mercury[7]	4.4	1.5	1.9	6.9	6.9	6.6
Tantalum	1.5	0.2	3.2	1.9	1.3	1.1

1. Aluminium Group (metal content). 2. Metal Grade, Jamaica Type and Surinam Type. 3. Sponge. 4. Dioxide, Battery Grade group. 5. Molybdenum Group (metal content). 6. Vanadium Group (metal content). 7. Bearing Materials Group (metal content).
Source: *Stockpile Report to Congress*, Washington (July–December 1970; July–September 1976; October 1979–March 1980).

The stockpile of the US Government consists at present of 93 metals, minerals and other raw materials, of which the Government disposes of part as surplus and aims to effect purchases to make up existing stocks. Since 1973 there have not been any substantial sales but Congress in 1980 concluded legal procedure for approval of releases from strategic reserves, including 35,000 long tons of tin from a stockpile amounting to a total of 200,480 long tons. Already in 1978 such a motion had been tabled by the industry and in 1979 representatives of the mining sector urged Congress to sell surplus tin stocks from strategic reserves and to acquire copper for the stockpile from the proceeds in order to assist the domestic copper industry, which was then at a low ebb. In the view of the producer countries such a release ought only to be made after consultation with the International Tin Council and the producer countries, and tin sales only undertaken when the market situation permits.

The Federal Emergency Management Agency of the US Government, which is responsible for the administration of the strategic reserves, is planning for the period 1980–85 raw materials transactions within the stockpile amounting to a total of $4–6 billion on a revolving fund basis. Higher stockpile targets are planned for cobalt, manganese and tungsten, among other materials.

In other countries the laying down of reserves to safeguard supplies in case of shortfalls in delivery or of high short-term demand due to economic cycles is of fairly recent date or still at the planning stage, but the question of stocking up on raw materials is acquiring increasing importance in the industrialized nations.

France

In France the Government, under the impact of the 1974 oil embargo, passed a resolution in January 1975 to create national raw materials reserves and made available 100 million francs for the purpose. Despite stocking up to 250 million francs (approximately $50 million) no essential progress has yet been recorded, as no general agreement could be reached as to which raw materials should be included in the stocks and how these should be financed (budget allocation, shareholding in industry or currency reserves of the Bank of France were discussed). The administration of the national reserves is under the control of the Groupement d'Importation des Métaux (GIRM), the chief function of which is the import of copper for the French industry. In 1975 61% of French copper imports were dealt with by this organization, operating in the strategic reserves field assigned to it in the same way as a government body. In autumn 1975 purchases were made within the scope of the available resources, among which copper and nickel were quantitatively the most important products, although zinc, lead, tin and molybdenum were also procured (CIPEC, *Quarterly Review*, October–December 1976, p. 28 ff.). France will most probably complete its stocking of non-ferrous metals in the 1980s, in order to lay down national raw materials reserves equivalent to about two months' consumption of those metals for which the country is dependent on imports. The market conditions should largely determine future policy for stocking up on reserves.

West Germany

In West Germany the Government some time ago declared itself in favour of creating a raw materials reserve to safeguard supplies in case of unforeseen shortfall in delivery of the sensitive raw materials chromium, manganese, vanadium and cobalt (as well as asbestos). The West German Government has no intention at present of extending the provision of emergency stocks to other metals or minerals and it still remains uncertain when its programme for stocking up on essential raw materials will eventually be concluded. There likewise appears to be no consensus of opinion at present as to the volume to be stocked of emergency raw materials supplies of which replenishment would appear to be particularly threatened.

In the case of raw materials which are in particular need of safeguard, such as chromium, manganese, cobalt and vanadium, West Germany is already entirely dependent on imports. Because of the lack of adequate stocks, German industry, especially the stainless steel industry and subsidiary branches of production, would be highly vulnerable to a breakdown in supplies. As early as

March 1979 the Federal German Bank declared it was prepared to make available DM 600 million as part of a credit limit (cash line) to the Reconstruction Loan Corporation for the purpose of stocking up on indispensable industrial materials. But efforts to discharge the government function of accomplishing the required stockpiling, mainly according to market principles with minimum government intervention and with industry itself assuming responsibility, proved extremely difficult. The nucleus of the probable German stockpile system to ensure stocking up on supplies of especially sensitive raw materials over the span of one year, with the firms acting on their own responsibility as far as possible, will be a joint contract between the West German Government and a consortium of firms which at the present time appears roughly as follows:

(a) The individual firms will purchase additional stocks in the name and to the account of a consortium still to be set up (Rohstoffbevorratungs-GmbH – Raw Materials Stockpile Ltd), which they themselves will store. In order to avoid major disruption of the market, a period of three to five years is considered necessary for building up stocks – in the case of cobalt probably even longer.

(b) To provide funds for additional stockpiling, the consortium will receive a credit from the Reconstruction Loan Corporation, of which the interest is to be borne by the Federal Budget, while the consortium would assume costs of storage and care of the raw materials.

(c) In order to prevent demands being made on the additional stocks acquired at every shortfall in supplies, the Government will decide when the firm may dispose of the stocks. This requires a very close watch on the market on the part of the Government as it has to prevent firms relying on emergency stocks to keep their own stocks at a lower level than previously. In the contracts, therefore, basically the level should be specified at which the stocks should be held by the firms as necessary for their own operations (*Wirtschaftswoche*, 1980, p. 18).

Recently it was reported that the projected plan for raw materials reserves in West Germany is not to be pursued for the time being. As this mode of stockpiling raw materials tends to resemble the national stocking procedure devised for state reserves in the agrarian sector, although not absolutely modelled on it, preference is often given by industrialists and politicians to safeguarding essential raw materials by tax concessions for the building up of special stocks by firms who are hence given an incentive to take the initiative.

Sweden

Sweden furnishes an example of how the government provides incentives to the holding of private stockpiles by means of tax measures. These involve depreciation allowances in the year of procurement for a large proportion of the storage costs, and aim to protect the taxpayers from paying taxes on purely inflationary gains and to cushion them against harsh price falls. Even though the prime object of the system is 'to stabilize cash flow business and promote economic efficiency', it has the side effect of encouraging the formation of larger private stocks than would otherwise be held. For some time now doubts have been cast on the efficiency of these private stocks as a substitute for a national stockpiling policy (International Economic Studies Institute, 1976, p. 272).

Spain

In Spain the Director General for Mining in the Department of Industry in October 1976 announced the formation of a Stockpile Commission which would be composed of members of the Government and of private industry and which was designed to work out an action programme for the supply of individual sectors of industry in Spain. In the field of non-ferrous metals the main emphasis was on studies relating especially to copper and bauxite. So far nothing has yet been made public on the volumes of materials in the stockpile and their financing. Spain considers the function of stockpiling primarily a means of counteracting economic price spirals (CIPEC, *Quarterly Review*, October–December 1976, p. 29).

The United Kingdom

In the United Kingdom to date no measures of any kind have been taken to stockpile strategic raw materials. British industry has admittedly expressed its approval of such a measure in principle, but considers that its practical implementation would present major problems, owing to the costs entailed and the financing of such a stockpile, which, owing to the steep rise in metal prices and the high level of the interest rate, it feels it is not in a position at present to create. Should the Government – as in the United States or France – assume the entire costs, there would be no real objection to the building up of emergency supplies.

Japan

Japan during the last six months of 1976 drew up a comparatively restricted stockpile programme, with financial resources amounting altogether to US$100 million, for copper, lead, zinc and aluminium. The aim of this programme was 'to contribute to the economic development of the developing countries and the stable supply of raw materials from overseas'. A stockpiling organization was set up comprising the Metal and Mineral Stockpile Association (for copper, lead and zinc) and the Light Metal Stockpile Association (for aluminium). A banking syndicate, guaranteed by the Government, has made funds amounting to US$100 million available to the Metal Mining Agency of Japan, and the Stockpiling Foundation was granted the same amount. The credit bears an interest rate of 9%, but government funding reduces the effective net interest rate for the stockpile to only 6.5%. Purchases and sales require the consent of the Government and sales may only be made when stocks exceed a half-month's production. The smelter and refinery producers, however, are demanding that the strategic raw materials reserves should be increased. Of the financial resources used 80% are allocated to reserves of copper, 10% to aluminium and 10% to lead and zinc (cf. CIPEC, *Quarterly Review*, October–December 1976, p. 28). In 1978 a stockpile programme for nickel was also drawn up, using exchange credits; stocks, however, have meanwhile been run down again. At the beginning of 1979 the Japanese Ministry of Finance and the Ministry for External Trade and Industry, at the request of the producers, granted an extension of the stockpile programme for non-ferrous metals until August 1981, with the stipulation that the producers should buy back one-sixth of the stockpile volume every six months. According to the ratio of procurement costs and interest paid to the respective producer prices, this may cause difficulties. The state stockpile today covers copper, zinc and aluminium; there also exists a private stockpile of copper and zinc.[1]

South Korea

South Korea's Government also intends to lay down stocks of raw materials to assure domestic supplies and stabilization of prices. Stocks are planned of domestically produced raw materials to the value of approximately US$346.5 million, which the State will buy up in case of a fall in demand and dispose of again with heavier demand or a worldwide increase in prices. The stockholding comes under the responsibility of the Supply Office with the stipulation that a maximum possible increase or decrease in stocks should not exceed 10%. In the field of non-ferrous metals stocking up is planned of 9,000 tonnes aluminium, 2,000 tonnes lead, 100 tonnes tin and 1,900 tonnes nickel.

India

It is learned that the Indian Government has decided on the creation of an aluminium stockpile. The volume to be stockpiled should be sufficient to cover three months' supply and it was intended to begin at the end of 1979 with purchases made via the national trading company MMTC.

---

[1] The buy-back of part of the stockpiled zinc by Japanese smelters, planned for 1979–80, has been postponed for the time being, in view of the changed market situation and the weaker prices, or only implemented to a very limited extent.

8

Trends in world trade in non-ferrous metals

8.1 ORIGIN AND DETERMINING FACTORS

It was only in the early phase of industrialization that the non-ferrous metal consumer and producer countries were largely identical, as at that time the first countries to become industrialized could still to a considerable extent cover their comparatively small requirements for metallic materials from their own domestic ore basis. With the rapid rise in consumption of metals these countries, however, had increasingly to make use of foreign resources for their raw materials supply. A feature of this development was the vigorous expansion of world markets in which the trend towards higher turnovers in external trade in non-ferrous metals has continued unabated up to the present day. It differs only in pace and extent for individual metals.

The broad expansion of world trade was accompanied by continual changes in the economic network of international trade which was influenced by factors both of supply and demand. The reasons for this include political events such as wars and their aftermath, block alignments among countries and shifts in currents of trade due both to economic and financial adjustments in the world metal economy and to environmental protection regulations. The principal reasons, however, were the following:

(a) differences in the overall economic and industrial growth of the consumer countries, with consequent variations in the increase of consumption and demand;
(b) changes in the structure of world industry during the course of industrialization both by countries and by branches of industry, and their repercussions on demand;
(c) changes in the type and quality of the primary materials required;
(d) changes in the availability of primary raw materials, either because of progressive mining of domestic mineral deposits up to exhaustion or because the deposits used in the consumer countries, compared with mining of resources in overseas territories, had become uneconomic;

188 *Non-ferrous metals*

(e) differences in the development of mine output in the countries producing raw materials, also influenced by the degree of concentration and success in exploration activities;
(f) changes in the development and expansion of smelter and refining capacities as well as shifts in the foreign sources of supply of primary materials;
(g) changes in the type and quality of market supplies of mine and smelter products.

8.2 ESSENTIAL FEATURES AND CHANGES IN THE STRUCTURE OF TRADE

Owing to the lack of statistical data it is not possible to give a complete indication of the trend of world trade in non-ferrous metals during the initial decades of industrialization. The network of international trade in non-ferrous metals and the form it assumed during the course of the industrial process can only be traced for the most recent period (see section 8.3 below). For the individual metals, however, the following analysis of the international pattern of supply and demand still clearly indicates the essential features and changes in the world situation of supplies and purchases during this period. Apart from the data given in *Metal Statistics* for 1929–50, the figures are largely based on the Report of the Paley Commission, who for their studies at that time had access to the best possible sources of information.[1]

Copper

Under the influence of the industrialization process this was the first non-ferrous metal to develop worldwide trade relations (see Appendix, Table A7). As this metal was already an indispensable material in the early stages of technology and development, the copper deposits in some European countries, although intrinsically of no great importance, were soon worked out and could no longer adequately satisfy the rapidly expanding requirements for copper. In this early phase of industrial development only the copper trade of Chile with Europe was of worldwide importance. As a share of world supplies it reached its peak in the 1860s and 1870s. During the 1880s the United States entered the field, with the opening up of its copper deposits at the Great Lakes and other reserves in the country. It had initially imported the bulk of its copper requirements but now became an export country in the copper trade and soon, as the biggest copper producer, acquired an influential position in the world market.

As the United States in course of time also brought the Chilean and other Latin American copper mines under its control financially and economically, the production of those countries accordingly became primarily directed towards refining and subsequent export, which accounted for around 66% of

[1] Paley Report, 1952.

world exports at that time. The copper production which had begun in the Congo was also for the most part refined in the United States (Gibson-Jarvie, 1976, p. 39). Thus, copper exports from Chile to Europe were soon surpassed by exports from the United States, likewise mainly destined for Europe, and the United States around the turn of the century and up to the outbreak of the First World War became the largest copper exporter in the world.

For a whole century the Old World was the only important import region for copper, which came predominantly from the western hemisphere. With an overseas turnover of unrefined copper of 38% copper smelter production in the world, some 90%, according to the annual averages from 1924/26, was imported into Europe from overseas, mainly from the United States, Chile, Peru, Canada, Mexico and the Congo (*Metal Statistics*, 29th year).

A new phase in world trade in copper began to take shape in the mid 1920s, when copper production in Latin America was vigorously expanded and, with the opening up of the extensive copper reserves in Africa and Canada, new and cheaper supplies made their appearance. At the same time the rapid increase in copper consumption in the United States at first brought about a decline in exports and finally compounded with net imports. A profound change in the structure of the copper trade resulted from a far-reaching polarisation developed between the eastern and western hemispheres: the United States became the chief purchaser of copper from Chile, Mexico, Canada and Peru and the European consumer countries increasingly covered their copper requirements from African producers. Direct trading in copper between the two leading industrial regions of North America and Europe remained comparatively slight up to the Second World War and transatlantic trade in the pre-war years consisted mainly of shipping of Latin American copper, which was refined in the USA and then exported to European countries (Grunwald and Musgrove, 1970, p. 158).

Yet another change in the structure of world copper trade began a decade after the Second World War, when the demand for copper increased more slowly in the United States than world demand and the rapidly expanding copper consumption in Europe could no longer be covered from the traditional sources. Europe thus soon became the most important sales outlet for Latin American production of refined copper. In subsequent years, however, this export from Latin America shifted increasingly to direct export to Western Europe, which today takes approximately 30% of the copper ores and concentrates with the rest going predominantly to Asia, in particular Japan.

Recently a new geographical trend has become apparent in world copper trade: under the influence of progressive industrialization in Third World countries, new sales outlets are opening up in the most advanced countries. One of the results of this, up to the present time, has been increasing intraregional trade in refined copper in Latin America: for example, in 1978 13% of Chilean exports were destined for Brazil.

To sum up, it may be observed that the bulk of world imports of unrefined copper in the early phase of the industrialization process went to the industrial nations of Europe, which possessed few raw materials of their own. The United States, however, although relatively well endowed with domestic resources, soon became one of the leading groups for copper import. Throughout the entire period under review, 1929–78, Chile remained with a considerable lead the most important supply country for the United States, with a peak share of American imports of 43% in 1965, which decreased during the course of the nationalization measures in the Chilean metal industry but still made up 34% in 1978 with a maximum value by volume. Mexico occupied second place as a supplier country to the United States up to the outbreak of the Second World War, but then lost importance as a supplier, compared with other countries such as Canada, Zambia and Peru – possibly as a result of 'Mexicanization' of its mining and smelting industry or because of its increasing domestic requirements in the course of growing industrialization.

Germany up to the end of the 1930s occupied second place in the world output of unrefined copper, for which the United States was the most important supplier, followed by Chile, Rhodesia (Zimbabwe) and the Belgian Congo. After the Second World War Germany only regained this position during the course of economic reconstruction of the country and in 1978 recorded the highest output worldwide of copper – considerably ahead of the United States in this respect – of which approximately two-thirds of imports of copper were supplied by Chile, South Africa, Poland, Zambia and Belgium-Luxemburg.

The United Kingdom, France, Belgium-Luxembourg and Italy have traditionally ranked among the chief importing countries, joined during the last decade by Japan, the bulk of whose imports are from Zambia, Chile, Peru and Africa.

Lead

World trade in lead (see Appendix, Table A8) is characterized by the fact that lead ores have traditionally been smelted for the most part in the country of ore mining. Only ores for which the domestic smelters were not equipped to separate their by-products had to be exported, so that only a relatively small proportion of lead ore production in the world (20% in 1976) was available for smelting in the jobbing smelters of countries which do not possess their own ore basis (World Bureau of Metal Statistics, 1976). The European countries, despite a large volume of their own production, were the largest importers of soft lead and lead bullion up to the end of the 1930s. In the mid 1920s Europe imported one-quarter of lead smelter production of the world from overseas, chiefly from Mexico, Canada and Australia and, before the world recession, the United States. The United States was then largely self-sufficient, but since the 1950s has been an import country for lead on the world market and was in

1978 ahead of the United Kingdom, West Germany, Italy and Japan. In the lead export trade West Germany took third place in 1978, after Australia and Canada and before the United Kingdom and Peru, but the USSR also temporarily became an important supplier during the period 1960–78.

Zinc

The export quota for zinc ore (see Appendix, Table A9) is considerably higher than that for lead ore: in the mid 1930s approximately 37% of zinc ores mined were exported for smelting and even recently this proportion is hardly less, showing that the raw materials basis of the mainly European jobbing smelters of zinc is considerably more extensive than that of lead. The most important countries for zinc are traditionally the major European industrial countries, headed by the United Kingdom, West Germany and France. Since the 1950s the United States has also belonged to this group, which today, by a considerable margin, records the maximum import of zinc in the world. Since the mid 1960s, however, the USSR has also been represented among the major zinc-importing countries.

Up to the outbreak of the Second World War world trade in zinc was transacted predominantly within Europe, as in export Poland, Belgium, Germany, Norway and the Netherlands also took precedence beside Canada and Australia. Since 1950 non-European countries have steadily been gaining ground, including (1978) Canada, in first place, followed by Australia, with high shares of their mine and smelter production; Mexico, Peru and the USSR are also represented in the top group with Belgium, the Netherlands, West Germany and Spain.

Tin

In world trade tin (Table A10) is the most constant of the non-ferrous metals in the structure by countries, subject to the regional concentration of raw material deposits and also depending on the location of smelter capacities. Apart from Malaya, the raw materials countries have until recently exported their tin in the form of concentrates for smelting. In the 1930s around 55% of tin metal in the world was produced in three smelters in Malaya, which smelted ores from Burma and Thailand as well as domestic ores. Approximately 10% of world smelter production was supplied by Banka and Billington in the present-day Indonesia and around 30% in five smelters in the United Kingdom, Belgium and the Netherlands, countries which maintained close trade links with the producer countries of mine products through political links and foreign possessions. Smaller amounts of tin were also produced in present-day Zaire. The United States up to 1941 had no significant smelter capacity but then, however, set up a large smelter for the processing of imported ores, chiefly from Bolivia. Today the smelter industry is somewhat less concentrated, because of the construction of plants in Brazil,

Nigeria, Indonesia and Thailand (Grunwald and Musgrove, 1970, p. 231).

The traditionally most important exporting country for crude tin is the present-day Malaysia. By far the most important European exporting countries – the United Kingdom, West Germany, Belgium, Luxembourg and the Netherlands – base their exports on imported materials. The United States, Japan, the Netherlands, India and Taiwan are the most important sales outlets for Malaysia. The United Kingdom sends most of its foreign crude tin exports to the USSR, while West Germany, Belgium, Luxembourg and the Netherlands supply predominantly European purchaser countries. The most important countries are today the United States, leading by a considerable margin, West Germany, France, the USSR, the United Kingdom and Italy.

Aluminium

This metal only became a commodity of world trade after the First World War, but until 1938 in still comparatively small volumes (see Appendix, Table A11). International exports in the annual averages recorded for 1924/26 were estimated at approximately 10% of aluminium production, i.e., some 18,000 tonnes. Even in the 1930s, of the five quantitatively most important non-ferrous metals aluminium had the greatest volume of domestic sales. Around 75% of aluminium production in the world was further processed in the countries with smelter production and only 25% was exported (*Metal Statistics*, 1927, p. vi; 1935, p. ix). Foreign trade was still largely one-way business, the countries concerned participating in world trade by either imports or exports, so that the data on exported or imported volumes usually also indicates approximate net positions. Up to the advent of the world recession Canada, Switzerland, the United Kingdom and France were the most important exporting countries, which in 1938 also included Norway and the United States. Of these only France and the United States could rely on their deposits of bauxite, the most important raw material for aluminium recovery, whereas the remaining countries had to develop their smelter production on the basis of imported raw materials. The principal importing countries were the European industrial nations, the United States and Japan.

The very marked one-way export trade in aluminium was still to be observed over a long period even after the resumption of world trade following the Second World War. The major exporting countries already mentioned (which were joined by the USSR after 1960) at that time did not engage in any appreciable imports and, conversely, the most important importing countries, the United States, the United Kingdom, West Germany, Belgium-Luxembourg, Sweden, the Netherlands and Spain recorded only very insignificant exports. The principal exception here was Switzerland, which on account of the reduction and fabrication plant of Alusuisse on the German border displayed a complex structure in external trade in aluminium. In Italy, also, trade flows in both directions were recorded during the period to a greater extent than in the other countries (in the 1960s, however, Italy became solely an importer of aluminium (Brubaker, 1967, p. 120 ff.)).

This basic pattern of world trade in aluminium was then transformed by an enormous expansion in turnover, extending up to recent times, so that the most important net import countries today, the United States, the United Kingdom, West Germany, France and Japan, have also increasingly become aluminium exporters. The trade network in this sector of the world metal economy has therefore considerably intensified with progressive industrialization. In this respect a market regional orientation of exchange relations has become apparent. The European exporting countries, with Norway, the Netherlands, West Germany, France and the United Kingdom in the top international group, transact their main business in Europe, whereas the external trade of Canada and United States is concentrated mainly on North and South America and Asia. The strongly marked orientation towards domestic sales which is traditional in the aluminium industry has continued up to the present day, however, as only some 21% (1976) of world production of aluminium goes for export, whereas the main bulk of production also undergoes secondary processing in the producer country.

8.3 THE REGIONAL PATTERN OF TRADE

In the decades following the Second World War, during which the industrialization process was resumed with a powerful upswing, the growing needs of the industrialized countries under this impetus resulted in a further vigorous expansion of world trade in the metal industry sector. From 1955 to 1976 world exports of non-ferrous metals (SITC 68) – conditional on prices – have increased altogether sixfold from $3.6 billion to $21.7 billion. This trend was accompanied by considerable shifts in the international currents of trade. These have become even more pronounced in the course of time and up to the present day have resulted in the following 'pattern of trade' in the world metal industry (see also Table 43):

(a) The predominant share of world trade in non-ferrous metals is taken up by the industrial regions of North America, Japan and Western Europe. Their share of global exports increased still further in the post-war years from 55% in 1955 to 60% in 1976.
(b) The share taken by the developing countries in world exports on the other hand declined during the same period from 34% (1955) to 25% (1976).
(c) The Eastern Bloc countries were able at the same time to step up their participation in world trade and in 1975 recorded a share in world exports of 9% (7% in 1955).

Table 43. World trade in non-ferrous metals by regions, 1955–76
Trade between regions

Destination region		Western industrial regions[1]			Oil-exporting developing countries			Other developing countries			Eastern Bloc countries			World	
			Share of			Share of			Share of			Share of		Total exports of supplier regions	
Supplier region	Year	Total ($ billion)	Exports of supplier region (%)	Imports of destination region (%)	Total ($ billion)	Exports of supplier region (%)	Imports of destination region (%)	Total ($ billion)	Exports of supplier region (%)	Imports of destination region (%)	Total ($ billion)	Exports of supplier region (%)	Imports of destination region (%)	($ billion)	(%)
Western industrial regions[1]	1955	1.72	87.7	56.6	—	—	—	0.17	8.7	79.0	0.07	3.5	25.0	1.96	55.2
	1970	6.11	85.9	59.8	0.08	1.1	80.0	0.59	8.2	64.1	0.33	4.6	39.2	7.11	58.9
	1976	10.85	83.1	64.4	0.40	3.3	66.7	1.10	9.1	47.8	0.60	5.0	34.3	12.95	60.5
Developing countries	1955	1.16	95.9	38.2	—	—	—	0.05	4.1	21.7	—	—	—	1.21	34.1
	1970	3.22	91.0	31.5	0.02	0.6	20.6	0.22	6.2	23.9	0.08	2.3	9.5	3.54	29.3
	1976	4.10	77.4	24.3	0.10	1.9	16.7	0.90	17.0	39.1	0.20	3.8	11.4	5.30	24.8
Eastern Bloc countries	1955	0.04	16.0	1.3	—	—	—	0.01	4.0	4.3	0.20	80.0	71.4	0.25	7.0
	1970	0.44	48.4	4.3	—	—	—	0.04	4.3	4.3	0.43	47.3	51.2	0.91	7.5
	1976[2]	0.95	57.7	5.6	0.01	1.1	1.8	0.08	4.3	4.0	0.87	47.0	49.7	1.85	8.6
World[3]	1955	3.04	85.6	100	—	—	—	0.23	6.5	100	0.28	7.9	—	3.55	
	1970	10.21	84.6	100	0.10	0.8	100	0.92	7.6	100	0.84	7.0	—	12.07	
	1976	16.75	78.3	100	0.60	2.8	100	2.30	10.7	100	1.75	8.1	—	21.40	

Note: Values of trade expressed as US $ f.o.b.
1. North America, Japan, Western Europe. 2. 1975 figures for exports other than to Western industrial regions.
3. Including Australia, New Zealand and South Africa.

Table 43. (cont'd)
Exports of the industrial regions

Destination region			World	North America		Japan		Western Europe		Oil-exporting countries		Developing countries		Eastern Bloc countries	
Supplier region		Year	($ billion)	($ billion)	(%)	($ billion)	(%)	($ billion)	(%)	($ billion)	(%)	($ billion)	(%)	($ billion)	(%)
North America		1963	1.10	0.42	38.2	0.03	2.7	0.50	45.5	0.01	0.9	0.14	12.7	–	–
		1970	2.44	0.81	33.2	0.14	5.7	1.16	47.5	0.02	0.8	0.29	11.9	0.02	0.8
		1976	3.15	1.55	49.2	0.15	4.8	0.95	30.2	0.10	3.2	0.35	11.1	0.05	1.6
Japan		1963	0.04	0.02	50.0	–	–	–	–	–	–	0.02	50.0	–	–
		1970	0.25	0.08	32.0	–	–	0.04	16.0	0.01	4.0	0.09	36.0	0.03	12.0
		1976	0.67	0.15	22.4	–	–	0.05	7.5	0.08	11.9	0.35	52.2	0.04	6.0
Western Europe		1963	1.59	0.23	14.5	0.02	1.3	1.10	69.2	0.02	1.3	0.11	6.9	0.11	6.9
		1970	4.42	0.31	7.0	0.07	1.6	3.50	79.2	0.05	1.1	0.21	4.8	0.28	6.3
		1976	9.03	0.75	8.3	0.10	1.1	7.05	78.1	0.22	2.4	0.40	4.4	0.51	5.6

Note: Values of trade expressed as US $ f.o.b.
Source: Compiled and calculated from GATT, 1977 and 1978 (Tables A3 and B3).

(d) The industrial regions have an even greater supremacy in world imports than in world exports, even though their share has declined from 86% in 1955 to 78% in 1976.
(e) The volume of imports of the developing countries (including the oil-exporting countries) on the other hand increased during the same period from 7% (1955) to 14% (1976).
(f) The Eastern Bloc countries record a development in global imports approximately proportional to the expansion of world trade: their share in 1976 at 8% was only slightly higher than in 1955.

Another salient feature of international trade in non-ferrous metal ores, concentrates and smelter and refinery products is that the exchange of goods operates mainly within the industrial regions; looking at import shares of the industrial regions as a percentage of their exports, 83% in 1976 compared with 88% in 1955, the interregional network has scarcely diminished. Of the exports of the developing countries the individual regions took only 77% in 1976 (96% in 1955), while the exchange of goods within the Third World has considerably intensified with increasing industrialization of these countries, showing a share of exports from 19% in 1976 compared with 4% in 1955. The exports of the developing countries to the Eastern Bloc increased in 1976 to take a share of 4% (2% in 1970). The non-ferrous metal exports of the Eastern Bloc countries to the industrial countries in 1976 was 58% (16% in 1955) and to the developing countries 5% (1975), while the percentage of exports within the Eastern Bloc countries amounted in 1975 to 47% (80% in 1955). Of world exports within the Western industrial regions, a decreasing share of 20% went to North America in 1976 (29% in 1963), an increasing share of 8% to Japan (3.7% in 1963) and 72% to Western Europe (68% in 1963).

North American exports to the oil-exporting countries in 1976 were 3.2% (0.9% in 1963), to the Eastern Bloc slightly up at 1.6% (0.8% in 1970) and to the developing countries roughly the same, at 13% compared with 11% in 1970. Exports to Western Europe declined between 1963 and 1976 proportionately from 46% to 30%, although this still represents by far the most important external trade relationship of North America in the field of the metal industry.

Japan's comparatively low exports of non-ferrous metals in 1976 were mainly concentrated on the developing countries (64%) and North America (22%). Western Europe, with a share of 8%, has lost ground relatively as a purchaser region, with a somewhat higher volume of trade, and the Eastern Bloc (6%) has also declined in importance as a sales outlet for Japan since 1970.

The intraregional share of non-ferrous metal exports amounted in 1976 to 78% (69% in 1963). Exports of the Western European countries by value are almost three times as great as those of North America. In export to the other regions North America took the lead over the developing countries with an 8% share in 1976, including the oil-exporting countries (7%), the Eastern Bloc countries (6%) and Japan (1%).

9

Pricing in the non-ferrous metal markets

9.1 PRICING AT THE METAL EXCHANGES

9.1.1 The London Metal Exchange

The fact that there was generally wide geographical separation between the natural sources of supply and the industrialized areas of demand in the non-ferrous metals sector at an early date resulted in the formation of commercial centres for the quantitatively most important metals. A metal exchange was established in London as early as 1862, at a time when the United Kingdom was the world leader in metallurgy and the metalworking industries. With the exploitation of new ore deposits and with progressive industrialization, considerable changes took place in the production and marketing structure of the world's metal economy and this process of change is still continuing. London has nevertheless remained the internationally most important centre of exchange trading in metals.

The London Metal Exchange (LME) began its commercial activity in January 1877. It was established in legal form as a company limited by shares in 1881, and it still operates in this form today. Exchange trading was only suspended during the two world wars; it was resumed in stages from November 1949 to August 1953. The London Metal Exchange is owned by the Metal Market & Exchange Company Ltd, whose members are the shareholders of the Exchange. Membership can be on an individual basis (Individual Subscriber) or as representative of a firm or company (Representative Subscriber). The members elect the Exchange Council and appoint a committee of members as the executive body of the exchange. The daily assessment of the prices prevailing in exchange trading is now the duty of the Quotations Committee. Traditionally the heavy metals copper, lead, zinc and tin have been permitted for official trading at the London Metal Exchange. Aluminium has also been traded there since 2 October 1978, and forward dealings in nickel were introduced on 23 April 1979, spot dealings in this metal commencing on 20 June 1979. Since February 1968 there has again been a silver market at the LME, after two previous suspensions. Special privilege is needed to participate in dealing in the 'Ring' – traditionally so named from the admission marking that used to be drawn with chalk in the hall of the Exchange at the opening of dealings. This privilege is only granted to firms legally registered in the United Kingdom and depends among other things on the fulfilment of high financial requirements (including liquidity and bank guarantees each at £500,000), to ensure the traditional system of principal's dealings. In this trading the members of the Exchange conclude contracts directly with each other without clearing house facilities or global guarantee on the part of the Exchange. The LME merely settles the daily balances by way of warrant clearings, but the individual contracts remain in existence until maturity.[1] Reciprocal protection for the members of the Ring – and therefore also for their clients – is provided by the LME Compensation Fund, which receives contributions from the members of the Ring.

The London Metal Exchange is also a physical market at which metals are bought and sold and are not only traded on the basis of warrants. The metals delivered or imported are deposited in officially registered LME warehouses and taken from them when a sale is made. From the point of view of customs law these may be 'free-port' transit or internal warehouses. Up to autumn 1963 the metal reserves of the LME were stored exclusively in British warehouses. So that the significance of the Exchange as an international trading centre would not be impaired in the course of the moves for European integration, warehouses for copper and tin were also set up on the continent of Europe (October 1963 in Rotterdam, February 1965 in Hamburg and November 1965 in Antwerp). At present there are 15 licensed European LME warehouses. Their location was at first restricted to the United Kingdom and the North Sea coast of the Continent, but an LME warehouse has since been operated in Genoa (Italy); extension to other producer and consumer centres of the world has not so far been considered appropriate on theoretical and practical grounds, including transport and foreign exchange problems (Gibson-Jarvie, 1976, p. 154 f.).[2]

Trading at the London Metal Exchange is based on standard contracts, which in addition to the prices lay down all the important terms of business,

---

1 This business principle differs fundamentally from that of a 'true' clearing house. Such a function is performed, for example, by the International Commodities Clearing House (formerly London Produce Clearing House), which has been in existence nearly as long as the LME, and handles contracts on a clearing basis at nearly all raw material markets in London – apart from the LME – and also some foreign exchanges (Gibson-Jarvie, 1976, pp. 22–26 and 142).
2 The Japanese Mitsubishi Metal Co. has urged the LME to set up a warehouse in the Far East (Tokyo or Singapore), because this would enable Japan and other Asian countries to participate in the pricing of metals and Japan as a user country could then play a more active role in the world marketing structure for non-ferrous metals. The present warehousing costs in Europe could then be drastically reduced.

such as qualities, sizes, mineral contents, delivery dates, places of delivery and conditions of payment. The LME contracts stipulate delivery in lots of a fixed weight, namely 25 tonnes for aluminium, copper, lead and zinc, 6 tonnes for nickel and 5 tonnes for tin; the lot weights may be 2% above or below these figures. The standard contracts are valid for dealings with a term of three months;[1] commitments for a longer term are covered by what are known as 'White Contracts', which are also subject to the LME rules, but are not effected by the warrant clearing that exists between the members of the Ring.

Originally there were four standard contracts, differing according to the term for copper and tin, from which the prototype of the standard contract developed, i.e. sale of metal at an agreed prompt delivery date. The first change was made in 1888, when 'good merchantable brands' (GMB) were made the basis of the standard warrants, which covered various grades of unrefined ('rough') and refined copper registered with the LME committee; the metal had to assay not less than 93% copper content and satisfy prescribed quality tests. In the year 1898 the grade 'refined', with 99–99.3% Cu, was declared as standard copper for the contract and a system of premium for electrolytic copper and discounts for 'rough' copper (below 94% Cu) was introduced. Until 1963 this standard contract remained the only copper contract in the LME. Then, in an attempt to adapt the contract conditions to the needs of industry, three contracts were introduced for wirebar, cathodes and for fire-refined copper, the first being split into two grades, 'electrolytic bars' and 'high-conductivity fire-refined (HCFR) bars'.

The early LME tin contracts were similar to the copper contracts; they were replaced in 1891 by a 'good merchantable quality' (GMQ) contract, which permitted the supply of Australian and Straits tin only. A second contract was introduced in 1897 for 'mixed tin', and included Banka and Billiton tin. The standard tin contract was introduced in 1912; because of the narrow market it permitted deliveries of various quality grades with corresponding price discounts up to at least 99% tin content. This minimum purity was further reduced to 98.5% in 1935, primarily in order to include the growing supply of tin from China. In 1958, however, the contract was again made stricter in regard to quality requirements, until finally a maximum tin content of 99.75% was demanded and the brand had to be permitted and registered by the committee. In 1974 the 'high-grade contract' was introduced (minimum 99.85% tin content). In 1903 the 'Good soft pig lead' contract for lead was introduced, and in 1915 the 'virgin spelter' contract was introduced for common spelter, though neither of these contracts stipulated anything

---

1 The LME has no plans to extend the contract period for the metals it deals in beyond the present term of three months. The reason for this lies in the consumer-orientated character of the LME, since the market is more exposed to speculative forces when contract periods are longer. Moreover, the entry requirements should not be raised, because the speculative element is less than on the US forward markets. According to the latest report of the Bank of England the participation of non-market circles in the LME was below 20% for all metals.

concerning the standards of the metal that could be delivered; for zinc, 'good ordinary brand' (GOB), with 98% metal content, was customary. Both metals were traded officially in the Ring for the first time in 1920. It was not until after the Second World War that the contracts for lead and zinc were altered so that the deliverable material was restricted to certain permitted brands. The warehouse warrant first became a transferable document in LME dealings in 1960.

The lead and zinc contracts are judged to be less satisfactory from the consumer's point of view with regard to their quality requirements and the permissible tolerances for impurities, because the consumer is not so much interested in the level of impurities but their nature, and this is not directly discernible from the contracts. This is an example of the fact that contract requirements as the basis for physical deliveries may be completely different from those for the purpose of forward exchange guarantee.

Initially copper and tin, on the one hand, and lead and zinc, on the other, were dealt with separately, because the latter still lacked the necessary standardization of quality categories and accordingly of contracts; only after the First World War were they brought together in one large ring. The practice at that time has recently been discussed again as a possibility for adopting trade in certain of the minor metals – despite the same two reservations – especially as most dealers in the Ring do not deal only in the six basic metals.

The special dealing in the Ring is limited to five minutes twice a day for each metal, during which spot and forward transactions[1] are concluded. The official LME quotations depend on the Bid and Offer prices called last in the second session of the Ring, and these are adopted as the basis for sales throughout the world until the next session of the Ring. Immediately after these prices have been announced, the kerb market begins, in which dealing is continued and the 'separate rings' are extended to about half an hour. The afternoon exchange also takes place – as a continuation of the kerb – in separate rings for the individual metals; by this time the Commodity Exchange (COMEX) in New York has already started business. The physical volume of sales at the New York market is relatively small, but the investment and arbitrage transactions with London are appreciable, so that the COMEX market may have considerable effects on the dealing at the LME.

The price quotations at the London Metal Exchange are important for the metal industry in two respects:

(a) The official settlement quotation serves as the price basis for sales contracts between semi-fabrication works and producers.

1 The technique of hedging on the London Metal Exchange is described in detail by Gibson-Jarvie (1976, p. 7 ff.), who also explains the terms 'contango' – the discount for spot purchases compared with three-month purchases – and 'backwardation' – the premium for spot goods on the London Market, as well as other exchange operations, such as carries, options, back-pricing, etc., and the main technical terms involved.

(b) The forward quotations for deliveries and sales form the basis for the hedging operations of the consumers, dealers and producers.

All transactions at the LME are based on the settlement price, which is identical to the spot selling price for that particular day; it also serves as the basis for sales contracts concluded between producers and customers directly.

The large producers had always endeavoured to repress exchange trade in favour of direct sales at firm prices, even at appreciably under LME quotations, so that, for example, the copper prices at the LME were sometimes only representative of a fraction of sales, as they were for zinc after introduction of the producer price in July 1964. In the first few years after the Second World War, volume of sales at the LME failed even to reach the pre-war share: for example, in autumn 1964 only about one-tenth of copper supply was sold in trading at the LME, the other nine-tenths being sold in direct trading.[1] Since then there has been a progressive worldwide increase of trade at the LME; in the case of copper, the proportion of sales at the LME in the Western world was estimated at 15% at the beginning of the 1970s.[2] Admittedly the volume of sales (see Table 44) cannot be determined completely, because the business concluded between the members of the Ring is not known, but it is certainly correct to say that the LME is primarily a 'pricing' market rather than a 'delivering' one. This is also the basis for the undoubtedly important guidance function of the LME, as is evident from the fact that its quotations serve almost exclusively as the price basis even for sales that are not effected through the Exchange.[3]

9.1.2 The New York Commodity Exchange (COMEX)

The New York Commodity Exchange Inc. (COMEX) was formed in 1933 as a result of the merger of four special exchanges, among which the National Metal Exchange had already carried out trade in metals. The members of COMEX (over 400) from the metal trade and – in contrast to the LME – also from the metallurgical industry and finance institutions, buy their seat in the Exchange as joint property. Metals traded are copper, lead, zinc[4] and tin, the

---

1 *Die Metalle*, 1965, p. 50.
2 Cissarz, *et al.*, 1972, p. 497.
3 This is also confirmed in the statistics published by Metallgesellschaft AG, Frankfurt-am-Main, which say: 'The metal markets, especially the LME, have developed into an establishment where prices are formed on the basis of smoothing out the peaks and the need for protection of consumers and producers. In this way they fulfil an important task and it certainly does not seem imperative that sales of metals dealt in by the Exchange are effected entirely or predominantly through the Exchange, as the Exchange quotations form the basis for pricing almost exclusively even in sales not effected at the Exchange' (*Metal Statistics*, 1968, p. x).
4 The COMEX zinc contract appears recently to have become insignificant, as a result of lack of sales; it is already an appreciable time since any transactions have been effected on its basis and so far no suggestions for its reactivation have come either from the exchange or from industry.

Table 44. The London Metal Exchange, turnover and stocks, 1970–79 (tonnes)

	Lead	Zinc	Copper	Tin	Nickel	Aluminium
Turnover						
1970	568,955	263,425	1,479,125	124,525	–	–
1971	671,825	576,925	1,904,250	129,005	–	–
1972	746,575	781,175	1,818,950	144,130	–	–
1973	1,106,525	1,059,730	3,006,150	147,490	–	–
1974	842,300	1,023,850	2,278,775	204,395	–	–
1975	809,725	998,575	2,720,400	169,695	–	–
1976	994,350	1,107,050	3,801,250	255,815	–	–
1977	1,510,130	1,065,500	3,394,625	305,565	–	–
1978	1,443,150	1,105,950	4,310,185	288,380	–	87,375[1]
1979	1,859,610	1,137,050	4,658,420	232,995	74,790[2]	1,062,710
Stocks						
1970	23,375	13,775	72,600	2,006	–	–
1971	55,225	16,150	140,300	6,059	–	–
1972	17,900	34,800	183,050	6,850	–	–
1973	21,625	8,075	34,825	2,580	–	–
1974	19,900	13,500	125,900	2,190	–	–
1975	85,300	69,750	496,975	7,225	–	–
1976	65,875	89,175	603,475	5,350	–	–
1977	66,925	64,525	641,175	4,085	–	–
1978	15,475	69,550	373,650	1,585	–	–
1979	17,525	46,000	126,500	1,740	5,700	17,450

1. October–December. 2. April–December.
Source: Date from Metallgesellschaft AG, Frankfurt am Main.

last with a pause from 1959 to April 1964 because of insufficient sales. The most important aspect of the New York Exchange is long-term forward business up to a maximum term of 14 months (Cissarz et al., 1970, p. 50), though spot prices are also quoted. The quotations at this commodity exchange are freely formed market prices; they also influence the domestic prices set by the American producers.

Like the London Metal Exchange, COMEX also maintains licensed copper warehouses. Turnover at COMEX, however, does not reach that of the London Metal Exchange. The major proportion of the copper requirements in the United States is similarly covered in direct trade between consumers and producers. Apart from this, copper is supplied by importers, trading companies and remelting works – and recently also by some copper producers – primarily on the basis of daily quotations. The importance of COMEX is largely limited to the American market.[1]

1 This is also why Chile, for example, bases its copper prices on the quotations of the LME. ENAMI, the Chilean government corporation for smaller and medium-size mines, which began trading on the LME in May 1979, bases its copper acquisitions on a price corresponding to the LME average of the previous month.

9.1.3 The Metal Exchange in Penang

For international trade in tin, in addition to the exchanges in London and New York there is also a kind of exchange in Penang (Malaysia).[1] Pricing in Penang differs from the pricing at the London Metal Exchange in that the former is not a stock exchange organization in the true sense, but rather the companies of the two tin smelting works, Sharikat Eastern Smelting and Straits Trading in Kuala Lumpur, establish the price daily by way of an auction where the material offered by the ore suppliers on each particular day is marketed.

The offers made by the purchasers to the two smelting works (at the market price or on a firm price basis) are effected through international tin dealers, such as Amalgamated Metal, Phibro and Billiton, some large American fabricators (including US Steel and Bethlehem Steel) and also local dealers. Pricing is then effected thus: starting with the highest bid price, all offer prices are gone through until a price is reached at which all the ore lots offered on that particular day — including offers to buy at a higher offering price — can be sold in the form of metal. Some levelling of peaks finally takes place between the two smelting works. Deliveries take place within two months after smelting the concentrates. No information is published on the deals made in Penang, but according to the amounts exported by Malaysia and Singapore, which are largely identical with the exchange sales (of which there is very little domestic consumption), the effective trading there might be greater than at the LME in London (Stodieck, 1970, p. 37). This is primarily because the exchange in Malaysia is in a more favourable location for the major producers, and is also reflected in the decision of the International Tin Council (4 July 1972) to take the quotations in Penang as a guide for the price limits of the International Tin Agreement. The price was given there up to 1980 in Malaysian dollars per pikul (133.3 lb) 'ex warehouse', and since January 1981, for metal that is smelted by the smelting works from the concentrate offered within 45–60 days, in Malaysian ringgit per kg 'ex smelter'.

9.2 PRICING OUTSIDE THE METAL EXCHANGES

Apart from the pricing pattern at the exchanges an important part has always been played by the autonomous pricing by supplier firms on the market. Such producer prices, for example the 'European Zinc Producers Price', are published separately by the large firms as list prices. The usually slight differences found between individual producer prices are due to the fact that these are homogeneously interchangeable commodities which do not permit of wide price disparities. It is also encouraged by the fact that price variations generally succeed each other at very close intervals of time, take the same

---

[1] In Singapore, until 1965, the Straits Trading Co. determined a price from the cassiterite concentrate proposals and the dealers' purchase offers. With the departure of Singapore from the Federation of Malaysia this exchange was transferred to Penang (Gocht, 1974, p. 250).

direction and are relatively of the same magnitude. For smaller producers the list prices of the major producers serve as reference prices for granting of discounts on the conclusion of contracts. For metals traded on the exchanges, the producer prices are in competition with the exchange quotations. According to the market situation premiums are sought or discounts granted on producer prices. Producer prices are frequently set for a specified period for forward purchase contracts – usually one year. This applies especially to metals for which there is no quotation on the exchanges. This form of pricing is also fully intentional, as producer prices are aimed to offer particular metals at a comparatively stable price, as opposed to the price discounts of exchange quotations, and to afford the fabricators a more constant basis for calculation. The producers, however, seek by their pricing policy to inhibit undesirable substitution processes and feeble demand, in order to ward off a price collapse, with its undesirable repercussions on mining activity and smelter operations.

In the current system of producer prices a price setting leadership occurs under certain circumstances. Because of the closely-knit association of metal markets, producer prices are inevitably oriented towards the prices of the internationally more powerful producers who because of their high shares of production virtually dominate market supply in the Western world. The lack of competitive exchange trading makes price setting easier, as for example in the case of aluminium up to October 1978 and nickel up to April 1979.

9.3 THE CURRENT PRICE STRUCTURE

The price structure in the world metal industry is very highly differentiated in accordance with the wide variety of market forms and market regulatory practices in existence. The following kinds of price, categorized according to the basic principles by which they are determined, can be found:

(a) price freely quoted on the exchanges;
(b) exchange prices which are influenced by quantitative measures for the regulation of the market supply under international agreements;
(c) list prices set by price setting leadership;
(d) free prices agreed between purchasers and producers (e.g., for special metals).

After the rescinding of the almost universal government price controls imposed during the Second World War and the re-opening of trading at the London Metal Exchange, the following price structures were established for the principal non-ferrous metals.

Copper

Copper quotations on the London Metal Exchange are almost exclusively the price basis for purchasing transactions in the Western world, outside the

United States. In West Germany, in addition, the so-called DEL-Notice (German quotation for electrolytic copper for conductor purposes) is issued daily in Düsseldorf. This is determined on the basis of notifications made by the major producers, dealers and fabricators on their business transactions. Because of the price orientation to be noted generally on the LME this Notice runs parallel to the London quotations (Forster, 1976, p. 53).

There have been constant attempts on the part of the producers – including those outside the United States – to introduce fixed prices independent of pricing on the London Metal Exchange. Thus the RST Group (Rhodesian Selection Trust) in 1955 adopted their own producer price; the other African Commonwealth producer Anglo-American continued to base its trading on the LME quotations and the RST Group discontinued this practice after a few years (Gibson-Jarvie, 1976, p. 44). In 1961 the major producers in Chile and Africa agreed on a selling price as a means of avoiding constant fluctuations in the exchange price. This fixed price, which was also prompted by anxiety over increasing substitution of copper in different fields of application, in particular by aluminium in the electrical sector, soon proved to be too low, however, and with the economic upswing this attempt to introduce a producer price was abandoned. Free prices from January 1964 onwards climbed to over twice the producer price and continued to soar even above the 'modified' prices of the respective producers. In particular, the CIPEC countries (Chile, Peru, Zambia, Zaire), whose earnings from copper production played a dominant part in their national budgets, in 1966 were no longer satisfied with earnings based on the comparatively low producer price at a time of high LME price quotations. Even on the part of the consumers uncertainty grew because it was not at all clear whether the long-term, forward buying contracts – which had hitherto been more auspicious – would turn out to be unfavourable. The Agreement was first broken by Zambia and then by Chile, which first adopted the three-month quotations of the LME and then the spot price as the basis for their transactions.

The reasons for the failure to introduce a producer price for copper are certainly very varied – even the recycling supply position enters into the question – but ultimately the factor which tipped the scales was the problem of short-term inelasticity of supply and demand on the non-ferrous metals market (Sies, 1976, p. 14 ff.).

Copper trading in the Western world outside the United States is therefore carried on almost without exception on the basis of LME quotations – which does not imply that the purchases are made on the LME. In the United States a number of special prices are applied. Of most significance are the US producer prices for copper, which are formed on the principle of cost-orientated selling prices of the major concerns in copper mining (mine-smelter prices) and – as is typical of oligopoly prices – are uniformly fixed, or at least generally show no great disparities. These producer prices are traditionally adjusted to market prices from time to time and in the interim, if necessary, applied with mark-ups or discounts. Recently, however, flexible producer prices have been evolved, which take greater account of fluctuations on the London Metal Exchange and the COMEX in New York. As the anticipated dire consequences of the diminishing influence of 'stable' producer prices have largely not materialized, the chances of United States copper producers reverting to a fixed price structure are considered very remote. The same applies to the US jobbing smelter price and the US producer price for exports. On the other hand, there are still the copper quotations of the New York Commodity Exchange (COMEX), which not only are of importance as a reference system but have also been applied by producers with mark-ups as their selling prices after abandonment of their fixed price, as, for example, in 1978 by the Anaconda Company and the Phelps Dodge Corporation (*Blick durch die Wirtschaft*, 16 August 1978). Of some interest are also the 'E & MJ Quotations' published in *Engineering and Mining Journal*. Over the short term considerable differences may occur between individual prices, from which copper fabricators may profit if they close transactions at the more favourable price or can exert pressure on suppliers. Under the influence of the international price connection inevitably adjustments are required to give a largely uniform price pattern over the long term. This is also confirmed by the fact that copper – unlike lead and zinc – is one of the 'Exchange Commodities' which are exempted from the voluntary price restriction imposed within the framework of the anti-inflation programme of the USA, because their price variations have hitherto approximated more closely to the price trend in an (organized) free market at home or abroad.

Lead

The price structure on the lead market is very similar to that of copper:

(a) In Europe purchases are transacted almost exclusively on the basis of London Metal Exchange quotations.
(b) In the United States there are a largely uniform producer price for lead, price quotations on the COMEX and free market prices.

In Europe efforts have constantly been made by the lead producers to obtain fixed prices, in view of falling lead quotations such as those in 1971/72, which were obviously modelled on the regulation procedures successfully practised for many years for zinc. With an improvement in the sales situation, however, these quotations have now been discontinued, because a producer price could hardly be maintained on a long-term basis in view of the multitude of producers and the importance of lead scrap.

In the United States there is no very close association between producer prices and free market prices, and this has induced the Council for Wage and

Price Stability, for instance, to place lead and zinc within the price controls enforceable under the government anti-inflation programme.

Zinc

On the zinc market in the Western world outside the United States there are the quotations of the London Metal Exchange and the 'European producer price for slab zinc'; in the United States (as also for copper and lead, and sometimes running parallel) there are the US producer price, the zinc quotations on the COMEX and free market prices. The European producer price for slab zinc has since 13 July 1964 been published by the major European and Canadian producers as a list price on which, depending on the market situation, discounts must be granted or premiums can be required. A clear-cut price-setting leadership is not apparent, although a certain coincidence in the timing and the extent of price variations is to be observed. The producers cite as the principal aim of their pricing policy the sale of their commodities at a comparatively stable price, hence affording the fabricators a better basis for calculation than the violently fluctuating quotations of the London Metal Exchange. They also aim to forestall substitution, which might be stimulated on price grounds and which can be counteracted by a sharp price fall in the event of slackening demand and its adverse repercussions on mining and smelter operation. The free market for zinc (outside the United States) is less important than for copper and lead, as sales of producers are predominantly based on producer prices via long forward contracts, whereas only 15–20% of copper transactions are effected at exchange prices. The practice adopted by the zinc producers is, therefore, on the whole to be regarded as positive. It appears, however, that it is coming increasingly into conflict with cartel law regulations, and the European Commission in Brussels is examining price setting from the point of view of fair trading and the law on competition.[1]

In the United States there is no close association between producer prices and free market prices. Zinc and lead therefore come under the price controls of the government anti-inflation programme.

Tin

Tin is quoted on the exchanges in London and Penang. The leading tin market was traditionally London and the International Tin Agreement decided on the LME spot price as the standard base for buffer stock transactions. It was only with the floating of sterling (1972) that the quotation in Penang was accepted by a resolution of the International Tin Committee as the reference price. Unlike the LME quotation this is not a true exchange price but one formed by a special auction (see p. 204). The quotations in London and Penang are

[1] The producer price may also be jeopardized by the international trend in foreign exchange rates, because it is calculated in dollars and consequently suffers when the dollar is weak.

largely parallel, however, because of the interchangeable nature of the supplies of this commodity. Another idiosyncrasy of the tin market is the fact that business transacted in tin is effected on the basis of the prices obtaining in both exchanges. Suppliers and consumers, from the initial Bandoeng Pool (1920) up to the Fifth International Tin Agreement in force today, at first with governmental consent and since the post-war period by means of government contracts, control an institutionalized instrumental body enabling them to influence the trend in the exchange prices by joint agreement.

Aluminium

The pricing pattern for aluminium has been determined for decades in accordance with the oligopoly structure of the market under the strong price-setting leadership of the major American producers, which together are responsible for over 60% of Western smelter production. This also applies to the setting of minimum prices under the European Aluminium Cartel. Apart from the aluminium list prices – on which invariably considerable discounts are granted or premiums requested – there are also free price quotations, such as the US market price (determined since October 1971) and the European free market price, which are mainly applied to materials from the Eastern Bloc and the market range of the smaller producers. These prices (admittedly fixed on the basis of comparatively smaller volumes), unlike the producer price, which aims at long-term stability, function as an index to scarcity and surplus situations on the aluminium market and because of this alone make it more difficult for list prices to be adopted (Forster, 1976, p. 119). Although the fixed price policy for many decades was made easier by the lack of exchange terminal transactions, this situation changed when aluminium trading began at the London Metal Exchange on 2 October 1978. As well as forward trading on a three-month basis, since the beginning of January 1979 spot dealings also have been transacted. The trend since then shows that quotations on the London Metal Exchange and the free market prices have largely moved into alignment.

Nickel

Among the six most important non-ferrous metals by volume the nickel market remained for the longest time without competing exchange quotations, but at the end of April 1979 nickel trading also commenced on the London Metal Exchange. It was from an early date a divided market, with an oligopoly structure over by far the larger market sector and a small number of producers, among which the International Nickel Company Ltd (INCO) was clearly the price leader under the cartel agreements, on the basis of its large but nevertheless sharply declining market share.[1] The other producers sometimes

1 1950 – 88%; 1960 – 68%; 1974 – 40%; 1975 – 36%; 1976 – 35%; (*Metal Bulletin*, 20 December 1977, p. 22).

granted more favourable freight conditions which amounted in effect to a price discount. There was also a considerably smaller free nickel market supplied by the Eastern Bloc countries and by smaller producers – including those from Cuba, South Africa and Rhodesia – as well as from surplus tonnages of nickel consumers.

The prices obtaining are published daily in *Metal Bulletin* (London) according to information supplied by the principal dealers. Unlike the longer, forward producer price which is maintained at a relatively stable level, these prices reflect the changing market situation.

During recent years the free market price on the nickel market has acquired greater importance as a factor influencing prices, at first due to an inadequate supply of producer nickel and since 1971 because of a general over-supply, interrupted only in 1974 by a brief steel boom (Forster, 1968, p. 161; Gebhard and Knörndel, 1977, p. 89).

Forward trading in nickel was officially introduced on the London Metal Exchange on 23 April 1979 and spot dealing on 20 July 1977. At first the leading nickel producers boycotted the market. They had already been opposed to the practice of exchange trading because they considered it might damage the relationship of trust between producers and purchasers and also feared that severe price fluctuations might arise, due to speculative transactions or the vulnerability of other metals traded on the London Metal Exchange. They were also anxious about variations in foreign exchange rates on the international currency market. The USSR, however, immediately entered as a seller.

10

The price trend in the non-ferrous metal markets

10.1 THE FUNCTIONING OF THE MARKETS

One of the special features of the world metals economy which is a determining factor in the price trend of non-ferrous metals is that during the progress of industrialization the world markets which have evolved for individual metals are usually not uniform and self-contained. With all metals there is in fact a tendency towards the formation of market segments:

(a) Horizontal segments are shown geographically in intensive sales and supply relationships between specific consumer countries or regions and those of preferred producer countries (for example, the Western world of the American and European copper market).

(b) Vertical segments are formed for products at different production stages (metals, semi-manufactures, scrap).

Although very varying pricing processes are to be observed in these market segments and the price trends in the short term never coincide, the reciprocal influence of these movements is clearly reflected in the long-term price trend. An important factor for the independence of the markets is the greater market transparency provided by the institution of exchanges, because the exchange quotations then make it possible for all involved in the market to calculate the respective movements and grouping of supply and demand.

The interdependence of the horizontal market segments has a levelling effect on price differences existing between them. Adaptation does not operate unilaterally, by means of a step-by-step approximation of prices formed outside the exchanges (e.g., producer prices) to exchange quotations, but always in a mutual feedback process, because oligopolistic strategies affecting market segments, cartel agreements and other practices for manipulating the market are bound to have an effect on exchange business.

In the vertical market segment for individual products the interdependence is particularly close when it already operates at the production end. This means that a direct price connection exists between the markets for basic metals and those for semi-manufactures (e.g., between exchange copper and rolled wire), as is plainly reflected in the comparatively small fluctuations in the price relationships for these products. A close association also usually exists between markets for new metals and for scrap, although occasionally the opposite tendency can be observed. When prices for new metals are rising there is a strong demand for scrap metals, which are still at first cheaper, so that prices of scrap are then pushed up. When scrap prices eventually rise more rapidly than those of new metals, and allowance is made for additional costs of remelting of old scrap, the price gap between primary and secondary metals narrows until finally it appears more worth while to use new metals again. The decline in demand for old scrap, with ample supplies, then results in a fall in scrap prices. Consequently, the supply of old scrap metals tends to decrease with increasing demand and rising prices for new metals until the cycle just described begins all over again. The prices of old scrap, therefore, follow new materials prices and they in turn influence the exchange quotations.

These forms of interdependence in the market segments are also a feature of the structure of world metal markets. Metals on the market already are dependent on the associated geology and production methods. On the consumer side other relationships also arise which have an influence on market business. The use of metals in specific connotations may be dictated by possible production methods, in the production of alloys, for example, or, on the other hand, there may be substitution of metals for each other. Many factors therefore contribute to the fact that price trends in individual metal markets seldom depart widely from each other[1] (see Figs 14 and 15, pp. 216 and 217). During the course of technical development and changing conditions of shortage, or as a result of varying long-term trends in production costs, there may be a complete change in the price structure of the metals industry – as has happened already in the regional prices for copper and aluminium during the course of industrialization – but the close connection, already described, between market and prices remains unaffected in principle.

A particular phenomenon in the price trend of international metal markets is the strong influence exerted by special factors such as wars, political unrest, strikes, laying down of strategic reserves, speculative transactions or measures to regulate supply. To these must also be added the extensive fragmentation of the markets of the Eastern Bloc compared with those of the Western countries. These factors can only trigger off the characteristic price changes in metal markets because of the inevitable time lag in adapting supply to demand, due to the time and costs involved in starting up new production facilities or closing down existing plants, unless of course these changes in demand can be met by higher or lower utilization of capacities or by stockpiles.

Another feature of the world trend in metal prices is its pronounced cyclical

1 Althaus and Baack, 1977, p. 14.

nature, except when it is subject to special outside influences. This is due to the fact that the demand for non-ferrous metals derives from the demand for end products, which is highly dependent on economic cycles, since the prime consumers of metals are in areas such as the electrical industry, the automotive industry, mechanical engineering and the building industry. If these sectors of industry, as a result of an upsurge in the economy, increase their demand for non-ferrous metals, this then leads to higher production and hence greater utilization of existing capacities, to investments for the creation of additional capacities and, because of rising prices, to stockpiling on the part of consumers and traders. During an economic downturn with declining demand, despite a run-down of utilization of capacities and falling prices, an over-supply may occur, resulting in increasing stocks held at the exchanges by producers and consumers as well as by traders. With economic recovery, however, shortages may then occur, because of both the previous lack of inclination to invest and increasing demand after dispersion of stockpiles, with the result that existing capacities are again fully utilized and new ones created. The consequent effects on price movements in the non-ferrous metal markets are further accentuated by the lack of short-term price elasticity on both sides of the market.

The demand for a metal generally has little effect in the short term on rising prices and does not diminish proportionately with falling prices. Even if the use of non-ferrous metals is dictated by technical considerations, the share taken by the non-ferrous metal component in the value of the end product is still comparatively slight. Thus, in automotive engineering, even with a strong short-term rise in lead prices per production unit, no change is made in equipping the vehicles with lead batteries and, conversely, falling lead prices do not necessarily lead to a rise in vehicle production and hence to an increased demand for lead in batteries. Price elasticity of supplies in the short term, apart from possible adjustments to stocks, is likewise slight, because of the comparatively long time required for investments to expand capacity in mining and smelting and also because of the high burden of fixed costs associated with a cutback in production, which, at least over the short term, is not reversible. Combined production of one metal with other metals – for example, lead and zinc or copper and mixed ores – leaves the producer with very little scope to react to price changes, with the result that extreme price fluctuations are encouraged (Althaus and Baack, 1977, p. 14).

The result of pricing taking place under such conditions is hectic price mark-ups with increasing demand or slashes with a decline in demand. This trend is aggravated by the impossibility of short-term response in metal consumption: substitution cannot suddenly be made if prices rise nor new applications opened up for the metal concerned if prices fall. Even interventions in the market, such as those, for example, under the International Tin Agreement, were only occasionally able to hinder the effect of specific price determinants on world markets.

A factor of increasing market influence during recent years has been found to be growing purchases by the Eastern Bloc countries, especially the USSR. Whereas until recently this group of countries had largely met their needs from their own production, so that the metal volumes transferred annually by individual countries to the West differed widely, in 1979 large net imports were made by the Eastern Bloc, especially of lead and tin. To what extent a future import trend may be inferred, in view of the raw materials reserves of the Eastern Bloc countries, will largely depend on whether they are able to expand mining, smelting and refining capacities to keep pace with demand. From previous experience it may be expected that non-ferrous metal trading with the Eastern Bloc will show strong fluctuations as the result of sporadic demand arising or existing surpluses and will continue to represent an instability factor in world markets (Hoffmeyer and Schrader, 1979, p. 119 ff.).

10.2 THE PRICE TREND

The price trend for non-ferrous metals during industrialization was determined by the combined action of a number of endogenous and exogenous factors influencing supply and demand to varying degrees in the course of time. The basic direction of the long-term price trend, on which short-term fluctuations are superimposed, has been governed, on the one hand, by the brisk increase in demand for raw materials from the industrial countries (and in recent decades also by growing demand on the part of the developing countries) and, on the other, by technical advances in mining and smelting which, owing to reduced production costs, made it possible to offer increasing metal volumes at falling or steady prices in real terms.

The trend in nominal prices for the most important heavy metals by volume during the course of industrialization over the past hundred years shows an increase of 3–4% per annum, with tin advancing more strongly than lead, zinc and copper. Aluminium for the same period had a slightly downward tendency. The period as a whole falls into two distinct phases with differing price trends (see Table 45 and Figs 14 and 15). From the beginning of the period under observation (1881 or 1895) up to 1950 the price trend for zinc, lead and tin shows a much weaker movement than for the period as a whole, for copper it is basically almost stagnant and for aluminium shows a slight decline. Since the end of the Second World War this tendency has changed in the case of the heavy metals, in that the upward trend rises much more steeply than in the previous period, and even aluminium in the long-term trend shows a marked upward tendency. From 1950 to 1979 the upswing was most marked in the case of tin (annual average 7%), followed by copper (5%), zinc 4.9%, lead (3.9%) and aluminium (2.8%). It should be noted, however, that during the period when these prices were recorded on the London or New York exchanges the purchasing power of the pound sterling and of the dollar was

Table 45. Non-ferrous metal prices at the London Metal Exchange 1881–1979 (regression estimates)

	Coefficients a	Coefficients b	R²		Coefficients a	Coefficients b	R²
Aluminium				Zinc			
1895–1979	3.353	−0.002	0.02	1881–1979	2.407	0.027	0.66
1895–1950	3.702	−0.017	0.62	1881–1950	2.835	0.011	0.20
1950–1979	2.914	0.028	0.68	1950–1979	4.217	0.049	0.50
relative change				relative change			
1895–1977	4.781	−0.023	0.81	1947–1977	5.175	0.007	0.03
1895–1950	4.972	−0.032	0.79	Tin			
1950–1977	3.238	−0.002	0.03	1881–1979	3.965	0.036	0.85
Lead				1881–1950	4.352	0.023	0.72
1881–1979	2.078	0.030	0.69	1950–1979	6.254	0.069	0.76
1881–1950	2.451	0.016	0.28	relative change			
1950–1979	4.260	0.039	0.40	1947–1977	7.167	0.009	0.17
relative change							
1947–1977	5.359	−0.026	0.42				
Copper							
1881–1979	3.404	0.026	0.63				
1881–1950	4.000	0.004	0.05				
1950–1979	5.241	0.050	0.79				
relative change							
1947–1977	5.996	0.005	0.03				

Notes: Prices for lead, copper, zinc and tin = LME quotations; for aluminium = US producers' list price. All calculations performed on basis of a logarithmic trend. Relative changes calculated from Index of Wholesale Prices, UK (1947 = 100) or US (1967 = 100). Figures significant to 5% probability of error.
Source: Calculated from *Metal Statistics*, various years.

exposed to severe fluctuations and losses. If a deflation of the nominal prices is applied by reference to the wholesale price indices in London or New York, the relative price movements according to the basic trend between 1947 and 1979 show only a slight increase for tin and copper in the basic trend (less than 1%), and a decline in the case of lead (2.6%), zinc (0.7%) and aluminium (0.2%).

A detailed analysis of the nominal price trend shows a decline in prices during the second half of the nineteenth century, followed by a general increase at the turn of the century, in the wake of accelerating industrial development and expanding demands for non-ferrous metals that could not be matched by supply in the short term. Under the influence of a cyclical slackening of the economy, there was soon a slump in prices. The economic recovery in 1906–1907 was then the prelude to a brief boom, which soon levelled off until the First World War, with its high demands for raw materials, caused an enormous jump in metal prices. At the end of the war problems relating to economic reconstruction and the resumption of international trade also overshadowed the trend in the non-ferrous metals industry. Prices remained low at first, but, as a result of the exceptional upswing in metal consumption

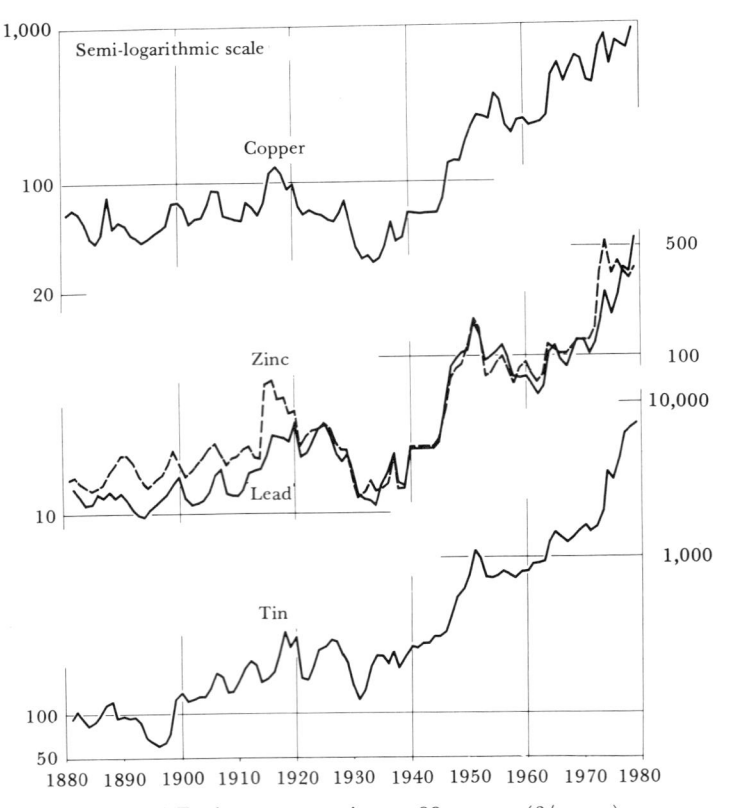

Fig. 14. London Metal Exchange quotations, 1881–1979 (£/tonne)
Sources: *Metal Statistics*, various years; *Non-Ferrous Metal Data*, various years.

and metal production, which held until 1929, prices reached a peak in the mid 1920s. The world slump and Great Depression put an abrupt end to this period, with a resulting price collapse for non-ferrous metals, except aluminium, to below the previous low of 1921.

The foreign exchange and trading policy measures adopted, such as the devaluation of the pound sterling and suspension of the Gold Standard in 1931 and the exchange control restrictions imposed by many countries in the 1930s, also had a critical effect on the price trend in international metal markets. They not only resulted in discrepancies between world market prices and national prices (depending on the respective extent of devaluation and of trade protection policies) but also largely restricted the orientation and lead given by exchange prices, particularly those of the London Metal Exchange. The Second World War then plunged the world metal market into a state of emergency and to virtual suspension of the markets.

The initial post-war years heralded in a period of rapidly fluctuating prices for non-ferrous metals. One cause of these erratic price movements was the limited convertibility of currencies, with consequent variations in exchange rates. This caused many countries to introduce exchange controls of various kinds (tariffs, import and export quotas and non-tariff restrictions), which inevitably affected the general price situation. The first major upturn in world metal markets in the post-war years was occasioned by the boom in demand during the Korean War and the associated stockpile purchases made in 1951. It was, however, of only comparatively short duration and already in 1952–53 prices had again fallen sharply. After fluctuating tendencies brought about by cyclical influences, prices on world metal markets only began to rise again substantially in 1964. This price rise continued, with short interruptions, until 1970–71. In the middle of 1972, under the influence of marked worldwide economic buoyancy, there occurred a boom in demand of a size unprecedented in the post-war period, which produced a meteoric rise in non-ferrous metals prices. At the end of 1973 there were signs of slackening in the world economy under the influence of the sharp increase in oil prices and fears of world shortages inspired by the Middle East War at that time. This prompted a flight into raw materials which was instrumental in again pushing up prices. By May 1974, i.e., within the space of two years, prices for non-ferrous metals – as for other industrial raw materials – had approximately doubled, without, however, drawing level with the far greater price increases in crude oil. Nevertheless, prices soon declined on a broad front, under the influence of the rapid sagging of the world economy, to the mid 1973 level, at which they then

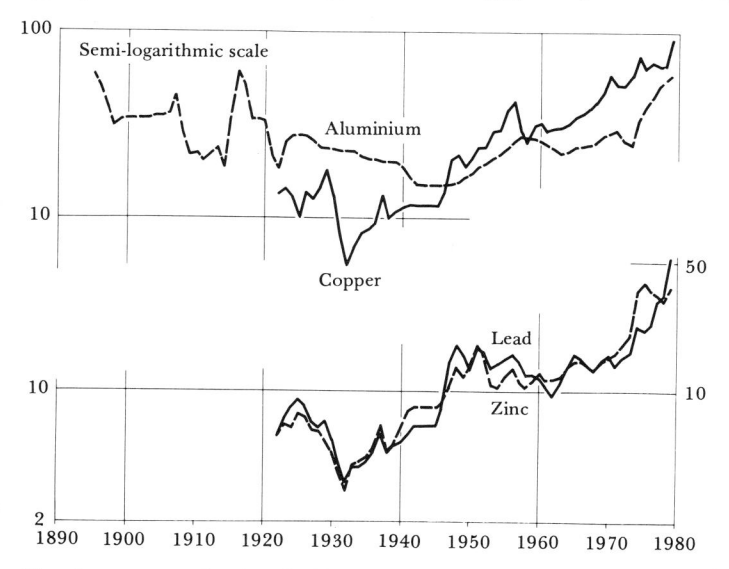

Fig. 15. Non-ferrous metal prices in New York, 1895–1979 (cents/lb)
Sources: *Metal Statistics*, various years; *Non-Ferrous Metal Data*, various years.

stabilized and on the whole remained steady until the middle of 1978.

During 1978 the trend in non-ferrous metal markets took a new turn. At first, considerable surpluses in supplies and very high stocks, which sometimes resulted in production cutbacks (e.g., in copper and zinc), caused depressed prices. In particular, American copper smelters and refineries restricted production to gear it to demand and to reduce excess stocks. Demand then expanded, both in the wake of economic cycles and as a result of a strong bullish tendency in speculation because of widespread uncertainty as to exchange rates, to such a level that, with production still lagging, world reserves had now been run down to below consumption requirement (Hoffmeyer and Schrader, 1978, p. 115 ff.). The marked fluctuation in the exchange rate of the US dollar led to at least short-term falls in prices[1] (converted to the currency of the country). Among the 'hard-currency' countries this had very adverse repercussions on demand in raw materials markets. The extent to which the decline in the dollar rate affected non-ferrous metal prices is demonstrated by the abrupt interim price reversal registered in November 1978, as a result of the announcement of American measures to support the dollar and to combat inflation. The overall price rise for non-ferrous metals only eased during 1979, although tendencies varied in the individual markets. Copper suppliers clearly made efforts to consolidate their market position as a result of the considerable running down of stocks, whereas the still very abundant stocks of zinc had a levelling influence on zinc prices. In the lead markets a price boom prevailed owing to a high level of demand and a lack of short-term flexibility, but towards the end of the year this deteriorated into a sudden collapse in prices. The powerful expansion of the aluminium markets was governed by continuing full order books for smelters and by shrinking world reserves. For tin also the upward price trend continued as a result of production deficits which had been in evidence since 1972, despite only moderate expansion in consumption (Hoffmeyer and Schrader, 1979, p. 118 ff.).

The boom in metal prices at the beginning of 1980, which attained new records for aluminium, copper and tin, was almost entirely due to speculative demands, which, starting with precious metals, were now operating in the non-ferrous metals sector. The widespread adoption of an 'inflation mentality' and the associated escape into raw materials led to a sustained upward trend. This was initially marked by severe fluctuations in metal prices, aggravated still further by the extremely low level of stocks maintained previously because of high financing costs. After the speculative tendencies had subsided, metal

---

1 The long-term prospects are different. According to the raw materials price index of the Institut für Weltwirtschaft (Institute for World Economy) (1970/72 = 100) raw materials prices rose between 1972 and 1979 by on average 130% (excluding crude oil); the non-ferrous metals were on average 138% more expensive. Allowing for the upward revaluation of the DM against the US $ (1972–79 58%), raw materials prices in DM show considerably smaller rates of increase.

prices declined sharply up to the middle of the year and then rallied again under the influence of feverish movements in the precious metals markets. Over the long term higher prices are to be anticipated in any case, especially as in the period 1975–79, in contrast to previous post-war economic cycles (i.e. after the Second World War), production capacities in the metal industry have not been appreciably expanded. The reason given for this is the high capital costs and an inadequate profits trend.

Especially noteworthy is the trend in price relationships between the individual non-ferrous metals during the course of industrialization. These reflect not only the respective permutations of supply and demand but also substantial changes in production costs and, especially in the short and medium term, differences in the pricing policies of the producers. The trend in price ratios of the respective metals to each other have important effects on their use. A relative price increase for one metal stimulates substitution by other metals of equal suitability for a particular purpose or, if replacement is technically impossible, has the effect of intensifying efforts to develop more labour-saving processes.

It is already apparent from the price trends indicated that during industrialization considerable shifts have occurred relatively in the prices for individual metals. A remarkable feature is that these have predominantly run counter to changes in metal consumption. Especially important here is the *volte-face* in the price ratio of aluminium to copper. Up to the beginning of this century aluminium, even after a rapid decline in its price, was still considerably more expensive than copper. Since the Second World War its price is now very much below that of copper. This decisive price advantage of aluminium, however, can only be utilized to a limited extent in production, because the differing physical and technical properties of the heavy metals usually do not permit their substitution by light metals, or only to a very limited degree.

Price relationships of lead and zinc have repeatedly changed since the end of the previous century. Lead was originally more expensive than zinc, but from the 1870s up to the Second World War lead prices at times dropped considerably below those of zinc, alternating in the interim, and even in the mid 1970s zinc prices were up on lead; recently, however, lead prices have again advanced ahead of zinc. The price relationships between nickel and tin have also undergone similar displacement during the past ten years and today the traditionally less expensive tin is over two-and-a-half times as dear as nickel. Admittedly, as industrialization progresses changes in price relationships between individual metals are to be expected. According to current estimates of probable reserves and resources of the different metals, taking into account the present level of technology in mining and metallurgy, major displacements in individual metal price ratios, such as those observed in the past century, are hardly to be anticipated.

11

Attempts at regulation in the non-ferrous metal markets

A characteristic feature of the international metal markets is their great instability, which makes price trends and earnings largely incalculable. At an early date attempts were made at national and international level to restrict free competition and to manipulate the market. The following chapter presents a survey of such attempts at regulation in the markets for copper, lead, zinc, tin, aluminium and nickel and of the objectives of the developing countries in the field of metallic raw materials under their 'Integrated Programme for Commodities' announced in 1976.

11.1 ATTEMPTS AT CONTROL OF THE COPPER MARKET

Ever since founding of the London Metal Exchange copper has been one of the metals traded there. In co-operation with the European copper fabricators it soon became possible to match supply and demand on the LME, so that changes in the pattern of production and consumption were reflected in the freely traded copper price on the Exchange. The first drastic slump in copper prices, which continued over a period of some years, occurred when American market suppliers of 'lake copper' joined existing suppliers from Chile, Spain and Portugal at the Exchange, following the mining of new copper finds in Michigan, at a time when the market was not yet able to absorb this influx of extra production, especially as consumers were at the same time cutting back their stocks, which were steadily depreciating in value. The price slump soon led to restrictions on production and in turn to a diminution in the supply position at a period when, with the growth of the electrical industry, consumption of copper was beginning to recover. As a result, in 1887 copper stocks on the London Metal Exchange fell to 15,000 tons, leaving insufficient assets even to conduct hedging transactions. In this predicament the copper market made its first attempt to establish a form of market control.

11.1.1 The Sécrétan Syndicate (1887–89)

In autumn 1887 the bottleneck situation prevailing in the world copper market induced Pierre Sécrétan, manager of the French Société Industrielle et Commerciale de Métaux, one of the leading European consumers of copper, to engage in the speculative purchasing of available copper on long-term (three-year) contracts. In mid 1888 the Sécrétan Syndicate held in this way contracts totalling some 75% of the world's copper production. This constituted the first registered 'corner' (i.e., speculative forward buying in a terminal market) on the London Metal Exchange. The price boom set in motion by these transactions, however, was followed by an acceleration of production, as well as an unexpectedly abundant supply of secondary material. Finally, the powerful market forces prevailed over the Syndicate's not inconsiderable pegging actions and the copper corner eventually collapsed with the stocks of the Sécrétan Syndicate standing at 75,000 tonnes. The Syndicate halted its buying operations in February 1889 and the London copper price slumped from a record high of £105 to £35 within only a short period. The Syndicate's stocks were taken over by the Banque de France, and their liquidation extended over a period of several years, as the market could not have absorbed such large quantities of copper without the risk of depressing prices further (Gibson-Jarvie, 1976, p. 35 ff.).

It should merely be recorded here that this first attempt at market control was destined to founder, because the Sécrétan Syndicate had not only underestimated production and price elasticity in the supply position of primary and secondary copper outside the 'corner', but had totally misjudged the sensitive reaction of consumers to price fluctuations. Much less had it even considered the possibility of a co-ordinated buyers' strike.

11.1.2 The Amalgamated Copper Company (1899–1901)

The next attempt at regulation of the copper market was initiated by a producer group. To this end, in 1899, the Standard Oil Company and the National City Bank founded the Amalgamated Copper Company and the United Metals Selling Company as marketing company of a cartel, whose membership was made up of some 20% of the American producers. Again, favourable conditions prevailed for 'bullish' speculation, owing to renewed expansion in the electrical industry and an upturn in shipbuilding at a time when the copper price was depressed. Subsequent events resembled those in the case of the Sécrétan corner: the Amalgamated group curbed shipments and the copper prices jumped from £51 to over £75. To maintain this price level the producers had to resort to supportive purchasing for a time at least, but continuing high demand, even at these price levels, prompted the independent producers to step up production, causing increases in reserve stocks of secondary copper, with the result that the supporting purchases became steadily more costly and the stocks of the cartel piled up to a total of some 200,000 tonnes. The more plentiful supply position now brought about a price decline, which in turn led to the collapse of the Pool in 1901 (Gibson-Jarvie, 1976, p. 38 f. and Ramms, 1959, p. 154).

In the course of the first decade of this century further attempts were made by the Amalgamated Copper Company to withhold supplies of copper for speculative reasons, so that the hectic development of prices continued until the economic recession in the United States also affected the copper market, with a rapid fall in copper prices.

11.1.3 The Copper Export Association (1919–23)

The First World War had produced a vigorous expansion of production capacity in the copper industries of the West (some 65% above that of the pre-war period), which, together with the large stocks of primary copper maintained as war reserves in the United States and the flood of secondary material on the market, depressed the market appreciably, and after decontrol allowed the copper price to slump below the pre-war level. In this tense situation some 95% of American copper producers banded together into an organization to be known as the Copper Export Association. This cartel endeavoured to liquidate the stocks with the producers (together with some of the surplus stocks taken over by them) on the best possible terms commensurate with prevailing market conditions, with the long-term objective of securing a rise of copper as a hedge against steep increases in production costs.

The orders were shared out among the producers on the basis of their output during the preceding year, and production quotas were also imposed. In consequence of these measures, the major producers (with production in excess of 30,000 tonnes) had succeeded in cutting their output to a relatively uniform 42% each. The mines in Chile, Mexico and Canada under their control were only affected to a small degree by the cutback in production. The liquidation of stocks proceeded successfully, not least probably on account of the ever-increasing demand for copper in world markets. Following the winding-up of the cartel in 1923, the copper price dropped only slightly, but copper was the only metal whose price in 1925 was below the level it had been in 1913.

Not only did the end of the First World War leave the United States in a powerful situation in the world copper economy, but the following years enabled it to strengthen this position still further. In 1926 the United States supplied some 53% of world mining production of copper and refined about 72% of world copper production (the Minière du Haut Katanga in the Belgian Congo, for instance, had nearly a half of its production of copper ore refined there). In addition, American capital controlled over 47% of mining production abroad, so that about 75% of world copper production was under the control of the United States and, moreover, concentrated in the hands of a very few large concerns, including Anaconda, Phelps Dodge, Kennecott, American Smelting & Refining Co., American Metal Co., and Nichols Copper Co. Furthermore, the major proportion of mine production controlled by the American companies in Chile and other countries in Latin America was destined for refining in the United States and was exported from there. At that time the United States produced approximately 66% of the world's exports of copper.

11.1.4 Copper Exporters Incorporated (1926–32)

The anticipated scarcity in the copper supply position, following the liquidation of surplus stocks at a time of increasing demand arising from progressive industrialization (in particular, electrification schemes), was taken as a pretext for American concerns, in view of their position of supremacy, to set up a new cartel, Copper Exporters Incorporated. Apart from American and Chilean producers, its membership included the Rio Tinto Company, the Belgian mining corporation Minière du Haut Katanga (Congo) as well as German concerns, so that it represented some 95% of world production. The declared aim of the cartel was to support copper prices by excluding exchange trading and by direct selling at fixed prices. The tonnage sold to consumers outside the United States was to be limited in order to minimize sales of surpluses by consumers at the LME. Surplus stocks in circulation on the market were acquired by the cartel and also by consumers anxious to hedge against rising monopoly prices. As a result, copper stocks held at the LME fell from 50,000 tonnes in 1926 to less than 5,000 tonnes in 1928.

The price of electrolytic copper had risen sharply by 1929; *force majeure* declarations had tightened supplies in some cases. This prompted customers to clamp down on demand. Under pressure from its own members, the cartel lowered the export price in spring 1929. The final break-up of the cartel came about with increasing availability of secondary material, delivered against the standard contract on the London market, and cartel members dropped out by making offers from their own vast surplus stocks. As this liquidation coincided with the spread of the world recession, despite cutbacks in production a price slide to an all-time low in 1932 could no longer be averted, especially as independent producers from Canada and Rhodesia now appeared as strong suppliers. This producer cartel certainly had to operate under the extremely adverse conditions of the Great Depression. It should be put on record however that it ultimately failed – like the Sécrétan corner organized by banks and consumers before it – because of lack of flexibility (Gibson-Jarvie, 1976, p. 42).

The worldwide economic slump finally resulted in a split in the world copper market. The American market was virtually closed to imports by a tariffs barrier, the United Kingdom enjoyed the protection of preferential tariffs for imports from Commonwealth countries, France and Belgium relied more heavily on supplies from their overseas territories, particularly Africa, while lack of foreign exchange and moves to achieve self-sufficiency in Germany, Japan and Italy brought about a severance of these countries from the world market. Nevertheless, the United States, under the pressure of its swollen stocks, succeeded in boosting exports, a policy encouraged by the restrictions on domestic sales from stocks and the maximum quotas for sales from new production. Copper prices in England and Germany, therefore, did not reach rock-bottom until 1934.

11.1.5 The International Copper Cartel (1935-39)

The founding of the International Copper Cartel in 1935 was prompted by efforts to stabilize the copper market which during the years of world crisis and the Great Depression had fallen sadly out of joint. Members of this cartel included all the major producers except Canada and the United States (the American firms were barred from entry by the Anti-Trust Law). It represented – excluding US domestic production – about 70% of world production. The members agreed to curb output to 75% of their capacity on the basis of a quota system and by limitation of American imports. Demand soon began to recover, particularly in the wake of production expansion, so that with a slow advance in prices production and import quotas were steadily raised. When in 1936/37 they culminated in a raw materials boom the Cartel at first reacted over-cautiously, so that quotas only rose when demand was already slackening off and a surplus situation ensued, bringing deteriorating prices. Up to the outbreak of the Second World War the influence of government bodies on the copper industry increased everywhere. Copper trading was suspended at the London Metal Exchange on 1 September 1939. Pricing by government authorities began in all countries and largely persisted until the resumption of copper trading on the London Metal Exchange on 5 August 1953.

11.1.6 The Intergovernmental Council of Copper Exporting Countries (CIPEC)

CIPEC was founded in 1967 by Chile, Peru, Zambia and Congo-Kinshasa, the present-day Zaire; in 1975 Indonesia became a full member and Australia, Mauretania, Papua-New Guinea and Yugoslavia are now associate members without voting rights. These countries today account for approximately 51% of mine production of copper and 22% of world production of refined copper, as well as some 70% of exports of mine and smelter products.

CIPEC is an association of countries at government level whose function is primarily consultative. To this end market studies are carried out, reports drawn up on trends in the world copper market and advice and assistance given to the member countries individually or jointly, with the ultimate aim of preventing extreme fluctuations in copper prices (Schroeder, 1975, p. 295). CIPEC was confronted with a critical situation in May 1974 when the sudden steep rise in copper prices, which had set in at the end of 1972, was followed by a complete price collapse; between April and the end of December 1974 copper prices fell by around 55%. At the end of 1974 CIPEC for the first time took active steps to control prices by means of a plan for cutting back copper exports, at first by 10% and later by 15%. This plan was suspended on 30 June 1976. The export figures show that it did not achieve its goal or even have any marked effect on prices. The result was a crisis for CIPEC. Chile rejected any further restriction agreements as previous arrangements had not been observed by some countries. (The reduction in exports by Zambia and Zaire were not deliberate policies but the consequence of internal and political problems.) In addition, it was expected that the present depressed prices could only be remedied by an upswing in the principal consumer countries. The Ministerial Conference of CIPEC countries in Paris in 1976 failed, therefore, because of differences of opinion: Zambia, Zaire and Peru supported cutbacks in production in view of the surplus stocks of copper, while Chile declared it was not prepared to support this policy. The chronic surplus situation in the copper market had its origin in the comparatively high market prices in the second half of the 1960s, which had stimulated a marked expansion in mining activities between 1971 and 1974. The following cyclical slump in the major consumer countries admittedly brought about a decline in utilization of capacities to about 80% but this did not prevent a further over-supply on the market, so that copper prices between April 1974 and the end of the year fell sharply. The slight price increase in 1976 already then triggered off a 5% higher utilization of smelter capacities with a resulting further increase in stocks at all stages of production.

The complete impotence of CIPEC was evident from these developments and it was clear that its efforts had so far failed to exploit its supply position, on the OPEC model, for the purpose of regulating prices and tonnages. There are many reasons to account for this: the greater geographical dispersal of copper deposits throughout the world, the wide range of uses for copper and the possibilities open for substitution, as well as the massive reservoir of recycled material in the industrial countries. Another weakness of CIPEC is that the United States, with the largest mine production of copper, Canada and other important producer countries, especially the Eastern Bloc (in particular Poland), are not members. An added difficulty for CIPEC in attempting to influence the copper supply situation is that – in contrast with OPEC's position and the ease of turning off the oil tap – cutbacks in mining raise a host of technical, economic and social problems for the countries concerned, problems which are the more acute if these countries rely mainly on copper exports for their foreign exchange earnings and are heavily dependent on this source of income for their national budget. For instance, copper exports (SITC 283.1 and 682.1) as a percentage of total exports amounted on average in 1977–79 to 50.1% in Chile, 20.0% in Peru, 38.3% in Zaire and 87.9% in Zambia.

Negotiations for an international copper agreement – after 18 meetings of representatives of producer and consumer countries – have so far yielded no result. A plan has been put forward by Indonesia for three development stages, each covering a two-year period. The first stage is earmarked for collection of data with the aim of providing greater market transparency. In the second stage buffer stocks would be provided to introduce a further control mechanism in the final stage. The plan was adopted almost unanimously by the exporting countries and some importing countries, including Finland, Norway and Sweden, signalled their approval. Doubts were expressed, however, by the European Economic Community and Japan.

11.2 ATTEMPTS AT CONTROL OF THE ZINC AND LEAD MARKETS

11.2.1 The European Spelter Convention (1908–14)

The situation towards the nineteenth century in the lead and zinc industries was by no means auspicious, with a very adverse earnings/costs ratio. This did not cause producers to cut back on production, however, as had been seriously expected. It was not until 1908 that, at the instigation of Germany, the question of a producer cartel was discussed, resulting in the setting up of the European Spelter Convention. The aim of the Convention was to exert control over zinc production by a quota system, to be adjusted when stocks rose above a certain level and/or the London Metal Exchange price fell below £22 per ton. In 1911 the Convention was prolonged for three years and the expansion trend was highly satisfactory for European producers. The quota control was not applied, however, owing to increasing demand. When in 1914 it was resolved to impose restrictions on output and quotas were allocated, the partners to the contract were reluctant to accept these. When the Convention was dissolved in August 1914 it is doubtful, therefore, whether it would have survived in any case.

11.2.2 The International Zinc Cartel (1931–34)

After the First World War there was a boom in the early 1920s, with epoch-making highs in prices, followed soon, however, by a sharp falling off as the new, modern production capacities in Australia and Canada began to exert pressure on European suppliers. In May 1928 a new zinc cartel was formed, whose members included not only Germany, France and the United Kingdom but also Belgium and Poland. It was wound up at the end of 1929 as the new, rapidly expanding production of electrolytic zinc in Australia, Canada and Mexico continued to exert pressure on the European market. Drastically falling zinc prices then led to the decision to form the International Zinc Cartel (July 1931) of which all the main producers outside the United States were members. As a result, output was reduced to 55% of the recognized capacities and consequently in 1932 production fell to below the world consumption level, stocks declined and prices rose. Currency and trading policy manoeuvres of a number of member countries then led to temporary suspension of the Cartel in 1932 and it was finally disbanded at the end of 1934, as a common policy was no longer practicable.

11.2.3 The Lead Smelters' Association (1909–14)

At the same time as the measures affecting zinc, an agreement was reached on the initiative of Metallgesellschaft AG for a cartel in the lead industry with the major Belgian and Spanish producers – the Lead Smelters' Association (1909). This differed from the zinc cartel in that marketing of the entire production of the cartel members was in the hands of Metallgesellschaft, which controlled the major portion of production in Germany and outside America and exercised market control over prices by regulating the volume of sales (not production). Agreements with the American Smelting and Refining Company (Asarco) neutralized the effect of cheaper American supplies, so that the European price level was successfully pushed up until this cartel also ceased operating on the outbreak of the First World War in 1914.

11.2.4 Other lead cartels before the Second World War

In the 1920s the situation in the lead industry was similar to that of zinc. After 1925 there was over-production and high stocks, which by 1930 sent prices plummeting to a new low. In April 1931, therefore, the Lead Producers' Reporting Association was founded, to which the majority of non-American producers belonged. Restrictions on output and help in financing stocks successfully prevented a further price fall, but this producer cartel also came to grief in March 1932, mainly because of the foreign exchange and trading policy measures taken by the United Kingdom. During the next few years, from 1934 onwards, as a result of steps taken to stimulate industrial activity in the major consumer countries lead prices picked up again. A renewed easing off resulted in 1938 in the founding of the Lead Producers' Association. The curbs on production which were forecast, however, no longer appeared to be necessary up to the dissolution of this cartel on the outbreak of the Second World War.

11.2.5 Post-war attempts at regulation of the zinc and lead markets

Lead dealings were resumed at the London Metal Exchange on 1 October 1952 and very soon, after an initial heavy fall in prices and a short-lived recovery, a world surplus in lead was recorded which induced some producers to impose protective measures. Zinc trading resumed at the London Metal Exchange at the beginning of 1953 and after a sudden price drop, developed more favourably. In the 1950s the price trend was sustained by growing demand and by stockpile purchases by the United States, until in this industrial sector also a marked deterioration in prices set in. In view of this situation the United Nations in 1959 took steps to set up the Lead and Zinc Conference, which in 1961 became the International Lead and Zinc Study Group. The founding of this Group followed a United Nations Commodity Conference for the purpose of co-operation within the framework of the United Nations but, after the sudden cessation of the Korean boom, the lead and zinc industries suffered a persistent worldwide recession. The declared function of this Study Group, with the collaboration of the major producer and consumer countries,[1] was to achieve transparency in the worldwide supply and demand situation in order to lend vital support to countries and firms in their policies. It was aimed to open up new uses for lead and zinc and to defend them against competing products.

No official resolutions were passed to make interventions in the market. The declaration by a number of major producer countries in 1959 that they were willing to cut back production was not therefore a mandatory measure but voluntary adaptation to the market in an existing critical situation (Althaus and Baack, 1977, p. 11 ff.). This policy had already been revoked for zinc by 1960 and for lead by 1961, because the participation of the producers was too small and consequently the decrease in production too low to have any appreciable effect on prices. Zinc prices in 1962 touched rock bottom. In 1966/67 producers again cut back on production but it was not a concerted action and no effects on the trend in capacities were to be observed (Grunwald and Musgrove, 1970, p. 216). Under the influence of worldwide economic buoyancy in 1964 zinc prices advanced to a new high (£148.10 per tonne). This induced the Imperial Smelting Company, who considered this price too high and were anxious to ward off substitution by other products, to announce their own 'realistic' price. This European producer price, which acts as a 'fixed price', does not follow short-term fluctuations on the LME, but, when required, is revised at relatively infrequent intervals.

In the case of lead – which is offered by most US lead producers at list price

---

[1] The International Lead and Zinc Study Group at present comprises the following countries: Algeria, Australia, Austria, Belgium, Bulgaria, Canada, Czechoslovakia, Denmark, Finland, France, Hungary, India, Italy, Japan, Mexico, Morocco, the Netherlands, Norway, Peru, Poland, South Africa, Spain, Sweden, Tunisia, the USSR, the United Kingdom, the United States and West Germany.

or according to the prevailing average price for the current month of delivery, as published in *Metals Week* – violent price fluctuations during the next ten years remained the order of the day. Not until the economic upswing in 1973/74 were peak prices reached, but these slid down again in the following years as the economic situation deteriorated, and the process could not be halted by supportive purchases on the part of producers on the LME.

11.3 THE INTERNATIONAL TIN AGREEMENTS

11.3.1 Early attempts at regulation of the tin market

The first international control in the tin market[1] arose as a result of the high surplus tin reserves recorded in the production areas at the end of the First World War. In order to 'normalize' the market, the Governments of the Dutch East Indies and the Federation of Malay States in December 1920 created the Bandoeing Pool for the purpose of buying up surplus tonnages of tin and, for the time being, keeping these off the market. At the beginning of 1921 some 19,000 tonnes were taken off the market in this way, but from 1923 to the end of 1924 these gradually found their way back again. This happened with only a slight reduction in output and – because the demands of industry had recovered during this time – at a profitable price. Consumption soon exceeded current production, however, with consequent signs of scarcity, leading in 1926/27 to an appreciable 'tin famine', which was reflected in an advance in prices. A speculative boom in tin production was the result and expansion was accelerated by technical progress and by the opening up of new deposits. When, in response to further increases in demand, stocks again rose and tin prices began to fall, there was growing readiness on the part of producers to come to an agreement for fear of ruinous competition. The initiative was taken at the beginning of 1928 by the Anglo-Oriental Mining Corporation (founded as a holding company) which set up the Malayan Tin Trust. This acquired major shareholdings in 16 mining companies in Malaya, took over the capital of Anglo-Malayan Tin Ltd and acquired important mining territories in Nigeria. By withholding its production from the market the company in 1929 achieved a short-lived price rise and at the end of 1929 took the lead in founding the Tin Producers Association (TPA). This Association included producers in Malaya, Australia, Burma, Siam (Thailand) and Nigeria. The Patino concern in Bolivia offered its co-operation; the Dutch group in the Dutch East Indies and the independent Malayan producers (Gopeng Group) did not join, however. The aim of this producer association was to restrict output on a voluntary basis but the curtailments undertaken in the face of the worsening world recession proved inadequate, with the result that stocks continued to grow and prices could not be maintained.

1 See International Tin Council Annual Reports.

11.3.2 The International Tin Agreements 1931–47

A number of factors appeared to have favoured international control of the tin market, including in particular:

(a) the concentration of tin mining in very few countries (British Malaya, the Dutch East Indies, Bolivia and Nigeria in 1930 accounted for around 90% of world production);
(b) the high financial interdependence in tin mining;
(c) the wide separation generally between the producer and consumer countries;
(d) the specific properties of tin (comparatively low differences in quality, low coupled production, limited possibilities of recovery, low risk of substitution).[1]

Under the impression made by increasing weakening of the market for tin the First International Tin Agreement (Agreement on the International Control Scheme) was concluded at the beginning of 1931. This was signed by all the major producer countries (British Malaya, the Dutch East Indies, Bolivia, Nigeria and – in the same year – Siam) and controlled some 90% of total world production of tin. The declared aim of this Agreement organized at government level was to institute a 'relation between production and consumption which would prevent rapid and severe oscillations in price'. Each member country was allotted a standard tonnage on the basis of its production in 1929. The quotas could be varied each quarter and adherence to them was enforceable if necessary by the respective governments.

To implement the Agreement, the International Tin Committee was established, in which representatives of the individual governments co-operated with a Technical Advisory Committee. The restrictions began with production quotas of 78%. Cutbacks by firms under these was to be decided by the individual states. An unexpectedly sharp decline in tin consumption, particularly in the United States, resulted in a further increase in stocks and sagging prices; the restrictions were first increased in 1932 to 56% then to 33% of the standard quota and curbs imposed on exports. This policy was maintained even when there was a slow revival in demand and stocks fell, because the stocks held by the International Tin Pool (built up simultaneously with participation as partners in the Agreement) had not yet been dispersed. This only occurred at the end of 1933 after prices had risen by some 50%. Although the member countries of the International Tin Restriction Scheme largely observed the agreed restrictions – which entailed closing down production at a number of mines, especially in Malaya and Bolivia – this was bound to have an effect on the independent countries: their share of world export increased between 1929 and 1933 from 10% to 27%. However, efforts

---

1 Unless otherwise stated, these observations are based on Schöllhorn, 1955.

to extend the Agreement, which was also supported by the World Exchange and Economic Conference in July 1933, at first remained unsuccessful.

The Second International Tin Agreement (1934) was signed by the previous member countries. In July 1934 they were joined by four other producer areas, French Indo-China, the Belgian Congo, Portugal and Cornwall, so that the only major producer country still absent was China. The restrictions planned for a further three years were meanwhile raised to export quotas of 54% of the standard quotas, but, owing to the renewed demand and price decline at the end of 1934, these were restored to 44%. In order to support the restrictions policy under the Agreement for the Tin Buffer Stock Scheme, concluded in July 1934, it was agreed to form a stabilization reserve, by the use of which it was possible to exert a more rapid influence on fluctuations in supply and demand than by changing the quota. The Buffer Pool policy, which was leading virtually to a scarcity of supplies on the market, aroused increasing criticism on the part of the consumer countries as the supply position became worse, but it was not until 1936, after a phased increase in quotas to 80% and later further easing to 110%, that production for the first time exceeded consumption. Nevertheless, tin remained scarce during the succeeding period, especially as deliveries in many cases often still remained under the quotas, owing to the difficulty of increasing production at short notice.

The Third International Tin Agreement (1937) prolonged tin control by a revised specification of standard quotas, mainly at the expense of the original contract partners. The transfer of non-used quotas and the exceeding of quotas were regulated and, from now on, the producer countries were allowed to hold stocks of 25% of their standard tonnages in order to ensure that they would have sufficient capacity to supply if quotas were raised. An innovation was the official inclusion of consumers' representatives in the Agreement (without voting rights, however); in addition, the rule requiring unanimity for passing a resolution was relaxed, to make a majority vote sufficient.

The trend in the tin market after the 1936/37 boom showed declining demand and falling prices as a result of the general economic recession in 1937/38. Following initial retention of the 110% quotas this led to renewed restrictions, with a reduction in export quotas to 35% of the standard tonnage. Nevertheless, in view of the growing surpluses, the Second Tin Buffer Pool (1938) was agreed upon, likewise stocked from deliveries made by members and not by purchases on the free market. A new feature, however, was the concept of ensuring a specific price level by introducing a range of prices within which intervention was permissible – in this case price limits fixed between £200 and £230 per long ton. The tin price was to be maintained within these limits by means of purchases or sales from the stabilization reserve. As the price was below £180 per long ton when the agreement came into effect, there was understandable opposition from consumers, because the scheme was obviously designed to protect producers at their expense. Speculators naturally exploited the possibility offered by this margin for price rises and private pools were also established.[1] With a renewed reduction of product quotas, a price of £230 was reached by measures complying with the Agreement. The tin supply from the Buffer Pool, however, was insufficient to maintain this price, because of exhaustion of buffer stocks, due to increasing demand triggered off by tension in the world political situation.

Following the outbreak of the Second World War the Tin Committee still remained in existence even though international tin control had become impossible. The International Tin Agreement was prolonged for another five years in 1942 in order to provide a control mechanism for continued regulation of the world tin market up to the end of the war. This prolongation, however, had no longer any practical significance.

If a critical assessment is made of the international regulation of the tin market in the 1930s it must be observed that, despite the numerous drastic restrictions, it was ultimately of no disadvantage to producers. When cost per production unit increased, as a result of lower utilization of capacities, they were always able to offset this by closing down uneconomic plants and resorting to other cost-saving expedients. As it was also possible to maintain tin prices during this period at a level considerably higher than that of the other non-ferrous metals, the major tin companies were still able to make higher profits during periods of restriction. However, the attempts to eliminate rapid and severe oscillations in price did not succeed. It may well be argued that in fact a destabilizing effect was exerted by the scarcity of tin deliberately induced, combined with an unqualified quota determination and – owing to the great instability of prices – the risks involved in stockholding by the industrial fabricators and the reduction in tin reserves by the Buffer Pool. The regulatory measures in the tin market operated quite clearly at the expense of the consumers, who were exposed to a control mechanism dictated by producers anxious to rescue a production sector which had fallen into a precarious situation through over-expansion.

11.3.3 The International Tin Agreements since 1954[2]

Problems of over-production soon cropped up again for the tin industry after the Second World War. The reconstruction after the devastation in Eastern Asia was embarked upon with such zeal that the limits of previous capacity were reached in 1948 and mine production of tin in the Western world was already higher in 1951 than during the pre-war years. Consumption, however, fell sharply after the Korean boom at the beginning of the 1950s, either because of widespread adoption of the electrolytic process, which represented a

---
[1] Gibson-Jarvie, 1976, p. 59.
[2] International Tin Council Annual Reports.

considerable tin saving in the principal field of application of this metal, or because of increasing substitution of tin by other materials, particularly aluminium and plastics. The result was continually growing production surpluses, which were at first still absorbed to a great extent by the stockpile purchases of the United States. Tin prices up to July 1953 declined by almost one-third of their February 1951 level (when they were under the influence of the Korean crisis), and touched the lowest level since the reopening of the London Metal Exchange in November 1949. The attempts to control the international tin market were therefore renewed and, after fruitless discussions in 1948 and 1950, the required unanimity was reached at the conference held at the instance of the Economic and Social Council of the United Nations. After preliminary work by the Tin Study Group, set up under the auspices of the United Nations in 1947, of which almost all the major tin producing and consuming countries were members, in 1954 the First International Tin Agreement (ITA) of the post-war period was concluded; it came into effect on 1 July 1956 for a five-year period. The Agreement was signed by six producer countries and fourteen consumer countries: the producer countries represented about 90% of tin mining in the Western world, whereas the signatories among the consumer countries accounted for only about one-third of world consumption.[1] Important consumers such as the United States, West Germany, Sweden, Switzerland and Norway, which were responsible for some 53% of world consumption, were absent.

The main objectives of the First International Tin Agreement (1954) were as follows:

(a) to prevent or reduce unemployment which may arise in the tin producing areas due to imbalance between supply and demand;
(b) to reduce excessive fluctuations in tin prices and achieve stabilization of prices at one level, which over the long term makes it possible to achieve an equilibrium between supply and demand;
(c) to guarantee adequate supplies of tin at 'reasonable' prices;
(d) to increase the profitability of tin production and prevent wastage of natural resources.

The list of objectives in the Agreement was sadly lacking in precision however, as the frequently employed terms 'reasonable', 'adequate' and 'fair' were certainly open to a wide range of interpretation (Stodieck, 1970, p. 130).

The instruments employed by the 1954 International Tin Agreement were: to continue the Agreement of the 1930s; to establish stabilization reserves and introduce production and export controls on the following lines.

[1] Producer countries: Belgian Congo, Bolivia, Malaya, Nigeria, Indonesia, Thailand. Consumer countries: Australia, Belgium, Canada, Denmark, Ecuador, France, India, Italy, Japan, Lebanon, the Netherlands, Spain, Turkey, the United Kingdom.

Stabilization reserve

The formation of a buffer pool amounting to 10,000 minimum and 25,000 maximum long tons is incumbent upon the producer countries; this is done by means of metal supplies and capital investment in relation to the votes allocated to them in proportion to their share of production. Regulation of the market is the responsibility of the International Tin Committee (ITC) in which producer and consumer countries have an equal share of votes. The employment of the buffer pool depends on the trend in tin prices on the London Metal Exchange: if prices move within the upper third of the agreed stabilization range, then tin is to be released from the reserve, and if it falls in the lower third, stocks are to be replenished by tin purchases on the exchanges in London, Singapore or New York; if it moves in the middle zone the buffer stock manager may not intervene without the express permission of the ITC. If the price rises above the ceiling fixed, the entire buffer stock tonnage, if necessary, is to be sold at the market price, providing the ITC does not revoke this obligation. If the price falls below an absolute floor price, tin must be bought up, using all available resources; the introduction of export quotas for a limited period is also possible.

Export control

The Tin Committee determines the export quotas of the exporting countries on the basis of quarterly notifications of stocks and estimates of requirements by the consumer countries. If the quota is exceeded by more than 5%, the exporting country is required to allocate a quantity of tin to the stabilization reserve corresponding to the over-export. If the quota is not adhered to, it will be curtailed. Export restrictions can only be introduced when the stabilization reserve has reached a continued lower level. The acquisition of additional quotas is possible by earmarking a corresponding volume of tin to the reserve or by a cash deposit.

Production control

A direct restriction of output – as in the Agreement of 1931 – was not envisaged. The stocks in the producer country, however, should not exceed 25% of exports during the last 12 months.

The First International Tin Agreement (1954) differs fundamentally from the Agreements in the 1930s in that it includes consumer countries, which means that a separate majority of votes is required for the two market partners, as resolutions can only be passed with a majority of representatives from the consumer countries. Although the Agreement is not strictly a producer cartel, the net result, because of the higher concentration of the tin supply, is still in fact a greater influence by producer countries. The more flexible regulation mechanism in this Agreement must be rated as a decisive improvement.

Instead of fixed production and export quotas, market supply and export are agreed after consultation with the consumer countries on the supply position. The other new condition, namely that the quotas of the least profitable producer countries should be reduced at yearly intervals by 20% respectively and the quotas of the countries producing more cheaply raised correspondingly, has in fact acquired no practical significance. One of the reasons for this is that the economic and social circumstances have to be taken into account in the case of such decisions.

The First International Tin Agreement (1954) was confirmed in the years 1961, 1966, 1971 and 1976. The aims of the Agreement, which had remained unchanged, were supplemented by an endeavour to increase export proceeds from tin to assist the economic development of the producer countries. It was stipulated that the contributions of members to the buffer stock were to be in cash, not metal. The price limits were increased respectively in line with the LME prices; also, since the Third Tin Agreement (1966) the upper and lower limits of the range of intervention (i.e., the ceiling and floor levels) and also the middle range have been declared discretional ranges. Moreover, the Tin Committee was empowered to impose export quotas on the producer countries when the buffer stock manager found himself compelled to sell at least 5,000 tons of tin (Gibson-Jarvie, 1976, p. 66). The Fourth Agreement (1971) granted him so much freedom that he could now utilize all the opportunities offered by the exchange according to his own discretion.

In the Fifth Tin Agreement of July 1976, in order to extend the latitude for buffer stock operations, the contributions of member countries (in physical deliveries or cash contributions) were doubled to 40,000 tons. This represented about a fifth of world production. Supplementary funds can also be taken up by the Tin Committee at merchant banks against the hedge of tin stocks. Since the conclusion of this Agreement, however, the tin market has become a buyer's market and possible buffer stock operations have again been inadequate to defend the agreed ceiling price (Goreaux, 1978, p. 25). The United States would not consent in May 1979 to the raising of the intervention range of the International Tin Committee buffer stock, because the market supply would be reduced by the control policies of the tin-producing countries and tin prices would therefore be pushed up to an artificially high level. In July 1979 the International Tin Committee resolved to raise the tin intervention prices drastically, and they were raised again in May 1980.

The number of member countries has risen considerably in the course of time. At the Fourth Agreement (1971), Australia was present as a producer country; the USSR and other Eastern Bloc countries and West Germany were signatories as consumer countries. The Fifth Agreement (1976) was also joined by the largest consumer country, the United States (its entry having been opposed hitherto because of objections from the tin-consuming industry) as well as Norway and Denmark. The International Tin Agreement therefore now comprises seven producer and 23 consumer countries. According to the Amendment made at the Meeting of the International Tin Committee in March 1980, to take effect from 1 July 1980, the allocation of votes to each is now 1,000.

In order to administer the International Tin Agreement in accordance with its declared objectives, frequent adjustment was found necessary of the agreed price stabilization levels to the rising trend in tin prices at the metal exchanges: between 1956 and 1978 the maximum highs and lows for interventions had to be revised upwards eighteen times. Nevertheless, the Agreement was not very successful in maintaining the price ceiling: in the years 1961, 1964–66, 1974, 1976 and 1977–78 the market price rose over the respective upper intervention point, after selling of all available stocks from the buffer stock (the last time in January 1977), so that the manager of the buffer stock had to refrain from intervention. The prices fell below the floor price on only one occasion after 1956 – at the end of 1967, for a very brief period. On four occasions export quotas had to be imposed. From December 1957 to September 1960 exports were reduced by nearly a third, while controls from September 1968 to December 1969, January to September 1973 and April 1975 to June 1976 extended from holding exports at the same level to a curtailment of around 18%. The practice of export controls has had the effect of depressing the trend in tin mining development, especially as the release of some 148,200 tonnes tin from strategic reserves by the United States swelled the supply on the world market between 1962 and 1979.

Experience, therefore, shows that the International Tin Agreements in the form adopted hitherto have only had very limited success in achieving their object of price stabilization. Price increases above the upper intervention limit were only delayed temporarily, if at all, in the short term, but in the 25 years' operation of the Agreements they could not be effectively slowed down and the decline in prices below the intervention limit could only be prevented by restricting output and exports. The tin cartel has certainly contributed to the fact that tin has recorded scarcely any increase in consumption for 50 years.

11.4 CARTEL POLICY IN THE ALUMINIUM MARKET

11.4.1 Aluminium cartels before the Second World War

Efforts to establish market control in the aluminium industry began very early, soon after the development and patenting (in 1886) of the molten salts electrolysis process had paved the way for rational mass production. As consumption did not at first, however, expand on the same scale as production, the price of aluminium tumbled sharply – which no doubt contributed to technology and industry finding new uses for the metal. After discussions the four major producers in Europe and the United States nevertheless managed to come to an agreement on the co-ordination to some degree of the volume of production with trends in consumption. Later the aluminium producers formed rings. The European ring comprised Aluminiumindustrie AG (AIAG), with works in Neuhausen (Switzerland), Rheinfelden (Germany) and Lend (Austria), and the French and British aluminium works, and it virtually dominated the European aluminium market. The American ring was chiefly represented by the Pittsburgh Reduction Company, which after taking over the General Bauxite Company also monopolized the American sources of raw materials for aluminium production and from 1907 onwards, as Aluminium Company of America (Alcoa), controlled the principal American aluminium works as well as a works in Canada (Haening, 1910, p. 434 ff.).

The First European Aluminium Cartel (1901–1907) originated from the European ring. This, under the leadership of AIAG Neuhausen was joined by all European producers and the Canadian producer in order to defend themselves in the changing market situation at a time when special patents were expiring and more and more outsiders were entering the field. The principal arrangements concerned:

(a) the safeguarding of the respective domestic markets for each producer;
(b) the contractual partition of the foreign market;
(c) the fixing of minimum prices for primary (i.e., smelter) aluminium at home and abroad.

The cartel was successful in securing considerable price increases, encouraged by the growing demand for aluminium, but the price increase also accelerated the development of new capacities. Of the seven new producers entering the market, four were bought up by members of the cartel; the remaining three firms were of less importance. The market supply from outsiders – Alcoa did not join the cartel – contributed, however, to a price reduction of 30% and finally set in motion the dissolution of the cartel (Ramms, 1959, p. 327). The price competition of the former cartel members was only interrupted in the next few years by short-term agreements and in 1911 the price of aluminium touched rock bottom.

Renewed negotiations led to the conclusion of the Second European Aluminium Cartel (1912–15). It profited from growing demand under the influence of advances in alloying techniques, so that it was possible to disperse the stocks which producers had accumulated in the interim, utilize capacities to better advantage and raise the price of smelter aluminium. This price and regional cartel ended in 1915 with the onset of the First World War.

The Third Aluminium Price Cartel was formed in Europe in 1923 by the major producers in France, the United Kingdom and Switzerland. It proved to be no match, however, for the keen competition to meet the worldwide expansion of demand and was superseded by the Fourth European Aluminium Cartel (1926–31). This cartel was formed by producers from France, Germany, the United Kingdom and Switzerland with the aim of jointly making suitable price reductions (as price levels could not be maintained owing to rapidly expanding production) as an alternative to even greater competitive price cuts, and of opening up new markets with the assistance of a stable pricing policy. The agreements were planned to cover the following points.

(a) Fixing of sales quotas for individual members as percentage shares of total sales of primary aluminium and alloys at home and abroad. These were allocated approximately as follows: France 30%, Germany 27%, Switzerland 25% and the United Kingdom 20%.

(b) In the event of sales quotas being exceeded, the member concerned was to buy up the remaining quotas of those members who had lagged behind.

(c) Every producer was entitled to depart from the uniform price agreement in order to fix prices in his domestic market appropriate to demand. He had sole selling rights there within the quota allocated to him. A surplus domestic demand in a country was to be passed on to the other members.

These agreements enabled price competition in European markets to be eliminated, especially as the cartel refrained from an attempt at price undercutting on the American market, so that the European cartel price was also recognized by non-members (Alcoa, Aluminium Ltd), although not in third-party markets. Nevertheless, an expansion of capacity could not be prevented, because the price control extended only to primary aluminium and the producers were able to hedge on semi-manufactures and finished goods. The world economic crisis and depression then caused producer stocks to rise again so that an attempt was made to impose tighter controls on production and a new cartel was formed.

The Alliance Aluminium Compagnie von Basel (1931–39) was based on much more rigorous agreements than the previous cartels. The agreement was concluded for 99 years (!), with the right to give notice, and member countries participated in the AAC by the takeover of the share capital corresponding to their relative production. Many important producer countries were missing – for example, the United States, the USSR, Italy and Germany (in so far as the domestic market was concerned). Instead of the previous sales quotas, production quotas for primary aluminium – irrespective of use – were decided under the supervision of an independent auditing body. A change in quotas was only to be made on the basis of new products which appeared suitable for opening up new markets, but not because of expansion of capacities. The selling price of primary aluminium was declared mandatory on all the markets. The financing of surplus stocks was the responsibility of the AAC.

Even though market supremacy of this European cartel was limited by the independent suppliers, the price level could in fact be maintained even in the years of depression, although the (unofficial) practice of price differentiation, by means of (relatively high) list prices on markets with comparatively inelastic demand or offering little scope for substitution, and by price rebates where there was elastic demand, was customary. It also succeeded, despite the relatively rigid cartel price, in limiting the decline of European production up to 1932 to some two-thirds of the 1929 production level, whereas in the United States a decline to less than a half was recorded (Ramms, 1959, p. 329). The brisk revival of demand which began in the following years, together with the realization that it was impossible to impose absolutely watertight controls, then led to a drastic revision of Cartel policy. In 1935 the system of production quotas was abandoned and Cartel members were permitted to decide on their own production. The outbreak of the Second World War put an end to the activities of the AAC.

11.4.2 Market regulation after the Second World War

In the aluminium industry, after the lifting of state controls, with fixed prices, enforced in almost all producer countries during the Second World War and the early post-war years, agreements aimed at market regulation and interventions were not reinstated. Mention should be made, however, of the 'gentlemen's agreement' entered into by Western aluminium producers in 1968, with the aim of being a defensive measure against dumping by the Eastern Bloc and of stabilizing prices with falling demand. It has induced the EEC Commission in Brussels to consider bringing an anti-trust action against some large aluminium producers in the European Economic Community because of presumed infringement of Article 85 of the Treaty of Rome.

In this context we should also mention the International Bauxite Association (IBA) founded on 8 March 1974, with headquarters in Jamaica. The eleven member countries – Australia, the Dominican Republic, Ghana, New Guinea, Guyana, Haiti, Indonesia, Jamaica, Yugoslavia, Sierra Leone and Surinam – currently represent over 70% of bauxite production in the world. A hold over the primary materials market for aluminium, not codified by binding agreements, is the main preoccupation of this group; the aim of the bauxite supplying countries is to improve their income by conducting themselves in the manner of a cartel on similar lines to OPEC. A certain measure of success may be reported here, too, as some countries in recent years have increased the mining royalties payable (mainly by foreign companies) and/or their export prices for bauxite, have raised their tax rates on earnings or introduced special levies on bauxite export and thus have been able to increase their earnings. The organization had already recommended a minimum price for bauxite to its members in 1978 (in 1979 it amounted to 2% of the US list price for primary aluminium) and one was adopted for alumina which in 1980 worked out at 14–16% of the average primary aluminium price (99.5% Al) published by *American Metal Market*. In both cases this is a recommendation which is not binding on members. Both aluminium prices are, incidentally, below the normal level of 2.5–3% for bauxite and 16–19% for alumina. The possibility that lasting damage might be inflicted by individual producer countries or even a group of countries in regard to supplies of aluminium to smelters is considered to be very slight, because bauxite occurs abundantly in the world, as do the alternative raw materials shale and clay. It is true that the latter have a lower Al_2O_3 content, but they largely occur in the consumer countries themselves. With rising prices it is now becoming worthwhile to mine such deposits, even if extraction of aluminium from primary materials other than bauxite is not yet considered competitive with conventional production methods for the 1980s (Sies, 1976, p. 7).

11.5 CARTEL FORMATION AND CONTROL OF THE NICKEL MARKET

An international nickel cartel, the Entente du Nickel, was already in existence in Paris in 1900. It included the Canadian, French and British producers. With the position of market supremacy of the International Nickel Company of Canada (Inco), which was further strengthened technically and economically in 1928 by the merger with Mond Nickel Company, and which up to the end of the 1950s accounted for approximately three-quarters of world production, the cartel was hardly more than an agency of Inco. Despite its fairly lax rules, the dealings of this cartel, which hardly made any public appearance, were more effective and uniform than other international cartels with apparently stronger organization. Even though there was a relatively small free nickel market, Inco or the cartel dominated by it virtually controlled prices and tonnages of the world nickel supply, obviously without exploiting this position of supremacy at the expense of the consumers (Berg and Friedensburg, 1944, p. 59 ff.). The Inco position nevertheless became weaker during the course of time because of new suppliers, and this made it easier to introduce exchange trading in nickel; at the end of April 1979 this was accepted on the London Metal Exchange.

11.6 ATTEMPTS TO REGULATE METALLIC RAW MATERIALS WITHIN THE FRAMEWORK OF THE INTEGRATED PROGRAMME FOR COMMODITIES

A new phase in international commodity policy began when the United Nations General Assembly passed, in May 1974, the 'Charter of Economic Rights and Obligations of States' and the developing countries announced a programme of action for a 'new world economic order'. The real turning point was marked in 1976 by the Fourth World Trade and Development Conference (UNCTAD IV) in Nairobi, at which the developing countries, in putting forward their programme, took the initiative towards realising their plans for reordering the economic relations between the industrialized and the developing nations. The Integrated Programme for Commodities, which aims especially at an increase in the transfer of resources from the developed to the developing countries, signifies a renunciation of the previous classic pattern of separate agreements between states. It relies on a comprehensive system of interventions in the commodity markets, carried out simultaneously and financed from a Common Fund. The Common Fund calls for joint contributions from the industrialized and the developing countries, in the expectation that better results will ensue from stabilizing commodity prices at a level tailored to suit both sides, and also in the hope of political advantages in avoiding conflict. The Programme is intended to help realize the following aims of the developing countries (Resolution 93/IV of the 1976 UNCTAD Conference in Nairobi):

(a) To create stable price relationships in raw materials trading at a level which is acknowledged as worthwhile and just for the producers and as 'fair' to the consumers, and which takes into account the general international price trend (indexing) as well as achieving a balance between demand and supply.
(b) To improve and stabilize the export earnings of developing countries.
(c) To improve the marketing of commodities by means of multilateral purchasing and supply commitments.
(d) To assist subsequent fabrication of raw materials in the developing countries and promote diversification of production.
(e) To bring production of synthetic substitutes for raw materials in industrial countries into harmony with the production of natural raw materials in the developing countries.

The scope of these objectives is embodied in their integrated application and the instruments for their realization. As interpreted by UNCTAD, these objectives should in principle cover every commodity for which stabilization measures appear necessary in the interests of the member countries (UNCTAD TD/B/C.1/184). The Nairobi Conference in the first instance envisaged 18 agrarian, mineralogical and industrial commodities of special interest for the developing countries for inclusion in international commodity agreements to which both the producer and consumer countries would be signatories. Among the ten 'core commodities' chosen as the key materials for international control, the non-ferrous metals are represented by copper and tin. In the second group the first non-ferrous metals selected were lead, zinc and aluminium, i.e. raw materials of which the industrial countries have the largest world market shares, and, finally, bauxite and manganese were also named among the core commodities to be included in the first instance in the joint commodity programme.

International buffer stocks and export and production quotas were planned to be the mechanisms for stabilizing earnings. It is aimed to set up a common fund for financing these and as a bracket for individual commodity agreements. At the same time, this would function as a catalyst for conclusion of future agreements, framed on the principle of global membership with joint responsibility of all signatories in the international commodities sector.

The function of the Common Fund is not confined merely to financing buffer stocks and promotion of individual agreements. Apart from this 'first window', there is to be a 'second window' to help finance other suitable measures in the fields of research, development, diversification, marketing and the infrastructure. The joint financing of the buffer stocks, the volume of which will be decided under the individual agreements, will be administered by a committee empowered to remove an over-supply by drawing one-third of the Common Fund in cash and, if required, be given a credit for the remaining two-thirds. It is hoped by this arrangement to make available adequate funds in the case of some agreements to be applied to financing interventions in other agreements. The Articles of Association provide for the present 120 developing countries, who make up the 'Group of 77', to be given 47% of the votes and the industrialized countries 42%, while the Eastern Bloc countries will have 8% and the People's Republic of China 3%. The payments, therefore, are predominantly (up to 68%) from the industrial countries. The Eastern Bloc countries provide 17% and the People's Republic of China 5%, while the combined contribution of the developing countries amounts to 10%.

Even though the basic contract for the Common Fund was finalized in Geneva only in the summer of 1980 after four years of negotiation, this controversial instrument has still not cleared every hurdle. The agreement will only come into effect when 90 states, with a share of at least two-thirds of the mandatory contributions (totalling US $470 million), have ratified their entry. The outstanding balance of US $280 million will then be furnished by voluntary contributions. The 'first window', designed to finance stocks of raw materials, can only be opened when agencies for the agreements on individual commodities have joined the Fund. According to the UNCTAD plans there will initially be 18 such individual agreements. Possibly the first of these would be the one for tin, which is currently being negotiated. Until the individual agreements have been concluded, however, much greater practical importance attaches to the 'second window'. The US $350 million allocated to this (of which US $280 million comes from voluntary contributions) is to be applied in particular to the improvement of quality and productivity and the promotion of marketing and fabrication, or to greater diversification of the product range, in developing countries. Since the Nairobi Conference in November 1976 only one agreement, on rubber, has been concluded to date and this still requires ratification by the national legislature. According to the present state of negotiations, therefore, the progress that has been made is not very encouraging in view of the aim of UNCTAD to draw upon the Fund as from 1982. Up to February 1981 only 24 countries had signed the agreement and only 47% of the required mandatory contributions had been paid. Thus, it should still be some years before the value of the Fund and its effects on international commodity markets will become apparent.

It is not proposed here to discuss the prospects of realization of the agreements envisaged; the negotiations for the Sixth International Tin Agreement are an eloquent example, however, of the difficulty of reconciling the different interests of the producer and consumer countries. We can merely indicate the effects and problems that arise without examining them in detail:[1]

(a) The price stabilization which it was aimed to establish at a level diverging from the market equilibrium price will tend to aggravate the imbalance between demand and supply. Consequently, utilization of surpluses for inferior purposes will increase or bottlenecks will prevail over longer periods than they would otherwise. The efforts of the developing countries to secure as narrow a range of price fluctuations as possible and measures to influence the price trend increasingly hamper the operation of the market as a guiding mechanism. This means there will be less inducement to adapt the supply on offer in the developing countries to market demands. The policy of the developing countries to encourage horizontal and vertical diversification of the product structure, with a consequently broader spectrum of the export range, will also be prejudiced, because centralized bureaucracies lack both the information and the imagination to introduce such changeovers with any prospects of success.

(b) Use of a common fund for the basic financing of buffer stocks might well represent a saving compared with the separate financing of individual agreements. Even so, estimates of the money required for price stabilization would have to be considerably higher than the funds earmarked for it hitherto (see the comprehensive studies and calculations by Baron et al., 1977, p. 15 ff.).

(c) The fundamental weakness of the Integrated Programme for Commodities lies in the difficulty of price forecasting. Because of the uncertainty involved in predicting a price trend this may well present a problem to each buffer stock manager which is ultimately insoluble. Calculations of the 'critical forecasting error' have also shown that the tolerance threshold in the case of copper (0.37% of the 1975 price), aluminium (1.20%) and tin (1.72%) is only very slight, so that even a fractional over-estimation of the price trend would entail adverse effects on income for the world. In the event of an erroneous forecast the industrial countries stand to lose far more than the developing countries would gain, and this would eventually have serious repercussions on the sales prospects of the latter for their raw materials (Baron et al., 1977, p. 40 ff.).

(d) Finally, it is feared that the agreements finalized may be extremely difficult to adapt to changing circumstances and that even greater efforts will be needed for regulation and control because of the intrinsically dynamic nature of such systems.

1 In this context, see the very comprehensive studies made by Donges, 1976 and Kebschull et al., 1977.

Compensation for losses of export income, i.e., stabilization of raw materials export earnings, was already urged by the developing countries in 1964 at the First World Trade and Development Conference (UNCTAD I) in Geneva and was also included in the aims of UNCTAD IV in Nairobi. It was given less prominence, however, in the international discussions on the problem of commodity prices, but in 1969 at UNCTAD V in Manila it was reaffirmed as an objective by the developing countries. The stabilization of export earnings is understood by these countries to be an important component of the Integrated Programme and even in the case of 'stable' commodity prices they consider it should compensate for losses in export income which are due to a decline in demand or a decrease in the market supply.

The potential regulation of the system of compensatory financing proposed for the Integrated Programme for Commodities, to ensure a steady flow of foreign exchange income for the developing countries, may here find a model in the Minerals Regulatory Measure (MINEX) for stabilizing earnings from mine products, which applies to the non-ferrous metals included in the Programme. This measure is envisaged in the Lomé II Agreement, concluded on 31 October 1979 between the European Economic Community and the ACP States (the nations of Africa and the Caribbean and Pacific areas). Today 58 developing countries out of the 119 with voting rights in UNCTAD are parties to this agreement.[1] The terms of the Lomé I Convention of 1975 made provision for stabilization of earnings from the sale of agrarian commodities and iron ore. Lomé II, which now covers 44 commodities, also includes other minerals. With support from a special fund, amounting to a total of 280 million ECUs, the following mine products of the non-ferrous metals range will receive aid in future: copper, cobalt, manganese, bauxite/aluminium oxide and tin.

The compensatory payment under MINEX does not, however, provide for payment of an automatically calculated sum intended largely to maintain the foreign exchange income of a country at a constant level. It differs in this respect from the agrarian products, for which an ACP country was entitled to receive a contribution when proceeds from sales of products making up a specific percentage of its exports fell below a certain figure (a minimum of 6.5%, in some cases less, with a few exceptions). The new system for safeguarding exports of mine production is designed rather to provide rapid and effective first aid measures for contingencies, such as technical problems, arising from natural disasters, political events or a decline in proceeds which would jeopardize the very existence of an essentially sound and profitable mining capacity. Payments would be made when production is effectively at

1 Meyer, 1980, p. 85; Strizek, 1980, p. 7. The procedure departs from the system of compensatory financing from the IMF (International Monetary Fund) and also from previous UNCTAD proposals, which among development policy criteria offer no satisfactory solution for a viable earnings stabilization scheme (cf. the synoptic representation of different systems and critical discussion by Baron et al., 1977, p. 88 ff.).

risk (as, for example, the case of the copper mines of Shaba, Zaire, in 1978), but not merely when there is a drop in export takings. The assistance is tied to the project.

This system of compensatory financing provided under Lomé II is supplemented by agreements on the development of the mining potential of the ACP states, for which, as well as funds generally available from the European Development Fund, commercial credits (covered by public guarantees) of the European Investment Bank totalling altogether 200 million ECUs are available. This has the following advantages:

(a) Its viability and efficiency do not depend on price forecasts.
(b) The market mechanism is not invalidated, because only the level of the payment flows is influenced and not the price on the commodity market.
(c) It avoids the undesirable effect in the developing countries of allocating subsidies to unprofitable mine production enterprises.
(d) A certain measure of control of its application is possible.
(e) Compensatory financing can help offset an undesirable decline in investment in mining.
(f) The transfer of resources can be controlled in such a way that benefit particularly accrues to the most needy developing countries, insofar as they are suppliers of raw materials.

As a general policy, however, care should be taken to ensure a two-way operation of the system of compensatory financing and thus keep the subsidy element within limits (Donges, 1977, p. 28 ff.; Baron et al., 1977, p. 81).

12

Development prospects and problems of the world metal economy

12.1 MEDIUM- AND LONG-TERM PROSPECTS FOR SUPPLIES OF RAW MATERIALS

The world metals economy, with the increasing pace of industrial expansion on an ever broader scale, has been marked by enormous growth in the supply and demand for non-ferrous metals. A feature of this process is that alloys and special metals have tended to gain steadily in importance at the expense of the heavy metals which had previously dominated industry. Nevertheless, there have been unmistakable signs recently that growth is slowing down in the world metals economy. Since the age of technology began non-ferrous metals have always been key raw materials for industrial products, for their specialist properties rather than in terms of volume, and have remained so in spite of, or because of, technical progress and of innovations affecting their application. Their future development during anticipated further industrialization will largely depend on the availability of the most important of these minerals for industrial purposes, in sufficient quantity and quality.

Identification and exploration of world reserves of mineral raw materials have long been essentially the domain of the geologists. This is partly due to the fact that the supply of mineral commodities, in the volume and types required during industrialization, has never previously been an overall limiting factor. The increasingly rapid expansion in world consumption of materials since the Second World War, however, has focussed greater attention on the problem of ensuring supplies of non-renewable metallic raw materials for the world's industries. At the same time the wide area of overlap between the economic and geological sciences has become clearly apparent (Bender, 1976, p. 9).

At the time of the Korean War a study was commissioned by the President of the United States on the essential 'resources for freedom'. This study, presented as the Paley Report, was carried out jointly by a number of experts from the fields of science and technology. It represents the first broad-based attempt at long-term global forecasting of the future trend in supply and demand for the prime economic commodities and includes also an estimate of reserves of non-ferrous metals for the years 1950 and 1975. A number of other estimates followed in the 1960s and 1970s, of which that by the US Bureau of Mines deserves particular mention.

A note of alarm and urgency in the discussion on the supply of raw materials and their importance for the future development of the world economy was sounded in the Report of the Club of Rome on the predicament of mankind (Meadows et al., *The Limits to Growth*, 1972), which indicated the supposed threat to raw materials and the limits of an exponential growth rate. For some non-renewable raw materials, including essential non-ferrous metals, it was estimated that with present growth rates in consumption, the reserves will already be in short supply by the end of this century and indeed, even with a considerable increase in known reserves, some valuable non-ferrous metals will not be sufficient to meet the anticipated demand within the next few decades (*The Limits to Growth*, p. 63 ff.). In just under 15 years after the concept of the affluent society was mooted (Galbraith, 1958), inspired by the rapid surge in economic growth during the post-war years, the Club of Rome painted a gloomy picture of prospects for the supply of non-renewable metals. This certainly contributed in large measure to the pessimistic assessment of future supplies of raw materials, including the major non-ferrous metals. The booming conditions in commodity markets in 1973–74, with prices at sustained high levels, and the drastic increases in the price of oil by the OPEC countries in 1973 were regarded in many quarters as confirmation of this. The sequel to this development would be a further risk to economic growth due to the threat to long-term supplies of essential non-renewable, primary non-ferrous metals arising from steadily increasing consumption by a rapidly growing world population. A contributory factor here is the transformation of the former buyer's market of the past into a seller's market. It was argued that the countries exporting raw materials might, under this new pattern of events and as a result of unilateral changes introduced or contemplated among the principal mining countries during the post-war period, restrict their deliveries, either to secure price advantages from an artificial scarcity or to extend the life-span of their non-ferrous metal deposits, particularly for domestic consumption as their own industrialization took shape.

The raw materials debate at the beginning of the 1970s was coloured by the concept that reserves of the major mineral commodities would become depleted by the economic growth to be expected within the next few decades. It was also feared that the supply situation of the consumer countries would be under short-term strain because of attempts on the part of individual commodity producer countries or groups of countries to manipulate the market, possibly by setting up cartels on the model of OPEC. Since the onset of the recession in 1974 and the drop in raw materials consumption, with falling prices, discussions on commodities have given first priority to problems associated with the regulation of the metal markets, as this is regarded by producer countries of the Third World as advantageous in boosting their national income and hence of furthering their economic development. Even with the renewed upsurge in the economy, the question of scarcity of non-renewable metallic commodities nevertheless lost none of its topicality and the prospect for satisfying the demands of a world population numbering 6 billion by the year 2000 (50% more than today) continued to be a topic of discussion.[1] In this connection the OECD project carried out between 1975 and 1978, 'to study the future development of advanced industrial countries in harmony with that of developing countries', including also the non-ferrous metals sector, should be particularly noted (*Interfutures*, 1979).[2] No less important in this context is the comprehensive study *The Global 2000: Report to the President Entering the Twenty-First Century* (Washington 1980).[3] Of some interest in this context are the estimates by Leontief, Carter and Petri on the basis of a world model of future supplies of mineral raw materials, which was developed with the help of mathematical methods. On the basis of estimates of income levels and the production structure in 1948 – which, in line with the estimates of the Bureau of Mines, were multiplied by an additional 'reserve expansion' factor – and allowing for an increase in relative prices, which would curb demand, the conclusion was reached that the demand for lead and zinc would exceed the supply of these minerals in the 1990s. It was deduced from this that interregional trade in these two minerals would cease after 1990 and that by that date all countries without domestic reserves would have found substitutes for them. For the remaining non-ferrous minerals included in the world model – bauxite, copper and nickel – no shortages were calculated, at least not at a global level (Leontief *et al.*, 1977). A critical examination of these results within the scope of an expert report at the Institute of World Economy, Kiel, on the other hand, assuming a fully functioning market, showed that the authors of the model had omitted to note that adequate supplies of mineral raw materials would be assured if ocean mining, in particular, were to be included in the calculation (Argawal *et al.*, 1978, p. 5 ff.).

An attempt to quantify the reserves of non-ferrous metal ores must necessarily be based in theory on the volumes of metal existing in the earth's crust. The average concentration of all elements in land masses of the earth's crust today is largely known. The most important non-ferrous metals for

---

1 The Mannheim Working Conference of the Gesellschaft für Wirtschafts- und Sozialwissenschaft – Verein für Sozialpolitik, held in September 1979, deals exhaustively with the subject of 'non-renewable resources'. The Proceedings and discussion have been published in full (Siebert, 1980).
2 See also Michaelski, 1978. The following remarks are largely based on the above publications and on *The Global 2000* (1980).
3 The values given in *The Global 2000* and *Interfutures* understandably diverge in having a different annual base (1974 and 1976 respectively). Considerable agreement may be noted, however, in the trend shown.

industry are shown in Table 1, p. 8. These geochemical data permit the calculation of the theoretical metal volumes available in the entire surface crust of the earth to a depth of 1,000 metres, the maximum depth attainable by metal recovery methods today. The calculated volumes amount to many times the present reserves in presumably exploitable deposits (for copper for instance, over 50,000 times and for all metals of any kind over 10,000 times). For cost reasons, however, these enormous volumes calculated to exist in the normal rocks of the earth's crust are of very little practical interest as metal reserves for the foreseeable future, since the only economically recoverable ores today are those having a metal content far in excess of the average content of the earth's crust. An evaluation of the theoretical pay content of these metal volumes as recoverable resources is therefore ruled out not only for the immediate future but also for the years beyond 2000 (see the calculations and remarks in Bender, 1976, p. 10 ff.).

If a considerable proportion of the metals occurring in the natural rocks are not, therefore, feasible as long-term resources for the recovery of non-ferrous metals, it is all the more urgent to consider the extent of workable mineral reserves available today and in the immediate future and how long they will last as industrialization progresses. It is necessary, then, to estimate the resources of raw materials containing non-ferrous metal which offer prospects of economic recovery, and also to quantify the location, volume and quality of the prospected reserves for which economic extraction would be currently feasible.

The estimated world reserves of non-ferrous metals for the period 1950–79 (see Table 46) show that, despite the considerable volume of mine production during this period, the reserves in 1979 are considerably greater than those forecast for this period in previous years. The resources of these metals, however, are without exception many times greater than the reserves indicated as suitable for economic recovery. The reason for this is that the latter are estimated according to given technical and financial potentialities of particular mining projects planned for the immediate future.

The higher reserves estimated may be regarded as due to the exceptional level of exploration activity since 1950, but these estimates also confirm the extreme difficulty of making forecast projections for most non-ferrous metals. The main reasons are as follows:

(a) With increasing prices of raw materials it is now feasible to work deposits which were formerly disregarded on economic grounds, either because the metal contents were too low or because ore dressing and smelting techniques at that time were too difficult.
(b) Higher prices have also enlarged the scope for research in the mining, preparation and smelting of non-ferrous metals.
(c) The continual rise in raw materials prices has involved switching to

Table 46. Estimated world reserves and resources of non-ferrous metals, 1950–79 (million tonnes)

Metal	Reserves						Resources	Ratio of resources to reserves
	1950	1965/66	1974	1975/76	1977	1979	1977	1977
Copper	100.0	195.0	408.2	408.2	456.0	543	726	1.6
Lead	40.0	93.4	149.7	150.0	124.0	157	1,360	11.0
Zinc	70.0	75.3	235.9	135.2	150.0	240	1,800	12.0
Tin	6.9		10.2	10.2	10.2	9.7	37	3.6
Bauxite	1,400	5,964		17,272		22,700		
Aluminium			3,483.5	3,483	5,000		7,600	1.5
Titanium			341	340.1	394		2,015	5.1
Chromium			2,414[1]	523.4	523.2	820	3,692	5,300	6.5
Cobalt				2.5	2.4	1.5	3	4.5	3.0
Manganese			1,826	1,814.0	1,814	5,443	3,265.5	1.8
Molybdenum		2.2	5.9	6.0	9.0	8.4	31.7	3.5
Nickel			54.4	55.3	54.4	56.7	127.7	2.3
Vanadium			9.7	9.7	9.7	15.8	56.2	5.8
Tungsten	1.9		1.8	1.8	2.0	2.5	3.4	1.7
Niobium					10.7		14.6	1.4
Tantalum			0.07	0.07	0.06	0.06	0.26	4.3
Bismuth			0.06	0.06	0.08	0.1	0.13	1.6

Note: Figures refer to metal content, except for bauxite.
1. As Cr_2O_3 content.
Sources: EEC *Interfutures*, p. 43 f.; Michalski, 1978, p. 14 f.; US Department of the Interior, Bureau of Mines, *Mineral Facts and Problems*, 1976, p. 32; *Mineral Commodity Summaries*, 1980.

primary materials which were hardly ever used in the past for economic reasons (e.g., from bauxite to aluminium oxide).

(d) By extending the areas prospected and using modern methods of exploration, terrestrial deposits have been found which could be economically recovered when the infrastructure has been developed.

(e) Oceans and the sea bed represent still largely unexplored and untapped reservoirs of non-ferrous metals: at present only 2–3% of all mineral raw materials are obtained from this source (Prewo, 1979).

Experience has shown that progress in technology also increases the workable reserves of non-ferrous raw materials. This adds to the difficulty of estimating the reserves and countless examples have shown that technical development in the industrial field in the long term is extremely difficult to forecast (Casper, 1975, p. 8). Long-term estimates of the supply of non-ferrous metals are rendered even more uncertain by the possibility of recycling and, depending on price trends, by re-utilization of non-ferrous metals for scrap and remelted material. In the event of pressure due to scarcity of primary raw materials, the proportion taken up by these sources in total supply could certainly be substantially increased by improved technology and expansion of capacities in this field.

An added difficulty in estimating the life of reserves of non-ferrous metals is the problem of predicting potential demand. Changes in the pattern of consumption of non-ferrous metals depend on developments in industrial production, technical progress and/or changes in consumer habits. Moreover, comparatively high prices for a metal are conducive to reducing specific consumption of the metal by applying new technologies or by replacing it by cheaper metals or other materials. On the other hand, depending on prices and rarely for technical reasons, the opposite development may occur. The wide range of such alternatives, which can be extended by technical progress in an unprecedented manner, again adds considerably to the uncertainty of forecasting trends in demand. This explains why previous forecasts in the early 1950s did not correspond to actual development. The main source of error in the global survey of stocks made in the undoubtedly very praiseworthy Paley Report was the underestimating of the pattern of consumption for non-ferrous metals between 1950 and 1975 in the Western European countries and, particularly, in Japan; in addition, the prediction of demand in the United States was only correct in the case of aluminium, and the effective consumption of refined lead and copper, and of zinc (excluding remelted zinc), tin and nickel, was lower than the forecast (*Metal Statistics*, 1974, p. v ff.).

Even in the case of very recent forecasts for the years 1985 and 2000, for which more reliable statistical data and improved analytical and projection methods were available, wrong estimates of this kind, relating to the expansion in consumption assumed for the group of developing countries (which has been put at too low a figure) cannot be excluded. This risk is also expressly emphasized in *The Global 2000*, which, in the words of the authors, presents a picture 'that can be painted only in broad strokes and with a brush still in need of additional bristles'. With this proviso, projection for world consumption has been carried out on the basis of estimates by the US Bureau of Mines and of Wilfried Malenbaum (1977). The results for nine non-ferrous metals are given in Table 47. The biggest increase in world consumption is expected for aluminium, with an annual average of 4.3%, followed by manganese with 3.4% and also chrome ores, tungsten, lead and zinc, likewise with some 3%, whereas the annual average increase predicted for copper and nickel is 2.9% and for tin 2.1%.

In connection with the regional trend the following should be noted especially:

(a) For the United States an expansion in consumption in line with the increase in world consumption is only anticipated for aluminium, whereas for the other metals under review a considerably lower increase is expected.

(b) For Western Europe a somewhat over-proportional increase is forecast only for refined copper and chrome ore, while otherwise expansion is expected to lag slightly behind the global trend in consumption of non-ferrous metals.

(c) In Japan the increase in consumption of the non-ferrous metals under review (with the exception of zinc) is higher than for the world as a whole.

Table 47. The consumption of non-ferrous metals: estimated average annual increase and regional distribution, 1971–2000 (%)

Metal		Western Europe	USA	Japan	Other developed countries[1]	USSR	Eastern Europe	Africa	Asia	Latin America	China	World total (thousand tonnes)
Refined copper												
Increase	1975–2000	3.0	2.1	3.4	2.7	2.5	3.1	4.8	4.0	4.5	4.8	2.9
Share	1971/75	30.6	23.8	11.6	4.5	13.8	6.8	0.3	1.4	3.5	3.7	(7,923)
	1985	30.4	23.0	12.0	4.7	12.7	6.9	0.3	1.6	4.2	4.3	(11,341)
	2000	31.1	19.0	13.0	4.2	12.4	7.1	0.4	1.8	5.2	5.7	(16,839)
Lead												
Increase	1975–2000		1.4									3.1
Share	1971/75		27.4									(3,392)
	1985		23.3									(5,160)
	2000		20.2									(7,570)
Zinc												
Increase	1975–2000	2.7	2.1	3.0	3.1	3.3	3.0	4.3	4.0	4.4	4.0	3.1
Share	1971/75	27.6	20.6	11.9	5.6	14.8	8.0	0.4	3.7	4.0	3.4	(5,636)
	1985	26.4	19.4	12.5	5.6	15.7	7.6	0.5	4.2	4.6	3.6	(8,253)
	2000	25.9	16.6	12.0	5.9	16.1	8.0	0.6	4.8	5.7	4.4	(12,022)
Tin												
Increase	1975–2000	1.9	0.9	2.5	2.4	2.1	2.5	6.4	2.1	3.2	2.7	2.1
Share	1971/75	29.6	22.8	14.2	5.2	7.7	7.3	0.9	3.4	3.0	6.0	(233)
	1985	28.0	19.6	15.6	5.0	8.0	7.6	2.3	3.7	3.7	6.6	(301)
	2000	28.2	17.1	15.8	5.6	7.9	8.1	2.5	3.6	4.1	7.1	(393)
Aluminium												
Increase	1975–2000	3.9	4.3	5.2	4.3	3.7	4.3	5.5	4.4	5.1	5.0	4.3
Share	1971/75	23.4	35.8	10.2	4.3	12.2	6.8	0.3	2.4	2.7	1.9	(12,249)
	1985	22.5	36.0	11.7	4.4	11.4	6.5	0.3	2.2	2.9	2.1	(20,590)
	2000	21.3	35.8	12.8	4.3	10.6	6.7	0.4	2.4	3.3	2.3	(36,516)
Chrome ore												
Increase	1975–2000	3.4	1.3	4.1	3.6	1.4	4.0	4.2	4.1	5.4	4.2	3.3
Share	1971/75	27.0	16.5	16.2	10.7	10.8	10.7	0.7	2.7	1.6	3.1	(6,941)
	1985	28.8	13.1	17.9	11.1	7.4	12.2	0.8	2.9	2.2	3.7	(10,623)
	2000	27.8	10.0	20.2	11.7	6.8	12.8	0.9	3.3	2.6	4.0	(16,018)
Manganese												
Increase	1975–2000	2.7	2.9	3.7	1.8	3.2	3.4	4.5	4.0	4.9	4.5	3.4
Share	1971/75	20.3	9.5	8.2	5.4	31.6	5.7	2.4	6.8	5.3	4.9	(20,339)
	1985	18.6	9.8	8.6	3.9	31.4	5.9	2.7	7.5	6.3	5.5	(30,239)
	2000	17.4	8.3	8.9	3.6	30.6	5.8	3.1	8.0	7.7	6.6	(48,060)
Nickel												
Increase	1975–2000	2.8	2.2	3.6	2.7	3.2[2]		4.0	4.9	4.9		2.9
Share	1971/75	27.5	26.0	15.7	2.8	25.7[2]		0.6	0.6	1.1		(618)
	1985	27.2	23.3	17.1	2.7	26.7[2]		0.9	0.9	1.4		(905)
	2000	26.3	21.3	18.6	2.6	27.4[2]		0.8	1.1	1.8		(1,314)
Tungsten												
Increase	1975–2000	2.9	2.4	3.7	3.0	3.1	3.6	3.8	4.8	4.9	3.8	3.3
Share	1971/75	28.8	16.2	6.9	1.4	16.5	9.5	1.7	2.1	3.4	13.4	(40,182)
	1985	28.0	14.0	7.2	1.4	16.6	10.1	1.8	2.5	4.2	14.3	(60,207)
	2000	26.4	13.0	7.6	1.4	15.9	10.4	2.0	3.1	5.1	15.2	(92,637)

1. Australia, Canada, Israel, New Zealand and South Africa.
2. Includes Eastern Europe and China.
Source: Compiled and calculated from *The Global 2000*, 1980, p. 206 f.

(d) Consumption of non-ferrous metals (with the exception of manganese) in the developed Western-type countries (Australia, Canada, Israel, New Zealand and South Africa) will differ only slightly from the increase in the world trend as a whole.
(e) The increase in consumption in Eastern Europe will tend to accelerate more rapidly than in the world as a whole and also than in the Soviet Union.
(f) The most marked expansion in consumption may be expected in Africa, Asia, Latin America and China, in fact to a considerably greater extent than in the world as a whole.
(g) World consumption, even in the year 2000, will still be accounted for predominantly by the Western industrialized countries (the United States, Western Europe and Japan) with shares of 70% of aluminium, over 60% of refined copper, nickel and tin and almost 60% of chrome ore, although only 35% of manganese. The shares of the Eastern Bloc countries are usually estimated at about 20% and only in the case of manganese at 30%, somewhat higher than in the industrialized countries. The developing countries in Africa, Asia and Latin America, although increasing their share of world consumption of non-ferrous metals, will still remain on the whole regions of secondary importance.

There are two possible methods of calculation of the life span of non-ferrous metals, on the basis of estimates of consumption and of reserves:

(a) statistical calculation, in which it is assumed that consumption will remain constant in future;
(b) dynamic calculation, which is based on a putative expansion in consumption.

The extent to which the life-span of the reserves is curtailed in the dynamic calculation is apparent in a comparison with results of the static calculation (Table 48). Even according to this, however, it can hardly be concluded that there will be a general physical shortage of aluminium, titanium, chromium, niobium, manganese and vanadium in the future. The life-span for copper, lead, tin, zinc, molybdenum, tantalum and tungsten is considerably less, but certainly much longer than for bismuth and mercury. The estimates are only of limited reliability for some metals which are calculated to have a very small life-span, because firms only keep reserves of these to a very limited extent. It is also to be expected that when metals become more expensive there will be greater substitution and recycling. The drying-up of supplies of other comparatively scarce non-ferrous minerals, such as bismuth, barium, germanium and indium (which, however, is hardly likely), might certainly be remedied in most cases by appropriate technology (*Interfutures*, 1979, p. 45).

Generally, however, a scarcity of supplies will not occur overnight but will invariably be heralded by comparative price increases so that substitutes or new technical solutions can be found. A few vital applications will then be given priority and hence the life-span of these non-ferrous metals will be

Table 48. Estimated availability of reserves of selected metallic raw materials (million tonnes metal content)

Metal	Resources 1975/76	Reserves 1975/76	Availability of 1975 reserves[1] (years)	Ratio of 1975 reserves to cumulative demand 1974–2000
Copper	1,500	408.2	62	1.3
Lead	300	150.0	49	1.2
Zinc	245	135.0	41	1.1
Tin	37.0	10.2	44	1.3
Bauxite	5,700	3,483	> 200	4.0
Titanium	1,234	340.1	> 300	4.4
Chromium	1,049	523.2	> 200	5.7
Cobalt	4.3	2.4	78	2.1
Manganese	3,265	1,814	197	4.9
Molybdenum	28.6	6.0	65	1.4
Nickel	129.7	55.3	77	2.1
Vanadium	56.2	9.7	300	7.5
Tungsten	5.2	1.8	46	1.2
Niobium	14.6	10.0	> 800	> 10
Tantalum	0.26	0.07	49	1.1
Bismuth	0.13	0.06	22	0.5

1. Reserves in relation to demand 1975.
Source: Compiled from Michalski, 1978, p. 14 ff.

prolonged for uses for which they are indispensable. A general shortage of non-ferrous metals is therefore improbable in the immediate future. It should be possible to overcome specific problems unless the economic and technical transition period is adversely affected by sudden unforeseen events. According to all indications, therefore, we can hardly predict any problems of physical shortages of non-ferrous minerals arising in the future (*Interfutures*, 1979, p. 45 ff.).

We cannot, on the other hand, say yet whether the consumer countries of non-ferrous metals will always maintain these in the necessary volume at reasonable prices, as political risks to supplies may arise from the high regional concentration of the reserves. In the case of two of the 17 most important industrial non-ferrous metals studied, chromium and vanadium, 90% of the identified reserves are in the hands of two countries only; in the case of manganese three countries dispose of over 90%. The six most important reserve countries combined have 90% of molybdenum, tungsten, lithium, rhenium, tantalum and yttrium reserves and over 80% of reserves of cobalt and bismuth. Only in the case of copper, zinc, tin and lead is the share of the six major reserves countries between 66% and 77% (Table 49). The question of regional distribution of raw materials reserves of non-ferrous metals should therefore be considered as of greater importance than the global reserves situation and the life-span of individual metals. The EEC and Japan, in particular, are highly dependent on imports of most ores and metals but the

Table 49. Regional distribution of world reserves of non-ferrous metals, 1979

Metal	World reserves (million tonnes)	Share taken by the leading countries (%) Individually				In total
Copper	543.0	Chile	19.7	Zambia	6.8	65.5
		USA	18.6	Canada	6.5	
		USSR	7.4	Peru	6.5	
Lead	157.0	USA	26.8	Canada	12.7	77.1
		Eastern Bloc	7.4	Mexico	3.2	
		Australia	14.0	Yugoslavia	3.2	
Zinc	240.0	Canada	25.8	Eastern Bloc	10.0	70.0
		USA	20.0	Peru	2.9	
		Australia	10.0	Mexico	1.3	
Tin	9.7	Indonesia	16.0	Thailand	12.4	76.7
		China	15.5	USSR	10.3	
		Malaysia	12.4	Bolivia	10.1	
Bauxite	22,700.0	Guinea	28.6	Jamaica	8.8	74.9
		Australia	20.3	Greece	3.1	
		Brazil	11.0	Guyana	3.1	
Chromite	3,692.0	South Africa	65.8	Turkey	0.1	97.9
		Zimbabwe	29.0	Philippines	0.1	
		Eastern Bloc	2.9			
Cobalt	3.0	Zaire	39.4	USA	10.6	84.8
		Eastern Bloc	13.6	Philippines	6.1	
		Zambia	12.1	New Caledonia	3.0	
Manganese ore	5,443.0	Eastern Bloc	50.0	Gabon	2.8	97.7
		South Africa	36.7	Brazil	1.6	
		Australia	5.5	India	1.1	
Molybdenum	8.4	USA	48.7	Canada	5.9	96.9
		Chile	28.9	Peru	2.7	
		Eastern Bloc	10.7			
Nickel	56.7	New Caledonia	24.0	Cuba	5.4	55.2
		Canada	13.8	USA	4.3	
		Eastern Bloc[1]	7.7			
Vanadium	15.8	South Africa	49.4	Chile	0.9	98.2
		USSR	46.0	USA	0.7	
		Australia	1.2			
Tungsten	2.5	Eastern Bloc	66.1	Australia	4.3	89.7
		Canada	9.6	Turkey	3.0	
		USA	4.9	South Korea	1.8	
Lithium ore	1.9[2]	Chile	52.6	Zaire	10.5	99.2
		USA	21.1	Zimbabwe	3.2	
		Canada	10.5	Australia	1.3	
Rhenium	0.003	USA	37.1	USSR	7.1	97.0
		Chile	37.1	Peru	5.7	
		Canada	10.0			

Table 49. (cont'd)

Metal	World reserves (million tonnes)	Share taken by the leading countries (%) Individually				In total
Tantalum	0.06[2]	Zaire	61.2	Malaysia	6.0	95.5
		Nigeria	11.9	Brazil	5.2	
		Thailand	7.5	Australia	3.7	
Bismuth	0.1	Japan	24.0	USA	9.6	79.8
		Australia	18.3	Eastern Bloc	7.7	
		Bolivia	14.4	Canada	5.8	
Yttrium	0.05	India	52.4	Brazil	6.5	94.3
		Australia	15.7	Canada	6.3	
		USA	9.2	Eastern Bloc	4.2	

1. Excluding Cuba. 2. Western countries only.
Source: Compiled and calculated from *Mineral Commodity Summaries*, 1980.

United States also, although comparatively well endowed with raw materials, has to rely on imports of certain minerals. The majority of the Eastern Bloc countries and some 70% of developing countries likewise have only very limited reserves of non-ferrous minerals at their disposal. For the 19 most important non-ferrous metals in 1979, world reserves were distributed approximately as follows: (share %):

	Industrial countries	Developing countries	Eastern Bloc
Heavy metals	48	40	12
Light metals	30	60	10
Alloying and special metals	45	25	30

This distribution of reserves and the concentration of supplies in the markets should, however, imply only partial risks for the consumer countries largely lacking in raw materials, in particular molybdenum, chromium and nickel and also titanium, cobalt, niobium, tantalum and vanadium. For most non-ferrous metals producer cartels are hardly feasible, as the interests of the different countries possessing the reserves are usually opposed to such an arrangement. The concentration in smelter production has to be evaluated variously according to those countries with relatively free markets and those which are mainly state-controlled. Politically motivated temporary restrictions on supplies cannot be excluded on the part of the latter. A concentration of supplies with private firms should offer little risk to the consumer countries as the major international concerns are especially concerned, in the interests of long-term sales, to maintain fully functioning markets.

12.2 SUPPLY POLICY RESPONSIBILITIES

Fears that we are threatened in the immediate future with a world shortage of raw materials in the non-ferrous metals sector are not supported by geological and economic data on reserves and resources, nor by predictions of the future trend in world consumption of the metals. These fears are further dispelled if, in addition to the calculations based on the concept of availability, allowance is made for the fact that suppliers or purchasers will probably take steps in good time to adapt themselves to changes in price/cost relationships. When high prices prevail there is likely to be more intensive exploration, prospecting and exploitation of new deposits, and conversely, when signs of shortage appear, the price mechanism should stimulate greater use of substitution processes and recycling will probably make a greater contribution to raw materials supplies by use of improved technology and expanding capacities. Finally, we may expect in future that the comparative decline in metal consumption per unit of industrial production to be observed in the past, will continue, as reflected in the lower growth rate of non-ferrous metal production compared with industrial production as a whole. This trend will be further stimulated by the advances to be expected in technology. There is no doubt, from all experience acquired to date, that the time limits set today to industrial exploitation, according to clearly unsatisfactory methods of estimating, will be prolonged. There are no general grounds, therefore, for pessimism about growth, in so far as this is related to availability of non-ferrous metals, at least in the next few decades.

Nevertheless, this should not persuade the consumer countries that they can be entirely complacent in regard to future continuity of supplies for their non-ferrous metal requirements and the attendant circumstances making this possible. A high risk factor for continuity of supplies is that the consumer countries in the long term will have incessantly to turn to the mining countries of the Third World because of depletion of their former supplies. It has been apparent in recent years that the highly unstable political and legal conditions in some of these countries are capable of causing interruption of supplies. Military operations intercepting vital transport routes have been the main problem. The expropriation of privately owned foreign property in mining and smelter works and the nationalization of these assets have also caused losses in production and export. Other forms of state intervention, such as restrictions on imports and the imposition of high taxes and levies on foreign firms, amounting in effect to dispossession by 'cold war' tactics, have also proved to be disruptive factors. Moreover these countries, which are usually making great efforts to promote their own industrialization, naturally wish to work more of their ore themselves in their own country by creating new capacities, rather than exporting.[1] Although there will probably be technical and economic limitations to such plans, at least in the short term, there are latent risks in this situation for the consumer countries in the procurement of their raw materials.

These and other risks which are to be ascribed to the producer countries, as well as possible moves on the part of the consumer countries to introduce restrictive practices on access of manufactured goods to their markets, may well jeopardize the international commodities economy. They imply that fears regarding the smooth pattern of trade between producer and consumer countries would appear to be fully justified. Outside influences and the varying interests of these groups of countries, or of individual countries within these groups, do not exclude the possibility of shortages in supplies or indeed temporary deficits and panic reactions. Possibly, too, in future the instability of the international non-ferrous metals market will tend to increase.

Moreover, in all probability the costs of ore and metal recovery will escalate over the medium and long term, so that in future additional funds will be needed for new consumption and replacement of non-ferrous metals than hitherto. The principal reasons for this are as follows:

(a) The prospecting and exploration operations required will be considerably more expensive, because they will inevitably be concentrated to a greater extent in geological areas with difficult conditions of terrain and on ores of low metal content.

(b) The opening up of such deposits will probably involve extensive development of the infrastructure, such as roads, housing schemes, energy and water supplies.

(c) Preparation of lean ores of comparatively low metal content is technically more complicated and expensive and requires the appropriate production resources.

(d) Unit wage costs, due to higher pay rates and social security contributions, will probably increase if they cannot be offset by higher productivity. This will apply particularly to the exploitation of comparatively small- and medium-sized deposits.

(e) Substantially higher costs will be incurred in meeting energy requirements than in the past, and production costs will also be pushed up by the need to comply with environmental protection regulations.

---

1 The effects to be expected on income and employment are usually over-estimated however. Estimates of the vertical diversification potential of the developing countries in regard to exports expansion, in the event of these countries fully utilizing the advantages of their location for secondary processing of raw materials, have shown (model calculations based on volume and prices for 1973) that this potential is highest for secondary processing of bauxite and alumina to aluminium and comparatively high for zinc. In the working of copper, lead and tin the vertical diversification potential may now be regarded as utterly exhausted. According to the analysis of the effects on employment resulting from additional export earnings, the greatest number of additional jobs arising from increased diversification in secondary processing was likewise expected for aluminium and zinc, whereas for copper, lead and tin these are estimated as comparatively slight. It should be noted that these values vary from one country to another, depending on the conditions prevailing (Hoffmeyer and Neu, 1978, p. 89).

(f) Higher oil prices to be expected will be reflected in increased freight charges for overseas transport of mass-produced commodities.

(g) The raw materials countries who are anxious to benefit to a greater extent from the exploitation of their mineral wealth might raise taxes and levies on exports of raw materials which will have the effect of forcing up prices.

The obvious conclusion to be drawn from this probable trend is that the consumer countries should in future be more thrifty than in the past with these indispensable, non-renewable, metallic raw materials. This implies not only constant efforts towards more rational use of scarce materials but also greater utilization of recycled materials. The effect of this form of 'above-ground mining' on raw material supplies for the consumer countries should not be underestimated.

Nevertheless, we need hardly stress that a globally effective raw materials supply has to encompass a very wide radius of action. Policies to safeguard supplies naturally differ from one country to another, depending on the availability of domestic mineral raw materials, the probable pattern of consumption of non-ferrous metals as industrialization progresses and the degree of procurement risk. The latter depends to a considerable extent on the importance attached by the raw materials countries to obtaining industrial products supplied by a particular consumer country and the extent to which they rely on this. As a general policy the supply of raw materials to consumer countries cannot merely be directed towards meeting temporary shortages. This would mean they would avoid making necessary adaptation in their pattern of consumption and would serve to perpetuate unstable structures. A policy geared to the permanent safeguarding of raw materials for the consumer countries, which is also in the interests of those supplier countries who have to rely on sales of their products to obtain foreign currency for their consumer needs, industrial products and oil requirements should rather seek to achieve a fair balance of interests between suppliers and consumers and to foster more intensive medium- and long-term co-operation between these blocks of countries on a partnership basis.

It would be of advantage for raw materials trading between the consumer and producer countries to secure long-term raw materials supplies during the progress of industrialization on the lines suggested by the Tripartite Expert Group, a group of independent economists from North America, Japan and the EEC (*Weltrohstoffversorgung*, 1974, p. 39). Of particular value in this context would be internationally agreed rules of conduct for ensuring non-discriminatory access to raw materials markets with free price formation, to which a natural rider would be the consent of the consumer countries regarding their imports of processed and fabricated products from the countries producing raw materials. It is questionable whether international agreements on individual raw materials, to include provision of funds mainly by industrial countries for financing stocks of particularly sensitive products to minimize or prevent variations in production, with consequent extreme price mark-ups, would hold out great hopes of success according to the experience with the International Tin Agreements.[1] Agreements on stabilization of earnings, on the contrary, should be given priority. Efforts should be made, however, to reach agreement on improvement of the general climate of investment in the field of metallic raw materials.

Even though such skeleton agreements might go a long way towards removing discrepancies between the natural distribution of resources and the interests of the consumer countries, their realization today according to experience of recent international raw materials conferences must be regarded with reservation. The interests of the industrial and the developing groups of nations, and of individual countries within these groups, were found to diverge greatly on many major issues. The necessary international consultative procedures are also usually too cumbersome to produce a system of rules and conduct in the form of skeleton conditions.

It would indeed be a disaster for both consumer and producer countries if they were to postpone or, indeed, fail to take, necessary action to meet rising consumption of mineral commodities in the coming decades and merely waited for international agreements or for global measures creating a 'new world economic order' on the lines advocated by the developing countries. Significant increases in reserves and mining capacities are needed to keep pace with probable future world demand, and, owing to the time-consuming nature of prospecting ventures and maturing of investments, an 8–10 year period has to be allowed for mining projects to be realized. Neglect of prospecting for new deposits today will mean bottlenecks in a few years' time (see *Mineralische Rohstoffe*, 1979, p. 22).

An important contribution to safeguarding essential supplies of raw materials in the Western world will also have to be made in future by the firms which in the past bore the brunt of worldwide development in the non-ferrous raw materials with their vision, flexibility and willingness to take risks, in spite of the many setbacks due to wars, political unrest, expropriation of assets and restrictions on their activities. Operations of the major international mining companies in countries of the Third World will certainly be inhibited by the lack of compensation or inadequate indemnity for dispossession of foreign ownership in mining and smelting works during the post-war decades. The reluctance of industry to invest in countries or regions which are regarded as politically or legally unstable is understandable. This has already resulted in firms investing once more on a larger scale in the industrialized mining

---

1 Finally it should be repeated here that the effect of buffer stocks, quite apart from cost and financing problems, is obviously overrated, as unavoidable errors in forecasting of buffer stocks are not identified or are underestimated. It should not be forgotten that a buffer stock can also reinforce the prevailing market trend. The market contenders are aware of the stocks, and this is necessarily reflected in their behaviour to which metal markets have a very sensitive reaction.

countries and those considered 'safe', such as the USA, Canada and Australia. A consequence of this is that countries which dispose of high-grade deposits, such as Africa, now record declining production.

The recent advertising to be observed by some producer countries for renewed involvement of the former dispossessed firms in their mining and smelting industry may possibly underline how dependent these countries still are on the transfer of capital, technical know-how, engagement of managerial staff in production and experience in marketing of the products so important for their country. Whether this will be sufficient to revive activity of private firms in any of the countries of the Third World to the desired extent remains to be seen.

There are still no universally valid international rules for the protection of private investment in countries of the Third World, such as those advocated by industry and the banks in West Germany since the 1950s, despite the continual efforts of the EEC and the World Bank to this end. The Charter of Economic Rights and Obligations of States passed in 1974 by the General Assembly of the United Nations between the developing countries and the industrial countries, under pressure from the developing countries, but with a number of important industrial countries voting against it, would appear to have made the climate for foreign investment even worse, because of nationalization demands on the part of the development countries contained in it (Juhl, 1976, p. 191 ff.). The fact that the industrial countries were unsuccessful in securing global protection for private investment may probably be due in some measure to many countries of the Third World being afraid that a charter similar to GATT in the investment sphere would severely hamper their sovereign rights. West Germany has so far tried to find a way out by concluding bilateral protection agreements with the countries concerned (with 38 countries by September 1978). Nevertheless, any losses or deficits still occurring are covered wherever possible by a special insurance scheme. Investors would appear to be better served in the short term with such agreements than by waiting for international rules to be negotiated, which can usually be circumvented in any case. The EEC is also at pains to include clauses for the protection of private investments in contracts concluded with the member countries.[1]

One main ingredient for success – as in the case of West Germany – is

[1] Relevant studies have indeed shown that instruments of promotion such as bilateral investment agreements have hardly any noticeable effects on foreign investment activity. Thus in African countries bi- and multi-lateral investment protection agreements did not stimulate a greater influx of foreign capital, whereas Latin America, where virtually all countries on constitutional grounds are not prepared to sign such agreements and hence are not represented on the World Bank Convention, shows a strong concentration of international direct investments in developing countries. Assuming political risks to be equal in the two groups of countries, it is doubtful whether this will also extend to mining investments, which are not directed primarily towards the market potential of the investing countries but towards exploitation of regional ore deposits in the nature of grass-roots assets (Juhl, 1979, p. 77 ff.).

undoubtedly that the raw materials countries themselves participate in framing the protection clauses because this emphasizes the desired partnership nature of their co-operation. This would also apply to any proposed Free Investment Area on the initiative of the leading Western industrial countries, which the countries of the Third World could join. Direct investors from member countries would then enjoy a full ownership guarantee, as member countries are under an obligation not to expropriate foreign capital assets, or only to do so according to generally accepted principles (Juhl, 1976, p. 194 ff.). The advantage of such a multilateral protection agreement compared with bilateral contracts would be that investments which were the joint responsibility of investors from several different countries would no longer be subject to a large number of possibly varying bilateral agreements. This does not imply criticism of the merits of national systems, which can take account of the special circumstances of the contracting partners. They do raise special problems, however, in the case of international group investments when these, as in mining and smelting, require very high capital investment for the implementation of the project. Presumably many producer countries of the Third World take a cautious approach to entry into a Free Investment Area because they are afraid that taking on such obligations will place a restraint on their sovereign power and at the same time they rate the economic benefits of such membership as only slight.

A pragmatic solution will have to be found to the problem of how to ensure sufficient activity on the part of the industrial countries in exploration and opening up of mines, ore concentration and possibly smelting of non-ferrous metals to match the trend in consumption. This will have to offer an acceptable basis of co-operation to those countries of the Third World which are willing to co-operate but lack the financial resources and/or technical know-how necessary for the utilization of their mineral resources. If consumer countries with many years' experience of the raw materials economy do not find it appropriate, for political or other reasons, to make direct investment at their own risk to create capacities in countries possessing abundant raw materials, an alternative solution is for companies to finance and manage such projects on a partnership basis. A compromise will then have to be made between the expectations of the respective partners. For investors from the consumer countries, apart from ensuring raw materials supplies, interest centres on the profitability of the capital invested, while the recipient countries expect the foreign investment above all to make a contribution to solving their development and employment problems.

In view of the enormous requirement for capital and technical know-how, an exceptionally promising field of activity is therefore open to the consumer countries of the Western world, in co-operation with the producer countries, for the prospecting and exploitation of their mineral deposits – always within limits, however, to prevent new and undesirable forms of dependence arising on the part of the producer countries. Apart from capital shareholdings, management and consultancy contracts, which likewise respect both the sensitivity of the producer countries towards foreign investors and the understandable reluctance of potential investors to enter into commitments in the Third World because of increasing nationalistic movements, the answer frequently lies in joint ventures specifically tailored to the circumstances of the recipient country. International consortia, to include both raw materials producers and consumers, also appear to offer a viable solution, particularly in the industrial countries; an example of this is the continuous wire casting plant for copper existing for many years in West Germany in which Chile, a so-called 'threshold' country, has a shareholding. There are tentative efforts also in this direction in other countries. They indicate one way in which developing countries can acquire the necessary know-how and accumulate the practical experience required for the development of the raw materials sector (*Industriemagazin*, July 1980, p. 19).

International consortia of the consumer countries would appear to be a feasible form of co-operation wherever raw materials problems are concerned at international level, such as in the case of ocean mining. Direct foreign investment in the non-ferrous metals sector of the Third World will in all probability represent a diminishing factor and may only be allowed to operate under more rigorous restrictions. Responsibility for implementing mining projects, too, is likely to be increasingly transferred to government institutions of the countries concerned. Nevertheless, the international companies traditionally engaged in this field, with their wealth of experience and strong capital resources, will continue to play an important part, in the form of complex consortia (Tilton, 1977, p. 24 ff.).

In view of the exceptionally high capital requirement for global supplies of raw materials, the necessary funds required to safeguard sufficient supplies to meet increasing world demand for non-ferrous metals should not be regarded as the sole responsibility of companies in the consumer and producer countries. The solution would appear to be that adopted in West Germany and other countries, namely a system of guarantees to cover political risks of capital investment abroad combined with government funding for prospecting and exploration projects to support the mining companies. Other assistance is also provided in West Germany under the Foreign Investment Law and the Developing Countries Taxation Law, as well as geological co-operation between state and industry in the practical field. Special financial credits to the mining concerns active in the developing countries are offered by the (government-controlled) German Society for Economic Co-operation (DEG) and by the Reconstruction Loan Corporation (*Mineralische Rohstoffe*, 1979, p. 29).

A greater contribution will have to be made, however, by the international development organizations for the promotion of exploration, opening up and exploitation of deposits in developing countries,[1] even if they usually take the smaller share of the overall total capacity requirement. Nevertheless, their stronger commitment should contribute to reconciling the specific efforts of the developing countries and the commercial interests of the firms participating from the industrial countries. This could also be achieved by mobilizing risk capital on the part of the consortia of companies, banks and government agencies or by increased technical assistance and agreements aimed at minimizing conflicts.

It is certainly true to say that investments should only be made in mining and smelting that may be regarded as profitable over the long term and hence independent of state funding or international financial assistance. The time-span to be allowed here is considerably greater than in the fabrication industry. Among all the possible or necessary measures taken to safeguard supplies of raw materials, depending ultimately on more intensive international co-operation, the main emphasis should always be on maintaining effectively functioning markets so as to minimize any adverse effects on world trade. Prohibitions and official orders, whether by governments, centralized bureaucracies, cartel-type syndicates of producers or restrictive practices by consumers usually serve only to prop up uneconomic structures and prevent necessary, even if sometimes painful, adaptation processes. It has always been found, and the situation will not change in the future, that free formation of prices and unhampered international capital movements are the most appropriate instruments of economic control for optimization of long-term market behaviour. The conditions required to deal with increasing world demand for raw materials can only be achieved by unbiased market mechanisms, which will then ensure the economic viability of unremitting prospecting, opening up and utilization of new non-ferrous metal deposits and the development of technologies to conserve raw materials and hence extend the life of existing finite resources. Producer countries should be given the necessary technical support by the consumer countries for opening up additional supplies of metallic raw materials and also sufficient capitalization to enable development to keep pace with demand. There should be greater awareness of the need to abandon worldwide dirigist policies in this economic field and to allow broader scope for entrepreneurial initiatives in exploiting experience and creativity.

---

1 Up to 1973 the total contribution of the multilateral and bilateral financial assistance institutions was under US $750 million, or less than US $75 million per annum. This represented just under 1.5% of total investments, or 5% of mining investments, in the developing countries. The lion's share of this was provided by the World Bank, followed by the Export-Import banks of the United States and Japan, the Reconstruction Loan Corporation of West Germany, the European Investment Bank and the Inter-American Development Bank (Bosson and Varon, 1977, p. 49).

Appendix

EXPLANATORY NOTES ON THE TABLES

The statistics used in this book are mainly based on the *Metal Statistics* of Metallgesellschaft AG. The statistics by volume generally relate to 'new metal'. Old metal, i.e. metal recovered from scrap and other used materials, is not included in the production statistics owing to the difficulty of obtaining an exact coverage. Any departures from this policy are indicated where appropriate.

In an analysis extending over so long a period as in this book, a great many problems arise. A comparison of the data is not always possible, as some countries were, or are, included in world consumption and world production for which comprehensive statistics were not available in the past and in many cases are still lacking today. Discrepancies occur therefore in the early statistical material and consequently in the tables based upon it.

The terms below are defined, in accordance with *Metal Statistics*, as follows:

Mine production: Analytically determined metal content of the exploitable (prepared) ores; (for West Germany and some other countries) recoverable metal content of the ores. The production statistics for bauxite relate to the gross weight and not the aluminium content.
Smelter production: Metal recovery by the smelters from German and foreign ores. The production of remelting and alloying smelters is not included. The form of calculation is not uniform for the individual countries and in many cases an estimate only is given of the recoverable metal content of the ores. The production data for aluminium relate only to products from alumina. The production of lead covers refined soft lead and refined antimonial lead (also remelted lead and scrap). The data for copper also include production from direct use of the copper content of the scrap.
Consumption: Production + Imports − Exports ± Changes in stocks, i.e. volumes of crude metal available for consumption, irrespective of whether the products fabricated from these are for domestic consumption or for export.
Imports and exports of crude metals: Covers unrefined and refined metal.
Remelted metals and metals recovered from scrap: The volumes used in the secondary smelters, foundries and fabrication works.

For ease of reference countries have generally been given under their current names. The data given however relate to the status and sovereign territory of the countries concerned for the respective year.

In the smelter or mine capacities for non-ferrous metals by concerns (company groups) and companies (Tables A1–A8):

> The shares of capacity have been calculated respectively by capital shareholding: marketing agreements for larger production shares have been disregarded.
>
> In the case of firms only the major producers of the Western world are included, which account for 80% of total capacity.
>
> The shareholders given are only principal shareholders.

Table A1. Smelter capacities for primary aluminium by groups and companies, at the end of 1979

Groups and companies	Country	Capacity (Tonnes per annum)	World share[1] (%)	Major shareholders (%)
Groups				
Alcoa	USA	1,542,000		
Suralco	Surinam	66,000		Alcoa (100)
Alcoa of Australia	Australia	51,000		Alcoa (51)
Brasil Alcominas	Brazil	45,000		Alcoa (50)
Elkem A/S	Norway	79,700		Alcoa (45)
Aluminio SA de CV	Mexico	20,000		Alcoa (44.3)
		1,803,700	13.07	
Alcan	Canada	894,000		
Alcan UK	UK	125,000		Alcan (100)
Alcan Aluminium	W. Germany	48,000		Alcan (100)
Alcan Aluminio do Brasil	Brazil	60,000		Alcan (100)
Aluminio do Brasil Nordeste	Brazil	28,000		Alcan (100)
Alcan Australia	Australia	47,600		Alcan (70)
Indian Aluminium Co.	India	65,300		Alcan (55.3)
Nippon Light Metal Co.	Japan	109,500		Alcan (50)
Endasa	Spain	31,000		Alcan (25) State (25)
Aluminio Español	Spain	26,300		Alcan (14) Pechiney (26.6) Endasa (55)
		1,434,700	10.40	
Reynolds Metals	USA	885,000		
Canadian Reynolds	Canada	159,000		Reynolds (100)
Aluminio del Caroni	Venezuela	60,000		Reynolds (50) State (50)
Volta Aluminium	Ghana	20,000		Reynolds (10)
Hamburger Aluminium Werke	W. Germany	33,000		Reynolds (33)
		1,157,000	8.38	
Kaiser Aluminum	USA	657,000		Kaiser Ind. (38)
Volta Aluminium	Ghana	180,000		Kaiser Al. (90)
Anglesey Aluminium	UK	75,700		Kaiser Al. (67) RTZ (33)
Kaiser Aluminium Europe	W. Germany	36,000		Kaiser Al. (50)
Comalco Ltd.	Australia	51,800		Kaiser Al. (45) CRA (45)
Hindustan Aluminium	India	27,000		Kaiser Al. (26.7)
New Zealand Aluminium	New Zealand	34,200		Kaiser Al. indirect (22.5)
Aluminium Bahrain	Bahrain	21,300		Kaiser Al. (17)
		1,083,000	7.85	

Table A1. (cont'd)

Groups and companies	Country	Capacity (Tonnes per annum)	World share[1] (%)	Major shareholders (%)
Pechiney	France	430,000		
Aluminium de Grèce	Greece	143,000		Pechiney (100)
Alucam	Cameroun	55,000		Pechiney (100)
Pechiney Nederland	Netherlands	145,000		Pechiney (85)
Aluminio de Galicia	Spain	61,600		Pechiney (67)
Aluminium of Korea	Korea	9,000		Pechiney (50)
Aluminio Español	Spain	50,000		Pechiney (26.6) Alcan (14)
Eastalco Aluminum	USA	79,000		Pechiney (50)
Intalco Aluminum	USA	118,000		Pechiney indirect (50)
		1,090,600	7.90	
Alusuisse	Switzerland	83,000		
Aluminiumhütte Rheinfelden	W. Germany	64,000		Alusuisse (100)
Leichtmetall-Ges mbH	W. Germany	126,000		Alusuisse (100)
Salzburger Aluminium	Austria	12,000		Alusuisse (100)
Icelandic Aluminium	Iceland	77,000		Alusuisse (100)
Sor Norge Aluminium	Norway	52,500		Alusuisse (75)
Conalco	USA	99,000		Alusuisse (60)
Ormet Corp.	USA	92,700		Alusuisse indirect (39.6)
Aluminio Veneto	Italy	30,000		Alusuisse (50)
Alusaf	S. Africa	18,500		Alusuisse (22)
		654,700	4.74	
Companies				
Aluminum Co of America	USA	1,542,000	11.17	
Alcan Aluminium Ltd	Canada	894,000	6.48	
Reynolds Metals Co	USA	885,000	6.41	
Kaiser Aluminum & Chemical Corp	USA	657,000	4.76	Kaiser Industries (36)
Aluminium Pechiney	France	430,000	3.12	
Sumitomo Aluminium Smelting	Japan	355,000	2.57	
Ardal og Sunndal Verk	Norway	330,000	2.39	State-owned
Vereinigte Aluminium-Werke AG	W. Germany	330,000	2.39	State-owned
Anaconda Aluminum Co.	USA	327,000	2.37	Atlantic Richfield (100)
Mitsubishi Light Metal	Japan	307,000	2.22	
Venalum	Venezuela	280,000	2.03	State-owned (80), Japanese (20)
Efim/MSC	Italy	256,000	1.86	State-owned
State enterprise	Yugoslavia	245,000	1.78	State-owned
Intalco Aluminum Corp.	USA	236,000	1.71	Alumax (50) Howmet Aluminum (50)
Ormet Corp.	USA	234,000	1.70	Conalco (66) Revere (34)
Showa Aluminium	Japan	223,000	1.62	
Nippon Light Metal	Japan	219,000	1.59	Alcan (50)
Volta Aluminium Co. Ltd	Ghana	200,000	1.45	Kaiser Aluminum (90) Reynolds (10)
Martin Marietta Aluminum Inc.	USA	191,000	1.38	Martin Marietta Corp. (82.7)

Table A1. (cont'd)

Groups and companies	Country	Capacity (Tonnes per annum)	World share[1] (%)	Major shareholders (%)
Aluminio Español	Spain	188,000	1.36	Pechiney (26.6); Alcan (14); Endasa (55)
Revere Copper & Brass Inc.	USA	184,000	1.33	
Elkem A/S	Norway	177,000	1.28	Alcoa (45)
Pechiney Nederland	Netherlands	170,000	1.23	Pechiney (85); Hunter Douglas (15)
Consolidated Aluminum Corp.	USA	165,000	1.20	Alusuisse (60); Phelps Dodge (40)
Mitsui Aluminium Co.	Japan	164,000	1.19	
Canadian Reynolds Metals Co.	Canada	159,000	1.15	Reynolds Metals (100)
Eastalco Aluminium Co.	USA	158,000	1.14	Pechiney (50); Alumax (50)
New Zealand Aluminium Smelters	New Zealand	152,000	1.10	Comalco (50); Showa Denko (25); Sumitomo (25)
Aluminium de Grèce	Greece	143,000	1.04	Pechiney (100)
British Aluminium Co.	UK	141,000	1.02	Tube Investments (58)
Aluar	Argentina	140,000	1.01	Fate (52); Alcan, Kaiser, Pechiney minorities
Noranda Aluminum Inc.	USA	127,000	0.92	Noranda Mines (100)
Leichtmetall-Gesellschaft mbH	W. Germany	126,000	0.91	Alusuisse (100)
Aluminium Bahrain	Bahrain	125,000	0.90	State-owned (58); Government of Saudi Arabia (20); Kaiser (17)
Alcan (U.K.) Ltd.	UK	125,000	0.90	Alcan (100)
Endasa	Spain	124,000	0.89	State-owned (50.5); Alcan (25)
Aluminio del Caroni S.A.	Venezuela	120,000	0.87	Reynolds (50); State-owned (50)
Indian Aluminium Co.	India	118,000	0.86	Alcan (55.3)
Comalco Ltd.	Australia	115,000	0.83	Kaiser Aluminum (45); CRA (45)

1. Share of effective utilizable capacity of Western world (13.8 million tonnes).
Sources: The Spector Report; Aluminium Industry Service, Oppenheimer & Co. Inc., New York, February 1980; reviews by Metellgesellschaft AG, Frankfurt am Main.

Table A2. Smelter capacities for copper by companies, at end of 1979

Company	Country	Capacity (Tonnes per annum)	World share[1] (%)	Major shareholders (%)
Memaco[2]	Zambia	800,000	8.79	Majority state-owned
Roan Consolidated Mines				
Nchanga Consolidated Mines				
Codelco/Enami	Chile	765,000	8.40	State-owned
Gecamines	Zaire	525,000	5.77	State-owned
Phelps Dodge Corp.	USA	445,000	4.89	
Noranda Mines Ltd	Canada	435,000	4.78	Brascan Ltd (16.3)
Kennecott Corp.	USA	420,000	4.62	Curtiss Wright (13.5)
Asarco Inc.	USA	380,000	4.18	Bendix Corp. (approx. 20)
Nippon Mining Co.	Japan	360,000	3.96	
Metallurgie Hoboken-Overpelt	Belgium	330,000	3.63	Union Minière (45)
Mitsubishi Metal Corp.	Japan	283,000	3.11	
Amax Inc.	USA	280,000	3.08	Standard Oil of California (20)
Norddeutsche Affinerie	W. Germany	240,000	2.64	Metallgesellschaft AG and Degussa (40 each)
Anaconda Co.	USA	230,000	2.53	Atlantic Richfield (100)
Magma Copper Co.	USA	180,000	1.98	Newmont Mining (100)
Inco Ltd	Canada	180,000	1.98	Cons. Gold Fields
Sumitomo Metal Mining Co.	Japan	180,000	1.98	
Mount Isa Mines Ltd	Australia	155,000	1.70	Asarco (48.9)
Bor	Yugoslavia	150,000	1.65	State-owned
Minero Peru	Peru	150,000	1.65	State-owned
Mitsui Mining & Smelting Co.	Japan	147,000	1.62	
Dowa Mining Co.	Japan	139,000	1.53	
Palabora Mining Co.	S. Africa	130,000	1.43	Rio Tinto-Zinc (39); Newmont Mining (28.6)
Cobre de Mexico	Mexico	120,000	1.32	
Rio Tinto Minera	Spain	105,000	1.15	Rio Tinto-Zinc (49)
Hüttenwerke Kayser	W. Germany	85,000	0.93	L. Possehl & Co. (97.4)
Copper Range Co.	USA	80,000	0.88	Louisiana Land & Exploration (100)

Note: Owing to the high degree of state influence on some of the principal copper producers we have not attempted to list the companies by groups here.
1. Share of the effective utilizable capacity for refined copper, including electro-winning and alkaline cathodes, of the Western world (9.1 million tonnes). 2. Memaco is the Zambian State marketing company for the copper production of the two major Zambian copper companies Roan Consolidated Mines and Nchanga Consolidated Mines of which the State has a majority shareholding.
Sources: *Non-ferrous Metal Data*, 1979; American Bureau of Metal Statistics Inc., USA; *The World Copper Industry*, August 1979; Australian Mineral Economics Pty Ltd, Australia.

Table A3. Smelter capacities for tin by groups and companies, at end of 1979

Groups and companies	Country	Capacity (Tonnes per annum)	World share[1] (%)	Major shareholders (%)
Groups				
Straits Trading Co. Group	Malaysia	50,000	16.67	Chinese–Malaysian Group
Royal Dutch Group Shell/Billiton				
Thailand Smelting	Thailand	40,000		Shell/Billiton (100)
Billiton Metallurgie	Netherlands	2,500		Shell/Billiton (100)
Kamativi Smelting & Refining	Zimbabwe	1,200		Shell/Billiton (100)
		43,700	14.57	
AMC/Preussag Group[2]				
Datuk Keramat	Malaysia	30,300		AMC (50.5)
Makeri Smelting	Nigeria	6,700		AMC (55.8)
Associated Tin Smelters	Australia	2,700		AMC (33.3)
Williams Harvey	UK	3,000		AMC (100)
		42,700		
Peltim	Indonesia	32,000	10.67	State-owned
Companies				
Datuk Keramat Smelting	Malaysia	60,000	20	Amalgamated Metal Corp. (50.5)
Straits Trading Co.	Malaysia	50,000	16.7	Chinese–Malaysian Group
Thailand Smelting & Refining Co.	Thailand	40,000	13.3	Shell/Billiton (100)
Peltim	Indonesia	32,000	10.7	State-owned
ENAF	Bolivia	18,000	6.00	State-owned
Makeri Smelting	Nigeria	12,000	4.00	Amalgamated Metal Corp. (55.8)
Capper Pass	UK	12,000	4.00	Rio Tinto-Zinc (100)
Associated Tin Smelters	Australia	8,000	2.67	Amalgamated Metal Corp. (33.3)
Gulf Chemical & Metallurgical Corp.	USA	8,000	2.67	Assomet (Lissauer Group) (100)

1. Share of the effective utilizable capacity of the Western world (300,000 tonnes). 2. Preussag AG, Hanover, has a majority shareholding in AMC – Amalgamated Metal Corp., London.
Sources: International Tin Council, *Tin Statistics 1969–1979*, December 1979; reviews by Metallgesellschaft AG, Frankfurt am Main.

Table A4. Mining capacities for nickel[1] by companies, at end of 1979

Company	Country	Capacity (Tonnes per annum)	World share[2] (%)	Major shareholders (%)
Inco Ltd	Canada	250,000		Cons. Gold Fields
	Indonesia	22,000		
	Guatemala	13,000		
		285,000	39.75	
Falconbridge Nickel Mines Ltd	Canada	45,000		Superior Oil via McIntyre
	Dominican Rep.	30,000		
		75,000	10.46	
Le Nickel SLN	France			Imetal Group
	New Caledonia	75,000	10.46	
Western Mining Corp. Ltd	Australia	45,000	6.34	
Marinduque Mining & Industrial Corp.	Philippines	34,000	4.74	Sherritt Gordon (10)
Aneka Tambang	Indonesia	30,000	4.18	State-owned
Larco-Ste Miniere et Metallurgique de Larymna SA	Greece	30,000	4.18	Hellenic Mining

1. Mine production has been chosen as the form of representation in the case of nickel because this reveals the structure of the concerns more clearly.   2. Share in the effective utilizable capacity of the Western world (710,000 tonnes).
Sources: Company reports; US Bureau of Mines *Mineral Commodity Profiles*; reviews by Metallgesellschaft AG, Frankfurt am Main.

Table A5. Smelting capacities for lead by groups and companies, at the end of 1979

Groups and companies	Country	Capacity (Tonnes per annum)	World share[1] (%)	Major shareholders (%)
Groups				
Asarco Group	USA	263,000		
Industria Minera Mexico	Mexico	54,400		Asarco (34)
Britannia Refined Metals	UK	88,200		Asarco (49)
Federated Metals Corp.	USA			Asarco (100)
		431,600	8.90	
Penarroya/Imetal Group	France	225,000		
Peñarroya-España	Spain	70,000		Peñarroya (99)
Cobrac	Brazil	40,000		Peñarroya (98)
Cie Fse des Mines du Laurium	Greece	20,100		Peñarroya (67)
Assoc. Lead Manufacturers	UK	21,250		Peñarroya indirectly (25)
		376,350	7.76	
St Joe Minerals Corp.	USA	205,000	4.23	
Met Mex Peñoles	Mexico	190,000	3.92	Mex. owned, large state share (94)
Tonolli Group				
Blei- und Silberhütte Braubach	W. Germany	20,000		Tonolli Metallgesellschaft each (50)
A Tonolli	Italy	50,000		Tonolli (100)
Tonolli Sud	Italy	35,000		Tonolli (100)
Tonolli	Brazil	30,000		Tonolli
Tonolli Co. of Canada	Canada	14,000		Tonolli
Tonolli Corp.	USA	36,000		Tonolli
		185,000	3.81	
Boliden Group				
Boliden Metall AB	Sweden	55,000		
Preussag-Boliden-Blei	W. Germany	60,000		Boliden (50)
Paul Bergsoe	Denmark	3,000		Boliden (10)
Boliden-Bergsoe	Sweden	27,000		Boliden (90)
Bergsoe-Boliden	USA	9,000		Boliden (50)
Oy Bera	Finland	3,000		Boliden (60)
		157,000	3.23	
Yugoslav State Enterprises	Yugoslavia	(150,000)	3.10	State-owned
Cominco Ltd	Canada	145,000	2.99	Canadian Pacific Investment (54)
Metallgesellschaft Group	W. Germany			
Berzelius Metallhütten	W. Germany	100,000		Metallgesellschaft (100)
Blei- und Silberhütte Braubach	W. Germany	20,000		Metallgesellschaft (50)
Norddeutsche Affinerie	W. Germany	20,000		Metallgesellschaft (40)
		140,000	2.89	
Preussag Group				
Preussag AG Metall	W. Germany	45,000		Preussag (100)
Preussag Boliden-Blei	W. Germany	60,000		Preussag (50)
Norddeutsche Affinerie	W. Germany	10,000		Preussag via AMC (20)[2]
Ballast Metals	Canada	20,000		Preussag (50)
		135,000	2.78	
Rio Tinto Zinc Group	UK			
Broken Hill Assoc. Smelters	Australia	119,500		Conzinc Rio Tinto (70)
Capper Pass and Sons Ltd	UK	10,000		Rio Tinto-Zinc (100)
		129,500		

Table A5. (cont'd)

Groups and companies	Country	Capacity (Tonnes per annum)	World share[1] (%)	Major shareholders (%)
Companies				
Gould Inc.	USA	127,000	2.62	
Metallurgie Hoboken-Overpelt	Belgium	125,000	2.58	Union Minière (45)
Asarco Inc.	USA	263,000	5.42	Bendix Corp. (c. 20)
Broken Hill Assoc. Smelters	Australia	235,000	4.86	Conzinc Rio Tinto of Australia (RTZ) (70)
Soc Minière et Metallurg. de Peñarroya	France	225,000	4.64	Imetal/Rothschild, Paris
St Joe Minerals Corp.	USA	205,000	4.23	
Met Mex Peñoles	Mexico	190,000	3.92	(94) Mexic. owned, high state share
Britannia Refined Metals	UK	180,000	3.71	MIM Holdings (100)
Industrial Minera Mexico	Mexico	160,000	3.30	Asarco, USA (34)
Yugoslav State Enterprises	Yugoslavia	150,000	3.10	State-owned
Cominco Ltd	Canada	145,000	2.99	Canadian Pacific Investm. (54)
Amax-Homestake Lead Tollers	USA	127,000	2.62	Amax, Homestake Mining (50 each)
Gould Inc.	USA	127,000	2.62	
Metallurgie Hoboken Overpelt	Belgium	125,000	2.58	Union Minière (45)
Preussag-Boliden-Blei GmbH	W. Germany	120,000	2.47	Preussag AG, Boliden Metall AB (50 each)
Bunker Hill Co	USA	118,000	2.43	Gulf Resources & Chemical (100)
Berzelius Metallhütten GmbH	W. Germany	100,000	2.06	Metallgesellschaft AG (100)
Centromin	Peru	90,000	1.86	State-owned
SAMIM	Italy	86,000	1.77	State-owned
Tomolli	Italy	85,000	1.75	
Assoc. Lead Manufacturers	UK	85,000	1.75	Lead Industrie Group (Imetal 24.8)
Mitsui Mining & Smelting	Japan	78,000	1.60	

Table A5. (cont'd)

Groups and companies	Country	Capacity (Tonnes per annum)	World share[1] (%)	Major shareholders (%)
Tsumeb Corp.	Namibia	75,000	1.55	Newmont Mining (30); Amax Inc. (29.6); Selection Trust (14.25)
Schuylkill Metals	USA	75,000	1.55	Arrow Electronics
Seltzingers	USA	73,000	1.51	
Brunswick Mining & Smelting Co.	Canada	72,000	1.48	Noranda Mines (64)
Toho Zinc Co.	Japan	72,000	1.48	
Chloride Metals	UK	70,000	1.44	
Peñarroya-España	Spain	70,000	1.44	Imetal
General Battery Corp.	USA	69,000	1.42	
H. J. Enthoven & Sons Ltd	UK	60,000	1.24	Billiton (100)
Boliden Metall AB	Sweden	55,000	1.13	
Sanders Lead	USA	53,000	1.10	
Norddeutsche Affinerie	W. Germany	50,000	1.03	Metallgesellschaft AG, Degussa (40 each) Amalgamated Metal (20)
Preussag AG Metall	W. Germany	45,000	0.93	Westd Landesbank (40)
Blei-u-Silberhütte Braubach	W. Germany	40,000	0.82	Metallgesellschaft AG, Tonolli (50 each)
Cia la Cruz Minas	Spain	40,000	0.82	
Cubrac	Brazil	40,000	0.82	Peñarroya (Imetal) (98)
Ballast Metals	Canada	40,000	0.82	Preussag AG (50)

Note: Lead = refined lead.
1. Share of total effective utilizable capacity for lead smelting, including secondary but not remelted lead, in the Western world (4.85 million tonnes). 2. Financial participation by AMC/Preussag in Norddeutsche Affinerie. 3. Rio Tinto Corp. owns 72.6% of shares of Conzinc Rio Tinto of Australia.
Sources: *Annuaire Minemet*, Imetal Group, 1979; review by Metallgesellschaft AG, Frankfurt am Main.

Table A6. Smelter capacities for zinc by groups and companies, at the end of 1979

Groups and companies[1]	Country	Capacity (Tonnes per annum)	World share[2] (%)	Major shareholders (%)
Groups				
Mitsui Mining & Smelting Co.	Japan	255,000		
Akita Zinc	Japan	13,500		Mitsui Mining (10)
Hachinohe Smelting	Japan	35,000		Mitsui Mining (50)
		303,500	5.95	
Ste des Mines et Fonderies de Zinc de la Vieille Montagne SA	Belgium France	280,000	5.49	Union Minière (15.5) Soc. Gen de Belgique (38)
Cominco Ltd	Canada	235,000	4.60	Canad. Pacific Investments (54)
Metallgesellschaft Group				
Ruhr-Zink GmbH	W. Germany	145,000		Metallgesellschaft (100)
Berzelius Metallhütten GmbH	W. Germany	85,000		Metallgesellschaft (100)
		230,000	4.51	
Peñarroya/Imetal Group	France	100,000		Imetal/Rothschild, Paris
Pertusola	Italy	95,000		Peñarroya (100)
Preussag Weser Zink	W. Germany	28,800		Peñarroya (25)
		223,800	4.39	
Electrolytic Zinc Co. of Australasia Ltd	Australia	210,000	4.12	North Broken Hill Holdings
Canadian Electolytic Zinc Ltd	Canada	195,000	3.82	Noranda Mines (95)
Rio Tinto-Zinc Group				
Commonwealth Smelting	UK	61,700		Conzinc Rio Tinto (100)[3]
Budelco B V	Netherlands	56,300		AM & S (50) (Conzinc)
Sulphide Corp.	Australia	47,200		AM & S (100)
Broken Hill Assoc. Smelters	Australia	20,300		AM & S (70)[4]
		185,500	3.64	
Preussag Group				
Preussag Weser Zink	W. Germany	86,300		
Preussag AG	W. Germany	95,000		
		181,300	3.55	
Asturiana de Zinc SA[5]	Spain	155,000	3.04	
Toho Zinc Group	Japan	140,000		
Akita Zinc	Japan	6,800		Toho Zinc (5)
Hachinohe Smelting	Japan	3,500		Toho Zinc (5)
		150,300	2.95	
Outocumpu Oy	Finland	150,000	2.94	State-owned
SAMIM S p A	Italy	130,000	2.55	State-owned
Companies				
Ste des Mines et Fonderies de Zinc de la Vieille Montagne S A	Belgium France	280,000	5.49	Union Minière (15.5); Soc. Gen. de Belgique (38)
Mitsui Mining & Smelting Co. Ltd	Japan	255,000	5.00	

Table A6. (cont'd)

Groups and companies[1]	Country	Capacity (Tonnes per annum)	World share[2] (%)	Major shareholders (%)
Cominco Ltd	Canada	235,000	4.50	Canadian Pacific Invest.
Electrolytic Zinc Co. of Australasia Ltd	Australia	210,000	4.12	North Broken Hill Holding
Canadian Electrolytic Zinc Ltd	Canada	195,000	3.82	Noranda Mines (95)
Budelco B V	Netherlands	155,000	3.04	AM & S, Billiton (50 each)
Asturiana de Zinc S A	Spain	155,000	3.04	
Outocumpu Oy	Finland	150,000	2.94	State-owned
Ruhr-Zink GmbH	W. Germany	145,000	2.84	Metallgesellschaft (100)
Toho Zinc Co.	Japan	140,000	2.75	
Akita Zinc Co.	Japan	135,000	2.65	Dowa Mining (52); Nippon Mining, Sumitomo Metal (14 each)
SAMIM S p A	Italy	130,000	2.55	State-owned
Mitsubishi Metal Corp.	Japan	115,000	2.25	
Preussag Weser Zink GmbH	W. Germany	115,000	2.25	Preussag (75); Peñarroya (25)
Metallurgie Hoboken Overpelt	Belgium	110,000	2.16	Union Minière (45)
Soc. Min. et Metall de Peñarroya	France	100,000	1.96	Imetal
Cie Royale Asturienne des Mines	France	100,000	1.96	Union Minière (33)
Yugoslav State Enterprises	Yugoslavia	100,000	1.96	State-owned
Texasgulf Inc.	Canada	100,000	1.96	Canad. government (30.5)
Nippon Mining Co. Ltd	Japan	100,000	1.96	
Preussag AG Metall	W. Germany	95,000	1.86	Westd. Landesbank (40)
Ste Min. et Metall di Pertusola	Italy	95,000	1.86	Peñarroya (100)
Bunker Hill Co.	USA	95,000	1.86	Gulf Resources & Chemical Corp. (100)
Met Mex Peñoles	Mexico	95,000	1.86	(94) Mexic. owned, large state share
Asarco Inc.	USA	90,000	1.76	Bendix Corp. (c 20)
Berzelius Metallhütten GmbH	W. Germany	85,000	1.67	Metallgesellschaft (100)
Norzink A.S.	Norway	85,000	1.67	Boliden, BP (50 each)
Commonwealth Smelting Ltd	UK	85,000	1.67	Conzinc Rio Tinto of Australia (RTZ) (100)
Zinc Corp. of South Africa	South Africa	85,000	1.67	Cons. Gold Fields majority
Jersey Minière Zinc	USA	75,000	1.47	New Jersey Zinc (60); Union Minière (40)
Hudson Bay Mining & Smelting Co. Ltd	Canada	75,000	1.47	Anglo American Corp. Canada (45)
Sumiko I S P Co.	Japan	75,000	1.47	Sumitomo Metal Min.
Hachinohe Smelting Co.	Japan	70,000	1.37	Mitsui Mining (50); Dowa Mining (20); Nippon and Mitsubishi (10 each)
Centromin Peru	Peru	70,000	1.37	State-owned

1. The Belgian company Union Minière has a shareholding in the following zinc producers (t/year): Hoboken Overpelt 49,500; Asturienne des Mines 33,000; Jersey Minière Zinc 30,000; Vieille Montagne 43,400; as Union Minière is only a holding company however, and does not itself deal in zinc, it is not included in the list of zinc producers.   2. Share of effective utilizable production of Western world (5.1 million tonnes).   3. Rio Tinto-Zinc owns 72.6% of the shares of Conzinc Rio Tinto of Australia.   4. AM & S is 100%-owned by Conzinc Rio Tinto.   5. Changes in ownership that took place in 1980 have been taken into account.

Table A7. Trade in copper by supplier countries and destination countries, 1929–78

Year	Destination country	Imports (thousand tonnes)	Main supplier countries (%)								Other supplier countries (%)
1929	USA	353.9	Chile	38.1	Mexico	17.7	Canada	17.1	Peru	15.1	12.0
	Germany	194.6	USA	44.0	Chile	39.6	Belgium	11.7			4.7
	UK	147.7	USA	59.1	Chile	35.3					5.6
	France	146.8	USA	62.6	Chile	23.1					14.3
	Belgium	95.6	Belgian Congo	89.0							11.0
1938	UK	360.4	Chile	35.2	Canada	26.9	Rhodesia	25.3			2.2
	Germany	298.5	USA	25.8	Rhodesia	25.6	Chile	16.1	USA	10.4	19.0
	USA	160.4	Chile	34.5	Mexico	22.8	Canada	9.4	Belgian Congo	13.5	33.3
	Belgium, Lux.	104.8	Belgian Congo	39.6	Norway	16.7	Rhodesia	10.1			33.6
	Italy	77.3	Chile	39.8	Mozambique	21.7	USA	21.2			17.3
1950	USA	491.3	Chile	40.4	Rhodesia	16.1	Canada	9.6	Mexico	9.9	18.8
	UK	321.8	Rhodesia	47.3	USA	19.2	Canada	18.1	Belgium	7.5	7.9
	Belgium	156.5	Belgian Congo	74.7	UK	10.1	Rhodesia	8.6			6.6
	France	105.6	Belgium	38.4	Chile	21.5	USA	16.0			24.1
	Italy	61.7	Chile	31.0	USA	27.7	South Africa	14.8			26.5
1965	W. Germany	441.3	Zambia	44.3	Canada	17.2	Chile	16.3	USA	9.4	12.6
	USA	426.4	Chile	43.3	Peru	25.1	Canada	15.3	South Africa	9.6	6.7
	Belgium, Lux.	317.4	Zaire	61.9	South Africa	6.4	France	6.0			25.7
	UK	586.3	Chile	29.3	Zambia	21.3	Belgium, Lux.	12.4	USA	11.0	26.0
	France	266.7	Belgium, Lux.	35.5	Zambia	21.5	USA	14.6	Congo	10.2	18.2
	Italy	183.8	Zambia	28.2	USA	26.3	Congo	17.7	Chile	12.2	15.6
1978	W. Germany	538.0	Chile	28.0	South Africa	16.0	Poland	13.5	Zambia	9.8	Belgium, Lux. 9.8	33.9
	USA	487.4	Chile	34.0	Peru	18.5	Zambia	14.3	Canada	13.7		19.5
	UK	406.1	Zambia	19.0	Chile	18.4	Canada	17.7	W. Germany	8.3	Belgium, Lux. 8.3	28.3
	Italy	356	Chile	26.9	Zambia	14.2	Belgium, Lux.	8.8	Zaire	8.2	Yugoslavia 7.4	34.5
	Japan	330.8	Zambia	37.6	Chile	20.1	Peru	16.6	South Africa	7.3		18.4
	France	302.0	Belgium, Lux.	35.0	Zambia	19.2	Chile	9.7	Canada	6.7		29.4

Table A7. (cont'd)

Year	Supplier country	Exports (thousand tonnes)	Main destination countries (%)							Other destination countries (%)
1929	USA	373.4	Germany	21.7	UK	21.3	Italy	10.3		25.4
	Chile	300.9	USA	41.8	UK	16.5	France	14.0		15.7
	Canada	67.3	USA	88.7	Germany	11.1				0.2
	Mexico[1]	65.0								—
	Belgium, Lux.	35.9	Germany	81.6	France	8.4				10.0
	Germany	31.9	Czechoslovakia	30.0	USSR	19.4	UK	13.8		36.8
1938	Chile	349.3	UK	36.2	USA	19.2	Belgium	13.9	Italy	8.3	22.4
	USA	337.1	Japan	29.3	Germany	20.0	Czechoslovakia	9.0	France	8.6	UK 8.3	24.8
	Rhodesia	222.9	UK	41.0	Germany	34.3	Belgium, Lux.	4.8			19.4
	Canada	178.7	UK	55.0	Germany	13.9	USA	7.8	Czechoslovakia	6.8	Sweden 5.7	10.8
	Belgium, Lux.	117.7	USSR	32.0	France	28.0	Germany	20.1	Switzerland	4.9		15.0
	Belgian Congo	71.2	Belgium	54.1	Germany	44.0					1.9
1950	Chile	321.8	USA	77.9	Italy	7.1	France	4.9			10.1
	Rhodesia	295.4	UK	54.0	USA	24.9	W. Germany	5.4	Sweden	5.3		15.7
	Belgian Congo	166.9	Belgium	72.3	France	5.6	India	4.1			18.0
	USA	131.1	UK	51.4	France	12.7	Italy	1.5	India	6.3		18.1
	Canada	121.8	UK	48.0	USA	37.5	India	4.9			9.6
	Belgium	118.9	France	43.9	UK	20.1	Czechoslovakia	5.8	Sweden	5.5		24.7
1965	Zambia	683.5	UK	40.1	W. Germany	14.8	Japan	13.3	Italy	9.1	France 7.8	14.9
	Chile	491.3	USA	39.4	UK	16.8	W. Germany	14.6	Italy	5.0		24.2
	USA	304.6	UK	21.4	Italy	15.7	India	15.3	France	14.5	W. Germany 10.2	22.9
	Zaire	288.6	Belgium, Lux.	68.0	Italy	12.7	France	11.5				7.8
	Belgium, Lux.	263.2	France	35.4	W. Germany	20.6	Netherlands	15.0	Switzerland	5.8		23.2
	Canada	181.3	UK	53.1	USA	35.5	France	5.8				5.6

Table A7. (cont'd)

Year	Supplier country	Exports (thousand tonnes)	Main destination countries (%)								Other destination countries (%)
1978	Chile	865.4	USA	17.8	W. Germany	17.2	Brazil	13.3	Italy	10.4	Italy	4.0	41.3
	Zambia	575.5	Japan	23.9	UK	13.9	USA	10.7	France	10.6	UK	1.4	31.9
	Zaire[2]	447.7	Belgium, Lux.	78.3	Italy	9.6	France	3.9	Japan	2.7	Belgium, Lux.	6.1	4.1
	Peru	307.0	USA	27.9	Japan	15.9	UK	7.7	Brazil	6.7			35.7
	Belgium, Lux.	306.9	France	34.2	W. Germany	17.0	UK	11.3	Italy	10.6			26.9
	Canada	247.7	UK	28.1	USA	25.9	W. Germany	7.8	Belgium, Lux.	7.4	France	17.7	13.1

Note: Import: until 1950 raw copper; 1965 and 1978 refined copper with exception of France and Italy. Export: raw and refined copper.
1. No information for countries.   2. 1977.
Sources: Compiled and calculated from Paley Report, 1952, vol. 2, p. 1921; *Metal Statistics*, various years.

Table A8. Trade in lead by supplier countries and destination countries, 1929–78

Year	Destination country	Imports (thousand tonnes)	Main supplier countries (%)						Other supplier countries (%)
1929	UK	297.1	Australia	30.9	USA	23.3[1]	India[2]	18.1	Canada	15.9	11.8
	Germany	136.8	Australia	23.8	USA	23.0	Mexico	17.0	India	11.6	24
	France	96.6	Spain	32.6	Mexico	20.6	Tunisia	16.5			30.3
	Japan	60.6	Canada	53.0	USA	30.7	Australia	8.6			7.7
	Belgium, Lux.	31.3	Australia	39.0	Germany	11.5	Greece	8.6			40.9
1938	UK	414.0	Australia	46.1	Canada	26.4	Burma	15.1	Mexico	10.2	2.2
	Germany	84.4	Mexico	58.8	Peru	10.2	Belgium	10.1	UK	6.8	14.1
	France	42.0	Tunisia	38.1	Belgium	34.8	Mexico	20.0			7.1
	Belgium, Lux.	28.3	Mexico	80.6	South West Africa	6.0					13.4
	Sweden	25.7	Mexico	75.5	Peru	15.6					8.9
1950	USA	410.3	Mexico	48.8	Canada	23.8	Yugoslavia	9.7	Peru	7.1	10.6
	UK	174.6	Australia	80.0	Canada	7.4	Tunisia	6.4			6.2
	Belgium, Lux.	33.2	USA	73.5	Mexico	12.7	W. Germany	7.5			6.3
	Netherlands	27.7	W. Germany	40.4	Belgium, Lux.	37.6	UK	6.1			15.9
	France	17.1	Tunisia	58.5	Mexico	12.3	USA	8.8			20.4
1965	UK	218.7	Australia	56.6	Canada	24.9	South West Africa	6.5			
	USA	202.0	Mexico	33.0	Australia	23.0	Canada	14.3	USSR	2.9	9.1
	USSR	47.9	North Korea	34.7	Yugoslavia	28.0	Bulgaria	28.0	Yugoslavia	12.9	5.1
	Italy	45.9	Mexico	19.8	Peru	19.2	South Africa	16.1	Bulgaria	12.6	9.3
	Netherlands	42.8	Belgium, Lux.	45.6	Bulgaria	10.1	South Africa	9.1	Australia	8.6	32.3	26.6
1978	USA[3]	224.1	Mexico	35.9	Canada	31.8	Peru	11.5	Australia	7.3	13.5
	UK	192.2	Australia	75.3	Canada	20.0	North Korea	1.0			3.7
	W. Germany[4]	176.4	UK	21.1	Netherlands	14.4	Sweden	13.8	Belgium, Lux.	13.4	24.4
	Italy	146.7	W. Germany	23.8	South Africa	13.3	Australia	11.5	Mexico	10.0	11.7	41.4
	Japan	50.9	North Korea	36.7	Mexico	16.3	Australia	14.3	Peru	11.6	France	12.9	21.1

282 Non-ferrous metals

Table A8. (cont'd)

Year	Supplier country	Exports (thousand tonnes)	Main destination countries (%)							Other destination countries (%)
1929	Mexico	234.8	USA	31.9	UK	24.0	Germany	17.0	France	17.2	14.9
	Australia	156.5	Europe	94.5	Japan	2.9					2.6
	Canada	103.6	UK	45.4	Japan	34.6	Germany	4.9			15.1
	Spain[5]	99.6	France	32.6	UK	14.4	USSR	16.3	Italy	13.3	33.4
	India[2]	78.0	UK	84.2[6]	Japan	7.6					8.2
1938	Australia	216.4	UK	88.2	Germany	1.7					10.1
	Mexico	208.4	Germany	23.8	UK	20.3	Belgium, Lux.	10.9			45.0
	Canada	140.6	UK	77.2	Japan	11.2	China	2.4	Brazil	2.4	6.8
	Belgium, Lux.	67.1	France	26.5	Netherlands	26.2	Germany	18.6	Switzerland	4.9	23.8
	Peru	28.7	Germany	30.0	UK	24.7	USA	5.6			39.7
1950	Mexico[7]	205.7	USA	62.6	UK	23.0	Belgium	9.9	Japan	1.2	3.3
	Australia	127.6	UK	70.0	USA	12.4	India	7.6	New Zealand	6.0	4.0
	Canada	104.6	USA	91.1	UK	7.2	Brazil	0.8			0.9
	W. Germany	58.8	Netherlands	40.5	Belgium	16.7	USA	10.5	Sweden	5.4	32.3
	Belgium, Lux.	44.2	Netherlands	23.8	Brazil	20.8	Denmark	16.3	Switzerland	5.9	33.2
1965	Australia	159.1	UK	49.2	USA	27.4	India	7.2	Japan	7.0	New Zealand 2.8	6.4
	Canada	117.1	UK	46.9	USA	24.5	Netherlands	8.7	India	8.0	W. Germany 3.9	8.0
	Mexico	107.2	USA	92.2	Netherlands	2.7	UK	1.4	Italy	1.1		2.6
	USSR	102.5	E. Germany	37.2	Czechoslovakia	14.2	UK	10.0	Finland	8.2	Hungary 8.2	22.2
	Belgium, Lux.	62.6	Netherlands	40.3	W. Germany	28.9	UK	8.3	France	7.2	Switzerland 6.4	8.9
1978	Australia	295.9	UK	45.0	India	9.5	UK	5.5	Italy	5.0	Netherlands 4.4	30.6
	Canada	132.0	USA	50.0	UK	28.9	Italy	5.8	USSR	4.3	China 2.8	8.2
	W. Germany	123.6	Italy	32.9	France	11.8	Netherlands	11.3	USA	8.8	UK 6.9	28.3
	UK	105.2	W. Germany	22.8	Netherlands	17.0	Portugal	11.0	France	10.8	Belgium, Lux. 8.1	30.3
	Peru	91.2	USA	44.5	Italy	20.0	China	9.3	South Korea	8.3	USSR 6.6	11.3

1. Export includes larger quantities of lead of Mexican origin that were shipped via the ports of the United States. 2. Including Burma. 3. General import. 4. 50.5% of export is remelt lead, scrap and waste. 5. Including scrap and waste. 6. Estimated. 7. 1953.
Sources: Compiled and calculated from Paley Report, 1952, vol. 2, p. 1941; *Metal Statistics*, various years.

Table A9. Trade in zinc by supplier countries and destination countries, 1929–78

Year	Destination country	Imports (thousand tonnes)	Main supplier countries (%)								Other supplier countries (%)
1929	UK	144.7	Belgium	29.7	Germany	23.8	Canada	14.1	USA	12.2	Australia	8.9	11.3
	Germany	136.2	Poland	52.1	Belgium	18.1	Canada	7.9	USA	6.0	Australia	5.3	10.6
	France	39.3	Belgium	59.5	Canada	11.2	USA	9.2	Germany	8.4			11.7
	Japan	27.1	Canada	42.4	Australia	39.1							18.5
	Czechoslovakia[1]	13.4											
1938	UK	167.7	Canada	53.7	Belgium	22.2	Australia	9.5	Germany	3.9			10.7
	Germany	81.9	Poland	42.0	Belgium	30.5	Norway	19.5	Netherlands	3.5	Canada	1.1	3.4
	France	31.5	Belgium	45.7	Norway	25.7	French Indochina						
	Sweden	21.7	Poland	30.0	Norway	27.2	Belgium	13.3	Mexico	5.1			6.7
	Belgium	14.0	Netherlands	57.9	Norway	12.9	Mexico	21.7	Mexico	12.9	Netherlands	3.5	8.2
									Canada	11.4			4.9
1950	UK	144.2	Belgium	32.0	Australia	24.7	Canada	22.7	USA	11.0	Italy	2.2	7.4
	USA	141.5	Canada	69.8	Mexico	16.9	Norway	5.1	Belgium	2.3	Italy	1.7	4.2
	France	27.5	Belgium	73.8	Norway	10.9	Indochina	5.5	Netherlands	3.3			0.5
	Sweden	20.2	Norway	37.1	Belgium	35.6	Poland	10.9	Netherlands	5.9	Canada	2.5	8.0
	Netherlands	11.0	Belgium	72.7	Norway	14.6	USA	5.5	Netherlands	5.5			7.2
1965	UK	196.5	Canada	50.5	USSR	16.4	Australia	12.2	Bulgaria	5.3	Peru	4.2	11.4
	W. Germany	190.4	Belgium, Lux.	34.0	USSR	12.6	Canada	10.2	Netherlands	7.9	Peru	5.6	29.7
	USA	138.8	Canada	57.9	Japan	8.5	Mexico	8.4	Zaire	8.2	Peru	6.8	10.2
	USSR	58.8	Poland	82.3	North Korea	13.6	Romania	4.1					0
	Italy[1]	38.6											0
1978	USA	617.9	Canada	42.4	Spain	9.7	Mexico	8.3	W. Germany	6.0	Australia	5.6	28.0
	UK	181.6	Canada	26.3	Netherlands	24.8	Finland	20.9	Norway	8.2	W. Germany	6.3	13.5
	W. Germany	173.6	Belgium, Lux.	47.5	Netherlands	17.9	Norway	7.3	France	5.9	Finland	5.0	16.5
	France	82.5	Belgium, Lux.	33.6	Netherlands	14.6	Spain	6.6	W. Germany	5.5	Canada	3.6	16.1
	USSR[2]	44.5	Poland	85.8	North Korea	14.2							0
	Italy	43.1	W. Germany	23.9	Netherlands	16.7	Finland	14.9	Canada	11.8	Belgium, Lux.	10.0	22.7

284   Non-ferrous metals

Table A9. (cont'd)

Year	Supplier country	Exports (thousand tonnes)	Main destination countries (%)										Other destination countries (%)
1929	Poland	132.3	Germany	56.0	USSR	15.0	Czechoslovakia	8.5	UK	7.3	Sweden	4.9	8.3
	Belgium	71.5	UK	28.1	France	24.3	Germany	19.4	Switzerland	7.3	Netherlands	5.5	15.4
	Canada	61.3	UK	34.4	Japan	24.4	Germany	16.0	Argentina	6.2	France	6.0	13.0
	Germany	38.0	UK	64.7	Sweden	6.6	Argentina	5.5	France	3.2			20.0
	Netherlands[1]	22.6											
1938	Belgium	129.9	UK	29.1	Germany	22.7	France	11.1	Netherlands	5.4	Argentina	4.9	28.8
	Canada	119.9	UK	75.2	Japan	11.4	Belgium	4.0	France	2.2	USA	1.8	5.4
	Norway	44.4	Germany	39.2	France	18.5	Sweden	13.7	Spain	5.4	Czechozlovakia	4.7	18.5
	Australia	38.6	UK	41.2	India	31.9	Japan	24.1					2.8
	Netherlands	15.0	Belgium	44.0	Germany	31.3	UK	16.7	France	6.7			1.3
1950	Canada	133.2	USA	74.1	UK	24.6	India	1.3					0
	Belgium	113.8	UK	41.0	France	15.6	Netherlands	6.9	Sweden	6.5	Brazil	5.3	26.7
	Australia	43.7	UK	85.4	India	12.4	New Zealand	2.1					0.1
	Norway	33.1	UK	24.5	USA	23.3	Sweden	18.4	France	17.8	Denmark	4.5	11.5
	USA	11.7	UK	38.5	India	35.9	Brazil	6.8	Denmark	5.1			13.7
1965	Canada	239.7	UK	41.5	USA	34.7	India	8.8	Netherlands	5.1	W. Germany	3.3	6.6
	USSR	132.7	UK	23.1	E. Germany	22.5	Netherlands	19.4	Czechoslovakia	9.4	India	6.6	19.0
	Belgium	129.7	W. Germany	51.3	Switzerland	5.7	USA	5.6	UK	5.3	France	4.6	27.5
	Australia	88.4	India	32.5	UK	25.5	Thailand	7.1	Netherlands	6.9	Philippines	4.8	23.2
	Peru	56.5	Brazil	19.8	UK	17.2	USA	16.8	Netherlands	13.3	W. Germany	7.1	25.8
1978	Canada	439.3	USA	59.1	UK	12.1	India	2.8	Brazil	2.6	Philippines	2.5	20.9
	Australia	215.4	USA	17.7	Taiwan	16.8	Indonesia	16.0	Thailand	10.0	New Zealand	5.5	34.0
	Belgium	160.4	W. Germany	38.3	France	27.3	USA	12.7	Netherlands	4.9	Italy	3.9	18.9
	Netherlands	115.5	UK	39.0	W. Germany	23.6	France	10.8	Italy	6.8	USA	6.5	13.3
	Mexico	104.4	USA	48.9	Brazil	27.3	Venezuela	5.2	Japan	3.3	Columbia	2.8	12.5
	W. Germany	101.3	USA	25.4	Netherlands	16.6	Italy	12.9	France	8.2	Switzerland	7.1	29.8
	USSR	100.6	E. Germany	40.4	Czechoslovakia	21.7	India	13.3	Netherlands	9.1	Hungary	6.5	9.0
	Spain	81.8	USA	97.5	Belgium, Lux.	5.1	UK	5.1	India	3.1	Portugal	1.3	4.4

1. No figures for countries.   2. 1975.
Sources: Compiled and calculated from Paley Report, 1952, vol. 2, p. 196 f.; Metal Statistics, various years.

Table A10. Trade in tin by supplier countries and destination countries, 1929–78

Year	Destination country	Imports (thousand tonnes)	Main supplier countries (%)							Other supplier countries (%)
1929	USA	88.5	Brit. Malaya	66.9	UK	19.0	Netherlands	8.6	Australia 0.7	1.3
	Germany	17.5	Dutch E. Indies	45.7	UK	17.1	Brit. Malaya	13.7		14.9
	UK	14.9	Brit. Malaya	86.6	Belg. Neth. Dutch E. Indies	6.0				7.4
	France	12.4	Brit. India	40.3	UK	35.5	Dutch E. Indies	9.7		14.5
	Belgium	1.2	UK	66.7	Netherlands	16.7	Germany	8.3		8.3
1938	USA	50.5	Malaya	73.9	UK	6.5	Indonesia	6.1	Netherlands 4.6	4.7
	Germany	12.9	Indonesia	35.7	Netherlands	31.8	Malaya	14.0	China 7.0 China 5.4	6.1
	UK	11.9	Malaya	42.0	Netherlands	17.7	China	14.3	Belgium 8.4 Hong Kong 7.6	10.0
	France	9.4	Malaya	35.1	Netherlands	29.8	Belgium, Lux.	12.8	UK 8.5 Indochina 8.5	5.3
	Belgium[1]	3.9	Belgian Congo	59.0	Malaya	10.3	Hong Kong	7.7	Indonesia 7.7	15.3
1950	USA	84.2	Malaya	65.2	UK	10.2	Belgium	9.9	Netherlands 9.3	3.4
	W. Germany	8.8	Netherlands	44.3	Malaya	30.7	UK	12.5	Belgium 8.0 China 2.0	14.5
	France	5.8	Malaya	44.8	Netherlands	39.7	Belgium, Lux.	8.6		6.9
	UK	4.7	Malaya	97.9						2.1
	Italy[1]	4.3	Malaya	72.1	UK	11.6	Netherlands	7.0		9.3
1965	USA	41.5	Malaysia	78.3	Thailand	8.9	Nigeria	4.8	UK 2.4 Japan 1.2	4.4
	W. Germany	14.1	Netherlands	58.9	Belgium, Lux.	12.1	UK	7.8	Nigeria 7.8 China 3.6	9.8
	France	10.1	Malaysia	24.8	Netherlands	20.8	China	18.8	Belgium, Lux. 17.8 UK 10.9	6.9
	UK	9.4	Nigeria	61.7	Malaysia	24.5	China	3.2		10.6
	USSR	5.8	UK	37.9	Malaysia	27.6	Indonesia	24.1	China 8.6	1.8
1978	USA	46.8	Malaysia	51.1	Thailand	14.7	Bolivia	12.4	Indonesia 12.2 Brazil 3.9	15.7
	W. Germany	16.1	Thailand	36.7	Indonesia	32.7	Malaysia	11.2	Netherlands 5.0 Bolivia 4.4	10.4
	France	10.7	Malaysia	31.8	Indonesia	19.6	Thailand	16.8	Belgium, Lux. 9.4 Zaire 6.5	15.9
	USSR[2]	9.7	Malaysia	53.6	UK	27.8	Bolivia	17.5		1.1
	UK	7.8	Nigeria	33.3	Malaysia	26.9	Australia	20.5	Netherlands 11.5	7.8
	Italy	5.9	Malaysia	42.4	Indonesia	40.7	Thailand	6.8	W. Germany 3.4	6.7

Non-ferrous metals

Table A10. (cont'd)

Year	Supplier country	Exports (thousand tonnes)	Main destination countries (%)								Other destination countries (%)
1929	Brit. Malaya	103.7	USA	56.5	UK	15.0	Netherlands	10.0	France	5.5	Italy	4.3	8.7
	UK	30.9	USA	44.0	France	11.7	Germany	8.1	Sweden	4.5	Argentina	3.9	27.8
	Dutch E. Indies	13.6	Netherlands	60.0	UK	25.0	France	8.1					8.9
	Germany	5.1	USA	33.3	France	11.8	UK	9.8	Czechoslovakia	9.8	Austria	5.9	29.4
	Belgium	0.6	Germany	33.3	France	16.7	Italy	16.7	Switzerland	16.7			16.6
1938	Malaya	62.2	USA	55.0	Japan	14.0	UK	6.9	France	6.4	India	4.3	15.4
	Netherlands	25.3	USSR	26.9	Germany	25.7	France	9.5	USA	8.3	UK	7.9	21.7
	UK	12.5	USA	25.6	USSR	24.0	France	7.2	Sweden	5.6	Canada	5.6	32.0
	Belgium, Lux.	8.4	USSR	33.3	France	14.5	UK	13.1	Germany	11.9	Italy	11.9	15.3
	Germany	0.2	UK	80.0									20.0
1950	Malaya	83.1	USA	54.5	Italy	9.4	UK	8.9	Netherlands	5.3	France	4.0	17.9
	Netherlands	18.1	USA	29.8	W. Germany	21.6	France	12.7	Poland	6.6	Italy	4.4	24.9
	UK	15.7	USA	52.9	W. Germany	4.5	Denmark	4.5	USSR	3.8	France	3.8	30.5
	Belgium, Lux.	10.4	USA	75.0	Canada	9.6	W. Germany	6.7	France	4.8	Switzerland	1.0	2.9
	W. Germany	0.9	Netherlands	55.6	USA	44.4							0
1965	Malaysia	74.6	USA	42.9	Japan	17.7	Canada	5.4	Italy	5.0	India	4.8	24.2
	Netherlands	15.9	W. Germany	50.3	France	14.5	Italy	8.2	USSR	6.3	UK	4.4	16.3
	UK	7.0	USSR	27.1	France	14.3	USA	12.9	Poland	10.0	Romania	7.1	18.6
	Belgium, Lux.	4.0	France	45.0	W. Germany	40.0	UK	5.0					10.0
	W. Germany[1]	1.7	France	29.4	Belgium, Lux.	23.5	UK	11.8	Netherlands	11.8			23.5
1978	Malaysia	70.1	USA	33.5	Japan	22.8	Netherlands	17.8	India	4.6	Taiwan	3.9	17.4
	UK	7.0	USSR	60.0	Netherlands	14.3	Norway	5.7	Czechoslovakia	4.3	Argentina	2.9	12.8
	W. Germany	4.9	Netherlands	71.4	France	12.2	Austria	4.1	Italy	2.0			10.3
	Belgium, Lux.	2.3	France	52.2	Netherlands	8.7	W. Germany	8.7	Bulgaria	4.4	Hungary	4.4	21.6
	Netherlands	0.4	W. Germany	50.0	Belgium, Lux.	25.0		25.0					25.0

1. Including tin alloys. 2. 1975.

Sources: Compiled and calculated from Paley Report, 1952, Vol. 2, p. 191; *Metal Statistics*, various years.

Appendix

Table A11. Trade in aluminium by supplier countries and destination countries, 1929–78

Year	Destination country	Imports (thousand tonnes)	Main supplier countries (%)								Other supplier countries (%)
1929	UK	22.8	Norway	63.6	Canada	19.7	Germany	5.3	Switzerland	4.4	7.7
	USA[1]	22.0	Canada	58.6	Norway	18.2	Switzerland	10.9	UK	6.4	5.9
	Japan	11.9	USA	54.6	Switzerland	16.8	UK	10.9	France	10.9	6.8
	Germany	7.3	Switzerland	56.2	Austria	20.6	Canada	9.6	Norway	9.6	4.0
	Belgium[1]	3.1	Switzerland	45.2	Norway	22.6	France	9.7	W. Germany	19.4	3.1
1938	UK	47.0	Canada	65.7	Switzerland	20.6	Norway	11.5			2.2
	W. Germany	14.5	Canada	40.0	Switzerland	23.5	Norway	18.6			16.2
	USA	7.9	Norway	34.2	France	31.7	Switzerland	15.2	Canada	11.7	5.0
	Switzerland	3.8	Turkey	34.2	Italy	23.7	Germany	23.7	USA	13.9	7.9
	Belgium	3.8	France	26.3	Switzerland	26.3	Norway	23.7	Yugoslavia	10.5	10.5
1950	USA	160.4	Canada	87.8	Japan	4.3	Norway	2.6	Italy	1.1	3.1
	UK	143.5	Canada	85.5	Norway	9.8	France	4.7			0
	Italy	14.0	W. Germany	31.4	UK	22.1	Canada	16.4	Austria	1.1	13.0
	Belgium	8.7	France	58.6	Norway	13.8	Switzerland	9.2			10.3
	Sweden	8.4	Norway	60.7	Canada	22.6	UK	9.5			
1965	USA	476.1	Canada	65.5	Norway	17.3	France	6.4	Japan	4.6	3.5
	UK	321.8	Canada	51.5	Norway	20.9	USA	12.9	USSR	4.2	8.2
	W. Germany	169.5	USA	23.9	Norway	22.6	Canada	13.5	Italy	10.3	19.4
	Belgium, Lux.	117.0	France	79.1	USA	5.1	USSR	4.4	Canada	3.3	6.0
	France	65.5	Cameroun	46.6	USA	34.7	Norway	9.9	USSR	5.7	1.3
1978	USA	686.2	Canada	69.2	Ghana	11.7	Norway	7.3	Surinam	2.3	7.5
	Japan	598.1	Canada	20.8	New Zealand	20.3	Bahrein	17.5	Australia	9.7	22.8
	W. Germany[1]	410.9	Norway	41.1	UK	10.7	Netherlands	9.9	France	8.3	24.9
	Belgium, Lux.	266.8	Netherlands	49.2	France	14.3	Netherlands	9.9	France	8.3	24.9
	UK	190.9	Norway	66.8	Iceland	11.3	France	6.7	W. Germany	5.3	7.8
	Italy	190.5	W. Germany	31.1	France	18.1	Greece	13.8	UK	8.6	20.0
	France[3]	160.7	Netherlands	23.4	Greece	17.0	USSR	16.8	W. Germany	9.0	25.3
	Netherlands[2]	145.5	Norway	51.0	W. Germany	30.2	UK	8.3	Ghana	3.0	5.0

Table A11. (cont'd)

Year	Supplier country	Exports (thousand tonnes)	Main destination countries (%)										Other destination countries (%)
1929	Canada	33.1	USA	39.0	Japan	24.2	Germany	16.6	UK	9.4	Switzerland	4.2	6.6
	Switzerland[4]	13.2	Germany	26.5	UK	21.2	USA	13.6	Japan	13.6	Belgium	9.9	15.2
	UK	5.9	Germany	27.1	USA	25.4	Netherlands	23.7	Australia	11.9			11.9
	Germany	3.6	Czechoslovakia	16.7	UK	16.7	USA	13.9	Austria	11.1			30.5
1938	Canada	58.7	UK	52.5	Japan	24.0	Germany	9.5	USSR	3.2	Japan	11.1	10.8
	Norway	29.5	Japan	17.0	Germany	11.5	USSR	10.9	Sweden	8.8			51.8
	Switzerland	21.8	UK	37.6	Japan	28.0	Germany	11.5	Belgium	8.7			16.2
	France	14.0	UK	25.7	USA	23.6	Belgium	12.1	USSR	6.4			32.2
	USA	4.4	Germany	45.5	Switzerland	20.5	Japan	15.9	UK	3.6			4.5
	Canada	304.6	USA	47.8	UK	41.3	Brazil	1.6	Australia	1.5	Netherlands	1.3	6.5
	Norway	40.4	UK	34.7	Sweden	13.1	USSR	9.7	USA	9.7	Denmark	5.7	21.1
	Germany	34.3	Netherlands	39.7	USA	38.2	Italy	14.6	Belgium	4.4			3.1
	Japan	22.5	USA	59.6	Argentina	30.2	Canada	4.4					5.8
	France	16.6	Belgium	29.5	UK	28.9	Argentina	11.5	USA	8.4	Italy	6.6	15.1
1965	Canada	641	USA	49.2	UK	25.9	Japan	3.7	S. Africa	2.9	W. Germany	2.5	15.8
	Norway	242.4	USA	34.2	UK	26.3	W. Germany	14.7	Sweden	5.7	Italy	5.4	13.7
	USSR	229.0	E. Germany	38.1	UK	4.1	Czechoslovakia	9.0	Hungary	7.6	Yugoslavia	5.1	26.1
	USA	184.7	UK	21.8	W. Germany	13.8	France	12.3	Brazil	7.5	Argentina	7.2	47.4
	France	127.4	Belgium, Lux.	48.9	USA	19.3	W. Germany	10.1	Argentina	6.7	Egypt	3.1	11.9
1978	Canada	862.6	USA	56.8	Japan	19.0	China	8.9	Brazil	2.2	Spain	1.6	10.9
	Norway	630.2	W. Germany	26.8	UK	20.8	USA	10.9	Netherlands	10.9	Belgium, Lux.	5.4	30.2
	USSR[4]	502.4	E. Germany	22.8	Hungary	20.2	Czechoslovakia	18.0	Japan	8.5	Poland	6.6	23.9
	Netherlands	294.4	Belgium, Lux.	42.7	France	26.1	W. Germany	20.4	Rep. Ireland	4.5	UK	3.7	2.6
	W. Germany[1]	271.6	France	23.1	Italy	22.5	Netherlands	18.0	Belgium, Lux.	12.9	China	4.9	18.6
	France	160.7	Belgium, Lux.	11.6	W. Germany	11.1	UK	10.9	China	7.8	Brazil	3.2	55.4
	UK	160.5	Netherlands	40.4	W. Germany	10.5	USA	10.0	Japan	7.4	France	6.0	25.7
	USA	114.9	Japan	37.3	Mexico	17.2	Canada	9.6	South Korea	7.4	France	4.9	23.6

1. Including aluminium scrap ('old scrap') and aluminium alloys.   2. Including aluminium alloys.   3. Non-alloyed.   4. Including aluminium scrap ('old scrap'); USSR 1975.

Sources: Compiled and calculated from Paley Report, 1952, Vol. 2, p. 186; *Metal Statistics*, various years.

Appendix

Table A12. Non-ferrous metal exports as percentage of production, by countries, 1978

Country	Exports	Production	Ratio	Country	Exports	Production	Ratio
	(thousand tonnes)		(%)		(thousand tonnes)		(%)

Aluminium

Country	Exports	Production	Ratio	Country	Exports	Production	Ratio
Canada	826.6	1,048.5	82.3	Yugoslavia	61.4	176.0	34.9
Norway	630.1	656.9	95.9	Surinam	56.9	56.9	100.0
Netherlands	294.4	259.2	113.6	Japan	54.6	1,057.7	5.2
W. Germany	271.6	739.6	36.7	Sweden	38.5	82.0	47.0
France	166.4	391.4	42.5	S. Africa	37.4	81.1	46.1
UK	160.0	346.2	46.2	Switzerland	32.9	79.5	41.4
Bahrein	140.1	122.8	114.1	Venezuela	17.0	71.1	23.9
New Zealand	132.8	151.1	97.9	Austria	11.7	91.3	12.8
Ghana	111.3	113.5	98.1	Cameroun	11.6	41.3	28.1
USA	102.4	4,358.1	2.3	Spain	5.8	212.2	2.7
Greece	85.3	143.9	59.3	India	2.9	205.3	1.4
Italy	69.3	270.8	25.5	Taiwan	0.4	49.9	0.8
Australia	80.0	263.4	30.4	Iran	0.2	25.5	0.8

Copper mine production[1]

Country	Exports	Production	Ratio	Country	Exports	Production	Ratio
Canada	282.2	659.4	42.8	Zaire	35.0	423.8	8.3
Philippines	258.3	263.4	98.1	Malaysia	26.4	26.0	101.5
Papua New Guinea	195.1	198.6	98.2	Norway	24.6	29.1	84.5
Chile	112.4	1,035.5	10.9	S. Africa	18.1[2]	209.3	8.6
Indonesia	59.4	58.0	102.4	USA	17.5	1,357.6	1.3
Peru	48.1	366.4	13.1	Sweden	3.9	47.4	8.2
Australia	37.7	222.1	17.0				

Copper, refined

Country	Exports	Production	Ratio	Country	Exports	Production	Ratio
Chile	702.1	749.1	93.7	Japan	50.9	959.1	5.3
Zambia	549.9	627.7	87.6	Spain	46.5	147.0	31.6
Belgium	304.8	388.6	78.4	Sweden	27.1	64.4	42.1
Canada	247.7	446.3	55.5	Austria	17.2	31.9	53.9
Peru	173.7	186.2	93.3	France	17.2	41.3	41.6
W. Germany	148.7	404.5	36.8	Finland	16.0	42.7	37.5
Zaire	103.7	102.8	100.9	Yugoslavia	47.1	150.8	31.2
USA	95.3	1,832.0	5.2	Norway	14.6	15.6	93.6
S. Africa	77.8	152.5	51.0	UK	11.1	125.6	8.8
Australia	60.1	174.5	34.4				

Lead, refined

Country	Exports	Production	Ratio	Country	Exports	Production	Ratio
Australia	158.3	239.3	66.2	Tunisia	8.1	16.6	48.8
Canada	132.0	245.9	53.7	France	37.7	208.2	18.1
W. Germany	99.4	369.0	26.9	Zambia	10.0	12.9	77.5
Mexico	112.3	208.6	53.8	Japan	7.8	291.1	2.7
Peru	91.5	79.3	115.4	Netherlands	20.3	31.9	63.6
UK	86.2	345.8	24.9	Denmark	5.0	26.2	19.1
Belgium	74.8	104.2	71.8	Spain	5.2	122.2	4.3
Yugoslavia	41.0	116.7	35.1	USA	2.5	1,188.4	0.2
Morocco	28.5	30.0	95.0	Austria	0.7	17.6	4.0
Sweden	26.3	45.3	58.1	Greece	1.1	22.6	4.9

Table A12. (cont'd)

Country	Exports	Production	Ratio	Country	Exports	Production	Ratio
	(thousand tonnes)		(%)		(thousand tonnes)		(%)

Zinc

Country	Exports	Production	Ratio	Country	Exports	Production	Ratio
Canada	439.3	495.4	88.7	Yugoslavia	45.9	95.2	48.2
Australia	215.4	294.3	73.2	Peru	49.2	62.9	78.2
Belgium	152.2	232.9	65.3	Norway	48.2	71.6	67.3
Finland	109.7	132.9	82.5	Zaire	40.9	43.5	94.0
Netherlands	107.5	135.3	79.5	Zambia	39.5	42.4	93.2
Mexico	98.8	172.2	57.4	Italy	27.9	177.6	15.7
Spain	81.8[3]	175.8	46.5	UK	15.0	73.6	20.4
W. Germany	78.0	306.8	25.4	South Korea	5.7	59.0	9.7
Japan	57.8	768.0	7.5	USA	0.7	467.2	0.1
France	52.0	231.2	22.5	Austria	0.6	22.0	2.7

1. Exports including unrefined copper. 2. Including Namibia. 3. Including 'scrap zinc'.
Source: *World Metal Statistics*, Vol. 34 No. 2, 1981.

Bibliography

Achinger, Hans. *Wilhelm Merton in seiner Zeit*, Frankfurt am Main, 1965.
Agarwal, Jamuna P., Spinanger, Dean, and Stecher, Bernd. *The Future of the World Economy: an appraisal of Leontief's study*, Institut für Weltwirtschaft, Kieler Diskussionsbeiträge 54, Kiel, May 1978.
Ahlfeld, Friedrich. *Zinn und Wolfram. Die Metallischen Rohstoffe*, Stuttgart, 1958.
Althaus, Dieter, and Baack, Thomas. 'Zur Entwicklung der internationalen Bleiwirtschaft', in *Blei – Werkstoff mit Zukunft*, Metallgesellschaft AG Mitteilungen aus den Arbeitsbereichen No 20, Frankfurt am Main, 1977, pp. 8–15.
Avieny, Wilhelm. *Strukturwandlungen der Weltmetallwirtschaft*, Kieler Vorträge No 67, Jena, 1941.
Baron, Stefan, Glismann, Hans H., and Stecher, Bernd. *Internationale Rohstoffpolitik. Ziele, Mittel, Kosten*, Kieler Studien 150, Tübingen, 1977.
Bender, Friedrich. 'Metal-Rohstoffvorräte aus theoretischer und wirtschaftlicher Sicht', in *Die Versorgung der Weltwirtschaft mit Rohstoffen*, supplement to *Konjunkturpolitik* No 23, Berlin, 1976, pp. 9–24.
Berg, Georg, and Friedensburg, Ferdinand. *Die metallischen Rohstoffe*, Part 4, *Kupfer*, Stuttgart, 1941.
– Part 6, *Nickel und Kobalt*, Stuttgart, 1944.
– and Herbert Sommerlatte. Part 9, *Blei und Zink*, Stuttgart, 1950.
Boin, Udo, and Müller, Eberhard. 'Wirtschaftlichkeitsaspekte im Meeresbergbau', in *Manganknollen – Metalle aus dem Meer*, Metallgesellschaft AG Mitteilungen aus den Arbeitsbereichen No 18, Frankfurt am Main, 1975, pp. 44–49.
Bosson, Rex, and Varon, Bension. *The Mining Industry and the Developing Countries*, World Bank Research Publication, Washington, 1977.
Breidenbroich, Friedrich. *Die Strukturwandlung in der internationalen Kupferwirtschaft und die deutsche Kupferwirtschaft*, Frankfurt Dissertation, Würzburg, 1938.
Brockhaus der Naturwissenschaften und Technik, Wiesbaden, 1957.
Brockhaus Enzyklopädie, 17th fully rev. edn of *Der Grosse Brockhaus*, Vol. 1, p. 34, Vol. 3, p. 726 ff., Wiesbaden, 1966.
Brubaker, Sterling. *Trends in the World Aluminium Industry*, Baltimore, 1967.
Bundesanstalt für Geowissenschaft und Rohstoffe, Hanover, and Deutsches Institut für Wirtschaftsforschung, Berlin. Various enquiries: Hermann Kästner *et al.*, *Molybdän*, 1975; *Wolfram*, 1977; Hans-Jürgen Hildebrand *et al.*, *Mangan*, 1977; Manfred Kruszona *et al.*, *Kobalt*, 1978.

Cammarota, V. Anthony, Jr. *Zinc*, Mineral Commodity Profiles 12, Washington, 1978.
Casper, Walther. 'Zwischen Überfluss und Verknappung. Steuern Rohstoffe das zukunftige Wachstum?', in *Manganknollen – Metalle aus dem Meer*, Metallgesellschaft AG, Mitteilungen aus den Arbeitsbereichen No 18, Frankfurt am Main, 1975, pp. 7–11.
– 'Es gibt noch Bodenschatze im alten Europa', in Metallgesellschaft AG *MG-Information*, Vol 12 No 2, Frankfurt am Main, 1977, pp. 1–5.
CIPEC. 'National Stockpile Schemes, Existing or Proposed', in *Quarterly Review*, Paris, October–December 1976, pp. 26–31.
Cipolla, Carlo M. 'Die industrielle Revolution in der Weltgeschichte' in *Europäische Wirtschaftsgeschichte*, Vol 3 *Die Industrielle Revolution*, Stuttgart, 1976, pp. 1–10.
Cissarz, Arnold, et al., *Blei. Untersuchungen über Angebot und Nachfrage mineralishcher Rohstoffe*, Bundesanstalt für Bodenforschung und Deutsches Institut für Wirtschaftsforschung, Berlin, 1971.
– *Kupfer, ibid.*, 1972.
– *Aluminium, ibid.*, 1973.
– *Zink, ibid.*, 1974.
Däbritz, Walter. *Funfzig Jahre Metellgesellschaft 1881–1931*, memorial volume, Frankfurt am Main, 1931.
Donges, Juergen B. [1976 a] *Zur Neuordnung des Rohstoffhandels zwischen Entwicklungs- und Industrieländern*, Institut für Weltwirtschaft, Kieler Arbeitspapiere 45, Kiel, May 1976.
– [1976 b] 'Kritik der Pläne für eine neue international Rohstoffpolitik', in *Die Versorgung der Weltwirtschaft mit Rohstoffen*, supplement to *Konjunkturpolitik* No 23, Berlin, 1976, pp. 77–109.
– *Die Welthandelsordnung auf dem Prüfstand: Weitere Liberalisierung oder neuer Protektionismus?*, Institut für Weltwirtschaft, Kieler Arbeitspapiere 67, Kiel, January 1978.
Dumstorff, Helmut. 'Blei und Zink', in Werner Gocht (ed.), *Handbuch der Metallmärkte*, Berlin, 1974, pp. 194–226.
Ebeling, Günther K. A., Massion, Wolfgang P. J., and Michaelis, Hermann A. 'Aktuelle Standort- und Strukturfragen für eine Bleiproduktion', in *Blei – Werkstoff mit Zukunft*, Metallgesellschaft AG, Mitteilungen aus den Arbeitsbereichen No 20, Frankfurt am Main, 1977, pp. 56–59.
Eichmeyer, E. 'Metallverarbeitung', in *Meyers Handbuch über die Technik*, 2nd edn, rev., Mannheim, 1971, pp. 266–327.
Fabian, Harald. 'Kupfer', in *Ullmann's Enzyklopädie der technischen Chemie*, 4th edn., fully rev., Vol. 15, Weinheim, 1978, pp. 487–587.
Fachvereinigung Metallerzbergbau. *Jahresbericht 1979*, Düsseldorf.
Fischer, R.-E. and Bongers, U. 'Hüttenwesen', in *Meyers Handbuch über die Technik*, 2nd edn., rev., Mannheim, 1971, pp. 226–265.
Forster, Meinhard. *Struktur und Risiken der Deutschen Nichteisen-Metallversorgung, dargestellt am Beispiel Kupfer, Aluminium, Nickel, Zink, Blei und Zinn*, Institut zur Erforschung technologischer Entwicklungslinien (ITE), Hamburg, 1975.
Frey, Bruno S. Review of *Ökonomische Probleme der Umweltschutzpolitik*, (Schriften des Vereins für Socialpolitik, New Series, Vol. 91, Berlin, 1976), in *Kyklos*, Vol. 30, Basle 1977, pp. 759–760.
Friedensburg, Ferdinand [1965a]. 'Entwicklungstendenzen im Weltbergbau', *DIW: Vierteljahreshefte zur Wirtschaftsforschung*, Berlin, 1965, No. 1, pp. 86–96.

- [1965b]. 'Die Entwicklung der Bergwirtschaft in der Welt in den letzten hundert Jahren', in *Glückauf*, Vol. 101, No. 1, Essen, 1965, pp. 63–67.
- and Günter Dorstewitz. *Die Bergwirtschaft der Erde*, 7th edn., Stuttgart, 1976.
- and Rolf Krengel. *Die wirtschaftliche Bedeutung des Metallerzbergbaus und Metallhüttenwesens in der Bundesrepublik Deutschland*, Berlin, 1962.

Galbraith, John Kenneth. *The Affluent Society*, 3rd edn., London, 1977.

GATT, General Agreement on Tariffs and Trade. Networks of World Trade by Areas and Commodity Classes 1955–1976, in *Studies in International Trade*, No. 7, Geneva, 1978.

Gebhardt, Armin, and Knörndel, Klaus-Dieter. 'NE-Metallindustrie' in *Struktur und Wachstum*, IFO-Institut für Wirtschaftsforschung. Industrie series, Part 28, Munich, 1977.

Gibson-Jarvie, Robert. *The London Metal Exchange: a commodity market*, Cambridge, 1976.

Glebsattel, Hermann. *Die Entwicklung des Kupferpreises zwischen den beiden Weltkriegen. Untersucht auf der Grundlage der Strukturverschiebungen und Probleme der internationalen Kupferwirtschaft*, Dissertation, Kiel, 1949.

The Global 2000 Report to the President: entering the twenty-first century. A report prepared by the Council on Environmental Quality and the Department of State, Vols 1 and 2, Washington, 1980.

Gocht, Werner. 'Nickel und Kobalt', in Werner Gocht (ed.) *Handbuch der Metallmärkte*, Berlin, 1974, pp. 99–123.
- 'Sondermetalle', *ibid.*, 1974, pp. 336–369.
- 'Zinn', *ibid.*, 1974, pp. 226–252.

Goreux, Louis M. 'Der Einsatz von Bufferstocks' in *Finanzierung und Entwicklung*, Vol. 15, Hamburg, December 1978, pp. 23–27.

Grace, Richard P. 'Metals Recycling. A Comparative National Analysis', in *Resources Policy*, Vol. 4, Guildford, Surrey, December 1978, pp. 249–256.

Grebe, Willi-Herbert, *et al. Chrom*, in *Untersuchungen über Angebot und Nachfrage mineralischer Rohstoffe*, Bundesanstalt für Geowissenschaften und Rohstoffe and Deutsches Institut für Wirtschaftsforschung, Berlin, 1975.

Grunwald, Joseph and Musgrove, Philip. *Natural Resources in Latin American Development*, Baltimore, 1970.

Guyenz, Klaus. *Der Handel mit NE-Metallen in Deutschland unter besonderer Berücksichtigung der Einwirkungen nationaler und internationaler Organe*, Dissertation, Cologne, 1957.

Haenig, Alfred. *Der Erz- und Metallmarkt*, Stuttgart, 1910.

Harris, Keith L. *Tin*, Mineral Commodity Profiles, 16, Washington, 1978.

Heilmann, L. 'Bundesrepublik Deutschland: Die Aluminiumindustrie der Welt an der Jahreswende 1977/78', in *Aluminium*, Vol. 54, Part 1, Düsseldorf, 1978.

Hess, Margrit H. *Kupfer in der Weltwirtschaft mit besonderer Berücksichtigung der USA*, Volkswirtschaftliche Schriften, Part 17, Berlin, 1955.

Heubner, Ulrich. 'Das Zink in der Technik von heute und morgen', in *Erzmetall*, Vol. 31, No. 3, Stuttgart, 1978, pp. i–iv.

Hoffmeyer, Martin and Neu, Axel D. *Vertikales Diversifizierungspotential der Entwicklungsländer bei der Weiterverarbeitung von Rohstoffen*, Kiel, 1978.
- 'Zu den Entwicklungstendenzen der Energiemärkte', in *Die Weltwirtschaft*, Tübingen, 1979, Part 1, pp. 154–182 and 24*–28*.

Hoffmeyer, Martin, and Schrader, Jörg-Volker. 'Internationale Rohstoffmärkte', in *Die Weltwirtschaft*, Tübingen, 1978, Part 2, pp. 115–130.

- 'Teuerungswelle auf den internationalen Rohstoffmärkten', in *Die Weltwirtschaft*, Tübingen, 1979, Part 2, pp. 115–133.
Hornbogen, Erhard, and Warlimont, H. *Metallkunde*, Berlin, 1967.
IBRD (International Bank for Reconstruction and Development). *Commodity Trade and Price Trends*, Report No. EC-166/74, Washington, August 1974.
IMETAL. *Guide Minemet, Métaux non Ferreux*, Paris, 1977.
Industriemagazin – Management, Marketing, Technologie, Munich, July 1980.
International Economic Studies Institute. *Raw Materials and Foreign Policy*, Washington, 1976.
International Tin Agreement, HMSO, London, 1954.
International Tin Council. *Annual Report*, London, various years.
Jetter, Ulrich. *Recycling in der Materialwirtschaft. Stoffkreisläufe – Rückgewinnung – Abfallnutzung*, in *Expandierende Märkte*, Vol. 5, Hamburg, 1975.
Johnson, Harry G. 'The Elementary Economic Geometry of Buffer Stock Price Stabilization', in *The Malayan Economic Review*, Vol. 22, Singapore, April 1977, pp. 1–9.
Juhl, Paul-Georg. 'Zur Bewältigung politischer Interventionsrisiken in den Entwicklungsländern – Das Konzept einer "Free Investment Area"', in *Die Weltwirtschaft*, Tübingen, 1976, Part 1, pp. 191–201.
- *Deutsche Direktinvestitionen in Lateinamerika*, Kieler Studien 160, Tübingen, 1979.
Kästner, Hermann, et al. *Nickel*, in *Untersuchungen über Angebot und Nachfrage mineralischer Rohstoffe*, Bundesanstalt für Geowissenschaften and Rohstoffe und Deutsches Institut für Wirtschaftsforschung, Berlin, 1978.
Kebschull, Dietrich, Künne, Winfried, and Menck, Karl-Wolfgang. *Das Integrierte Rohstoffprogramm. Prüfung entwicklungspolitischer Ansätze im Rohstoffvorschlag der UNCTAD*, Hamburg, 1977.
Kieffer, R., Jangg, G., and Ettmayer, P. *Sondermetalle – Metallurgie, Herstellung, Anwendung*, Vienna, 1971.
Kirchgässner, Gebhard. 'Eine ökonomische Theorie des Recycling', in *Kyklos*, Vol. 30, Part 4, Basle, 1977, pp. 699–703.
Knoblich, Hans. *Der Kupfer-Weltmarkt*, Berlin, 1962.
Kollwentz, Walter. 'Die Erkundung von Mangan-Knollenvorkommen. Ein Beispiel mariner Prospektion und Exploration', in *Manganknollen – Metalle aus dem Meer*, Metallgesellschaft AG, Mitteilungen aus den Arbeitsbereichen No 18, Frankfurt am Main, 1975, pp. 12–26.
Kross, Günter. *Die Rohstoffe der Seltenen Erden. Vorkommen, Nutzung, Märkte*, Essen, 1974.
Krüger, Joachim and Schwarz, Karl-Heinz. 'Verhüttung von Manganknollen', in *Manganknollen – Metalle aus dem Meer*, Metallgesellschaft AG, Mitteilungen aus den Arbeitsbereichen No 18, Frankfurt am Main, 1975, pp. 37–43.
Leontief, Wassily W., Carter, Anne P. and Petri, Peter. *The Future of the World Economy*, New York, 1977.
Lilley, Samuel. 'Technischer Fortschritt und die Industrielle Revolution 1700–1914', in K Borchardt (ed.), *Die Industrielle Revolution*, Stuttgart, 1976, pp. 119–163.
Linden, Eike von der. 'Der Bergbau auf Blei', in *Blei – Werkstoff mit Zukunft*, Metallgesellschaft AG, Mitteilungen aus den Arbeitsbereichen No 20, Frankfurt am Main, 1977, pp. 32–39.
Lüpfert, Helmut. *Metallische Rohstoffe*, Leipzig, 1942.
LURGI Industries. *Lurgi-Handbuch*, Frankfurt am Main, 1960.
Maczek, Helmut and von Ropenack, Adolf. 'Die Zinkhütten der Metallgesellschaft', in

Metallgesellschaft AG, Mitteilungen aus den Arbeitsbereichen No 22, Frankfurt am Main, 1980, pp. 42–47.
Malenbaum, Wilfried. *World Demand for Raw Materials in 1985 and 2000*, Philadelphia, 1977.
Manthy, Robert S. *Natural Resource Commodities – A Century of Statistics*, Baltimore, 1978.
Meadows, Donella H. et al. *The Limits to Growth: a report for the Club of Rome's project on the predicament of mankind*, New York, 1972.
Meinberg, Harald. 'Stukturwandel im Bleigeschäft' in *Blei – Werkstoff mit Zukunft*, Metallgesellschaft AG, Mitteilungen aus den Arbeitsbereichen No 20, Frankfurt am Main, 1977, pp. 16–17.
Metal Bulletin, World Steel & Metal News, London, various years.
Die Metalle – Produktion, Verbrauch, Märkte, Schweizerische Bankgesellschaft, Bulletin 3/4, Zurich, 1965.
Metallgesellschaft AG. *Metal Statistics*, Frankfurt am Main, various years.
– *MG-Information: eine Zeitschrift für die Mitarbeiter im Bereich der Metallgesellschaft AG*, Frankfurt am Main, various years.
Metallurgische Technik, Rohstoffe, Verfahren, Produkte. Study of commodity security carried out on behalf of the Bundesministerium für Forschung und Technologie, by the Verein Deutscher Eisenhütteleute (VDEh) in collaboration with the Deutsche Gesellschaft für Metallkunde (DGM) and the Gesellschaft Deutscher Metallhütten- und Bergleute (GDMB), Clausthal-Zellerfeld, October 1975.
Meyers Enzyklopädisches Lexikon, Vol. 16, Mannheim, 1976, p. 125.
Meyers Handbuch über die Technik, 2nd, rev., edn, Mannheim, 1971.
Michalski, Wolfgang. 'Industrial Raw Materials, Physical vs. Political, Economic and Social Scarcity of Minerals', in *The OECD Observer*, No. 93, Paris, July 1978.
Mineral Commodity Summaries, Washington, various years.
Mineral Facts and Problems, US Department of the Interior, Bureau of Mines, Bulletin 667, 1975 edn, Washington, 1976.
Mineralische Rohstoffe, Bundesministerium für Wirtschaft, Bonn, January, 1979.
Minerals Yearbook, Vol. 1: Metals, Minerals and Fuels, US Department of the Interior, Bureau of Mines, Washington, various years.
Morgan, John D. 'The Non-fuel Mineral Position of the USA' in *Resources Policy*, Vol. 6, Guildford, Surrey, March 1980, pp. 33–43.
Neumann, Bernhard. *Die Metalle: Geschichte, Vorkommen und Gewinnung*, Halle an der Saale, 1904.
Non-Ferrous Metal Data 1979, American Bureau of Metal Statistics Inc., New York.
OECD. *Interfutures: facing the future*, Paris, 1979.
Paley Report, see *Resources for Freedom*.
Pasdach, Uwe-Jens. 'Kupfer', in: Werner Gocht (ed.), *Handbuch der Metallmärkte*, Berlin, 1974, pp. 162–194.
Petkof, Benjamin. 'Beryllium', in *Mineral Facts and Problems*, 1975 edn, Washington, 1976, pp. 137–146.
Prewo, Wilfried. 'Tiefseebergbau: Goldgrube, Weißer Elefant oder Trojanisches Pferd?', in *Die Weltwirtschaft*, Tübingen, 1979, Part 1, pp. 183–197.
Ramms, Hans-Wolfgang. *Wettbewerb und Preisbildung bei Nichteisen-Metallen*, Dissertation, Cologne, 1959.
Ratjen, Karl-Gustaf. 'Vom Standardartikel zum anspruchsvollen Produkt', in Metallgesellschaft AG, *MG-Information*, Vol. 11, Part 1, Frankfurt am Main, 1976, pp. 1–3.

- 'Zukunftsaspekte der Metalle', *ibid.*, Vol 13, Part 2, 1978, pp. 1-3.
Reinert, Max. 'Blei in der modernen Technologie', in *Blei – Werkstoff mit Zukunft*, Metallgesellschaft AG, Mitteilungen aus den Arbeitsbereichen No 20, Frankfurt am Main, 1977, pp. 67-75.
Resources for Freedom: a report by the President's Materials Policy Commission (Paley Report), Washington, 1952.
Rittinger, Peter, Ritter von. *Lehrbuch der Aufbereitungskunde*, Berlin, 1867.
Roethe, G. 'Wolfram, Molybdän, Vanadium', in Werner Gocht (ed.), *Handbuch der Metallmärkte*, Berlin, 1974, pp. 123-161.
'Rohstoffe – Titan wird knapp und teuer', in *Wirtschaftswoche*, No 32, Düsseldorf, 6 August 1979.
'Rohstofflager – Mahnung zur Eile', in *Wirtschaftswoche*, No 9, Düsseldorf, 29 February 1980.
Rolshoven, Hubertus. 'Nutzwert und Bedeutung der Metalle für den wirtschaftlich-technischen Fortschritt', in Werner Gocht (ed.), *Handbuch der Metallmärkte*, Berlin, 1974, pp. 1-5.
Rowe, J. W. F. *Primary Commodities in International Trade*, Cambridge, 1965.
Ryan, J. Patrick, and Hague, John M. *Lead – 1977*, Mineral Commodity Profiles 9, Washington, 1977.
Salzmann, Gunther. *Hundert Jahre Flotationspatent*, Gesellschaft Deutscher Metallhütten- und Bergleute (GDMB), Clausthal-Zellerfeld, 1978.
Sames, Carl-Wolfgang. *Die Zukunft der Metalle*, Frankfurt am Main, 1971.
Sandig, Harmut and Schmidt, Rudolf. 'Bleihalbzeug im Wandel der Zeiten – Produktion und Anwendung', *Blei – Werkstoff mit Zukunft*, Metallgesellschaft AG, Mitteilungen aus den Arbeitsbereichen No 20, Frankfurt am Main, 1977, pp. 76-83.
Schollhorn, Johann. *Internationale Rohstoffregulierungen*, Berlin, 1955.
Schroeder, Harold J. 'Copper', in US Department of the Interior, Bureau of Mines, *Mineral Facts and Problems*, 1975 edn, Washington, 1976, pp. 293-310.
Schwartz, Werner. 'Die Zukunft der Bleiverhüttung', in *Blei – Werkstoff mit Zukunft*, Metallgesellschaft AG, Mitteilungen aus den Arbeitsbereichen No 20, Frankfurt am Main, 1977, pp. 46-55.
Siebert, Horst (ed.). *Erschopfbare Ressourcen*. Schriften des Vereins für Socialpolitik; Gesellschaft für Wirtschafts- und Sozialwissenschaften, new series, Vol. 108, Berlin, 1980.
Sies, Walter. 'Die Märkte für NE-Metallerze und NE-Metalle' in *Glückauf*, Vol. 109, Essen, February 1973, pp. 227-234.
– *Aktuelle Probleme der Rohstoffmärkte*, paper delivered at the 10th Conference of the Bundesverband Materialwirtschaft und Einkauf e.V., Düsseldorf, 12 November 1976.
– 'Die Entwicklungsländer als Blei- und Zinklieferanten', in *Metall* No 9, Berlin, September 1977, p. 1009.
– 'Funktion der Weltmetallmärkte', paper delivered at the commercial and business seminar of the Wirtschaftsvereinigung Bergbau, Morsbach-Lichtenberg, 30 June 1978.
Snyder, Glenn H. *Stockpiling Strategical Materials: politics and national defense*, San Francisco, 1966.
Stainer, Julius. 'Blei und Zink werden immer gebraucht', in *Internationale Wirtschaft*, No. 47, Vienna, 19 November 1976.

Stamper, John W. and Kurtz, Horace F. *Aluminium*, Mineral Commodity Profiles 14, Washington, 1978.
Statistisches Bundesamt, Wiesbaden. *Bevölkerung und Wirtschaft*, Stuttgart, 1892–1972.
- *Statistisches Jahrbuch 1978*, Stuttgart.
Stevens, Richard F., Jr. 'Tungsten', in US Department of the Interior, Bureau of Mines, *Mineral Facts and Problems*, 1975 edn, Washington, 1976, pp. 1161–1176.
Stockpile Report to the Congress, Washington, various issues.
Stodieck, Helmut. *Bestimmungsgründe der Preisentwicklung auf dem Weltzinnmärkt*, Hamburg, 1970.
Strizek, Helmut. 'Die neue AKP-EWG-Konvention (Lomé II)' in Bundesministerium für wirtschaftliche Zusammenarbeit, *Entwicklungspolitik – Materialien* No. 66, Bonn, May 1980, pp. 6–10.
Tafel, Victor. *Lehrbuch der Metallhüttenkunde*, Vol II, Leipzig, 1929, p. 300.
Tilton, John E. *The Future of Nonfuel Minerals*, Washington, 1977.
Treue, Wilhelm. *Wirtschaftsgeschichte der Neuzeit*, Stuttgart, 1966.
United Nations, Interregional Workshop on Negotiation and Drafting of Mining Development Agreements. *Processing*, prepared by UN Secretariat, New York, October 1973 (ESA/RT/AC. 7/12.).
- *Monthly Bulletin of Statistics*, New York, various years.
- *Non-Ferrous Metals*, New York, 1972.
- *Yearbook of Industrial Statistics* (previously *The Growth of World Industry*), Vol. 1, New York, various years.
US Bureau of the Census. *Historical Statistics of the United States, Colonial Times to 1980*, Bicentennial edn, Parts 1 and 2, Washington, 1975.
Weisser, Johannes Dietmar. 'Bleilagerstätten', in *Blei – Werkstoff mit Zukunft*, Metallgesellschaft AG, Mitteilungen aus den Arbeitsbereichen No 20, Frankfurt am Main, 1977, pp. 28–32.
Die Weltaluminiumindustrie, IMB Conference for the Iron, Steel and Copper Industry, Lüttich, 22–25 September 1969.
Weltrohstoffversorgung: Konflikt oder Kooperation? Institut für Weltwirtschaft, Kieler Diskussionsbeiträge 36, Kiel, December 1974.
Wiesinger, R. E. and Schuchardt, P. B. 'Leichtmetalle', in Werner Gocht (ed.), *Handbuch der Metallmärkte*, Berlin, 1974, pp. 277–303.
Wincierz, Peter. 'Die Metalle', in K. Winnacker and L. Kuchler (eds), *Chemische Technologie*, Vol. 6, *Metallurgie*, Munich, 1973, pp. 1–24.
Winterhager, Helmut. 'Die industrielle und wirtschaftliche Bedeutung der Nichteisen-Metalle', paper given at the 4th Conference on 'Gaswärme in der Fertigung', Essen, 24 November 1955.
World Bank Atlas, Washington, 1979.
World Metal Statistics, Vol 34, No 2, London, 1981.
Woytinsky, W. S. and Woytinsky, E. S. *World Population and Production: trends and outlook*, New York, 1953.
Wuth, W. 'Mangan und Chrom', in Werner Gocht (ed.), *Handbuch der Metallmärkte*, Berlin, 1974, pp. 69–99.
Year Book of the American Bureau of Metal Statistics, 53rd Annual Issue for the year 1973, New York, 1974.
Zimmermann's World Resources and Industries, 3rd edn, New York, 1972.